WOMEN OF CHRISTIANITY,

EXEMPLARY FOR ACTS OF

PIETY AND CHARITY.

BY

JULIA KAVANAGH,

AUTHOR OF "WOMAN IN FRANCE," "NATHALIE," "MADELEINE," ETC.

With a new foreword by
James D. Smith III

"Pure religion and undefiled before God and the Father is this: to visit the fatherless and widows in their affliction, and to keep unspotted from the world."
—JAMES i. 27.

Wipf & Stock
PUBLISHERS
Eugene, Oregon

Wipf and Stock Publishers
199 W 8th Ave, Suite 3
Eugene, OR 97401

Women of Christianity
The Pioneer 1852 Narrative of Women's Lives in the Christian Tradition
By Kavanagh, Julia and Smith, James D.
ISBN: 1-59752-638-X
Copyright©1851 by Kavanagh, Julia
Publication date 5/1/2006
Previously published by D. Appleton & Company, 1851

Julia Kavanagh portrait by Henry Chanet (fl after 1874)
Julia Kavanagh, Novelist (1924-77)
Oil on canvas, 53x49cm
National Gallery of Ireland Collection
Photo©The National Gallery of Ireland

Foreword

Fifty years ago, editors from Harper & Brothers in New York City invited the journalist Edith Deen to write a sequel to her popular book *All the Women of the Bible*. With enthusiasm, she began researching the story of notable women throughout twenty centuries of Church history. In the introduction to her *Great Women of the Christian Faith* (1959), often considered the first volume of its kind, Deen speaks of gathering resources from an array of libraries and archives. One of the most helpful volumes, she acknowledges, was written a century earlier by Julia Kavanagh—*Women of Christianity*. Though largely unknown today, it remains the pioneer effort in telling the story of women's lives in the Christian tradition. Ranging from Dorcas in the Acts of the Apostles to Englishwomen Elizabeth Fry and Sarah Martin, Kavanagh's aim was to include "women remarkable for character, intellect and excellence who had flourished under the fostering influence of the Christian faith."

Kavanagh's name is well-known to students of Victorian literature (notably through her 1848 novel *Madeline*), and the details of her life are chronicled in publications such as the *Dictionary of National Biography*. She was born January 7, 1824, at Thurles, County Tipperary, Ireland, to [Peter] Morgan and Bridget [Fitzpatrick] Kavanagh. Baptized two days later, she remained a devout, lifelong Roman Catholic and (in her words) "Irish by birth and feeling." Her father was a poet and philologist and communicated this passion to Julia, an only child. With her parents she moved to London in early childhood, soon thereafter to Paris, and was largely educated in France. At her death in 1877, she was buried in the Catholic cemetery in Nice.

In 1844, she moved to London to pursue a literary career, first writing for periodicals, then publishing an initial book, *The Three Paths* (a children's tale) in 1847. The popularity of *Madeline*, drawn from the life of a peasant girl of Auvergne, helped establish her reputation in Europe and America. Among her twenty novels were *Nathalie, Daisy Burns,* and *Rachel Gray*. As feminist scholar Eileen Fauset (working on a full study) has noted, Kavanagh was astutely aware of the social and political double standards of the day, which she both revealed and challenged within the narrative of the patterned romance, a genre known more for entertainment than a prophetic, political voice. She questioned the ideal of marriage as a necessity for fulfillment in women's lives, identifying the value and character issues inherent in their life decisions. Single throughout her life, in these writings she drew deeply from personal experience. Being left the sole support of her invalid mother when her father deserted them, she felt the profound social burden—yet was enriched relationally and culturally by the disciplines of caregiving, study, and later seasons in France with occasional visits elsewhere (for example, Italy).

These life interests increasingly drew Kavanagh into the area of popular biography. In 1850, her *Women in France during the Eighteenth Century* was well received. Further research led, by 1862, to the publication of a two-volume *French Women of Letters* and a companion *English Women of Letters*. Early in this process, her interest in the story of Christian womanhood deepened as well. In exploring this, Kavanagh was aware of saints' lives in the Catholic tradition, but chafed under the "painful and wearisome similarity" so often found in the accounts. "The good are not alike, they differ from one another as much as other people. The fault must lie with the biographers who praised when they should have painted, and suppressed characteristic touches as undignified."

In the introduction to her *Women of Christianity*, Kavanagh also confronted the historical conventions of her era. Too often, she declared, men have filled the pages of history with their own deeds: daring in war, subtle in peace, magnificent in designs, triumphant in genius, revolutionary in faith and government—evidencing the old pagan spirit rather than the spirit of Christ. She was deeply convinced of the redemptive nature of the Christian message, which placed the idea of the equality of all before God in opposition to forces of tyranny and slavery. To be sure, the evils had not been wholly removed, but the principles by which they were to perish had been awakened. "Christianity freed woman, because it opened to her the long-closed world of spiritual knowledge."

In her survey, remarkably charitable and free of the periods' religious polemic, perhaps the most painful chapter addresses the Reformation era. There are accounts of Catholic women and Anglican, but none from Continental Protestantism. In summary, Kavanagh mentions that, from the close of the fourteenth century to the opening of the seventeenth, all women experienced an epoch of "great enterprises, religious changes and civil wars," which tended (with the exception of Teresa of Avila) to level downward their focused devotion.

Julia Kavanagh's *Women of Christianity*, appearing 150 years ago (with printings in London and New York), predates the great personalities and events of the women's movement of the later nineteenth century. Subsequent developments in critical historiography and feminist theory may leave contemporary readers disappointed with her work as a less sophisticated chronicler. Yet in her fervent desire to let the lives and voices of her sisters (in gender and faith) be heard, she is at one with many who have followed. Mary

Malone, introducing her recently completed three-volume historical survey, *Women & Christianity*, underlined the goal: "to extricate from the tradition the reality of women's lives." Over the past two decades, writers shouldering this two-millennia challenge have included Ruth A. Tucker, Barbara J. MacHaffie, Rosemary Radford Ruether, Margaret R. Miles, Amy G. Oden, Beverly Mayne Kienzle, and Elizabeth A. Clark. The republishing of this volume makes available the pioneer account of one who, in telling the story of Christian women across the ages, finds her rightful place within that story.

James D. Smith III
Bethel Seminary San Diego
University of San Diego
Feast of St. Catherine of Siena 2006

PREFACE.

WHEN I first conceived the idea of writing a work on the Women of Christianity, I contemplated including all the women remarkable for character, intellect, and excellence, who had flourished under the fostering influence of the Christian faith. I soon perceived that this design, if it were not too vast to be accomplished, would require the labor of years. I resolved, however, to execute at least a part of that great whole: a part complete in itself; to be followed by similar works or not, as circumstances and time might determine.

It was difficult to choose, difficult to decide, with whom to begin. How many great and heroic women suddenly seemed to rise from the barbaric gloom of feudal ages, or appeared mingling with strange daring in the strife, as deadly and as fierce, of recent generations! How many meditative spirits, living apart from a rude world that knew them not, heralded the dawn of civilization, gave to now forgotten idioms their sweetest strains, and nobly asserted in their day —not, it is true, so completely as they have been asserted in ours— the intellect and genius of woman!

But, from these women of action and thought, my mind turned to other women more lowly, though not less great.

For eighteen centuries I beheld them fervent in their faith, pure in their lives, patient when it was their lot to endure, heroic when they had to act or suffer; and I felt that these were essentially the " Women of Christianity," and that to them the first place belonged by right.

I need say little more concerning the aim of this work, save that it does not profess to include those women whose virtues went not beyond the circle of home, and whose piety was limited to worship. Love and adoration are beautiful, but sacrifice is the true spirit of Christianity.

The very foundation of our faith rests on an act of self-immolation: the death of Jesus on the cross. The women who have inherited this spirit, who have filled their lives with acts of self-denial, who, like their great Master, have gone about doing good, are those whom I have selected as examples of the women of Christianity.

Such is the object of the work. I do not wish to speak of the trouble I have had, or the pains I have taken in writing it. Some difficulties which I had anticipated, I did not find; others on which I had not reckoned, beset me in my task. I thought of the difficulty of procuring materials, not that the materials would often be imperfect. I did not know then, as I know now, that the good are quickly forgotten, and neglected in death as in life; that their history is too often written by the least gifted amongst those who write, and read by the most humble amongst those who read; that the limited sympathies of the biographer, and the fastidiousness of the reader, have united to keep in obscurity the most noble of their race; and that, so far as regards the past, the evil is irreparable. I have felt it much during the progress of this work: biography after biography have I read, and—with some interesting exceptions—I have been struck with their painful and wearisome similarity. Now, this need not be. The good are not alike: they differ from one another as much as other people. The fault must lie with the biographers who praised when they should have painted, and suppressed characteristic touches as undignified. I wish I could have changed this; but as I found things told, even so was I compelled to relate them.

The limits of this work have rendered it necessary to condense ; but I believe I may say, that no essential matter has been omitted, and no recorded incidents, necessary to develop the character further, or awaken a new sense of interest in the reader, have been excluded or overlooked. I did not think it desirable, in a work devoted to the active charity of Christian women, to enter into the minute detail of religious feelings and opinions; and I have forborne to touch on the difficult subject of supernatural manifestations. My object was to record those marvels of charity and devotedness which are the greatest boast of the Christian faith, and in which man has not as yet surpassed woman. Moreover, I wished to shun discussion, for which I had no room, and controversy, for which I had no inclination. It was my aim to relate simply and truly the history of women who were essentially simple and true ; and I desired that the spirit in which this work was written should accord with the subject, and be a spirit of charity.

JULIA KAVANAGH.

KENSINGTON, *December* 6, 1851.

CONTENTS.

6 CONTENTS.

PERIOD THE THIRD.—THE SEVENTEENTH CENTURY.

PERIOD THE FOURTH.—THE EIGHTEENTH AND NINETEENTH CENTURIES.

AUTHORS AND WORKS CONSULTED.

Abelly.
Acta Sanctorum.
Arvine.
St. Augustine.
Baillet.
Ballard.
Bareith.
Baxter.
Bede.
Bibliothèque des Chartes.
Biographie Universelle.
Biographie des Contemporains.
Brantôme.
Butler.
Campan.
Campbell.
Carron.
St. Catherine of Sienna.
Chateaubriand.
Choisy.
Christian Biography.
Clairfontaine.
Clarke.
Collet.
Congreve.
Coste.
Dover, Lord.
Dufresnoy.
Duncon.
Encyclopédie des Gens du Monde.
Eusebius.
Evangelical Biography.

Evelyn.
Fleury.
Ford.
Fordun.
Fry.
Genlis.
George.
Gibbon.
Gibbons.
Goodwyn.
Gregory of Tours.
Guizot.
Gurnall.
Halstead.
Hays.
Huntingdon.
Jardine.
St. Jerome.
Bishop Kenn.
Kohlrausch.
Lacroix.
Leroux de Liney.
Les Princesses de France.
Library of Christian Biography.
Life of Eleanor, Empress.
Life of Frances of Amboise.
Life of Jeanne Biscot.
Life of St. Margaret.
Life of Mrs. Rowe.
Life of St. Teresa.
Lingard.
Marabotto.
Martin.

Michaud.
Michelet.
Milner.
Montagu.
Montalembert.
Montyon.
More.
Moore.
Necker.
Pilkington.
Prescott.
Bp. Rainbow.
Reyre.
Ribera.
Richard.
Rose.
Sherman.
St. Simon.
San Severini.
Schnitzler.
Sismondi.
Starling.
Steele.
Strickland.
St. Teresa.
Tertullian.
Theodoric.
Thiebault.
Thierry.
Touron.
Tricalet.
Tyrone.
Villemain.
Walker.
Wilford.
Woodward.

WOMEN OF CHRISTIANITY,

PIETY AND CHARITY.

INTRODUCTION.

Christianity of Woman—Early Martyrs—Virgins and Widows of the
Primitive Church—Rapid Progress of the Faith.

WE find it recorded in the Acts of the Apostles, that whilst Peter tarried at Lydda, there dwelt in the neighboring town of Joppa "a certain disciple named Tabitha or Dorcas," and that "this woman was full of good works, and alms-deeds which she did." Dorcas sickened and died; Peter was summoned; he found her body laid out in an upper chamber, "and all the widows stood by him weeping, and showing the coats and garments which Dorcas made while she was with them."

Of the women who have walked in the steps of this woman of the first Christian age, consecrating their souls to God, their lives to the poor, what says history?

Men have filled its pages with their own deeds: their perilous daring in war—their subtle skill in peace—their designs vast and magnificent—the power of their ideas—the triumphs of their genius—the revolutions in their faith and government—all they have either done or undergone, has been faithfully recorded. Thus the past reads like a marvellous story of strange events and stirring deeds, succeeding one another with startling rapidity; and in a confusion that, seen from afar, seems both reckless and magnificent. Like Mirza, we look down on the wonderful vision, and behold at one glance the deeds, wars, glories, oppressions, and struggles of whole

1*

ages.   But in all this what have we?   The annals of nations, not the story of humanity.

What share have women in the history of men?   We hear of empresses and queens, of heroines and geniuses, and even of those women who won a perilous fame through the power of loveliness or surpassing grace; but woman in the peace and quiet beauty of her domestic life, in the gentleness of her love, in the courage of her charity, in the holiness of her piety, we must not hope to find.   History has been written in the old pagan spirit of recording great events and dazzling actions; not in the lowliness of the Christian heart, which, without affecting to despise the great, still loves and venerates the good.

The writer of the following pages has neither the power of supplying so great a deficiency, nor the ambitious aim of opening a new path in history.   Leaving the task to others, she intends no more than to record with truth and simplicity what is known of the pure and good women who have lived and died since the opening of the Christian era,—of those women who honored humanity, but whom the historian has rarely mentioned, whom the general biographer has too often forgotten.

The preaching of the Gospel is an era in the modern world. If we would know what it did for woman, we need only compare the earliest Christian women with those of the ancients in their purest days.   No doubt there were many noble women before the word of Christ was known or acknowledged in Europe,—women of lofty intellect and high character, accomplished Greeks or rigid Romans, fit to rule with Pericles, or worthy to suffer with Brutus.   But the difference is clear and striking—there was no Dorcas.

There could not have been one: the virtues of Dorcas were not those which formed the pagan ideal; and, at the time when she lived, that ideal was already a thing of the past. When the first dawn of Christianity appeared, the faith of the ancients had been failing them for several ages.   Epicurism, superstition, and a moral depravity too deep to bear record, held sway over the subjects of the wide empire; until suddenly a secret murmur, welcome as the glad tidings of liberty to the fallen, arose and spread from Jerusalem to Rome.

To the capricious tyranny of the emperors—to the slavery of thousands of human beings—to the subjection of many nations to one nation—Christianity opposed the equality of all before God, the spiritual freedom of which no bonds can deprive the soul, and the universal brotherhood of men. The evils were not removed, but the principles by which they were to perish had awakened. The "good tidings" were told to the lowly and the great; to the oppressed and the free; in the market-place and by the household hearth. There they reached woman : woman, alternately the toy or drudge of man, whom only birth, beauty, or genius, could raise to equality ; who, to be something, must be the daughter, wife, or mother of an illustrious citizen, and who seemed destined never to know the moral dignity of individual worth.

Christianity at first appeared to change little in the condition of women. It told them in austere precepts to obey their husbands, to dwell at home, to mind household duties, and to leave the great aims of life to man ; and yet it proved the charter of their liberty. We must not ascribe this fact to the widows, virgins, and deaconesses of the early church ; important as was the part they acted. Had not the pagan creed its vestals, priestesses, and prophetic sibyls ? Not there lay the difference. Christianity freed woman, because it opened to her the long-closed world of spiritual knowledge. Sublime and speculative theories, hitherto confined to the few, became—when once they were quickened by faith— things for which thousands were eager to die. Simple women meditated in their homes on questions which had long troubled philosophers in the groves of Academia. They knew this well. They felt that from her who had sat at the feet of the Master, listening to the divine teaching, down to the poorest slave who heard the tidings of spiritual liberty, they had all become daughters of a great and immortal faith.

Of that faith they were the earliest adherents, disciples, and martyrs. Women followed Jesus, entertained the wandering apostles, worshipped in the catacombs, or died in the arena. The Acts of the Apostles bear record to the charity of Dorcas, and the hospitality of Lydia ; and tradition has preserved the memory of Praxedes and Pudentiana, daughters of a Roman senator, in whose house the earliest Christian meetings were held at Rome. The wealth of the two virgins went to relieve the church and the poor; united in their lives and in their charity, they were not divided in death: they were buried side by side on the Salarian road. The church of Saint Pudentiana, erected on the spot where the palace of their father once stood, is held to be the most ancient in existence.

Many of those early Christian women won the crown of martyrdom. They were now beings with immortal souls; they suffered as such both worthily and willingly. The Elysium of the ancients was the home of heroes; the heaven of the Christians was open to the meanest slave. The new faith showed no favor of sex in its rewards; and the old, as if knowing this, made no exception in its cruelty. From the days when Nero raised the first general persecution against the church, and lit up the evening sky of Rome with the fires in which Christians were slowly consumed, women shared all the torments and heroism of the martyrs.

In every rank they suffered or perished bravely. Two near relatives of Domitian, both bearing the name of Flavia Domitilla, were banished from Rome by the emperor, and lingered many years in exile, for having embraced the faith. Sabina, a lady of Umbria, was converted by her slave Seraphia, and put to death at Rome under the persecution of Adrian. When Justin, once a heathen philosopher, was brought up before the Præfect for having become a Christian, a woman named Charitana was one of his companions, and like him having answered "that by the divine mercy she was a Christian," was scourged and beheaded.

They suffered not only for being Christians, but even for exercising Christian virtues: for giving aid and shelter to the living; for burying the dead martyrs; for reading the holy scriptures, and refusing to deliver up to the heathens the book on which their faith rested. They were included in all the calumnies vented against the professors of the new creed; accused of magic, of impiety, of unnatural affections, and of feeding on the flesh of infants. Their austere morality was a silent reproach on the profligacy of the heathen women, felt and not forgiven. In the purest days of ancient Rome, the institution of six vestals had been supported with the greatest difficulty; whereas numberless virgins were known to fill the primitive church. When Juvenal wrote, Roman ladies counted their years by their successive husbands; but Christian widows rarely—and never without a sense of shame—took second vows and belonged to more than one man. This purity, in the midst of a profligacy so deep that it sullies the pages in which it is recorded, was, like the love which united them, one of the distinctive marks of the early Christians.

They were of every race, and yet they formed in essential points a people more distinct than the ancient or modern Jews. They were known by their modest garments, mostly white; by their grave bearing; temperance, and chastity; by that love which made them call one another brothers and sisters, support the widows and orphans, and undertake long journeys from pure motives of charity. They fulfilled the duties of active life, but they were not seen in the theatres, public games, or sanguinary amusements of the heathens: they dwelt apart, worshipping God in lonely places—forests, cemeteries, or catacombs—bearing persecution patiently, ever ready to die, and silently protesting by their pure and austere life against the profligacy of their age.

It showed very forcibly the spirit of the new religion, that to women was chiefly intrusted the practice of its purity and charity in their severest and most extensive meaning.

From the times of the apostles many maidens consecrated themselves to God, and were designated as the virgins. The bishop gave them a blessed veil in the church, and this, with their black or gray garments, distinguished them from other unmarried women. In some places the consecration consisted in the virgin laying her head on the altar, and allowing her hair to grow unshorn, like the ancient Naza-renes. In Egypt and Syria, on the contrary, the virgin cut off her hair, as if to renounce one of the greatest charms of her sex, and with it the desire of being pleasing in the eyes of men.

Everywhere, before the establishment of convents, they led a retired and ascetic life. They seldom went out, and in the churches had places set for them, apart even from the other women. They lived in their own homes, or two or three together. Their days were spent in silence, retirement, poverty, labor, fasts, vigils, and orisons. Those who per-fumed their hair, wore garments that swept the ground, or adorned themselves with jewels, were not considered real virgins or esteemed as such. If they broke their vows and married, they had to perform a public penance.

The widows mentioned by the apostolic writers, led a more active though not less ascetic life than that of the virgins. Like them they prayed, fasted, and renounced worldly hopes and pleasures; but their years and experience gave them more liberty to go out. They visited sick people and prisoners, especially martyrs and confessors of the faith. They relieved the indigent, and practised hospitality. When they were rich, they spent their wealth thus; when poor, they were supported by the church. The most aged widows were made deaconesses by the imposition of hands, and included amongst the clergy. At first this office was not conferred on widows under sixty years of age, but they were ultimately admitted at forty. Virgins were sometimes made deaconesses, and then took the name of widows.

Their office resembled that of the deacons. They were intrusted with all the deeds of mercy that applied to their own sex. They visited and relieved poor women, instructed the catechumens, led them to baptism; helped them to undress for the ceremony, and, for some time after it had been performed, continued to see and exhort them. They kept watch at the entrance reserved to women in the churches, helped them to take their ranks, and saw that they behaved with propriety and reverence whilst the divine mysteries were celebrated. The deaconesses were subject to the government of the bishops, to whom they gave an account of the manner in which they performed their appointed tasks. Deaconesses existed as late as the twelfth century.

Purity and charity were enjoined to the virgins and widows, and expected from every Christian woman. The writings of the early Fathers show of what importance the whole sex had become. Virginity, widowhood, nay, even female attire, were favorite subjects with the gravest writers. Tertullian wrote two books on the ornaments of women: he advised them to abstain from paint, false hair, and other pagan modes of helping beauty. Christian women, he said, did not go to the temples, theatres, and festivals of the Gentiles; if they left home, it was to visit sick brethren, to go to the church and hear the word of God. " Cast off delights," he eloquently adds, "in order not to be oppressed by persecution. Arms accustomed to bracelets would not know how to bear the weight of chains; feet adorned with sandals could not endure fetters; and a head covered with pearls and jewels would leave no room to the sword."

Well might he say so. The sword never spared women when the time came, and the wrath of the persecutors kept pace with the increasing number of the Christians. The faith had journeyed rapidly along those wide roads which had marked the conquests of Rome: a few hundreds had, within a comparatively short space of time, become countless multitudes. As the same Father says so finely,—"It is true we are but of yesterday, and yet we fill all your towns, cities, islands, castles, boroughs, councils, camps, courts, palaces, your senate and forum,—we leave you only your temples."

PERIOD THE FIRST.—THE ROMAN EMPIRE.

CHAPTER I.

The First Christian Martyrs—Sufferings of the Church—Heroism of Women—The slave Blandina—Biblis—The Mother of Symphorian—Donata, Secunda, and Vestina—Vivia Perpetua and Felicitas—Potamiana—Mary—Julia, &c.—Greatness of the Persecution.

It lies not within our province to relate all the persecutions which the Church endured, from Nero down to Julian; and it would far exceed our limits to dwell separately on every one of the female martyrs who suffered during those four ages. A few traits, the most remarkable, and the best attested in church history, will bear sufficient testimony to the Christian heroism of woman in those early times.

In the year 177, Marcus Aurelius being emperor, there arose in Lyons and Vienna, cities of Gaul, a violent persecution against the professors of the Christian faith. It had been propagated there even in the time of the Apostles, owing to the facilities of intercourse between Marseilles and the ports of Lesser Asia. In an affecting letter, attributed chiefly to St. Irenæus, and which is to be found in the Ecclesiastical History of Eusebius, the sufferings of the Lyonese Christians are recorded with a touching mixture of force and simplicity. After a greeting from the "servants of Christ at Lyons and Vienna, in Gaul, to those brethren in Asia and Phrygia having the same faith and hope," the authors of the letter proceed to state how the persecution began by excluding the Christians from houses, baths, and market places, so that nothing belonging to them could even appear in public. They bore all patiently; "esteeming what was deemed great but little, they hastened to Christ, showing in reality that the sufferings of this time are not worthy to be compared with the glory that shall be revealed in us. And first they nobly sustained all the evils that were heaped upon

them by the populace : clamors and blows, plundering and
robberies, stonings and imprisonments, and whatsoever a
savage people delight to inflict upon enemies. After this,
they were led to the forum, and when they had been inter-
rogated by the tribune and the authorities of the city, in the
presence of the multitude, they were shut up in prison until
the arrival of the governor. Afterwards they were led away
to be judged by him, from whom they endured all manner
of cruelty."

"Ten of the Christians fell, and sacrificed conscience to
safety. Many who had remained free, and attended the
martyrs in prison, were in their turn arrested. The pagan
slaves apprehended with them, fearing lest they should be
included among the Christians, accused their masters of the
crimes of Thyestes and Œdipus. The fury of the people
and of the magistrates was roused to the utmost. It fell on
several of the Christian captives, and amongst the rest on a
female slave named Blandina; 'in whom,' as the authors
of the letter write, 'Christ made manifest that the things
that appear mean, and deformed, and contemptible among
men, are most esteemed by God, on account of her cherishing that love to him which evinces itself by fortitude, and
does not boast of mere profession; for whilst we were all
trembling, and her earthly mistress, who was herself one of
the contending martyrs, was apprehensive lest, through the
weakness of the flesh, she should not be able to make a bold
confession, Blandina was filled with such power, that her
ingenious tormentors, who relieved and succeeded each other
from morning till night, confessed that they were overcome,
and had nothing more that they could inflict upon her.
Only amazed that she still continued to breathe after her
whole body was torn asunder and pierced, they gave their
testimony that one single kind of the tortures inflicted was
of itself sufficient to destroy life, without resorting to so
many and such excruciating sufferings as these.'

"But this blessed saint, as a noble wrestler, in the midst
of her confession itself renewed her strength; and to repeat,
'I am a Christian: no wickedness is carried on by us,' was
to her rest, refreshment, and relief from pain."

The constancy of this noble woman was a living example
which the rest eagerly followed. Even a slave, named

Biblis, who had renounced the faith, awoke as from a deep. sleep, and instead of the accusations which her tormentors expected, boldly exclaimed, " How can it be imagined that they whose religion forbids them even to taste the blood of beasts should feed upon children ?" for the Christians of Gaul still observed the law of abstaining from eating blood enacted by the Apostles.

Many of the martyrs perished in the midst of the torments inflicted on them ; some died in prison, through the ill-usage they had received ; and others in the arena, in the presence and for the pleasure of a barbarous people. Blandina and a youth of fifteen, named Ponticus, were every day brought forth to witness the tortures of their friends. " Force," we are told, " was also used to make them swear by the idols ; and when they continued firm, and denied their pretended divinity, the multitude became outrageous at them, so that they neither compassionated the youth of the boy, nor regarded the sex of the woman. Hence they subjected them to every possible suffering, and led them through the whole round of torture, ever and anon striving to force them to swear, but were unable to effect it. Ponticus, indeed, encouraged by his companion, so that the heathen could see that she was encouraging and confirming him, nobly bore the whole of these sufferings, and gave up his life. But the blessed Blandina, last of all, as a noble mother that had animated her children, and sent them as victors to the great king—herself retracing the ground of all the conflicts her children had endured—hastened to them at last, with joy and exultation at the issue, as if she were invited to a marriage feast, and not to be cast to wild beasts."

We spare the reader the detail of the torments which closed the life of the heroic slave. Even amongst the heathens, no woman had been known to go through so great a course of sufferings with a courage so unshaken. Her remains, with those of the other martyrs, were deprived of burial by the hatred of their persecutors,—a hatred which death itself failed to appease. They were burned to ashes, and then cast into the Rhone. The heathens did this because they attributed to the Christian belief in the resurrection on the great judgment day, the ardent faith which led their victims undaunted through the whole array of human suffering.

In spite of all that persecution could do, the Christians remained true to one another. A poor widow exercised the noble and perilous duty of hospitality towards two fugitive Christians, Epipodius of Lyons, and Alexander, a Greek by birth. They were young, nobly born, fellow-students, attached friends, and brethren in the faith. They lay for some time undiscovered in the house of their hostess; but they were at length detected, apprehended, and executed, shortly after the martyrdom of Blandina and her companions.

In the course of the following year, this cruel persecution gave a Christian mother the opportunity of making to her God the sacrifice which proved the faith of Abraham. Symphorian, the son of Faustus, and of a mother whose name has remained unknown, descended of a noble Christian family in Gaul, young, accomplished, and virtuous, was led before the consul Heraclius for having refused to join in the impure worship of Cybele. "Why do you refuse to adore the mother of the gods?" asked Heraclius from his tribunal. "Because I am a Christian, and adore the true God in heaven," answered Symphorian. Neither threats nor torments could move him, and he was at length condemned to perish by the sword.

As they led him out of the town to the place of execution, his mother stood on the walls, to see him pass. True to her proud Roman-blood, she had come there: as those stoic matrons, from whom she was perchance descended, went to see their victorious sons led in triumph to the Capitol, so did she stand to behold him whom she had borne, on his way to the heavenly Jerusalem. When her voice could reach him, she raised it, and said in a clear loud tone, "My son, my son Symphorian, remember the living God, and be of good cheer. Raise thy heart to heaven, and think of him that reigneth there. Fear not death which leads to certain life."

The fifth general persecution was raised by the emperor Severus in the year 202. But, as there always existed a sufficient number of edicts against the Christians to authorize almost any amount of cruelty, we find that, two years before this persecution, twelve persons of Scillita, a town of Africa, had already suffered at Carthage. Amongst them were three women of remarkable constancy, Donata, Secunda, and Vestina. They were brought before the proconsul, who said to them, "Honor our prince, and offer sacrifice to the gods." Donata replied, "We give to Cæsar the honor that is due to Cæsar; but we adore and offer sacrifice to God alone." Vestina said, "I also am a Christian." Secunda said, "I also believe in my God, and will continue faithful to him. As for your gods, we will neither serve nor adore them." They were condemned to be beheaded, and giving thanks to God, were led to the place of execution, where, kneeling in prayer, they calmly waited until the sword of the executioner severed their heads from their bodies.

It was not always that woman's faith rose thus high. When, two years later, the great persecution began, Leonides, father of the celebrated Origen, was arrested in Alexandria, and cast into prison. His son, then a youth of seventeen, longed to share his glorious sufferings, and would have gone and delivered himself up as a Christian, if his mother had not conjured him to stay with her, and, to secure his compliance, kept him at home by locking up his garments.

This persecution reached Africa in the following year. Five catechumens were apprehended at Carthage. Two were women: Felicitas, a poor slave, and Vivia Perpetua, a lady of rank, twenty-two years of age, with an infant at her breast. The martyrdom of these two women is one of the most touching episodes in early church history. The father of Vivia Perpetua was a pagan. He was somewhat advanced in years, and loved his Christian daughter better than his other children. He visited her in her prison, and strove to shake her resolve: he failed, and parted from her in anger. When he heard, however, that the prisoners were to be examined shortly, he came again, and forgetting wrath in love, made one more effort. "Daughter," said he, "have pity on my gray hairs! have compassion on your father—on your child, that cannot survive you." He took her hands as he spoke—he kissed them—he called her no longer his daughter, but "Domina," his lady, and knelt weeping at her feet. The heart of Perpetua was pierced with exquisite sorrow, yet she remained firm, though not unmoved.

On the following day the prisoners were examined before Hilarian in an audience-chamber crowded with people. When it came to the turn of Vivia Perpetua to confess her

faith, her father, holding her infant in his arms, appeared
by her side. Again he pleaded, not for his own sake, but
for that of the innocent child ; the judge joined in his arguments and entreaties, and concluded with the exhortation :
" Sacrifice for the prosperity of the emperors." " I will
not," she answered. " Are you then a Christian ?" inquired
Hilarian. " I am," was her firm reply. As her father heard
the words which doomed her, he attempted to draw her off
from the platform on which she stood ; Hilarian commanded
him to be beaten away ; the wretched old man received a
blow with a stick, whilst the judge condemned the five Christians to be exposed to wild beasts. They returned to prison
rejoicing ; Perpetua, who had been in the habit of giving
suck to her child, asked for it in vain ; her father refused
to send it : she had seen the last of what she loved best on
earth.

The condemned Christians were reserved for the shows
with which the soldiers were amused on the festival of Geta.
Whilst waiting for the hour of martyrdom, Felicitas, who
was far gone with child, gave birth to a daughter. She suffered much, and could not always remain silent under her pain.
One of the guards mockingly asked what she would do when
exposed to the wild beasts. Felicitas answered : " It is I
that suffer what I now suffer ; but then there will be another
in me that will suffer for me, because I shall suffer for him."
A certain Christian woman took her child, adopted it, and
reared it as her own.

On the 6th of March the five Christians received the free
supper and last meal, which, according to an established
custom, the condemned always ate in public. They did their
best to convert it into the beautiful Agape or love-feast of
the early Christians. The room was full. Many had come
to look on : some, Christians in their hearts, were there to
gaze with reverence and love on the future martyrs ; others,
indifferent pagans, professors of a cruel and voluptuous
creed, found a strange pleasure in looking on those at whose
torments they were to clap their hands on the morrow. The
five Christians edified some, and astonished all, by the cheerful composure of their bearing.

On the following day they left the prison for the amphitheatre. Like all the martyrs of those times, they went

forth to death as to a bridal feast. Perpetua, the lady, with modest look and downcast eyes; Felicitas, the slave, scarcely able to contain her joy. When they reached the gate of the amphitheatre, the guards gave the men the red mantle of the priests of Saturn, and offered to the women the little fillet worn by the priestesses of Ceres. They refused these badges of superstition, and Perpetua, speaking for the rest, said they had come thither of their own accord, relying on the promise that they should not be forced to do any thing contrary to their faith. The tribune consented to let them appear habited as they were.

They entered the amphitheatre. Perpetua sang, like one who had already conquered; the three Christian men, turning towards the people, threatened them with the judgments of God. As they passed before the balcony where Hilarian sat, they said to him : "You judge us in this world, but God will judge you in the next." On hearing this there was but one cry amongst the people, who all called out for the Christians to be scourged. Each of the venatores or hunters, men whose office it was to encounter the wild beasts or whip the condemned, accordingly gave the Christians a lash as they passed before them. A leopard and a bear speedily ended their sufferings. Perpetua and Felicitas were stripped, put into nets, and exposed to a wild cow. But a murmur of disapprobation rose amongst the spectators, shocked by this mixture of indecency and cruelty. The executioners drew the women out, gave them loose garments, and again brought them to face the wild cow. Perpetua was the first attacked; the cow tossed her up; she fell on her back, but soon sat up; her clothes were torn and disordered; she gathered them around her, then got up, calmly fastened her loosened hair, and perceiving Felicitas lying on the ground much hurt, she helped her to rise. They stood together in the arena, quietly expecting the rest; but the people, more eager for blood than for pleasure, cried out that it was enough. They were accordingly led to the gate, where the swords of the confectores usually dispatched those whom the wild beasts had only tortured and not killed.

Rusticus, one of those faithful catechumens whom no peril could deter, was there to receive and comfort them to the last. Perpetua, awakening as from a dream, asked when

she was going to meet the wild cow : she believed with difficulty that the encounter was over. Contrary to the usual
custom, and in order to gratify the blood-thirstiness of the
spectators, the two women were again led forth into the
centre of the amphitheatre, to die there within view of all.
They gave one another the kiss of peace, and meekly sur-
rendered to their fate. An unskilful gladiator prolonged
the torments of Perpetua, by inflicting many slight wounds
before the final one. Her hand, more steady than his in
that awful moment, had to guide it to her throat, and direct
the sword that was to close her pure and brief life.

Perpetua and Felicitas are amongst the most illustrious of
Christian martyrs. For three centuries their venerable relics
were preserved in the great church of Carthage ; where, according to St. Augustine, their yearly festival drew to honor
their memory more than had gone to witness their martyrdom. The shrine is fallen, the relics are lost ; but the
memory of the two noble women still lives.

Amongst the names of early saints and martyrs, which the
Church has faithfully commemorated for many ages as her
greatest titles of honor, are those of Perpetua and Felicitas,
the lady and the slave of Carthage.

Many similar records are preserved : many little traits
of woman's nature, touching or sublime, have been transmitted by ecclesiastical writers and ancient Fathers of the
Church.

Potamiana of Alexandria, a female slave of exquisite beauty, having already received the first seeds of the Christian
faith from her mother, applied to Origen for further instruction. She was progressing under his teaching, when her
master, who had conceived a violent passion for her and failed in seducing her, delivered her to the Præfect Aquila, in
the hope of enforcing her compliance. Tortures having
failed to move her, she was condemned to be thrown into a
caldron of boiling pitch. The only favor she asked was to
keep on her garments ; she added that the executioners
might let her down by degrees, to see the patience with
which Jesus Christ gifted those who trusted in him. Both
requests were granted.

Amongst the martyrs who perished in Numidia in the year
259 was a reader in the Church, named Marian. His moth-

er Mary followed him to the place of execution encouraging him. When all was over, she kissed his dead body, and blessed God for having made her mother of such a son.

Centuries passed, and the same spirit still lived. When Genseric took Carthage in the year 439, a noble maiden named Julia was sold as a slave to a pagan merchant of Syria. She bore her fate with fortitude; performed every duty of her new state, and devoted to prayer and reading all her spare moments. Her gentle cheerfulness and fidelity endeared her to her master, who esteemed her the most valuable of his possessions. He took her with him in one of his voyages to Gaul. When they had reached Corsica, he went on shore to join in an idolatrous festival; Julia remained apart. Her absence was an implied censure, which Felix, the governor of the island, resented. He caused her to be brought before him, and offered to procure her liberty, if she would sacrifice to the gods. " I am free whilst I serve Christ," replied the undaunted slave. Felix, in a transport of rage, caused her to be first struck on the face, and then crucified. Painters generally represent this illustrious saint with the wreath and veil of virgins, standing by the cross through which she found both death and eternal life, bearing in one hand the palm of martyrdom, and in the other the open Scriptures, over which she bends in absorbed mood.

To the same heroic times belong names held dear by the faith of ages, and immortalized by Christian art with the Madonnas and penitent Magdalenes. Then perished the lovely Agnes, the type of youthful innocence; Catherine, the learned and royal virgin, the chaste patroness of schools and studious men; rapt Cecilia, whose sweet strains were said to draw down worshipping angels from heaven : a Christian muse worthy of being painted by Raffaelle. Spite of the obscurity thrown around them by legendary lore, they still embody the heroism and poetry of female martyrs, and lead us back to those far times when women were first called upon to embrace a faith, and held worthy to suffer.

How far they justified the trust, we have imperfectly recorded: those are not facts easily put in words or easily rendered credible. The history of the world offers no second instance of the things that then occurred daily. The wars and oppressions of ages gone often read like the strife

and tyranny of yesterday; but the persecution and constancy of the Christians stand alone.

Hitherto the hatred of triumphant Rome had spent itself
on conquered races: she crushed the nations whose gods
she admitted into her wide Pantheon.   Now it was not people against people, but faith against faith.   The contest lasted upwards of four centuries.   Whilst victims were sacrificed on the altars of paganism, Christians perished in the
amphitheatre.   For four ages the blood of martyrs flowed.
The hatred of one creed and the enthusiasm of the other
kept equal pace.   The heathens crowded the rows of the
circus with cruel eagerness, whilst the Christians entered the
arena with fervent joy.   It was indeed a strange sight: men
and women, whose days were spent in guilty indulgence,
coming to the public shows, where other men and women,
of pure and austere life, were ready to perish for their
pleasure;* and, stranger still, that the spectators of this
fierce pageantry should not be more eager to behold death
than the actors to die.

CHAPTER II.

Recluses—Female Relatives or Friends of the Greek Fathers—Christian
  Women of Rome in the Fourth Century—Paula—Eustochium—Marcella—Fabiola—Monica.

WHEN persecutions and martyrs ceased, religious fervor
asserted itself by extraordinary austerities and life-long acts
of penance.   Those were the times of Paul and Anthony
the anchorets, of Simeon Stylites, of saints whose abode was
the desert, and who sought a home amidst the grottoes and
ruined cities of the lonely Thebaid.

For three years Thaïs the courtezan wept over her sins
in a monastery; Mary of Egypt spent her penitent life in
the fields of burning sand which lie beyond the Jordan; and
Pelagia, the beautiful comedian, forsook the world for a
grotto on the Olive Mount.   Past errors were not always

* Chateaubriand, Etudes Historiques. Etude cinq.

needed to lead women into ascetic life. Syncletica, a rich and noble maiden of Alexandria, beautiful and of unsullied purity, early retired to a narrow cell, where she spent the remainder of her days in prayer and solitude.

Much that now seems exaggerated in all that is told of those penitents and recluses, we must ascribe to the ardor of the Eastern imagination and character. Christianity to them was more than a creed—it was a passion : there was passion in their austerity, mourning, and longing for solitude. That thirst of sacrifice, which to modern judgment appears extreme, then raised them above the rest, and filled even the heathens with respect and wonder : they felt truly that in their faith, there was nothing akin to the feeling which peopled the most dreary deserts of Egypt with worshippers of God.

But even admitting this, Thais, Mary, and Syncletica must be considered as exceptions. Another class of Christian women, differing from the first converts and martyrs, had arisen,—women of home, and home virtues. The mothers, wives, sisters, and daughters of saints or Fathers of the Church : saints themselves in life and name ; learned in holy things, pious, austere, and gentle; of ardent faith, and often of boundless charity ; giving to their sex a higher though calmer dignity than it had yet attained, and, for the first time, calling down on womanhood both the love and reverence of man.

Generations of Christians then edified the world with their faith, genius, and learning. During the persecution of Maximinus II. in 311, St. Macrina and her husband lost all their estates by confiscation, and lived for seven years hidden in the forests of Pontus. Their son, St. Basil, and his wife, St. Emmelia of Cesarea, had ten children ; of whom four— Macrina the eldest, who helped to rear her brothers and sisters in the love of God, the eloquent Basil, the judicious Gregory of Nyssa, and the charitable Peter of Sebaste—have been recognized as saints by the Church : the three sons were celebrated for their learning, and died bishops.

Macrina was deeply versed in the holy Scriptures. She led a pious and retired life, and after the death of her father, and of a young man to whom he had betrothed her, she induced her mother Emmelia to found two monasteries ; one

for men, the other for women, on their own estate near Ibora,
in Pontus. Emmelia and Màcrina lived in one house, Basil
and Peter in the other. The pleasant Iris flowed between
the two monasteries, and around both there spread plains,
valleys, and wooded hills of pastoral beauty and primeval
solitude. After the death of Emmelia, Macrina disposed of
all that was left of their estate in favor of the poor, and
lived by the labor of her own hands. Her resignation to
the will of God equalled her self-denial. She undertook to
console Gregory for the death of their brother Basil in 379.
From her arguments, and the subject of their discourse, he
composed a dialogue on the soul and on the resurrection, in
which he introduced her under the name of the mistress.
Within a few months she followed Basil. Gregory witnessed and recorded the fortitude of her last moments. The
house was so poor that, save her own garments, it held
nothing with which to cover the corpse of Macrina as it was
borne to the grave; Gregory threw his episcopal cloak over
it. So real was the poverty of the primitive convents, where
ladies of high descent and princely wealth, the sisters of
Christian bishops, chose to live and die.

Gregory of Nazienzen, the friend and countryman of Basil,
was, like him, the son and brother of holy women. His
mother Nonna converted her heathen husband, who became
a bishop of Nazienzen, and held the see forty-five years;
Gorgonia his sister, whose virtues in the married state Gregory has affectingly commemorated, was eminent for piety
and charity.

Anthusa, mother of the great St. John Chrysostom, remained a widow at twenty, in lovely and voluptuous Antioch; that capital of the East where Christian austerity and
heathen luxury both held sway. She would never contract
a second marriage, but divided her life between religion and
the education of her children. On hearing this from her
son, who studied under him, the heathen teacher of eloquence, Libanius, could not help exclaiming, as he turned
towards his audience: "Oh! gods of Greece! what women
there are amongst those Christians!"

Those Christian women, so noble and simple in their
purity, had not, like those of Rome or Sparta, cast away the
feelings of nature. When Chrysostom, seized with religious

fervor, wished to forsake the world, Anthusa took him by
the hand, led him into her room, and making him sit down
by the bed where she had given him birth, she began to
weep; then, as the saint afterwards expressed it, "said
things sadder than her tears."

Her tender and pathetic entreaties prevailed; Chrysostom
remained, became a celebrated archbishop, an eloquent
preacher, and died in exile. Whilst he held the see of Constantinople, Nicareta, Olympias, Salvina, Procula, and Pantadia, holy virgins and widows, whose names have been consecrated by the Church, acknowledged his spiritual guidance.
Olympias, the most celebrated, was a truly noble woman.
She was the daughter of Seleucus, a wealthy lord belonging
to the court of Theodosius the Great, and was married in
early youth to Nebridius, treasurer to the emperor. Twenty
days after their marriage, Olympias remained a widow. Her
wealth and beauty attracted many suitors, whom she inexorably rejected. Theodosius wished her to marry one of his
relatives; she refused to do so; to punish her, he placed
her property in the hands of the Præfect of Constantinople,
with orders to act as her guardian until she should be thirty
years of age. Olympias calmly thanked him, and said:
"Your goodness towards me has been that of an emperor
and of a bishop, in thus relieving me from the heavy burden
of my property. Add to that goodness, by dividing my
wealth between the poor and the Church. I have long
been seeking a fit opportunity to avoid the vanity of making
this distribution myself, as well as the danger of attaching
my heart on perishable goods, instead of keeping it fixed on
the true riches."

Theodosius admired the magnanimity of the youthful
widow, and feeling somewhat ashamed of the ungenerous
part he had acted, he caused all her property to be restored
to her in the year 391. The riches of Olympias were immense, and she distributed them with princely liberality.
Whilst she herself lived in a state bordering on penury, she
gave ornaments and sacred vases to the churches; relieved,
almost without ceasing, distressed monasteries, hospitals,
beggars, prisoners, and exiles; and set at liberty several
thousand slaves. Her alms were scattered over towns, villages, islands, and deserts, to the extremities of the then

known world. The poor of every land were to her as her children, and the most remote churches dear to her in the Lord. With time she became deaconess, and as such visited the sick, the poor, the aged, and the distressed of Constantinople.

Though good and pious, Olympias was not happy. She suffered from ill-health, and was through her whole life exposed to persecutions and odious slanders. Her greatest sorrow was to part from St. John Chrysostom. A pure and tender friendship united them for many years. This great and charitable prelate, who gave all the revenues of his church to the poor, and melted down the sacred vases for their relief in seasons of scarcity, had agreed to accept from Olympias the coarse and frugal food which formed his daily sustenance. When he was banished in the year 404, and bade his friends adieu in the great church of Constantinople, to which Olympias belonged as deaconess, the fortitude with which she had borne other sorrows forsook her, and she fell down at the feet and clung to the garments of the archbishop in a transport of grief.

Chrysostom was exiled for having wounded the vanity of Eudocia the empress; but other women were as faithful in their affection as she was in her hatred. For the sake of their beloved pastor, Olympias, Pantadia, and Nicareta endured many grievous persecutions. Nicareta left Constantinople, and ended her days in a remote solitude. Olympias lost all her property, was dragged by soldiers before the public tribunals with the grossest insults, and saw the little community of virgins over whom she presided rudely dispersed. Her exiled friend addressed to her no less than seventeen epistles, one of which contains the fullest account of his sufferings and his faith. The days of the once munificent and wealthy widow closed in sadness and poverty: the year of her death is unknown.

Olympias is not the first instance of a Christian woman faithful to friendship and opinion: many such cases occur in the history of the persecution of the Catholics by the Arians, or in the dissensions which early arose between civil and ecclesiastic power. Whilst the stern and orthodox Athanasius waged his daring and persevering war against heresy, he was repeatedly obliged to be concealed in Alex-

andria, then celebrated for its learning and frequent tumults.
A Catholic virgin of twenty, renowned for her loveliness, was
sitting alone at midnight in her house, when Athanasius suddenly appeared before her, and conjured her to grant him
an asylum. She immediately led him into her most retired
apartments, and intrusted the secret of his presence to no
other person. She waited on him herself, supplied him with
books and provisions, managed his correspondence, and behaved so discreetly, that, though for six years he made her
house his hiding-place in times of danger, his presence was
never suspected.

The East, where Christianity had first arisen, possessed
great attractions for the faithful of every land. Two noble
ladies of Spain, both named Melania—one was the grandmother of the other—left their western home to retire to
Jerusalem. Melania, the younger, was accompanied by her
husband Pinian, son of the Præfect of Rome. They parted
with all their estates in Spain, Gaul, and Italy; freed eight
thousand of their slaves, and gave to a relative those who
preferred the security of bondage to the chances of freedom.
They ended their days in Palestine, prayer and good deeds
their occupation, and the reading and transcribing of manuscripts their innocent amusement.

Paula and Eustochium are still more illustrious pilgrims
from the west to Holy Land. Their names are closely linked
with the name of a great Father of the Church, perhaps
the greatest: St. Jerome, author of the Latin translation of
the Old and New Testaments known as the Vulgate. Apart
from his piety and learning, Jerome was an extraordinary
man. His character, austere and melancholy, was inherited
from his Dalmatian ancestors; but in breadth and fire his
genius partook of the Eastern deserts, where he strove to
quench the passions of his youth; and where, full of days,
wearied of existence, he closed a life of many vicissitudes
and stupendous labors. Paula, her daughter Eustochium,
and their friends Marcella, Albina, Fabiola, women descended from those illustrious families which gave to Rome her
heroes, and to the world its masters, reverently claimed St.
Jerome as their spiritual father. They were worthy of the
relationship. The ascetic spirit of their teacher, his haughty
contempt of the world and its enjoyments, his learning, his

passion for solitude, were shared by these adopted daughters; though tempered by the gentleness of their sex and the tenderness of their charity.

In the year 381 Jerome came to Rome to attend a Council of the Church. He formed an acquaintance with Paula, who made him reside in her house. She was then about thirty-five, and had been a widow three years. There is great beauty in the character of Paula. She had a noble and passionate soul, affections deep even to weakness, and with all this the stoicism of a Roman matron ; making to faith and its aspirations the heroic and heart-breaking sacrifices her ancestors had made to pagan pride and Roman glory.

In no respect did she belie her illustrious origin. Her father boasted his descent from Agamemnon ; and her mother could, with more historic truth, trace Paulus Æmilius amongst her ancestors, and claim a share in the blood of the Scipios and of the Gracchi. Toxotius, the husband of Paula, was of that great Julian family which gave birth to Cæsar. They had five children, a son and four daughters. In 379 Paula lost her husband : his death threw her into such an agony of grief that she was herself near dying ; when she recovered, it was to give up her life and soul to God. Her wealth was great, but it had limits ; and her alms seemed to know of none : the poor—the sick—the infirm—were diligently sought out through the whole city, and relieved at her cost. She held herself defrauded if they received other alms than hers : even the indigent dead were laid out and buried at her expense. When relatives remonstrated, and asked what inheritance she would leave to her children,— "The mercy of God!" answered Paula. Jerome thought that, both in her alms to the poor, and in her own personal austerities—which were great—Paula went too far ; but his remonstrances could not induce her to lessen either her own privations or her liberality to others.

Prayer and reading had a large share in the daily occupations of the devout widow. Her ardent entreaties induced Jerome to allow her and her daughter, Eustochium, to read over with him the Old and New Testaments, which he explained to them as they went on. Similar assistance was asked and obtained by Albina and her daughter Marcella, both friends of Paula. They were deeply read in the Scriptures, and eager to learn more. They would never allow Jerome to leave them, without having first made him answer numerous questions on the true meaning of difficult passages or obscure texts. Albina was critical, acute, and so hard to satisfy, that Jerome protested she was more his judge than his pupil. Marcella was more docile; yet her own authority in such matters was so great, that she was herself consulted from every part, like a doctor of the Church. It was thus that she mainly contributed to the condemnation of the disciples of Origen.

When Jerome came to Rome, Marcella was advancing in life, and had been a widow for many years. Her husband died in the seventh month of their marriage; she was young, and celebrated for the beauty of her person. Cerealis, an old and wealthy consul, wished to marry her. Marcella refused; and to her mother, Albina, who observed that Cerealis being aged would not live long, and would leave her all his property, she replied,—"If I wished to marry, I should look for a husband, and not for an inheritance."

Marcella not only persisted in remaining single, but she also became the first nun in Rome; where monastic life was much despised. She braved the general prejudice, and founded a community of Roman virgins, devoted like her to prayer, the study of the Scriptures, and the relief of the poor. Paula was strengthened by her exhortations in the early part of her widowhood, and for some time Eustochium lived under her care. "What must have been the mistress who made such disciples?" exclaims St. Jerome. These ladies did not remain satisfied with reading the Scriptures in a Latin version; they studied the original Hebrew, and acquired rapidly the knowledge which had cost Jerome so many days and nights of labor. He records that they sung the psalms in Hebrew, without the least trace of a Latin accent.

Fabiola, less learned, surpassed these illustrious ladies in charity. She was descended and took her name from the noble Fabian family. Her first husband was a heathen, and a licentious man. Fabiola divorced him, and married another. After the death of this second husband, she was told that her last marriage, though legal, was contrary to

2*

the precepts of the Gospel. With admirable humility, she, of her own accord, went to perform public penance, and stood with other sinners, whom their errors excluded from the sacred edifice, beneath the porch of one of the Roman churches. From that time Fabiola forsook the world, and edified Rome with her liberal charity. Jerome, in recording her virtues after her death, styled her "the praise of the Christians, the wonder of the Gentiles, the mourning of the poor, and the consolation of the monks."

She founded the first hospital which had ever been known in Rome. In that luxurious and magnificent city, public liberality had until then been displayed in providing the citizens with occasional distributions of corn, licentious amusements, and sanguinary shows. Fabiola served the sick with her own hands; she carried them on her shoulders, and dressed wounds and sores which others had not even the fortitude to contemplate.

The ancients had no love and but little mercy for suffering humanity. Their ideal was one of glorious and godlike men and women; their pity, for heroic sorrows; they despised the poor and infirm as degraded beings. The change wrought by Christian charity is one of the greatest triumphs the new religion ever obtained. The long-contemned Lazarus of the parable, a beggar and a leper, was now acknowledged as a brother: he had once lived and died unheeded at the rich man's door; homes were now built to receive him, and the daughters of his oppressor made themselves his servants.

Towards the close of her life, Fabiola collected all that remained of her property, and uniting it with that of Commachius, son-in-law of her friend Paula—who, like her, was exclusively devoted to good deeds—they erected near Ostia a vast hospital, in which poor strangers were received and entertained. She died there, poor herself, in the year 400.

Jerome and Paula were then both residing in separate monasteries at Bethlehem. After the loss of two daughters, whose death again nearly brought on her own—for she loved passionately, and excessive grief was one of her infirmities—Paula resolved to leave Rome, and, like Jerome, to lead a life of monastic solitude in Holy Land. Her daughter Paulina was married; her son Toxotius remained under the care of relatives; Eustochium agreed to accompany her mother.

Before her departure Paula divided the greater part of her wealth amongst her children. They followed her to the water-side, beseeching her not to go : the youth Toxotius wept and clasped his hands in entreaty. Paula answered nothing, but raised her eyes to heaven as if imploring strength. When she had embarked, she refused to look at that shore where the loved ones stood, and which she was never to behold again.

In this journey to the East, the two Roman ladies visited places famous in ancient classic lore and in sacred history : the cell in the island of Pontia, where Flavia Domitilla had spent her exile ; voluptuous Cyprus ; Antioch ; Sidon ; the land of the Philistines ; Cesarea, the city of the apostles ; Jerusalem ; Bethlehem ; the banks of the Jordan ; and every spot, in city or wilderness, where Christ had once healed the sick, or fed the hungry multitudes. Paula resolved to fix her home in Bethlehem : with the remainder of her wealth she built two monasteries ; one for men, where Jerome dwelt —the other for women, where, with her daughter Eustochium, she took up her abode. She also erected, on the road leading to Bethlehem, hospitals for the sick and houses for strangers, so that none might need shelter in the place where Joseph and Mary had once sought for it in vain.

From his retreat Jerome continued to correspond with his friends in Rome. Marcella still questioned him on scriptural matters ; and so great was the renown of his knowledge, that Aglasia and Hebidia, two ladies from the furthest end of Gaul, sent a friend to Bethlehem for the express purpose of submitting twenty-three scriptural questions to his decision. His epistles show that he tried to lure Marcella and Fabiola away from Rome, with charming pictures of the rural home their friends possessed in Bethlehem, where the laborer and the reaper cheered their toil by singing the psalms of David. He failed, but did not cease to remember the two ladies with evident affection : friends who ask for copies of his works are referred to Fabiola and to "Marcella, who dwells on Mount Aventine." The end of the pious widow was sad. The Goths of Alaric took and plundered Rome in 410. They entered the house of Marcella, and enraged at not finding treasures, which she had long before distributed amongst the poor, they beat and scourged her cruelly.

Marcella rejoiced in the cause of her sufferings : she thanked God " that she had secured her wealth before, and that the loss of the city had found her poor, and not made her so." She did not long survive this event.

Paula had then been dead some time. After ruling her monastery with much wisdom and charity for nearly twenty years, she fell dangerously ill. Her end was serene and beautiful. On the last day of her life, Jerome heard her often repeating in a low tone verses from the psalms. He asked if she suffered ; she replied in Greek, that she was free from pain, and saw all things calm and peaceful. She said no more; and as if already contemning every thing mortal, she continued to repeat texts from Scripture until her last breath.

The room and the monastery were filled with bishops, priests, virgins, and monks ; yet when the saint expired, no cries, no lamentations were heard ; but psalms were sung aloud in the languages of many races. The palor of death had not altered the beauty of Paula's countenance : grave and majestic, she looked not dead, but sleeping. For three days psalms were sung, in Hebrew, Greek, Latin, and Syriac, around the corpse. Eustochium never left it. The mother and daughter had had but one heart : for many years they had never taken a meal or gone to sleep without one another. Eustochium had nursed her mother through her illness with the tenderest care ; she now remained near her, faithful to the last, kissing the closed eyes, and embracing the body of her who had given her life.

On the third day, bishops carried Paula to the grave ; other prelates accompanied, bearing lighted torches, and leading the singers. The poor and the widows were there too ; and, even as in the days of Dorcas, they showed the garments which she whom they named their mother had made " while she was with them." She was buried in the church erected on the spot, where, according to tradition, once stood the humble dwelling in which Mary gave birth to the Saviour.

It is through Jerome that we know Paula. He loved her very tenderly, and called her faults the virtues of others. To console Eustochium, he wrote an account of her mother's life, and touchingly explains how his own grief had long delayed and often interrupted the task. Paula died in 404, in

the fifty-sixth year of her age. Eustochium, who was chosen abbess in her stead, died in 419, three years after her
monastery had been burned down by Pelagian heretics.
Jerome—who was much attached to her, and as a token of
respect for her sanctity and virtues, styled her "his lady
Eustochium"—did not long survive her. They were both
buried near Paula. Their empty tombs are still shown to
travellers in that now stationary land, where ages slowly
pass, and seem to leave no trace.

These Greek and Roman ladies whose lives we have briefly
recorded, exercised a public and domestic influence which it
is difficult to understand, without bearing in mind that paganism, though declining, was not yet conquered. Læta, the
Christian wife of Toxotius, was the daughter of a priest of
Jupiter ; Paula, the younger, who afterwards became abbess
of the monastery of Bethlehem, was reared in a home where
heathen gods and Jesus Christ were both adored. She sang
Christian hymns in the arms of her pagan grandfather, and
lisped "Alleluia" in the midst of her childish endearments.
Jerome wrote an excellent letter to Læta on the education
of this child : he recommended that she should be carefully
taught Greek and Latin literature. The education of women
who were to act as missionaries of the faith in their homes,
was no unimportant matter. Almost every one of the ladies
we have mentioned was learned as well as pious. Læta was
one of the best beloved disciples of Jerome ; she emulated
the ardent charity of Paula, and finally converted her father
by the example of her many virtues.

We should, perhaps, have mentioned first, as earlier in
point of time, Marcellina, the sister of St. Ambrose, and
Monica, the mother of St. Augustine. Of the former little
is known, save that she reared her brother, and was a pious
virgin. Monica has been admirably painted by her son.

It was probably in Tagasta, a small town of Numidia,
that the mother of Augustine was born, in 332, of Christian
parents, who reared their children in the fear and love of
God. An old nurse, who had often carried the father of
Monica on her shoulders during his infancy, was now intrusted with the guardianship of his daughters. She was austere,
vigilant, and her authority was great. The young girls took
their meals at the frugal table of their parents ; they drank

no wine, and were allowed water but sparingly: their governess would never let them drink between their meals, howsoever great their thirst might be. When they begged hard for just one cup, the severe monitress inflexibly replied, "Now you want water because you cannot have wine; but when you are married, and mistresses of the cellar, you will despise water, and yet the habit of drinking will stick to you."

As Monica grew up, her parents, confiding in all the lessons of temperance she had received, intrusted her with the task of daily fetching, from the cellar the quantity of wine needed for the family. After filling her flask from the cup which she had dipped in the cask for that purpose, Monica could not resist the temptation of taking a sup, just to see how it tasted. She disliked it, but found it more palatable on the following day, and still more pleasant as she went on; she ended by liking it so well, that in the end she could drink off a cupful easily. This secret habit was fortunately checked by a quarrel with a maid-servant who accompanied her young mistress to the cellar, and who, in the heat of her resentment, rather disrespectfully called her "drinker of pure wine." The insult stung so deeply the proud soul of the young girl, that from that day she observed the most exact temperance.

Soon after this Monica received baptism, and being of marriageable age, was given by her parents to a citizen of Tagasta; an idolater, but a man of probity and honor. Such unions, though censured by the most devout, were not uncommon; and never was the precept, "Wives, submit yourselves unto your husbands, as unto the Lord," more faithfully followed than by this Christian wife of an idolatrous husband. Monica sought to convert him by the example of her own purity, patience, and gentleness; and the conversion was sadly needed. Patricius was hasty in temper and licentious in habits, yet he never once heard an impatient or reproachful word in his home: if he blamed her unjustly, Monica heard the reproof in silence, waited until his anger was exhausted, and then calmly justified her conduct. When ladies of Tagasta, whose husbands bore more likeness to Patricius than they to Monica, came to her with the marks of ill-usage on their faces, and complained bitterly of the vices and violence of those to whom they had been united, Monica scrupled not to say, "Lay the blame rather on your own tongues;" then with an appearance of pleasantry, under which she hid her perfectly serious meaning, she added, "Remember that when your marriage contract was read to you, you heard the contract of your servitude. Forget not then what you are, and strive not against your masters."

Few obeyed the austere and humble counsel. Four ages of Christianity had nearly elapsed, and woman had still only the choice of evils: submission to the caprices of a tyrannical and licentious master, or ill usage. Need we then wonder at those crowds of virgins and widows to whom their vows of chastity gave honor amongst men, and the freedom of hearts that owned no master save God? Alas! it was not always divine love that filled the cloisters of the olden time, and gave, for ages, so many brides to heaven.

Monica had three children—Augustine, another son, and a daughter, who died an abbess. Augustine was born in 354, and immediately numbered among the catechumens by receiving on his forehead the sign of the cross, and on his lips the mysterious and symbolic salt: infant baptism was not then in use. Spite of his many faults, Patricius loved his wife and children. Proud of the dawning genius of his eldest son, he strained his means to give him a good education; even the devout Monica, growing somewhat worldly for the sake of her favorite child, shared all his eagerness on this subject. Augustine was sent to the neighboring town of Madaura, to study belles-lettres and eloquence; he subsequently prosecuted his studies at Carthage, amidst all the dangers and the dissipation of a great city. Monica, in earnest and touching language, begged of him to lead a pure life, and above all never to attempt to seduce a married woman. In his Confessions the penitent saint acknowledges that he listened to her impatiently, and held her advice mere woman's talk, which he would have been ashamed to heed or obey.

Patricius died in 371. For a year he had wholly relinquished his dissolute courses, received baptism, and lived like a sincere Christian. The father rose from his slough, but the son fell: he became the slave of his passions, renounced the Catholic faith, in which he had been brought up, and embraced the creed of the Manicheans; who contended for the existence of two first principles, one good, the other evil. Yet in the midst of all his errors, Augustine continued to display that admirable genius which stamps every thing he has left and written with a lofty and eloquent tenderness. To relieve his mother from the expenses of his education he opened a school of grammar and rhetoric in Tagasta.

Monica mourned over him with deep and yearning grief. Shocked at his blasphemies, she would no longer allow him to reside under her roof, or to sit at her table; but she wept and prayed for him incessantly. Her dreams became the image of her waking thoughts. One of those nightly visions comforted her greatly: she saw herself sorrowfully standing alone on a rule of wood, when a youth, radiant with light, came up and asked her why she wept. When she answered that it was for the soul of her fallen son, he bade her look well, for that where she was she should see Augustine. She looked round, and beheld him standing on the same rule of wood with her. When she mentioned this dream to Augustine, he slighted it, and endeavored to interpret it in the sense that his mother would adopt his creed, and not that he should return to hers. "No, not so," very promptly replied Monica, "for it was not said to me, *where he is* you also are, but he is *where you are*." The quickness of the answer struck her son more than the dream itself; which, however, gave her so much hope that she once more allowed him to dwell in her house.

For nine years Augustine persisted in his dissolute life and false faith. Monica prayed for him, and omitted no human means of bringing him over to her belief. A certain bishop, urged by her to come and argue with him, discreetly refused, and said he would himself end by finding out the truth; but as Monica persisted, and with fervent entreaties and many tears besought him to make at least the attempt, he replied, as if weary of her importunities, "Continue as you have begun; surely the son of so many tears cannot perish." Struck with his words, Monica took them as a prophecy, and insisted no more.

The weariness of the world and its pleasures, of life and its aims—nay, of the heart itself, and of all its promised delights, is no new sorrow: it clings to humanity as the bitterest portion of the curse which fell on Adam and his posterity. This curse overtook Augustine, in spite of his fame, genius, and pleasures. His dearest friend died; the guilty love in which he had indulged for years was imbittered by quarrels and jealousies; fame when won seemed worthless; his very belief failed him, and no other faith came to fill the void of soul and heart. He was scarcely thirty; yet, in the strength of manhood and prime of life, the sweetness of existence was over, and nothing seemed left to quaff but the bitter dregs of the once enchanting cup. Wearied of Africa, he resolved to go to Rome. Monica was filled with grief. The shadow which darkened the days of the erring son, had fallen lightly on the pure life of the mother: patient beneath her hard destiny, she had made the happiness of life consist in the peace of home, and its ambition in the aspirations of her soul to God. Her heart still owned one human tie—her children. She followed Augustine to the sea-side, hoping that her tears would induce him to remain, or to take her with him. He wished to do neither; but she kept so close on his steps, that he was compelled to deceive the love he could not shake off. He assured her that in going on board he only meant to bid farewell to a friend, with whom he wished to remain to the last moment. The distrustful mother wept, and clung to his garments; at length she was persuaded to pass the night in a chapel consecrated to the memory of St. Cyprian. It stood on the shore, not far from the spot where the vessel lay at anchor. Whilst she spent the night in vigil and prayer, the ship set sail. Dawning day found her in the little oratory, and her son far away on the waters. She returned, sad and alone, to her home in Tagasta.

From Rome, Augustine proceeded to Milan; where his mother joined him ere long, braving the terrors of a long voyage to see him again. A great joy awaited her: after a long and bitter struggle, Augustine cast off the trammels of his former passions, until his soul at length stood pure and free before God, confessing the faith of Christ, and rejoicing in its liberty. Soon after his conversion, which he has himself admirably related in the memorable "Confessions," Augustine gave up the school of rhetoric which he held at

Milan, and retired to a country house at Cassiacorum, lent to him by one of his friends. Monica, his brother, two of his late pupils, and some friends, accompanied him. In this quiet retreat, devoting themselves to prayer, contemplation, and social converse, they spent that most pleasant part of the year in southern climates, the warm and genial vintage-time.

When the little household had prayed together, Augustine and his friends walked forth to enjoy the cool morning time. Monica remained within, engaged in household tasks. She however shared in the religious and literary conferences; of which some have been preserved by her son ; he speaks with admiration of her remarks, and of her firm and manly heart, strong in its faith. After the baptism of St. Augustine, this little society resolved to embark for Africa, and seek a home where they might all live together in religious and philosophic retirement. They began their journey in the autumn of 387, and stopped at Ostia, near the mouth of the Tiber, whence they thought to embark. Here Monica suddenly sickened and died.

The pages in which Augustine records the last hours and aspirations of this noble woman are amongst the best he ever wrote ; they breathe the very spirit of tenderness and prayer. But they must be read with what preceded : taken apart, the style seems peculiar and obscure—scarcely any thing of the charm remains. " The day now approaching wherein she was to depart this life," writes Augustine, " it came to pass that she and I stood alone in a certain window, which looked into the garden of the house where we now lay at Ostia ; and where, removed from the din of men, we were recruiting from the fatigues of a long journey for the voyage. We were discoursing then together, alone, very sweetly ; and forgetting the past in the future, we were inquiring between ourselves of what sort the eternal life of the saints was to be, which eye hath not seen, nor ear heard, nor hath it entered into the heart of man to conceive. But yet we longed with all our hearts after those heavenly streams of the fountain of life, that we might in some sort meditate upon so high a mystery. And then our discourse was brought to that point, that the very highest delights of the earthly senses, in the very purest material light, were, in respect of the sweetness of that life, not only not worthy of comparison,

but not even of mention. Raising ourselves with a more
fervent affection towards the eternal, we passed by degrees
through all corporeal things; even the very heavens, whence
sun, and moon, and stars shine upon the earth : yea, we
were soaring higher yet, by inward musing and discourse,
and admiring of Thy works ; and we came to our own minds,
and went beyond them, that we might arrive at that region
of never-failing plenty, where Thou feedest Israel forever
with the food of truth."

Thus soaring in spirit, they sought to imagine how it would
be if the tumult of the senses, and all they perceive of the
soul herself and her imaginings, were suddenly hushed : if
God spoke to her not through external signs, angel's voice,
or mysterious parable, but in living reality. Then compar-
ing her state to that rapid thought which for a moment had
raised them so high, they found that this bliss of intellect
and love surpassed all other, and they placed eternal happiness in the mere presence of the divinity.

" As we spake," adds Augustine, " this world with all its
delights became contemptible to us. My mother said, ' Son,
for mine own part, I have no further delight in any thing in
this life. What I do here any longer, and to what end I am
here, I know not, now that my hopes in this world are accomplished. One thing there was for which I desired to
linger for a while in this life—that I might see thee a Catholic Christian before I died. My God hath done this for
me, and more ; since I now see thee despising earthly happiness, and become his servant : what then do I here ?' "

Five or six days after this, Monica was seized with a fever.
Recovering from a fainting fit, she said to her sons, " You
will bury your mother here." The brother of Augustine,
knowing with what care she had formerly prepared her own
grave near that of Patricius, seemed to deplore that she
should die and sleep in a foreign land. Monica chid him,
and bidding both her sons lay her body wherever she died,
and not trouble themselves about it, she added but one request, " that they should remember her before the altar of
the Lord."

On the ninth day of her illness, and in the fifty-sixth year
of her age, Monica died. " I closed her eyes," writes Augustine, " and there flowed withal a mighty sorrow into my

heart." Time brought consolation, but not forgetfulness. It is strange and touching, after so many ages have passed away, to read the request which he addresses to all those who may peruse his Confessions, "that at the altar of God they may remember Monica, and Patricius her husband;" that so his mother's last request may be, "through the prayers of many, more abundantly fulfilled to her."

We have lingered too long, perhaps, over this life of a simple woman of the fourth century. Her existence was calm and domestic; happy because her soul was with God. Such as it was we give it, as one of the last glimpses of the sphere within which woman's hopes grew and died, or blossomed into immortality, until the great Barbarian invasion shattered to pieces the foundations of the old world; and, in the midst of seeming ruin, laid the seeds of that other civilization which has not yet run its course of ages.

CHAPTER III.

Christian Princesses from the Fourth to the Fifth Century—Helena—
Constantia—Flacilla—Pulcheria and her Sisters—Story of Athenais.

THE conversion of Constantine the Great to Christianity, in the early part of the fourth century, introduced a series of religious princesses, who differed more honorably from their predecessors on the throne, than their Christian husbands or fathers differed from the degenerate Cæsars whom they replaced.

First, and (save Pulcheria) greatest, was the Empress Helena, the mother of Constantine. She was the daughter of a British king, according to some authorities—of an innkeeper at Tarsus, according to others : she was certainly a pious and munificent princess, who, though converted to Christianity in old age, left, and deserved to leave, the name of a great saint. Her grand-daughter, Constantia, inherited her fervent piety. Ælia Flacilla, the gentle and worthy wife of Theodosius the Great, endeared herself to her husband and his subjects by many virtues. The beautiful and impe-

rious Eudocia, who persecuted St. John Chrysostom with
relentless hatred, had three daughters of eminent piety.
The eldest, Ælia Pulcheria Augusta, has left a name the
more worthy of record for appearing as it does through the
slow degeneracy of the Eastern empire, then ruled by imbe-
cile emperors and insolent eunuchs.

Virgin, empress, and saint, Pulcheria imparted to her long
sway the prudence, wisdom, and gentleness of her own character. Mildness was one of her favorite virtues; but in the
hour of need she could be both firm and vigorous. " She
alone," justly observes Gibbon, " among all the descendants
of the great Theodosius, appears to have inherited any share
of his manly spirit and abilities." Her father, Arcadius, died
in 408. Pulcheria was then about nine years of age : she
had two younger sisters, Arcadia and Marina, and a brother
a year younger than herself, Theodosius the Second. An-
themius, his tutor and minister, governed the empire in his
name for a few years.

The precocious wisdom and talents of Pulcheria were so
remarkable, that in 414, when she was little more than fifteen years of age, she was, in the name of her brother, declared Augusta and his partner in the imperial dignity ; and
from that day she governed the empire, and superintended
the education of Theodosius.

A child in years, a woman in gravity and wisdom, Pulcheria seemed to have passed unscathed through that ardent
period of life, which gathers within a space so brief, hopes,
dreams, and feelings enough to agitate a whole existence.
Her very piety was calm : the unquiet thoughts which so
often trouble the devotion of fervent hearts were unknown
to the youthful Augusta. Serene without coldness, she
seemed to temper her actions, and even her feelings, with
the sedate majesty of her rank.

One of her first acts as Augusta was very characteristic.
She knew and dreaded the evils which foreign alliances en-
tailed upon the State, and she resolved not to marry : her
piety, though quiet, was deep; it rendered self-denial easy,
and her firm mind could contemplate without fear a life of
solitude and liberty. With the natural ascendency of an intellect both calm and strong, Pulcheria induced her two sisters to follow her example. In the presence of the clergy

and of the people, the three youthful sisters of Theodosius solemnly consecrated themselves to God. Pulcheria caused their vow to be inscribed in large letters on a gold tablet adorned with precious stones, which was publicly offered in the great church of Constantinople.

The imperial palace now became as secluded and as sacred as a monastery. To authorize no suspicions, howsoever slight or groundless, the princesses received no men in their private apartments: it was recorded of Pulcheria that she never spoke to any man, save in public or open places. The three imperial virgins had no other society than that of the chosen maidens with whom they formed a sort of religious community. Their attire was simple and without ornament; they lived frugally, and fasted often; they divided their time between useful studies and light works of embroidery, and devoted several hours of the day and night to prayer and psalmody. They were assiduous in their public devotions, and liberal in their alms to the poor. One feeling animated them: they ate, worked, and prayed together, and whatever they did was marked with all the unity of religious and sisterly love. The only difference in the condition of the three sisters was, that Pulcheria alone ruled the State—a difference which Arcadia and Marina, conscious of her superiority, bore with modest humility. They were not Augustæ, like their sister, but nobilissimæ—"most noble." They lived with ascetic simplicity, but were called queens, and knew how to keep up royal dignity. Arcadia erected at her own expense the public baths of Constantinople, which took from her the name of Arcadian.

Pulcheria was excellently adapted to the exercise of that power which she had neither received nor taken, but which had been tacitly relinquished to her; and which she had as tacitly assumed, because she alone, of all the members of the imperial family, was equal to its duties. She transacted the affairs of the State with dispatch and indefatigable activity. Her extensive learning, her familiar knowledge of the Greek and Latin tongues, the elegance with which she could use both these languages on all the occasions of speaking or writing on public business—gave both ease and dignity to the exercise of her extensive power. But prudence still remained her great characteristic: in all her difficulties she prayed to Heaven for the aid of good counsel, then reflected maturely, and consulted with her ministers. Her measures were slowly conceived, but were carried out with promptness and decision. She took little or no honor to herself, and always acted in the name of her brother; to whom she ascribed the peace and prosperity of his long reign.

The education of Theodosius was one of her most important and least successful tasks. Pulcheria gave him the best masters; surrounded him with youths who were to share his studies and excite his emulation; and judiciously alternated his more serious pursuits with manly and military exercises. To herself she carefully reserved the task of instructing him in those arts of government, which her clear and vigorous understanding had learned without a master. But Theodosius the Younger, like his weak father, Arcadius, was made to be governed. Hunting, painting, carving, and the transcribing of manuscripts, were the only occupations for which he showed any taste. He had the piety without the talents or energy of his sister. Yet he was chaste, temperate and so merciful of heart, that he pardoned every criminal who implored his pity. When Pulcheria censured this indiscriminate mercy, "Ah! sister," replied Theodosius, "it is easy to make a man die, but God alone can bring him back to life."

It was only to exercise this amiable leniency that the young emperor interfered in the government of his dominions: all the real burden of ruling the State, therefore, fell on Pulcheria. The only relaxations which she sought were such as became the grave and austere devotion of a virgin consecrated to heaven. Unless when urgent business detained her, she always shared the pious exercises of her sisters, and devoted several hours of the day to the attentive study of the holy Scriptures. Such was her thirst of the divine word that she often forsook her lonely couch, consisting of a few boards covered over with a carpet, and pursued her uninterrupted studies through the silent night. Ages separate us from Pulcheria; the language which she spoke has died away, the empire which she ruled has long been fallen; but even through the lapse of centuries, the mind can look back and greet the pure vision of the virgin em-

press, forgetting sleep for wisdom, and sitting up alone to
meditate on the word of God.

Like her sisters, Pulcheria was liberal in her alms to the
poor. The praise of the historian, who asserted that the
generosity of the three sisters of Theodosius had banished
mendicity from his empire, may be exaggerated ; but it is
honorable to have rendered such praise probable. Gibbon
acknowledges that in Pulcheria " the piety of a Christian
virgin was adorned by the zeal and liberality of an empress.
Ecclesiastical history describes the splendid churches which
were built at the expense of Pulcheria in all the provinces
of the East ; her charitable foundations for the benefit of
strangers and the poor ; the ample donations which she
assigned for the perpetual maintenance of monastic societies ;
and the active severity with which she labored to suppress
the opposite heresies of Nestorius and Eutyches."

The romantic marriage of Theodosius displays the kind
and liberal feelings of Pulcheria—austere for herself, but to
others indulgent. When the emperor reached his twentieth
year, he asked his sister to find him a bride, " a virgin of
royal or patrician blood, more beautiful than all the maidens
of Constantinople ;" he confessed, however, that beauty was
much more important than a noble or royal origin. None
of the noble maidens whom Pulcheria, with a view to her
brother, had caused to be brought up in the palace, answered
his expectations ; she accordingly requested Paulinus, the
friend of Theodosius, to look out for such a young girl as her
brother wished to find.

Whilst Paulinus was engaged in this search, there died at
Athens a heathen sophist, named Leontius. He bequeathed
every thing he possessed to his two sons, and to his daughter,
Athenais, left only a hundred pieces of money ; declaring
that he gave her no more, " because her learning and beauty,
which raised her above her sex, were in themselves a sufficient fortune." Athenais was then twenty-seven years of
age ; but she was beautiful and very learned : her father had
instructed her in literature, in all the philosophy of the
schools, besides geometry, astronomy, and eloquence. This
eloquence proved fruitless when she besought her brothers
to give her a share in their father's inheritance : they turned
her out of doors ; and Athenais, having no other remedy,

came to Constantinople. and appealed to the empress. Her beauty, unblemished name, and accomplishments, impressed Pulcheria so favorably, that she promised to protect her : as an earnest of her favor she received her at once into the palace.

On the following day Pulcheria said to her brother : " I have found a maiden of pure morals ; her brow is well formed ; her hair curled and golden. She has fine eyes, a straight nose, a fair complexion, grace in every motion, and a modest bearing. She is a Greek, a virgin, and very learned." This categorical description inflamed Theodosius. His passion increased when, hidden by a drapery, he beheld the beautiful stranger conversing with his sister. Athenais was a heathen, but the prospect of a throne readily made her a Christian. Pulcheria instructed her herself, caused her to be baptized under the name of Eudocia, and, though the younger of the two by some years, adopted her as her daughter. Eudocia was married to Theodosius in 421. Two years later she gave birth to a daughter, and was raised to the rank of Augusta. Thus was realized a fortune far more splendid than any which the Athenian sophist could have foreseen for his daughter.

The only vengeance which Eudocia took of her unkind brothers, was to call them to court and raise them to the rank of præfects and consuls. Those studies and sciences which had charmed her youth in the solitude of her Athenian home, were still dear to her in the imperial palace of Constantinople. . She paraphrased in verse the first eight books of the Old Testament, and the prophecies of Daniel and Zachariah. . She also wrote a life of St. Cyprian, and composed a panegyric on the Persian victories of Theodosius. To these productions may be added a singular life of Christ, composed from verses of Homer : a common practice in that degenerate age. In the year 428, Eudocia undertook a pilgrimage to Jerusalem. Her progress through the East was marked by ostentatious magnificence. Seated on a throne of gold and gems, she pronounced, before the senate of Antioch, an eloquent oration, in which she gloried in sharing with them the blood of the Greek. She promised to enlarge the walls of Antioch, gave a considerable sum to restore the public baths, and accepted the statues which the

3

grateful city erected in her honor. When she reached the gates of Jerusalem, Melania, the younger, came forth to meet her; and the empress received the saint with every token of esteem and respect. After displaying throughout all Holy Land a zeal and munificence in charitable gifts and pious foundations which exceeded even the far-famed liberality of Helena, Eudocia returned in triumph to Constantinople.

The passionate fondness of the emperor for his wife increased with time; her influence at length superseded that of his sister, who had continued to govern the State with her usual zeal and prudence. Pulcheria has been accused of ambition and love of power; unjustly, we think; she ruled because the indolent emperor was unfit to rule, even in the simplest things. She injured herself to rouse him from this disgraceful apathy. Theodosius never read the papers which he signed daily; after many useless remonstrances, Pulcheria at length offered for her brother's signature a document by which he sold to her his wife. Shortly afterwards, Theodosius sent for the empress, who was then in the apartment of his sister; Pulcheria refused to let her go, and proved to her brother that he had sold Eudocia to her to be her slave. This practical lesson did not please Theodosius, and greatly offended his wife.

Eudocia had not a generous heart: she forgot how much she owed to her benefactress, and urged her husband to banish her from his court by forcibly conferring on her the rank of deaconess. It was then no uncommon practice to exclude thus from the world, women of rank who were found to be in the way. No less ungrateful than his wife, Theodosius consented: he summoned Flavian, bishop of Constantinople, and ordered him to make Pulcheria deaconess, by the imposition of hands. Flavian refused, and privately sent word to Pulcheria to keep out of his way, lest he should be compelled to do that which might displease her; she took the hint, and, leaving the palace, retired to a country-seat in the plains of Hebdomon. This happened in the year 447. Marina and Arcadia had both been dead some time.

Eudocia was superior in learning to Pulcheria, but she had neither her wisdom nor her experience. Her rule was marked by the greatest disorders, both civil and religious; it was brief. Theodosius, notwithstanding the mature age of his wife, suddenly became jealous of her, and accused her of a criminal intrigue with his bosom-friend Paulinus. In the heat of his resentment, he publicly separated from the empress; and, forgetting the clemency of his youth, caused Paulinus to be put to death. Eudocia took a second pilgrimage to Jerusalem, where she died in 460, solemnly protesting her innocence.

Pulcheria learned in her solitude the fall of Eudocia; but it required the heresy of the Eutychians and the entreaties of Pope Leo to make her come to court. She saw her brother, and spoke to him with so much force on the subject of his religious errors, and on the evils of the government of eunuchs which he sanctioned, that, yielding to her old influence, he restored her at once to her former power. He died soon after this in the year 450. Pulcheria was unanimously proclaimed empress of the East, and was thus the first woman to whose publicly recognized sway the Romans submitted. With a wisdom worthy of admiration, and an entire freedom from that ambitious vanity ascribed to woman, Pulcheria, instead of centering the power of the State in her own hands, resolved to share it with Marcian, an excellent general and statesman; and moreover a zealous Christian, eminent for his piety to God and his charity to the poor. The empress was then fifty-one, Marcian was sixty-five, and a widower; Pulcheria offered to give him her hand and raise him to the throne, provided he would agree to consider himself only her nominal husband. Marcian readily consented: they were married, and for three years these two great souls governed the empire in concert, and directed all their thoughts and efforts towards the public weal. Their union remained unbroken until the death of Pulcheria, on the 10th of September of the year 453. Marcian, who survived her four years, then remained sole master of the empire.

The end of Pulcheria was calm, and worthy of a life so noble and so dignified. Death had been one of the points of her daily meditation for many years: it found her prepared, as Christian and as sovereign, to go and surrender her long account to God. The poor, whom she had faith-

fully assisted in her lifetime, were the heirs to whom she
bequeathed all her riches and possessions. The name of
saint has long been bestowed on her by both Greeks and
Latins; and Pope Benedict XIV. (called the Protestant
Pope, on account of the little respect which he showed for
many names in the calendar), always professed a singular
veneration for St. Pulcheria.

A calmer glory than that which has rendered the names
of the Elizabeths and Catherines of later years so celebrated,
lingers around the gentle memory of the Greek princess.
She made no foreign conquests; she did not extend the
limits of the empire, but she preserved it in peace and
prosperity: her prudence warned off misfortune; her justice prevented rebellion. Like the wise virgins of the Gospel, Pulcheria carefully guarded the lamp that was to guide
her steps to the heavenly bridegroom: human passions never extinguished its pure flame, or darkened it with that be-
setting sin of the austere and the chaste—spiritual pride.
Whilst she embraced a life of solitude—the ideal type of
female purity—she forgot not humility, that other chosen
virtue of woman. The even flow of her days, the sedate
gravity of her character and actions, gave little scope to the
details in which biography finds its deepest charm; but
there is high moral beauty in this calmness and repose of a
life spent on a throne, amidst all the agitation inseparable
from the government of a large empire. We read in that
deep peace, the thoughtful wisdom which ruled Pulcheria,
from her early vow of virginity to her late marriage with
Marcian; and the wisdom which springs from motives so
excellent and so pure, is surely virtue before God.

Here closes all that seemed to us most worthy of record
in the history of Christian women for the first five ages of
their faith. They were eminent for fervor in the days of the
martyrs, and for learning and charity in the calmer times
which followed. Elegant and dignified as became the patrician daughters of an ancient civilization, they stand essentially apart from the barbarian princesses, and not always
gentle nuns, of succeeding ages.

Calm Monicas, dwelling in austere homes, where something of Greek elegance and old Roman virtue still lingers;
mild and yet impassioned Paulas; Fabiolas, great in charity;

imperial and learned Pulcherias, shall no longer rise before us. -Through the wild passions, brutality, and ignorance of barbarian races, must the native spirituality of woman now assert its claims. Long banished and oppressed, it shall dwell apart and seek convent solitudes; until awakens, after centuries of gloom, the impassioned adoration of the middle ages; when, for the sake of her who bore Jesus, every woman is dear and sacred to the heart of Christian chivalry.

PERIOD THE SECOND.—THE MIDDLE AGES.

CHAPTER IV.

Civilizing influence of Woman—Power of Geneviève—Early Converts—
Spirit of Proselytism—Clotildis—Bertha—Ethelberga—Necessity of
Convents—Radegonde—Hilda—Bertilla—Bathildis.

A LONG period of rude and ignorant barbarism followed
the decline of Roman power. Then seemed ready to perish
all that the old world had through ages gathered of learning and civilization. Wilder and far more ungovernable
passions than those which had ever troubled the republics
of Greece or Rome, decided the fate of races and empires.

Happily for the modern world, there still existed many
principles to prevent total degradation. Christianity, women, and monasteries, though with many degrees between,
exerted their respective influence. Christianity—we speak
now without reference to its divine origin—stood, a great
spiritual and moral power, in the very stronghold of the
barbarian world : women, who were themselves raised by
religion, softened and refined men ; whilst convents were
even as an ark where the studious took refuge, and which
carried down through many a stormy sea the venerable
classic lore of past ages. Many other causes no doubt
tended to modify the primitive rudeness and ferocity of the
barbarians, who had invaded Europe and triumphed over
Rome ; but it neither lies within our scope, nor is it our intention, to dwell upon them here.

We have already said, and we must repeat, that the women of whom we are going to speak have little in common
with the early Greek and Roman converts to Christianity.
From them we are descended, but what we are they were
not : religion to them was more than the exercise of gentle
and feminine virtues ; it helped them to subdue passions in
all their native strength, and which the stern and degrading

bondage of their masters had failed to tame. The blood which flowed in the veins of the daughters and mothers of the primitive and warlike nations could not be either calm or slow. Women have little share in the history of those times; but when they do act, what perfect embodiments they seem of the virtues, vices, and crimes of their race! The women of Sparta or Lacedæmon never showed a spirit more indomitable than those Gaulish matrons, who, on seeing their army defeated, murdered their children, and hung themselves from their chariots, sooner than fall into the hands of the Romans. We may search ancient or modern tragedy for a destiny and death more heroic than that of Boadicea, or for a hatred more relentless than the fierce contest of Brunehaut and Frédegonde, the two Frank queens.

Religion did not at once cool this ardent spirit—it rather modified than subdued it; and we must remember that the modification was slow. The progress of Christianity owes much, however, to these women. They embraced it for reasons similar to those which had instinctively impelled the first Christian converts, and which in their case were rendered more powerful by their degraded condition, their ignorance, and the harshness with which they were treated. To those whom this world has not favored, the glorious promises of the next will ever be most dear. Excluded from active and intellectual life, despised and oppressed in their homes, the barbarian women took refuge in a faith which soothes the heart and elevates the soul. They had little personal influence, and thus their action was not perceived at first; but the virtues of Christianity, purity, temperance, forgiveness, and resignation were essentially feminine virtues: they were more easily practised by women, than by men; and this gave to the weaker sex a moral superiority over the stronger one, which is visible even through the primitive rudeness of those dark ages.

Christianity had early penetrated into Gaul; it had there resisted the pagan worship of Rome, and with time it conquered the ruder idolatry of the barbarians, whose lawless power superseded the rule, civilized, though stern, which had once spread over the whole western world. The northern invaders oppressed their women, but they recognized in them something divine. This impression was strengthened by the pure and moral dignity they witnessed in those who had embraced the Christian faith. The Velledas and Druid priestesses of Germany and Gaul prepared the way for women of power as great, and of inspiration far more pure.

In the course of the fifth century, Geneviève, a simple shepherd girl of Nanterre, near Paris, was revered as the earthly providence of the city; which afterwards chose her for its heavenly patroness. Her charity in times of fever, famine, or danger, was unequalled. When Childeric, king of the Franks, besieged Paris, Geneviève boldly went out at the head of a brave little band to procure provisions, and brought back boats laden with corn to the starving citizens. Childeric became master of the city; but though a foe and a heathen, he respected the pious and patriotic maiden. It is said that he seldom refused any thing to her prayers, and that when there were any prisoners whom he did not wish to forgive, he caused the gates of Paris to be closed on the saint—a touching acknowledgment of her merciful influence. The power of Geneviève with heaven, was held to be still greater than that which she possessed over earthly sovereigns; and to her prayers the Parisians attributed the deliverance of their city from the threatened visit of Attila, "the scourge of God." She died advanced in years, universally venerated and beloved.

The important and interesting series of events described in ecclesiastical history as the conversion of nations, took several ages to accomplish. It is difficult to estimate now how far the personal influence of pure and revered women like Geneviève may have aided the work. It is at least certain that in those remote lands where the zeal of missionaries carried Christianity, the new religion derived its earliest triumphs from the enthusiasm of women. A divine instinct seemed to reveal to them how much they would owe to the faith; for they were ever amongst the first converted, and the most eager to convert. The charm of poetry and romance lingers around the legends of those early times. When the great apostle of Ireland fearlessly journeyed over the whole island on his mission of peace, he once chanced, with his companions, to rest for the night near a fountain. As day broke they began chanting the morning service; two royal virgins, Ethnea and Fethlimia, coming to the fountain to bathe, were surprised at the sight of these venerable strangers, clad in white garments, and holding books in their hands. A conversation ensued ; Patrick spoke so eloquently of the true God, that the princesses became converts, and received baptism at the fountain. Shortly afterwards they were consecrated virgins of the Church.

The first religious community of women in Ireland was founded by St. Bridget beneath the oak of Kill-dara ; thence other sisterhoods spread over the land, still acknowledging her for their spiritual mother. Many pious virgins leaving the isle of saints, crossed the seas, like missionaries of truth, to make their homes amongst nations still lingering in the darkness of idolatry ; and bequeathed their names to the veneration of foreign lands.

In Gaul and Britain, the wives of kings early led to the propagation of the faith. Clovis, king of the Franks, heard of the beauty and virtues of Clotildis, a princess of Burgundy, who had been spared by her usurping uncle in the massacre of her family. A messenger, disguised as a beggar, entered the remote castle where Clotildis was kept; when the pious princess had washed his feet, the messenger discovered his real errand, and offered her the ring of Clovis. She accepted it, and became the wife of the Frank king.

Clovis was a heathen, Clotildis a Christian. She was beautiful and beloved ; and she resolved to convert her husband. Whenever Clovis came to visit her in the peaceful though homely villas, more farms than palaces, where she resided whilst he and his rude chiefs were away at war, she spoke to him long and earnestly on the dogmas of the Christian faith. It required, however, a battle, in which he conquered, and attributed his victory to the power of the God his wife worshipped, to convince Clovis. Towards the close of the fifth century he was baptized with his sister and three thousand of his warriors. But the value of these conversions must not be overrated : Clovis, though a Christian, was still a barbarian. The recital of the passion of Christ roused him to fury, and made him exclaim : " Had I been present at the head of my valiant Franks, I would have avenged him." To the Frank chief, the sacrifice of mercy gave no thoughts save those of war and vengeance.

Clotildis, pious, charitable to the poor, and humble in the

3*

midst of greatness as she was, knew not the divine virtue of
forgiveness: after the death of Clovis she urged her sons to
avenge her murdered kindred. The evil passions which she
thus fostered wrought their own punishment: two of her
sons murdered their nephews and her grandchildren, for the
sake of their inheritance. It required ages of Christianity
and civilization to efface these savage and cruel instincts from
the barbarian races. Clotildis retired to a cloister, where
she died in 531.

This spirit of proselytism was carried down through several generations of pious queens. Bertha, grand-daughter of
Clotildis, married Ethelbert, king of Kent, and prepared her
husband to embrace the Christian faith when it was preached
in Britain by St. Augustine. Their daughter Ethelberga
was asked in marriage by Edwin, king of Northumberland.
Her brother Eadbald replied, "that a Christian maid could
not lawfully marry an idolater, lest the faith and its mysteries should be profaned by the company of one who knew
not the worship of the true God." Edwin having promised
that the princess should enjoy entire freedom of conscience,
the objection was waived, and Ethelberga was sent to him.
Pope Boniface entreated her by letter to convert her husband; and she contributed much to that great change, which
led Edwin to embrace the faith and die for it, in fighting
against Penda, the idolatrous king of Mercia. This persecutor of Christianity, who sought to extirpate it by the sword,
could not conquer it in his own home: his son Peada became a Christian to marry Alaflede, and his four daughters
consecrated themselves to God, in those calm retreats for
which Anglo-Saxon princesses already began to forsake the
rude palaces of their fathers.

Cloisters early formed a part of the social system. They
screened their wearied or timid inhabitants from the polished
corruption of the old world, or sheltered them from the strife
and tumult of the new. Their importance increased with
every succeeding age: these homes of prayer and learning
superseded the gardens of heathen philosophy. In classic
lands they often rose on the ruins of pagan altars: the retreat of Benedict, patriarch of the western monks, was
erected on Mount Cassino, on a spot where a temple to
Apollo had once stood; and a nunnery, governed by his

sister Scholastica, was situated within a short distance. In lands farther west, where the tide of barbarian invasion had flowed in more deep, convents arose on the brow of steep hills, or in wild and desolate places; it was only when the times grew more secure that monasteries were to be found in fertile plains and large cities. The recluses gave the chief portion of their time to religion and study: much of their leisure was spent in transcribing ancient manuscripts—a labor of time and love in which both monks and nuns were engaged.

We cannot give a better illustration of the causes which peopled those religious and learned asylums, than in the history of St. Radegonde, who founded the monastery of Holy Cross, in the town of Poitiers. Radegonde was the daughter of a king of Thuringia, and was carried off by Clotaire, king of Neustria in Gaul, who conquered and plundered her native land in the year 529. She was then a mere child, but exquisitely beautiful. Her master resolved to make her his queen on some future day; in the mean while he caused her to be carefully instructed in ancient and ecclesiastical learning. Radegonde grew up in the knowledge and hatred of the fate to which she was destined. She could not love the oppressor of her race; and her soul, elevated and refined by religion and study, could have no sympathy in common with a cruel and licentious prince, who disgraced the Christian faith which he professed. The young girl longed for a life of silence, prayer, and calm studies. She fled in terror when her marriage-day came, but was overtaken, brought back, and forcibly united to Clotaire.

The rude and often cruel amusements of her husband's court had no charm for Radegonde. Clotaire had presented her with the mansion in which she had been reared; she gave it to the poor and sick, whom she loved to serve with her own hands. She often introduced lepers into the royal palace, washed their feet, and waited on them, whilst they partook of the good cheer which she had caused to be prepared for these poor afflicted creatures. When these charitable tasks were over, the queen retired to her most remote apartments, and forgot her hard destiny in the gentle companionship of books—those kind and faithful friends whose power to charm away eare has been gratefully attested in every age. Learned clerks and bishops sometimes visited the court of Clotaire; and when Radegonde could converse with one of these welcome guests, she was happy. But those pleasant hours were few and far between: such visitors came seldom and soon departed; with them fled the brief happiness of the poor queen.

Clotaire cared little for the coldness with which his wife met his unwelcome love; but he resented her refined tastes and reserved habits. "I have got a nun, and no queen," he would say impatiently; and he scolded her, because, wrapt in her books and studies, Radegonde was always late at meal-times. They had no children; and the last tie between them was broken, when, in a fit of jealous policy, Clotaire caused the brother of his wife to be put to death.

Radegonde went to Noyon, seemingly to visit the bishop. On entering the cathedral where he officiated, she exclaimed, in words that show the passionate and long-repressed aspiration of her soul:—" Priest of God, I want to leave the world: consecrate me to the Lord." The Frank chiefs present drew their swords, and forbade the bishop to comply. Radegonde entered the sacristy, threw the robe of a nun over her royal garments, and coming forth, threatened the bishop with the judgment of God if he refused to grant her request. He then made her deaconess by the imposition of hands. Radegonde joyfully took off her bracelets, girdle, and other gold ornaments, and laying them on the altar, she solemnly presented them to the poor.

Clotaire at first threatened to take back his wife by force; but her entreaties and the remonstrances of the clergy prevailed: he allowed her to found in the town of Poitiers the magnificent monastery of Holy Cross, which she entered in 550, with a considerable number of maidens who wished to share her retirement. In this pleasant abode—soothing alike to the senses and the heart—there were gardens, baths, porticos, and galleries, besides a large church. The recluses prayed, read the Scriptures, studied ancient letters, and transcribed manuscripts, without neglecting needlework. Learned men visited them frequently; and, at certain times of the year, dramatic performances, the germ of the mysteries of the middle ages, took place in the presence of numerous guests.

It was thus that monasteries became asylums where the most spiritual and intellectual Christians loved to retire, and that their inhabitants rose into importance, even in the eyes of those who cared least to break the bonds of active life. Hilda, one of those Anglo-Saxon princesses to whom we alluded a few pages back, founded monasteries for both men and women; and from her convent decided on State matters, and shared in the councils of kings. In her presence, and in that of her sisterhood, a great religious controversy, concerning the time for celebrating Easter, took place at Whitby in the year 664.

The monastery of Chelles, near Paris, was one of the most celebrated. Thither resorted to live under the rule of the abbess St. Bertilla, princesses, and holy women of every land. Amongst others Hereswith, sister of Hilda, and queen of the East Angles; and St. Bathildis, the Anglo-Saxon slave, first queen-consort, then queen-regent, of the Franks; illustrious for her piety, and for the active zeal with which she endeavored to extirpate slavery.

Christianity, though essentially opposed to slavery, did not succeed in abolishing it at once: Christian nations long owned slaves, and trafficked in human flesh and blood. The Anglo-Saxons distinguished themselves by their avidity in carrying on this infamous commerce: their brethren and their children were to be seen in all the market-places of Europe; their sons were sold to till the soil of Ireland; their daughters to become the victims of foreign insolence and brutality. William of Malmesbury has left a harrowing picture of that slave-trade, as carried on opposite the Irish coast, where " whole rows of wretched beings of both sexes, fastened together with ropes, like cattle—many adorned with beauty, and in the bloom of youth—were daily offered up to any who chose to buy."

The same trade existed on the coast facing France; and thus it happened that a young Anglo-Saxon girl named Bathildis was sold by her parents in Kent to slave-dealers; from whom Archambauld, French mayor of the palace, purchased her for a small sum. According to another, but far less probable account, Bathildis was of royal blood, and had been carried away by pirates—a plausible story framed to justify her subsequent elevation. Archambauld proved an indulgent master : the only task of the Anglo-Saxon girl was that of cup-bearer to himself, his wife Lanthilde, and the Frank or Gaulish, lords who sat at his board. The beauty, modesty, and grace he thus daily witnessed in his young slave, gradually induced in the powerful mayor other feelings than those of mere indulgence. When his wife died, he eagerly pressed Bathildis to take her place, and assume a rank second only to that of queen; but the young girl had long sought in the aspirations of ardent piety, that only freedom and refuge then open to souls that looked beyond the rude pleasures and enjoyments of the world. She shrank from marriage with fear, left the palace of the mayor by stealth, and did not return until she learned that her master had taken another wife : then she came back, and quietly resumed her former station. This one act paints her character ; which nobly blended the pride and liberty of the woman with the humility and fidelity of the slave.

Archambauld showed no resentment : he even contributed to the greatness of her who had refused to become his wife. Clovis II., king of the Franks, saw and loved the beautiful girl who filled his cup every time he sat down at the board of his mayor ; Archambauld encouraged his passion, and urged him to marry her. This time Bathildis could not, or did not dare, to resist the joint authority of her master and her king : she yielded, and in the year 649 became queen. Such, we are told, was the fame of her virtues and endowments, that her elevation created no envy and scarcely any wonder. The latter fact is probable enough ; as the wives of the Frank kings were chosen from amongst princesses; or from the daughters of bondsmen, according as policy or inclination prevailed. Young, dissolute, and apathetic, Clovis was one of those degenerate Merovingians who allowed themselves to be ruled by the mayors of their palaces, and who still bear in history the degrading name of Rois fainéants.

A young woman, beautiful and energetic in her very gentleness like Bathildis, could not fail to obtain great influence over the weak and vacillating Clovis. She did not meddle in State affairs, but gladly undertook the exclusive direction of ecclesiastical matters, which then comprised the care and relief of the poor. She restored and endowed anew the celebrated female abbey of Chelles, near Paris, founded by Clotildis, the first Christian queen of France. On her request, Théodéchilde, abbess of Jouarre, sent her Bertilla, a learned and pious maiden, under whose spiritual rule Chelles became one of the most celebrated abbeys in Christendom. "In the monastery of Chelles, near Paris," observes the Protestant historian Michelet; "men and women heard with equal respect the lessons of St. Bertilla. The kings of Great Britain asked her for some of her disciples to found schools and monasteries. She sent them both teachers and books." Many legends are told of the piety and charity of Bathildis. Warned, it is related, by a vision, she once sold all her jewels for the benefit of the indigent: her gold bracelets, the distinctive badge of her royal rank, were the only ornaments which she retained. She imparted the same spirit to her husband during the severe famine which afflicted France under his reign. All their plate was sold, and the money distributed to the poor; in the zeal of their charity they scrupled not to strip the venerated tomb of St. Denis of the sheets of gold and silver with which the piety of their predecessors had adorned it, in order to relieve more fully the wants of the distressed.

Clovis II. closed his inglorious reign in 655. Clotaire, the eldest of his three sons, being then only five years of age, Bathildis became regent. She found the kingdom laboring under two great evils: simony and slavery. The Church then represented religious and moral law; she wielded immense power; it was most urgent that this power should be pure in its source. With the aid of the better portion of the clergy, the queen-regent succeeded in eradicating simony from the bosom of the Gallican Church. Slavery was more deeply rooted; in her struggle against it Bathildis labored alone, unaided, save by her own energetic spirit, and the living memory of the past. The Franks had found slavery established by the Romans in Gaul. They tolerated and adopted it; showing, however, a tendency to mitigate its worst features. In her elevation, the pious Bathildis had never forgotten the thousands whose miseries she had witnessed, and whose degradation she had once shared. She bought back a large number of the most oppressed and miserable slaves, and set them at liberty. When

the heavy taxes, then imposed on the poorer part of the pop-
ulation, compelled many unhappy beings to sell themselves
into bondage, in order to pay the sum exacted from them,
the queen acquitted their debt; but as the same cause ever
reproduced the same effects, she took a bold step, and abol-
ished the tax which lowered human beings to the level of
cattle. She gave to freedmen the right of property, and
declared them citizens of the State. Although it surpassed
her power to abolish slavery completely, she waged against
it incessant war. The law of the Gospel she held to be a
law of freedom, and would not suffer that Christians, whom
the pure blood of the Saviour had delivered from the bondage of sin, should bow beneath the yoke of mortal men.
She strictly forbade that any Christian should henceforth be
made a slave, and was amongst the first of those noble
spirits who, interpreting the Gospel in its purest meaning,
opened to future ages the broad path of liberty.

The consolation which she derived from these sacred tasks
atoned to Bathildis for the many trials and mortifications
which she found otherwise attached to the exercise of power.
So deep at length became her disgust of the world, that in
the year 665 she retired to the monastery of Chelles, and
there took the religious vows. From the day that she entered the convent, Bathildis showed herself the most humble
and submissive of the daughters of Bertilla. Deep sorrows
followed her in this calm retreat: the errors of her sons,
who refused to heed her wise counsel, the crimes of her enemies, and the cruel persecutions endured by those whom
she had most loved and trusted, saddened her heart, but
could not dismay her faith. One of her chosen and cherished tasks in the abbey of Chelles was to attend on the
sick sisters. She herself gave an example of heroic patience
during the last painful illness which preceded her death.
She died on the 30th of January, of the year 680, surrounded by the whole sisterhood, whom she exhorted to
holy charity and love of the poor. She has been canonized
by the Church, and the Anglo-Saxon girl is still highly venerated in France, and remembered by tradition in the neighborhood of Chelles.

The name of St. Bathildis is invariably mentioned by historians in terms of the highest praise. It is recorded (and

much is implied by the simple fact) that this pious and generous princess was the first to create in France the office of almoner, rendered necessary by the immense number of her charities. But no eulogy can be more noble or complete than the brief one of President Heinault: "Queen, she never forgot that she had been a slave; and nun, she never remembered that she had been a queen."

CHAPTER V.

Increase of Monasteries—Apostolic Labors of the Nuns—Lioba—Celebrated Nuns and Princesses—Austrebertha—Raingarda—Giselle—Hroswrta—Herrade—Theodelinda—Ludmilla—Dombrowka—Maud—Alice—Cunegondes—Margaret of Scotland.

Nuns, princesses, and queens are, for several ages, the only charitable and pious women of whose lives and actions there exists any record. Women of charity and household virtues no doubt existed then, as now; but they lived unheeded, and died unremembered: the veil and the crown eclipsed all else.

The importance of monastic retreats continued to increase. They arose in every land, and acquired a celebrity which endured for ages. In some cases the nuns were called upon to assume apostolic labors. St. Thecla, a nun of Winburn in Dorsetshire, was invited over into Germany by St. Boniface; and she became Abbess of Kitzengen, near Wurtzburg, about the same time that St. Lioba was appointed Abbess at Bischofsheim, St. Walburge at Heidenheim, in Bavaria, and Kynegild in Thuringia. These holy women were to instruct the new converts of their own sex, and train them up in piety and virtue.

The most illustrious of these nuns is Lioba, the relative, friend, and fellow-laborer of Boniface. In the year 719, Boniface left England, his native land, to go to Rome. There he begged the apostolic blessing of Pope Gregory II., and the permission of preaching the Gospel to the northern idolaters. Both requests were granted. Boniface crossed the

lówer Alps, and travelled through Bavaria and Thuringia,
baptizing infidels and reforming Christian churches on his
way. His labors extended to Friesland, whence he went
into Hesse and Saxony; he ultimately became Primate of all
Germany, and won the far more glorious title of Apostle of
the North.

To civilize the rude barbarians amongst whom he dwelt,
Boniface requested the assistance of religious men and women. His cousin Lioba left her monastery in Dorsetshire to
answer the call. She had long maintained a correspondence
with Boniface; her Latin epistles to him still exist. Lioba
was learned even for a nun : she spoke and wrote Latin, and
was familiar with the Scriptures, the Fathers, and every
point of ecclesiastical law. The Bible seldom left her hands :
she had it read aloud to her when she lay down to rest; so
ardent and constant was her thirst for the divine word.

It was not, however, so much by her learning as by her
cheerful bearing, hospitality, and great charity, that Lioba
seconded the designs of Boniface, and earned during her
lifetime the name of a saint. Boniface loved her very tenderly; before undertaking that last journey into Friesland
which ended with his martyrdom, he earnestly recommended
Lioba to his friend Lullus and his monks at Fulda. He requested that after her death she might be laid by him : " I
wish," he said, " to await near her the day of resurrection.
Those who have labored together for Christ should receive
together their reward." The request was complied with,
and during her lifetime Lioba was, by a special privilege,
allowed to enter the abbey and assist at the divine services
and conferences which took place within its walls.

Lioba survived the martyrdom of her friends twenty-four
years. Bishops often came to consult her in her monastery ;
her sanctity was acknowledged and venerated by Pepin the
Frank king, and his two sons Charlemagne and Carloman.
Hildegardis, the most amiable and best beloved of the five
wives of Charlemagne, had a great affection for Lioba, and
once induced her to come to Aix-la-Chapelle; but after a
few days Lioba returned to her solitude. She bade the
young queen a tender and last adieu : kissing her robe, her
forehead, and her mouth, she said : " Farewell, precious
part of my soul; may Christ, our Creator and Redeemer,

grant that we may see each other without confusion on the day of judgment."

She died, not long after this, in 779; having for some time relinquished the government of her monastery, as well as of the various nunneries which she had founded in Germany. Her remains were laid near those of Boniface, by the altar of Fulda: the two friends and apostles still sleep there peacefully, and wait side by side for the great judgment day.

Convents had many and well known abuses; our province is not to dwell upon them, but to speak of those recluses only whose virtues sanctified the monastic state. Nuns like Lioba certainly contributed much to the progress of Christianity; and it must be borne in mind that, in those early times, cloisters generally secluded, for many obvious reasons, the most generous, pious, and intellectual members of either sex. When the beautiful Icasia was rejected by the Emperor Theophilus, for having answered him with more wit than he approved of in a wife, she retired to a convent, where she lived peacefully engaged in literary pursuits. In the seventh century, Austrebertha, a noble maiden of the north of Gaul, caressingly said to her mother, who wished her to remain in the world: "Oh! my dear mother, you have given me a heart so tender that creatures can never fill it. Let me, then, be the bride of Christ, and of none other." Edburge, grand-daughter of King Alfred, on being offered in her childhood a royal robe and a religious habit, eagerly chose the latter, and remained faithful to the state thus early embraced. Editha, another Anglo-Saxon princess, refused, it is said, the chance of a crown, to live and die in the monastery where she had been reared.

Virgins who left home in all their early freshness and purity, and wearied widows, whose tasks in life were ended, thronged to these calm retreats. After the death of her husband, the pious and charitable Raingarda retired to the monastery of Marsigny. A train of noblemen and friends accompanied her; and even at the gates of the convent, they attempted to dissuade her from entering; but, turning towards them with a severe look, she said: "Do you return into the world, for my part I go to God."

The love of study and science drew many to the cloister.

It could not but be so, when an author who wrote on the education of war in the thirteenth century, limited their education to spinning and sewing, and expressly declared that, unless when she was intended to become a nun, no maid ought to be taught reading or writing. Giselle, the beloved sister of Charlemagne, abbess of the convent of Chelles, was the declared patroness of scientific and literary men. In the ninth century, the convent of Gandersheim, in Lower Saxony, was greatly celebrated for the learning and piety of the nuns. One of the abbesses, named Hroswrta, excelled in logic and rhetoric, and was an author of some fame. A young nun bearing the same poetic name (white rose) received in this convent a classical education, and composed six comedies, which modern learning has carefully analyzed, and pronounced the most remarkable productions of those times. In a later age Herrade of Landsberg, abbess of the convent of Hohenburg, perpetuated the fame of her predecessors, Relinde and Gerlinde. She composed for her nuns a Latin work, entitled "The Garden of Delights," in which she collected all the literary and scientific knowledge of her age. To the learning of a clerk, Herrade united the charity of a Christian woman: she caused to be erected, at the foot of a neighboring hill, a monastery, in which she founded a hospital.

We might give numerous instances in which learning and piety were thus united; but we have said enough. It now remains to us to speak of the queens who continued the pious task of Clotildis and Bertha, and of those who, for several ages, added the halo of the saint to the queenly diadem.

Towards the close of the sixth century, Theodolinda, queen of the Lombards, encouraged the apostolic labors of Columban, and extirpated the Arian heresy from her dominions. Christianity penetrated more slowly in the north than in the genial south : it was not until the ninth century that it reached Bohemia, then governed by Duke Bozivor ; who embraced the faith with his wife Ludmilla. After his death and that of her eldest son, she governed the State for her eldest grandson, Wenceslas ; but his mother, Drahomira, soon claimed and obtained the regency. Drahomira was a pagan : she persecuted the Christians, shut up their

churches, and forbade the priests to teach ; it was not, however, in her power to prevent Ludmilla from training Wén-
ceslas in the fervent piety that ultimately made him a saint
and a martyr.

Drahomira hated her mother-in-law intensely ; and her
aversion increased when Wenceslas began to reign, and
preferred the advice of Ludmilla to that of his pagan mother.
She laid a plot to take away the life of the aged duchess ;
Ludmilla learned this, but she thought it either unworthy of
her, or too difficult, to shun her fate.   She calmly prepared
herself for death, by distributing her wealth amongst her
servants and the poor, and devoutly receiving the last sacraments of the Church.   The assassins sent by Drahomira
found Ludmilla praying in her chapel ; they strangled her
with her own veil, before the altar of the faith for which
she died, and which has numbered her amongst its martyrs.
A similar fate awaited Wenceslas : he was murdered as he
prayed in a church.   The last of the assassins who struck
him was his brother Boleslas ; the instigator of the crime
was their impious mother, Drahomira.   But the efforts of
both mother and son could not prevent the Christian faith
from prevailing in Bohemia.   Dombrowka, one of their
descendants, was married in 965 to Micislas, duke of Poland,
on the express condition that both he and his people would
embrace Christianity.   He agreed to this, and the princess
left Bohemia for Poland, accompanied by a considerable
number of priests, who were to teach the new faith to the
northern idolaters.   In 955, the Russian Princess Olga was
baptized at Constantinople, and on her return, contributed
much to the progress of the faith in the dominions of her
son Svientoslaf.

In the same age, Maud, empress of Germany, rendered
herself eminent for her charity to the poor.   After the
death of her husband, Henry the Fowler, her two elder
sons strove for the crown ; both agreed, however, in strip-
ping her of her dowry.   The pretence they took was, that
she squandered the revenues of the State on the poor.   It
was long before they consented to restore to her the wealth
which she applied to charitable purposes.   She died piously
in 968.

Her successor on the imperial throne, Alice of Burgundy,

was like her a princess of great charities and virtues. She married Lothaire, king of Italy, in her sixteenth year. Berengarius, margrave of Ivrea, poisoned Lothaire in 950, and insisted on marrying his son to the young widow. She refused, and was imprisoned by the tyrant in a strong castle, near the lake of Garda. A priest named Martin dug a subterranean passage, through which the captive made her escape. He took her to the other side of the lake; hid her in the reeds, and fed her with fish from the lake. The Lord of Canozza, warned by this faithful friend, came and carried off Alice to his impregnable fortress, built on a steep rock; where she remained until Otho I., son of Maud and Henry, invaded Italy, and freed it from the yoke of Berengarius. He met Alice at Pavia, and married her in order to conciliate the Italians, who felt deeply interested in the fate of the young and widowed queen. Like Maud, Alice incurred the reproach of prodigality, through a charity that knew no bounds: and like her she was persecuted in her widowhood by her son, who banished her from his court. After his death, she became regent, and governed the empire with wisdom and firmness. She died in 980. Her contemporary, the pious and learned Pope Silvester II., called Alice "the terror of kingdoms, and the mother of kings."

The virtues of Maud and Alice revived in Cunegondes, a sainted empress of the following age. During the lifetime of her husband St. Henry, Cunegondes distinguished herself by her charity and munificence. When he died in 1024, she retired to a monastery, where she spent the last fifteen years of her life in attending on the sick. She would never allow any distinction to be made between herself and the other nuns. As she lay dying on a bed of coarse haircloth, weak with disease, and exhausted by fasts and austerities, she perceived, whilst the prayers of the dying were being read to her, that a cloth fringed with gold had been prepared to throw over her corpse; the ex-empress changed color, and ordered it to be removed, nor could she rest until she had exacted and obtained a promise that she should be interred in her poor religious habit.

The most illustrious of these crowned saints is the gentle and pious Margaret, queen of Scotland. Though born far from England, Margaret was of Anglo-Saxon race; being the grand-daughter of the heroic Edmund Ironside; and the little niece of Edward the Confessor. In the year 1017, Edmund was assassinated by Count Edric, and Canute the Dane ascended the throne of England. He sent Edward and Edmund, the two infant sons of his predecessor, to the King of Sweden. This sovereign, in his turn, sent the young princes to the King of Hungary, by whom they were hospitably received and educated. Edmund died childless; but Edward married a princess named Agatha, by whom he had Edgar Atheling, Christina, who became a nun, and St. Margaret.

After the death of Canute and his son Hardicanute, Edward the Confessor was called to the throne in 1041. Some years elapsed before he thought of his exiled nephew, the rightful heir, and invited him over to England. Edward came, with his wife and children. He died before his uncle, and bequeathed his rights to his son Edgar Atheling, who had never the courage or good fortune to assert them. He was set aside by Harold, who perished on the fatal field of Hastings, and by the Norman William, who conquered England. Edgar thought it more prudent to flee than to engage in a doubtful struggle. The young prince secretly embarked with his mother and sisters; but they had not been long at sea when a tempest drove their ship into the Frith of Forth; they were then hospitably received by King Malcolm III.

The Scottish sovereign could sympathize with the hard fate of the royal exiles: his father was that "gracious Duncan," whose sad destiny has been immortalized by the genius of Shakspeare; and for seventeen years Malcolm wandered in foreign lands, whilst the usurper Macbeth held his kingdom. Edward the Confessor at length gave him ten thousand men, with whom, aided by his own friends, the prince recovered his crown. Gratitude, no less than the hospitable temper of his race, therefore, induced Malcolm to make the English fugitives welcome in his dominions. He refused to deliver them up to William of Normandy; with whom he engaged in a war for their sake. Margaret was virtuous and beautiful; her host fell in love with her, and offered her his hand; she hesitated, but her relatives pressed her and she complied. In the year 1072, she was married to Malcolm in the royal Castle of Dunfermline. Margaret was no portionless bride : her dowry consisted of immense treasures which she had brought away from England, besides many precious relics ; one of which, the black cross, was for several ages much venerated in Scotland.

At the time of her marriage, Margaret was twenty-four years of age ; her husband was much older ; but this did not prevent her from ever loving him with the deepest tenderness. She became celebrated for her conjugal love, no less than for those other virtues which she possessed in an eminent degree ; and which, though unobserved in the exiled princess, drew down universal love and admiration on the queen. Theodoric, monk of Durham, and her confessor, to whom we owe an excellent account of this amiable woman, speaks highly of her penetration, memory, and graceful eloquence. He often admired how the queen, who shared with her husband the cares of State, the diligent housewife, the attentive mother, could still find time for study ; and, as if her mind had never been otherwise engaged, enter with learned men into subtle theological discussions, in which none displayed a clearer intellect, or expressed themselves in more ready and elegant language. But it was perhaps still more remarkable that, though living in the world, and seemingly distracted by so many various occupations, Margaret never once lost the early fervor and tenderness of her devotion. "When she spoke to me of the sweetness of everlasting life," writes Theodoric, "her words were full of all grace: So great was her fervor and compunction on these occasions, that she seemed as if she would quite melt into tears ; so that her devotion drew also from me tears of compunction. In the church no one was more silent, no one more intent in prayer."

The piety of Margaret was eminently practical. She made the noblest use of the extensive influence which she derived from the love and esteem of Malcolm. She reformed church abuses, and earnestly labored to suppress simony, usury, sacrilege, and other sources of public scandal. She herself gave a living example of every Christian virtue to her subjects : and her conjugal love was proverbial. She early surrounded her six sons and two daughters with able masters, and often instructed them herself. "Fear the Lord, O my children," she would say, "for those who fear Him shall never want. If you delight in Him, children of my heart, He will bestow on you earthly happiness and eternal felicity with all the saints."

The favorite virtue of this excellent woman was charity: she gave away all her own money to the poor, and was often obliged to supply herself from the coffers of the king ; a liberty he allowed her to take. Every time she walked or rode out, troops of widows and orphans flocked to her as to a common mother. When Margaret had distributed all that she had brought with her for the use of the poor, she gave them the garments of her servants, so that none might go away sad and unrelieved. The hall of her palace was always filled with indigent persons, whose feet she washed. She never sat down to a meal without having first fed and waited on nine orphan children and twenty-four grown up poor. In the same spirit she frequently visited the hospitals, and attended on the sick herself. To this private charity, Margaret united the public liberality which becomes a queen : she freed debtors, helped families in distress, ransomed captives of every nation, but especially the English, founded hospitals for poor strangers, and churches and monasteries for her own subjects.

In all that she did the queen obtained and merited the approbation of her husband. From her Malcolm, who, though rough, was naturally inclined to virtue, learned to be just, merciful, almsgiving, and pious. He loved Margaret passionately, despised that which she contemned, and prized whatever she held dear. Though he was himself ignorant and careless of literary knowledge, he liked to see and hold the books in which his more learned wife read and prayed. So precious did he consider whatever her hands had touched, that he would often call in a jeweller, and bid him adorn with gold and gems some favorite volume, which he then carried himself to the queen. If he heard that there was any of these books which she prized more highly than the rest, he, too, liked to have it oftener in his hands, and would kiss it repeatedly. Those men of the middle ages, who now seem so rude and stern, felt suffi-

4

ciently secure of their own manliness not to exclude simple love and tenderness from their hearts.

Malcolm had reigned thirty-three years when he engaged in a war with England. He was treacherously slain by an English soldier; and his eldest son, Edward, was killed in attempting to avenge his death. Margaret was at that time lying dangerously ill, and well aware of her approaching end. "She had a foresight of her death long before it happened," writes Theodoric; "and, speaking to me in secret, she began to repeat to me in order her whole life, pouring out floods of tears at every word with unspeakable compunction, so that she obliged me also to weep; and sometimes we could neither of us speak for sighs and sobs. At the end she spoke thus to me:—'Farewell; for I shall not be here long: thou shalt stay some little time behind me. Two things I have to desire of thee: the one is, that so long as thou livest thou wilt remember my poor soul in thy masses and prayers; the other is, that thou wilt assist my children, and teach them to fear and love God. These things thou must promise me, here in the presence of God, who alone is witness of our discourse.'"

About six months after this Margaret died. She bore the pains of disease with humility and patience: she never uttered one word of complaint in the midst of all her sufferings. Four days before her death Malcolm was killed in Northumberland. On that day Margaret, who had vainly endeavored to dissuade him from this expedition, looked oppressed with sadness; and turning towards those who sat around her, she suddenly said—"Perhaps to-day there has befallen the kingdom of Scotland a greater evil than any this long time back." She did not explain her meaning, and none of those who heard these words understood their real sense, until tidings of the king's death arrived.

On the fourth day after uttering this prophetic sentence, Margaret, feeling somewhat better, rose, went into her oratory, and there received the viaticum. Her fever soon returning, she was obliged to lie down again; and whilst her chaplains read the psalms to her, she held the black cross, and, keeping her eyes fixed upon it, recited the Miserere. She was gradually sinking into unconsciousness, when her son Edgar, who had returned from the army, entered her

apartment. The dying queen roused herself from her agony
to question him concerning the fate of his father and brother.
Edgar replied that they were both well; but she, sighing
heavily, said,—"I know, my son, I know; by this holy
cross, by our consanguinity, I conjure thee to tell me the
truth." Thus solemnly adjured, Edgar related all. Margaret heard him without a murmur; and when he had done
she said,—"Thanks and praise I give to thee, Almighty
God, who, to purify me from my sins, sendest me so many
sorrows to endure in my last hour."

Not long after this, feeling the approach of her last moments, she said, in the words of the Church,—"Oh Lord
Jesus Christ, who by thy death hast given life to the world,
from all evil deliver me!" As she uttered the words " deliver me," she gently expired. This event took place on the
16th of November, 1093. Queen Margaret was then forty-
seven years of age. She was canonized in 1251 by Pope
Innocent IV. At the period of the Reformation her relics
were removed from Scotland to Spain, and deposited with
the remains of her husband in a chapel of the Escurial, built
to receive them by Philip II. "Saint Malcolm, king, and
Saint Margaret, queen," may still be read on the shrine beneath which the two sovereigns of Scotland sleep side by
side. "They were lovely in their lives, and in their deaths
were not divided."

A succession of saints adorned the posterity of this royal
couple; and from them descended some of the best Scottish
sovereigns. Their daughter Matilda, or Maud Atheling,
married Henry the First of England. It was through her
that the blood of the Saxon and Norman sovereigns first
blended in the royal line of England. Matilda was pious
and charitable, like her sainted mother, and to this day bears
in history the name of " Good Queen Maud."

CHAPTER VI.

Spirit of the Middle Ages—Its Exaggeration and Greatness—Causes—
Elizabeth of Hungary.

BEFORE proceeding further, we must beg our readers to
remember that the middle ages are characterized by a certain breadth or greatness, an exaggeration in good or in evil,
almost unknown to our modern times. There is now more
personal liberty, but there was then more individual independence of action, more indifference to opinion ; for religion was not a matter of opinion, but of faith : it was this,
and not human power, that rendered it so long inviolable
and sacred.

This era of great virtues and great crimes is past. We
may place our civilized coldness far above the exaggerated
spirit of our ancestors ; we may congratulate ourselves on
passions more calm, and tempers more sedate ; but we cannot change that which has been : we cannot efface from history the burning spirit which roused the whole western
world to redeem the sepulchre of Christ, and sent forth
countless multitudes to the land of their redemption : we
cannot banish into oblivion that strange and impressive train
of religious men and women, who astonished even their contemporaries by the singleness of their faith, and the might
of their charity ; whose lives, apart from every supernatural feature, read like marvellous romances, and, when the
first strangeness is worn off, impress us by the depth and so-
lemnity of feeling they reveal.

What shall we say to St. Mary of Oignies and her husband, both young, noble, and rich, who forsook the world to
make themselves servants of the lepers of Villembroke ? By
what standard shall we judge Francis of Assissi, who, fired
with the love of God, hailed every living thing as a brother,
and held nothing mean which the Almighty had thought it
worth his while to create ? Religion was then a passion, or
it was nothing : that calm modern feeling, that cold belief
which inspires not one great or good action, had not yet been
sanctified by the name of piety. If we wish to know the

difference between the present and the past, we may compare the lives of the saints of the middle ages with the religious biographies of modern times. Arrayed in combat against the temptations of this world, and the terrors of the next, they overcame their passions through spirits of evil; who to them were no symbols, but awful realities. No doubt we may boast of more wisdom, and of more moderation; but where is the generosity and the greatness?

These remarks are not intended to imply that people were infinitely better some five or six hundred years ago than they are now: but they were certainly very different; and we must know how to accept that difference. Good is the protest against evil, and great crimes call forth great virtues: the excess of oppression produces excess of pity. We have triumphed over much: many petty and vexatious tyrants are low; many cruel oppressions are gone and past; many sanguinary persecutions shall never be renewed: but have we not lost something? Why is faith so dead, or charity so low, that a sort of apology is needed for those who took the Gospel in its literal meaning?—who were not ashamed to trust in God, or to give one of their two garments to some suffering brother? We do not choose to imitate them: let that pass; but where is our right to ridicule or censure? Was it so difficult to add to our better regulated charity, not the actions, but the lofty and enthusiastic spirit of our ancestors? Admitting even that we cast aside that spirit, with a smile at our superior wisdom; was it then impossible to understand it? Why tax—as they have been taxed—with insanity and superstition, Radegonde, who kissed a leper, and Margaret, who washed the feet of beggars?—noble women, who thus professed the spiritual brotherhood and love which not even the most loathsome disease could repel,—the equality before God which rank could not efface; and who thought that in so doing they followed the very spirit of the Gospel. To those who think differently, we can only recommend to pass over the following pages: they have not been written without the knowledge that amongst our readers there are many who will feel more surprise than admiration.

In the beginning of the thirteenth century, Hermann, landgrave of Thuringia and of Hesse, and Count Palatine of Saxony, ranked amongst the greatest princes of Germany. He was allied to Frederick Barbarossa, to the houses of Bohemia, Saxony, Bavaria, and Austria; he made or unmade emperors at his pleasure, and ruled over vast dominions, that extended from the Lahn to the Elbe. Warned, it is said, by a prediction of the celebrated Klingsohr, minstrel and necromancer, the landgrave resolved, in the year 1211, to request, for his eldest son Lewis, the hand of Elizabeth of Hungary, then four years of age. An embassy of noble lords and ladies was sent to the court of the pious and warlike Andrew II., king of Hungary. Both Andrew and his wife Gertrude agreed to give their daughter in marriage to the son of Hermann. The little Elizabeth, clothed in a robe of silk, embroidered with gold and silver, was brought in a cradle of massive gold, and given up to the Thuringian ambassadors. "I confide her to your knightly honor," said the king to the Lord of Varila, the chief of the knights of Thuringia. After three days spent in rejoicing, the embassy, laden with rich presents, took away the young princess to the land of her future husband. She was solemnly betrothed to him immediately on her arrival, and brought up with him at the court of the landgrave. Lewis was then eleven years old, and the two children, according to the custom of the times, gave one another the tender and familiar names of brother and sister.

The childhood of Elizabeth was marked by a piety and purity both touching and rare: even then, God seemed the centre of her soul, heart, and desires. Her father allowed her a yearly income, worthy the daughter of a king; and all of it that was at her disposal went to the poor. Her propensity to give was irresistible: she drew down on herself the murmurs, and almost the aversion, of the officers of the household, by lingering about the kitchen and pantry, in order to pick up fragments of broken meat, which she bestowed in charity.

Elizabeth was about nine years old when the landgrave, who had always loved her very tenderly, died. Her betrothed was now sovereign prince; but he was still too young to rule his dominions, or to possess any power. With the landgrave, Elizabeth had lost her only efficient protector. Sophia, his widow, disliked her; and her daughter Agnes, vain of her dazzling beauty, looked down with contempt on

the humble Elizabeth, and plainly told her that she was only
fit to be a chambermaid or a servant: indeed all the courtiers agreed that there was nothing in her noble or princely.
Her love of retirement, her modesty of bearing, her tender
familiarity with the poor, and the affection she showed for
the young Hungarian attendants sent with her by her father,
were imputed as so many crimes to the little stranger.

Once, on the festival of the Assumption, the mother of the
young landgrave said to Agnes and Elizabeth, "Let us go
down to Eisenach, to the church of our dear Lady, and hear
the fine mass of the Teutonic knights: perchance they will
preach something about her. Put on your rich garments,
and your crowns of gold." The young princesses obeyed.
As they entered the church they knelt down. Before them
stood a large crucifix; on beholding it, Elizabeth took off
her crown, and prostrated herself bareheaded. The Princess
Sophia sharply reproved her, and asked if the crown were
too heavy for her? Elizabeth looked up, and humbly answered, "Be not angry with me, dear lady. Here, before
my eyes, is my God and my King, the mild and merciful
Jesus, crowned with sharp thorns: shall I, who am only a
vile creature, remain before him crowned with pearls, gold,
and precious stones, and by my crown mock his?" So saying, she began to weep with love and tenderness, and again
bowed down. To avoid a contrast that would have been noticed, Sophia and Agnes were compelled to follow her example.

Their hatred and ill usage of her daily increased, and the
haughty Agnes once went so far as to say, "Lady Elizabeth,
you strangely mistake if you imagine my brother will marry
you. For this you must become very different indeed from
what you are." It was to this—to break off the marriage
of the young stranger with the landgrave—that all the efforts
of her enemies tended; and since the family of her betrothed
looked coldly upon her, the mean instinct of the servile had
given Elizabeth enemies in the whole of that court, which
she had ever edified with examples of modesty, humility,
and devotion.

But, in the midst of this ungenerous persecution, Elizabeth
found a faithful and steadfast friend in her future husband.
Neither the influence of a mother, nor the sneers of courtiers,
could induce him to break the faith he had plighted to his

childish bride. He loved her for those virtues which drew down on her the envy and hatred of others; nor was she less dear to the generous and chivalrous heart of the youth for being persecuted by all save him. He would see and console her privately; and every time that, in the course of his travels, he saw some rare or precious object, he bought it for his betrothed: he never came back empty-handed. Beads of coral, a crucifix, an image of devotion, a little knife or purse, gloves, jewels, chains or pins of gold, were his usual presents. No sooner did Elizabeth hear of his return than she would all joyously run forth to meet him. The young man would then take her in his arms, and, caressing her tenderly, give her whatever he had brought, as a token of his love, and of the faithful remembrance he had kept of her during their separation.

It once happened that, being in company with some foreign knights, he forgot to bring his usual gift. Elizabeth was mortified; for her enemies publicly rejoiced at this proof of forgetfulness. The young princess confided her sorrow to an old friend, that Lord of Varila to whose honor her father had intrusted her; and he promised to mention the matter to the prince. A fit opportunity soon offered. As the Lord of Varila and the landgrave were resting from the chase, and lying down in the grass within the shadow of a wood, whence they could clearly see the Inselberg, the highest mountain of all Thuringia, the former said to the prince, "May it please you, my lord, to answer a question I shall put to you?" "Speak freely," was the answer. "Do you mean," resumed the Lord of Varila, "to marry the Lady Elizabeth whom I brought to you, or will you send her back to her father?" Lewis rose, and extending his hand towards the Inselberg, he said, "Seest thou this hill before us? Well, then, if it were of pure gold from the base to the summit, and that the whole of it should belong to me on the condition of sending back mine Elizabeth, I would never do it. Let the world think and say of her all it likes; I say this—I love her, and love nothing more. I will have mine Elizabeth: she is dearer to me, by her virtue and piety, than all the lands and riches of this world." The Lord of Varila asked and obtained the permission of repeating this to Elizabeth; and as a token of his faith, the prince commissioned him to present her with a little pocket mirror, double bottomed and mounted in silver, with an image of our Lord crucified, under the glass. Elizabeth smiled joyously as the Lord of Varila repeated the words of her betrothed, and gave her his present; and when she opened the mirror, and beheld within it the image of the Saviour, she kissed it, and devoutly pressed it to her heart.

In 1218, Lewis was dubbed knight; and, two years later, he married Elizabeth, in the midst of splendid festivities. The tournament alone, to which all the knights of Thuringia had been invited, lasted three days. Lewis was twenty, his young bride was thirteen; and both were remarkable for great personal attractions: the manly beauty of the young landgrave was celebrated amongst his contemporaries. His bearing was dignified and noble; and his long fair hair, transparent complexion, and mild countenance, gave him something of angelic serenity: his whole aspect inspired love; and nothing, it is said, could surpass the charm of his voice and smile.

Elizabeth, though so young, was not unfit to stand near him as his bride; for Heaven had been prodigal to her of the gifts which constitute the loveliness of woman. She was tall, and of a most noble and graceful figure: historians mention with admiration the matchless dignity of her mien, as well as the pure and perfect beauty of her face. Though a daughter of the North, she had the clear olive complexion of a southern maiden; hair of the darkest hue, and eyes full of tenderness and love.

The outward graces of this accomplished pair were far surpassed by the inward gifts of their high and noble natures. We have spoken of the youth of Elizabeth; that of her husband had not been less pure. He had early chosen as his motto, "Piety, chastity, justice;" and he remained true to all it implied. In him blended in a rare degree the virtues of the Christian, of the knight, and of the sovereign: he was faithful to his God, to his love, and to his people. He delighted in pious exercises, in the society of monks and learned men, in the relief of the sick and the poor; to whom he often gave his own garments. With all this, he was a valiant knight, excelling in all martial exercises; and so full of daring that, without arms,

4*

and by the mere might of his strong heart, he once quelled the rage of an escaped lion, and made him lie down cowed and subdued at his feet. To piety and bravery Lewis united a rare degree of modesty: a light word made him blush like a maiden. Both before and after his marriage, licentious courtiers vainly endeavored to seduce him into sin; he repelled their attempts with the calm indignation of a virtue nothing could move. Magnanimous, cheerful, and gentle, he had but one passion: justice. He held himself bound to redress the wrongs of his meanest subject, as well as to punish the crimes of the most mighty. Under his sway the prosperity of Thuringia rose to the highest degree it could attain, and her people spent their days in happiness and peace. This good and pious prince has never been canonized: but for several years after his death, the people came to his tomb in pilgrimage; and in history he is still designated as "The Saint."

The affection which united the landgrave to his wife was deep; it rendered their marriage a sort of heaven upon earth. They loved one another with divine and human love; and seeing them so pure, "angels," says an old German chronicler, "abode with them." The love which she bore her husband by no means diminished the fervent piety of Elizabeth. Every night whilst Lewis slept she rose to pray. When he woke and missed her, he chid her mildly, calling her "Dear Sister," according to that habit of their childhood which they had both preserved; he entreated her not to injure her health, and taking her hand gently, compelled her to return to rest. Sometimes he fell asleep in the midst of his entreaties, and the eyes of Elizabeth closed, spite of her wish to pray. Often when her women entered her room in the morning, they found her sleeping on the carpet by the bedside, with her hand still clasped in that of her husband.

It was seldom indeed that they could bear to be apart: contrary to the etiquette which already prevailed, they sat by one another at table; and unless when the journeys he took were too distant, Elizabeth always accompanied the landgrave. She braved heat, frost, snow, and overflowing rivers, the worst roads and most violent storms, for the pleasure of bearing him company. If he could not take her with him, she clothed herself in widow's weeds, and lived in deep retirement until the time of his return. Then indeed she adorned herself carefully, and ran forth to meet him with the joyful eagerness of love.

The landgrave deserved that love, by an affection and fidelity over which absence and temptation had no power. Whilst he was once travelling without his dear Elizabeth, some lords who accompanied him endeavored to render him unfaithful. He heard them silently, but as they insisted, he angrily replied : "If you wish for my good-will, speak thus no more. I have a wife, and am bound to keep my faith to her." On another occasion, when a perfidious host, wishing either to try or tempt him, introduced into the apartment of Lewis a young girl of singular beauty, the landgrave said to the Lord of Varila, "Send away this woman quietly, and give her a mark of silver to buy herself a new cloak, so that want shall no more make her sin. Verily, I tell thee, that even though such an action were not a sin against God and a scandal in the eyes of my brethren, yet should I never think of it, solely for the love of my dear Elizabeth, and not to trouble or sadden her soul." Shortly after his return, the Lord of Varila related this circumstance to Elizabeth in the presence of the landgrave ; kneeling with much emotion, she said : "Lord, I am not worthy of so good a husband ; but help us both to observe the holiness of wedded life, so that we may eternally abide together near thee."

We have hitherto dwelt more on the trials and joys of Elizabeth, than on those actions which show us the happy girlish bride under the pure and immortal aspect of a saint. Her austerities were great, but they never affected her natural cheerfulness : she was gay and merry in the very midst of penance. She saw no sin in innocent amusements, where she never placed her heart : she shared in the festivities of her court, and danced and played like other ladies. She blamed those whose gloomy and severe faces were a reproach to religion. "They look," said the cheerful Elizabeth, "as if they wished to frighten God. Let them give him what they can gayly, and with a willing heart."

This free and generous spirit by no means led Elizabeth to love or indulge in the vanities of the world. She once went to Eisenach magnificently clothed, covered with jewels, and wearing a golden crown; but as she entered the church, and beheld the image of the crucified Saviour, the same devout emotion which she had felt once before assailed her so violently, that she fell down in a swoon. From that day she resolved to renounce dress, unless when state occasions or the will of her husband should oblige her to assume it as a token of her rank. She gave up dyed stuffs, veils of bright colors, narrow-plaited sleeves, and long trailing robes, all of which were then articles of great luxury.

Though rigid to herself, Elizabeth was to others full of tenderness and charity. Her husband set no bounds to her liberality; yet she was ever short of money. Several times, when his court was visited by foreign princes and ambassadors, Elizabeth could not appear before them because she had given away all her rich garments to the poor: this was with her a constant practice. As she went down one day from the castle to the town, richly clad, and wearing her crown, she was beset by a great number of beggars; to whom she gave away the money she had about her. When she had thus distributed it all, a poor man came up, and plaintively asked to be relieved. Elizabeth was filled with pity; and, having nothing else to bestow, she took off and gave him one of her gloves, richly embroidered and adorned with jewels. A young knight who followed her, seeing this, turned back, and having bought the glove from the beggar, he fastened it to his helmet. From that day, as he afterwards declared, with the enthusiastic faith of the age, he conquered in battle and tournament. He joined the crusade, fought against infidels, and returned home unharmed; on his deathbed he attributed his success and glory to this token of a pure and sainted woman, which he had ever faithfully preserved.

In her canonization Elizabeth is styled "Patroness of the Poor." Her whole life shows how truly she deserved the title: her affection for them was constantly expressed; and she left her stately castle of Wartburg to visit them in their own wretched homes. She paid their debts, attended their wives in their lying-in, clothed their new-born babes, watched by the dying, laid out the dead, and piously followed to the grave the meanest of her subjects. At home it was still of the poor that she thought: she spun wool for them with her maidens; and often got coarse food prepared for herself, in order to know, by personal experience, how they fared. Elizabeth scarcely needed such knowledge.

The expenses of the landgrave's table were defrayed by certain taxes, which Lewis either thought just, or could not remove. The confessor of his wife, Conrad of Marburg, an austere, domineering priest—to whom cannot, however, be denied the merit of ever seeking to defend the oppressed—declared that this tax ground down the poor; and forbade his penitent to taste the food thus procured. Elizabeth obeyed; but as of all the dishes on her husband's table, there were only a few which she could touch, and as she did not wish to seem to make a difference, she was often starving in the midst of plenty. Once, being on the point of accompanying the landgrave on a journey, she could find nothing to eat save a piece of brown bread, so hard that it had to be soaked in warm water. That same day she rode sixteen leagues on horseback.

These privations were more welcome than painful to the devout princess: surrounded by riches, she yet preserved in her heart the love of Gospel poverty. Putting on the gray cloak and torn veil of a poor woman, she would gayly say to her ladies,—"Even thus should I be were I a poor beggar;" and she took evident pleasure in the thought. One night that both she and her husband lay awake, she said to him,—"Sir, if it annoy you not, let me tell you by what life we might serve God." "Speak, sweet love," replied Lewis, "what is your thought?" "I should wish," said Elizabeth, "that we had only one piece of land, that would give us wherewithal to live, and about two hundred sheep. You could thus plough the ground, lead the horses, and undergo these labors for the love of God; whilst I should mind the sheep, and shear them." The landgrave laughed, and said,—"Gentle sister, if we had so much land and so many sheep, we should not, methinks, be very poor; and many would certainly think us too rich."

But charmed, we are told, with the tender simplicity of his young wife, the landgrave mentioned this incident to a friend, through whom it became known to one of the early biographers of Elizabeth.

The many opportunities she found of exercising charity

did not satisfy her ardent heart. Leprosy, now so rare, was then a common disease; the lepers were, perforce, secluded from society. The sympathy of the Church and of their brethren followed them in their solitude; but with it ever blended repulsion and mysterious fear. Persons of eminent virtue often set aside this feeling, and braved the popular prejudice and the real danger, in order to restore these poor afflicted creatures to that kindly communion, of which, whilst surrounded by the living, they were as effectually deprived as the dead. Elizabeth delighted in visiting and consoling them: she fearlessly sat down by them, and exhorted them to patience, in soothing and tender language. Her maidens of honor once found her sitting in a retired spot of her orchard with a leper, whose head rested on her lap: Elizabeth had just been cutting off his hair, and was dressing his head, when her maidens surprised her. She only looked up, and smiled silently.

On another occasion, whilst Lewis was away, she carried her charity so far towards a poor leprous child named Elias, whom no one else would touch or assist, that, after washing him with her own hands, she placed him in the bed which she shared with her husband. The landgrave just then happened to return; and on learning this circumstance from his mother Sophia, he could not help feeling somewhat angered. Going up to the bed, he drew back the coverlet; but suddenly, says one of the early historians of the saint, "the eyes of his soul were opened, and instead of the leprous child, he saw Jesus Christ himself." This vision—typical of the true sense of Christian charity, that what is done to the meanest human being is really done to God—affected the landgrave so deeply, that he permitted his wife to build a hospital on the slope leading to their castle of Wartburg. Twenty-eight sick or infirm persons were admitted within its walls, and were daily visited by Elizabeth, who loved to bring them food herself, and thus spare them the trouble of climbing up the steep path leading to the castle. She often went down to the town on similar errands of charity; and, to shun observation, generally took a narrow and dangerous path, still called break-knee. As she once went down thus, loaded with bread, meat, and eggs, wrapped up in the folds of her mantle, she was, according to a popular tradition, met by her husband, who opened her cloak, and found it filled with red and white roses. This poetical legend is still told by the now Protestant inhabitants of the spot where the good Elizabeth once lived.

In the year 1226, the landgrave being then at the Imperial Diet, the province of Thuringia suffered extremely from the great dearth which afflicted all Germany. The poor ate roots, wild fruit, dead horses, and yet died by hundreds on the high-roads. The charity of Elizabeth was boundless. The treasury then possessed the large sum of sixty-four thousand gold florins; and she did not hesitate to distribute it all amongst the poor. Notwithstanding the strong opposition of all the officers of the household, she opened the granaries of her husband, and gave away the whole of the corn: it amounted to the value of several towns and castles. Elizabeth caused as much bread to be baked as the ovens of the castle would hold, and daily gave away the hot loaves to those that came to ask for them : their number often amounted to nine hundred.

We have already mentioned that the roads leading to the Castle of Wartburg were steep. The weak and the infirm, could not climb so high; but they were not neglected: Elizabeth went down to them every morn and evening. She founded two new hospitals in Eisenach, and attended on their inmates with a zeal nothing could check. In one of those hospitals sick or orphan children were received, whom Elizabeth treated with peculiar tenderness. They no sooner saw her than they ran to meet her, and clung to her garments, calling out, "Mamma, mamma!" She made them sit around her, gave them toys, and only caressed the more tenderly those that were most afflicted.

The three hospitals, which she now daily visited and attended, did not so much engage the time of Elizabeth but that she still found means to visit the homes of the poor. She once entered a cottage where a poor man lay sick and alone ; he begged of her to milk his cow, as weakness prevented him from getting up ; the good princess cheerfully made the attempt, but failed, from not being accustomed to such an office. The prisoners were not forgotten by her : she visited them frequently, prayed with them, dressed the wounds their chains had inflicted, and when they were de-

tained for debt, bought their liberty.. So great was her
charity in this season of sharp distress, that she ordered the
revenues of the four dukedoms belonging to her husband
to be exclusively devoted to the relief of the poor of his
dominions; and she sold all her jewels and valuables for the
same object. .

When the harvest-time came, Elizabeth gathered together
all the poor that were able to labor, gave them scythes, new
shirts and shoes, so that their feet might not be hurt by the
stubble fields, and then sent them to work. Those who
were too weak were dismissed with a little money and garments; often her own rich veils and robes, which she gave
them to sell. In the mean while, the landgrave, hearing of
the sad state of his dominions, obtained from the emperor
the permission of returning to Thuringia. As he approached Wartburg, all the officers of the household, fearing his
anger, went forth to meet him, and complained of his wife's
prodigality. The anger of the landgrave was indeed roused,
but against the accusers. "Is my dear wife well?" he
asked; "this is all I wish to know: what do I care about
the rest?" He added,—"I wish you to let my good little
Elizabeth give away as much as she likes: you must help,
and not thwart her. Let her only leave us Eisenach, Wartburg, and Naumburg; God will give us back the rest when
he thinks fit: alms will never ruin us."

With this the good prince hastened to meet his dear wife.
Never since their marriage had they been so long apart;
and her joy on seeing him again was extreme: she could not
weary of kissing and caressing him. As Lewis held her
clasped in his arms, he kindly said,—" Dear sister, how fared
thy poor people during this bad year?" · She gently answered,—" I gave to God what belonged to him, and God
kept us what was thine and mine."

Hitherto Elizabeth had known as much happiness as ever
fell to the lot of woman. . She had been married nearly sev-
en years, and the affection of her husband had rather increased than diminished. God had given her three children,
honors, great wealth, and every earthly blessing. Heavy
calamities were to follow this happiness and prosperity. A
crusade was preparing for the year 1227. Lewis took the
cross. He did not dare to tell his wife, who was then near

giving birth to her fourth child; and instead of wearing the cross openly, he kept it in the purse suspended from his belt. They were sitting together one evening, when Elizabeth, playfully putting her hand in the purse, drew forth the cross. On seeing it she fainted away with grief. When she was restored to consciousness, the landgrave vainly sought to console her. After long remaining silent, and weeping much, Elizabeth said,—"Dear brother, if it be not against the will of God, stay with me." "Dear sister," he answered, "allow me to go, for it is a vow I have made to God." She submitted at length, and the landgrave, having now no further reason for concealment, prepared every thing for his departure. He recommended his wife to his mother, brothers, and officers. The butler said,—"I know that the lady Elizabeth will give all she finds, and reduce us to misery." Lewis answered, "he did not care, for that God would know how to replace what his wife would give away." Unable to tear herself from him, Elizabeth accompanied her husband to the frontiers of Thuringia. They reached the limits of his dominions, and still she would not leave him: another day she journeyed by his side, and again another; until at length their old friend, the Lord of Varila, was obliged to separate them. The landgrave and his knights pursued their journey, whilst Elizabeth returned sorrowful and alone to the castle of Wartburg. Immediately on her arrival she put on widow's weeds. Her biographers narrate that a fatal presentiment was at her heart; and the event justified her fears: Lewis died on his way to Holy Land a few months after their separation. The news reached Thuringia in winter; and Elizabeth was kept in total ignorance of it until she had safely given birth to her fourth child.

As she sat one day in her apartment, her mother-in-law, Sophia, entered it with several ladies. When they were all seated, Sophia said,—"Take courage, dearly beloved daughter, and be not disturbed by what has happened to your husband, my son, through the will of God, to whom, as you know, he had wholly given himself up." "If my brother be captive," replied Elizabeth, "with the aid of God and of our friends, he shall be ransomed: my father, I feel sure, will help us, and I shall soon be comforted." "Oh, my dear daughter," resumed Sophia, "be patient, and take this

ring which he has sent you; for, to our woe, he is dead."
"Madam," cried Elizabeth, "what do you say?" "He is
dead," repeated Sophia. Elizabeth turned pale, then became crimson; her hands fell on her knees, and, clasping
them passionately, she exclaimed in a broken voice,—"Ah!
Lord my God! Lord my God! Behold the whole world is
dead for me: the world and all its delights."

Then she rose, and, like one bereft of sense, she ran through
halls and galleries exclaiming—"He is dead, dead, dead."
At length a wall opposing her passage, she stopped short,
and leaning against it, wept long and bitterly. Her mother-
in-law and the other ladies led her away and attempted to
console her; but she only answered in broken exclamations,
"I have lost all! Oh, my beloved brother—oh, the friend
of my heart—oh, my good and pious husband, thou art dead,
and hast left me in misery! How shall I live without thee?
Ah, poor lonely widow and miserable woman that I am;
may He who forsakes not widows and orphans console me.
Oh! my God, console me! Oh! my Jesus, strengthen me
in my weakness."

She asked for resignation, and it came not near her. She
had loved her husband with impassioned human love, with
all the tenderness of a saint and all the weakness of a woman.
She of whom a priest once declared that he had seen her
from the altar, lost in prayer, and shining with a divine light,
could yet, during the celebration of the most sacred mysteries of her faith, forget all around her in contemplating him
to whom her life was not more firmly bound than her heart.
She had loved him too much, perhaps, and he was now removed forever: no more would that fair yet manly face
charm her eyes and trouble her devotions. That pure fidelity
which the passions of youth could never shake, that love
which had protected her from childhood, that boundless
trust which grew the stronger with accusation: all, in short,
that could render conjugal affection dear and sacred, were
taken from her with him. Well might she weep and call
this world a desert.

On leaving his wife and children, the late landgrave had
confided them to the care and love of his two brothers.
They resolved to repay that trust by despoiling the widow
and her poor orphans of their lawful inheritance. Elizabeth

was mourning in her apartment with her mother-in-law, when insolent courtiers, sent by the princes Henry and Conrad, entered the room ; and, after accusing her of squandering the money of the State, ordered her, in punishment of her crimes, to leave the castle instantly. Elizabeth asked at least for a delay, whilst her mother-in-law, taking her in her arms, exclaimed,—"She shall stay with me : no one shall take her from me." Force was used to separate them. Sophia could not see her sons, and was only allowed to accompany Elizabeth to the gates of the castle. In the court, the widow of the late sovereign found her children and two of her maids of honor. She was not permitted to take away a single thing. On a bleak winter's day, carrying in her arms her young infant, and followed by the three other children (of whom the eldest, her little Hermann, was not more than four years old), Elizabeth descended that steep path leading from Wartburg to Eisenach, and along which she had so often gone down on errands of charity.

Her pitiless brothers-in-law had ordered that no house should be opened to receive her, and none of the ungrateful beings whom Elizabeth had so often assisted, dared to disobey : every door was closed against her. At length she stopped at a miserable tavern, which she refused to leave, saying it was open to all. The master of the house could not, or dared not, give her any other place to sleep in than a miserable hut ; from which he turned out his hogs to admit her and her children. The soul of Elizabeth only rose the higher with her trials : she wept ; but she also returned thanks to God for thus visiting her. At length a poor priest of Eisenach ventured to receive her ; but her brothers-in-law no sooner learned this, than they bade her lodge in the house of a lord who had always shown himself her bitter enemy. He treated her so cruelly, that she left on the following day. It seems that trustworthy persons offered to take charge of her children, for whose safety she feared, and that Elizabeth accepted, though nearly heart-broken by this separation : she thus remained alone with her maidens, earning a scanty living by spinning wool.

The poor and hospitable priest who had given her a night's lodging, is the only instance mentioned of any thing like sympathy received by Elizabeth in Eisenach : the people gener-

ally treated her with brutal ingratitude. One old woman,
whom she had often assisted, meeting her on a narrow bridge
thrown over a muddy stream, pushed her in, and said, "Thou
wouldst not live like a princess when thou wert one: lie now
in the mud; I shall not pick thee up." Elizabeth only
laughed at this, and saying, "This is instead of the gold and
jewels I wore formerly," she went and washed her garments
at a neighboring fountain.

Her calamities at length came to the knowledge of her
relatives. She first went to reside with one of her aunts,
abbess of the convent of Kitzingen-on-the-Mein; and afterwards with her uncle Egbert, prince and bishop of Bamberg:
he gave her the castle of Bottenstein; where, with her children and her two faithful maidens, she at length lived in
peace.

Elizabeth was little more than twenty; and her uncle
thought her too young to live single: he wished her to
marry the Emperor Frederick II., who desired the match
ardently, for she was one of the most beautiful princesses of
the day. She refused, with modest firmness. Her sorrow
for the loss of her husband had not yet subsided: besides
she had, of her own accord, solemnly vowed to Lewis never
to belong to any other man should he happen to die first.
To shun the importunities of her ambitious relative, she took
a pilgrimage to the monastery of Andechs; and, as a token
that she had now done with human love, she laid on the
altar her rich wedding-robe, which is still preserved in the
church.

Whilst Elizabeth resided at the castle of Bottenstein, the
procession, bearing the remains of her late husband, passed
by Bamberg on its way to Reinhartsbrunn. On her request
the coffin was opened. She kissed with impassioned tenderness all that was now left of him she had so much loved;
then, raising her soul to God, she exclaimed aloud, in words
that have been transmitted, "I give thee thanks, O Lord,
for having deigned to hear the prayer of thy handmaiden;
and for having granted my ardent wish of beholding again
the remains of my beloved; who was also thine. I give
thee thanks for having thus mercifully comforted mine afflicted soul. He had offered himself, and I had offered him
to thee, for the defence of thy Holy Land. I regret it not,

even though I loved him with all the might of my heart. Thou knowest how I loved him, who loved thee so much: thou knowest that to all the joys of this world I would have preferred that of his delightful presence; that I would have been glad to live with him, and beg with him from door to door through the whole world, merely for the happiness of being with him, if thou hadst permitted it. But now I abandon him, and I abandon myself to thy will; and I would not, even though I could, purchase back his life with one hair of my head, unless it were thy will, O my God!"

The lords who were bringing back the remains of Lewis to his native land were the bravest of his court, being those who had accompanied him in his crusade. They learned with indignation the treatment their Lady Elizabeth had received, and promised to see her and her children righted; they kept their word so effectually, that, shortly after their return, Elizabeth, who willingly consented to a reconciliation, re-entered the castle of Wartburg, from which she had been so cruelly expelled. The government of Thuringia was left to her brother-in-law Henry, but the rights of her son Hermann were acknowledged. A year after this, she asked Henry to give her a separate residence; he granted her the town of Marburg and its revenues.

We have not space to dwell at full length on the remaining years of Elizabeth. She filled them with deeds of an heroic charity that almost surpasses belief. She was now a wealthy lady; but her wealth was not her own—it belonged to the poor. She lived in a little house, and earned her livelihood by spinning wool, whilst thousands subsisted on her bounty, and the sick were cared for in the hospital which she had founded immediately on her arrival. The world called her mad, because her riches were not squandered in luxurious amusements; but she only smiled at the imputation. She once gathered together an immense number of poor people, and distributed abundant alms amongst them; their joy was so great, that they began to sing. Elizabeth heard them from her house, and exclaimed, in words that paint her heart, " Did I not tell you that we must render men as happy as we can !" and she went forth to rejoice with them.

Her confessor, Conrad, seems to have thought that she

found too much pleasure in such tasks : he had already forbidden her to take a vow of poverty, and he now forbade her to be so prodigal.   Elizabeth strove to elude his prohibition : he had told her to give only one farthing at a time, and she caused silver farthings to be struck.   The poor, accustomed to larger donations, complained ; but, with the finesse of a woman, she said to them, " I am forbidden to give you more than one farthing at a time, but I am not forbidden to give to you every time you shall come."   It need not be said that the hint was readily taken.   Conrad was much irritated, and, in his resentment, did not scruple to strike her.   It is painful to read how far this harsh and domineering priest carried his authority over his docile penitent.   In many things his prohibitions were justified, for he checked the excessive austerities in which Elizabeth had always been prone to indulge ; but the way in which he exercised his dominion was harsh, and often cruel.   He was indeed a stern father ; yet there is no doubt that, in his own austere way, he loved her, and held himself bound to treat her with severity for the greater good of her soul.   When he once thought himself near dying, his distress at the prospect of leaving her was great : he knew that, though he was only a poor monk, he stood between her and many enemies, who would take advantage of his death to work her ill.   The danger was averted : Elizabeth, though still in the prime of youth, was the first to die.

A burning fever seized and carried her off quickly.   Several times during the course of her illness she was heard to sing with ravishing sweetness.   She died in all the transports of a heavenly piety, on the 19th of November of the year 1231 ; being then little more than twenty-four.   Rarely has a life so varied and so brief been graced by so many virtues.   So great was the renown of her sanctity, that, a few days after her death and funeral, her tomb was already crowded with pilgrims, who waited not the sanction of the Church to proclaim her holy.   The stern Conrad, who had given her so many opportunities of practising the virtues of patience and submission, suggested her canonization to the pope ; and it took place four years later.   The translation of her relics drew immense crowds.   The emperor, Frederick II., whom Elizabeth had refused to marry, placed on her head a crown of gold, saying, " Since. I could not crown her living as my empress, I will at least crown her to-day as an immortal queen in the kingdom of heaven."

For several ages, the fame of Elizabeth continued to increase. The romantic interest of her story, and the heroic virtues which she practised, have rendered her one of the most popular saints of the Catholic Church. One of her daughters married, and left a son, from whom are descended the various branches of the house of Hesse. There are few of the reigning sovereigns of Europe who may not claim St. Elizabeth of Hungary as their ancestress. In the year 1539, Philip of Hesse, one of her descendants, who had adopted the doctrines of Luther, caused her shrine to be opened and despoiled of all its ornaments : the relics were buried at night in some unknown spot.

The land where Elizabeth lived has undergone great changes : the churches where she was honored, now hold another creed ; the mansions of charity which she founded, exist no longer. A modern traveller,* to whose enthusiasm for the character of this noble woman we owe the best biography of her that exists, has recorded with sorrow how few traces of her existence he found, in places whence the changes of time and religious opinion need not have effaced her memory : spots once named after her now bear the names of other princesses. One token, however, the traveller found both characteristic and touching. The hospital which Elizabeth built at Wartburg is there no more, but the little fountain that once belonged to it exists : the clear waters still flow in their stone basin, surrounded with grass and flowers. Here the wife of the landgrave was wont to wash with her own hands the linen of the poor. No other princess has come there to perform this humble office, and give her name to the fountain : it is still called " the Fountain of Elizabeth."

* Count Charles of Montalembert

CHAPTER VII.

Hereditary Virtues—Hedwiges, Duchess of Poland—Margaret of Hungary—Kinga—Elizabeth, Queen of Portugal—Isabel of France—Hedwiges of Hungary—Clare—Agnes.

WE have already had occasion to remark that piety and charity were often hereditary in families; the family of St. Elizabeth of Hungary may be adduced as another instance: for several generations it produced women of eminent piety and virtue.

The aunt of Elizabeth, Hedwiges, duchess of Poland, exhausted her revenues to relieve the poor; and in order to be able to assist them from the monastery, where she retired after the death of her husband, she took no vows. Her patience under heavy sorrows, her humility, her boundless charity, have been deservedly extolled.

Margaret of Hungary, the niece of Elizabeth, died in her twenty-eighth year, in odor of sanctity.

Her sister, Kinga or Cunegondes, was married to Boleslas the Chaste, sovereign of Lesser Poland. Whilst she was still a child, Kinga was in the habit of giving away to the poor her garments of purple and gold; and, as a princess, she loved to humble her pride and mortify her senses by attending on poor lepers. She carried this charity so far, that, although she remained unharmed in the midst of infection, her attendants refused to eat the food she had touched, or to approach her too nearly. A romantic legend relates, that as a reward for the peril which she so heroically braved, Kinga was once enabled to heal a leprous woman by a kiss of her pure lips. She died in 1292, deeply venerated.

Elizabeth, queen of Portugal, was the grand-daughter of Violante, sister of Elizabeth of Hungary; after whom she was named. She inherited many of her virtues, and had also a virtue of her own, which she found many occasions of exercising; and which might well entitle her to be styled "the Peacemaker," even as her relative was styled "the Patroness of the Poor." Her birth, in 1271, restored harmony between her grandfather, James I., king of Aragon, and her father, who was afterwards Peter III. It was perhaps owing to this circumstance that Elizabeth was so much beloved both by James and by her own father. Scarcely, however, had she reached her twelfth year, when Peter promised her in marriage to Denis, the young King of Portugal. He was the only reigning sovereign who sued for the hand of Elizabeth, and was for this reason preferred to his rivals.

The King of Aragon was, however, sorely troubled when he had to part from his favorite daughter. He accompanied her part of the way, and as they separated he embraced her, weeping much, and saying: "Was there ever seen a more miserable man than I am? Behold! I send away from me the thing I hold most beloved and most dear." Then he blessed her over and over, and said: "My daughter, thou seekest a strange country: I reared thee; I taught thee; in nothing more may I counsel thee. Assuredly I never saw a creature that could compare to thee with regard to the intelligence and virtues with which thou art dowered." "And thus," says an old chronicler, "the king went away from his daughter."

The arrival of Elizabeth in Portugal was marked by a characteristic incident. She reconciled her husband Denis to his brother, the Infant, with whom he was at variance. So great was her love of peace, that she did not merely seek to soften the animosity of contending parties by arguments and entreaties, but when money was the cause of quarrel, she restored harmony by giving whatever sums were needed. To this kind and amiable disposition the young queen united many other virtues. From the day that she became sovereign of Portugal, she devoted herself to the welfare of her subjects. All pilgrims and poor strangers were by her orders provided with food and lodgings. She founded a hospital near her palace at Coimbra, a house for penitent women at Torres-Novas, and a hospital for foundlings. She secretly assisted persons of gentle blood fallen into distress, portioned and married poor maidens exposed to temptation, and visited, to serve and relieve them with her own hands, sick and suffering persons. At home she employed all the time she could spare from her devotions in working for the poor: a pious task in which she was assisted by her maidens of honor.

5

Denis was a great and good king : he prepared the commercial greatness of Portugal, he was a patron of the arts and sciences, and history has deservedly styled him "the just," and "the father of his country;" but this good monarch was an indifferent husband, and stained his private life with a long course of licentiousness. Elizabeth endured his infidelities with great patience : such were her meekness and her love of peace, that she reared her husband's natural children as tenderly as her own. With time the king reformed ; but not before he had put his pure and virtuous wife to the strange trial of seeing her fidelity questioned. Denis soon became convinced that his suspicions were both ill-founded and disgraceful ; he discarded his mistresses, and in that way, at least, gave his wife no further cause of complaint. Other afflictions were in store for Elizabeth.

She had two children by the king : Alfonso, who succeeded his father, and Constantia, who married Ferdinand IV., king of Castile, and died in her youth. Elizabeth had to restore peace between her brother, James II. of Aragon, and her son-in-law. They were on the verge of making war, when her entreaties induced them to keep their forces for the common Moorish foe, and submit their quarrel to the arbitrament of her husband ; with whom she took a journey into Spain for that purpose. The reconciliation was happily effected ; and similar success awaited the praiseworthy efforts of Elizabeth when she interfered between her son-in-law, Ferdinand, and his cousin, Alfonso, who disputed his right to the crown. She soon had occasion to exercise in the bosom of her own family her zeal for peace. Her son, Alfonso, afterwards styled the Brave, was a prince of a proud and impatient spirit. Soon after his marriage with the Infanta of Castile, he quarrelled with his father. Elizabeth favored his escape ; but interceded in his favor with Denis, who was so much irritated against her that he banished her to the city of Alanquer. The queen bore this disgrace with great patience, and refused to side with the malcontents. After some time, the king recalled her to court, and she succeeded in reconciling him to their son.

The quarrel soon broke forth again. The Infant wanted to enter a town where the king resided, and Denis came forth to meet and prevent him. The armed followers of the

prince insisted on advancing, and the supporters of the king
forbade the way. An army was rapidly drawn up on either
side, and a combat began with an exchange of stones and
arrows. Some were killed, and many badly wounded. As
the strife began to wax warm, the queen suddenly appeared,
mounted on a mule, without a servant to hold the bridle, or
male or female attendant that dared to follow; she rode
fearlessly between the two contending armies, exposed to
the stones and arrows that flew around her from either side.
"God, whose service she intended," writes a pious biographer, "permitted her to pass thus unhurt." She reached
the presence of the king; from him she went to the Infant;
she thus journeyed alternately between father and son, until
at length Alfonso agreed to submit, and kiss the hand of
Denis, who consented to forgive him, and bestow on him his
paternal benediction. They parted reconciled; "and thus
on that day, through the intercession and prayers of this
queen, God chose to deliver many men of the kingdom of
Portugal from death, and other irreparable evils."

After reigning forty-five years, Denis fell sick, and died
in 1325. Elizabeth retired to a convent of poor Clares.
She did not take the vows, because she would thus have
lost her privilege of bestowing alms, and of supporting at
her cost a great number of poor people. "She practised
the seven works of mercy," writes one of her biographers;
"for she clothed the naked, she fed the hungry, visited the
sick, and supported hospitals; she caused the dead to be
laid out and buried, she released prisoners for debt, redeemed
captives, and brought back erring sinners to virtue." The
same biographer commends Elizabeth highly for several singular virtues, such as never resenting an offence, and never
once being seen to wear an angry face. He praises highly
her charity to the poor, and to unfortunate sinning women:
to keep them from temptation, the good queen provided
them with food and clothing.

Whilst Elizabeth resided at Coimbra, a great dearth fell
on the land. The queen caused bread, meat, and money to
be daily distributed amongst the people; but this did not
prevent many men and women from dying of hunger. Elizabeth saw to their burial; with a charity that extended beyond the grave, she caused the rites of the dead to be per-

formed over them, and masses to be offered up for their souls. So profuse were her alms, even in proportion to her great revenues, that her servants murmured amongst themselves, and reproved her, saying, "She would keep nothing for herself for the time yet to come." To whom the queen replied: "I would rather die of hunger myself than deny aid to the poor in this season, and thus become guilty of their death before God." One last act of charity crowned worthily this pure and noble life.

Whilst Elizabeth resided at Coimbra, a war broke out between her son, Alfonso IV., king of Portugal, and her grandson, Alfonso XI., king of Castile. Their armies were already on foot, but no encounter had taken place. Elizabeth resolved to attempt to reconcile them in person. Her attendants represented that, with her disease—she was afflicted with a tumor in one of her arms—such a journey taken in the burning heats of summer might prove fatal. Elizabeth replied that health and life could not be better expended than in seeking to save two kingdoms from the miseries of war. The news of her journey disposed the contending parties to a peace, which her presence at Estremoz, on the frontiers of Portugal and Castile, finally effected. She arrived ill of a fever, which rapidly increased, and soon became fatal. She died with the serene piety of a saint. As her daughter-in-law, Queen Beatrix, sat in her chamber by her bed, shortly before her death, Elizabeth suddenly turned towards her, and said: "My lady daughter, make way for that lady who is passing there by you." "My lady mother," answered Beatrix, wondering, "who is that lady?" "She who came in here clad in white garments," answered the dying queen. Beatrix looked, and saw no one; whence she concluded that the holy Virgin, whom Elizabeth had always much honored, had sent this lady to visit and comfort the sick queen. No more heavenly messengers came to soothe her pain, or summon her away; the hour of her departure had arrived; it found Elizabeth calm and prepared. She received the last sacrament of the Church with fervent piety, then repeated to herself the Creed and the Lord's Prayer, until the words died on her lips, and she quietly expired. She died on the fourth of July, 1336, in the sixty-fifth year of her age.

Another royal family of the same age, offers the same instances of female virtue and piety which we have traced in that of Hungary. Elizabeth of Hungary left a son, who died young: poisoned, it is said, by one of his uncles. Before his death he visited the court of France, where Blanche of Castile received him kindly. Out of reverence to his mother, the French queen often kissed the brow which the lips of the sainted Elizabeth had pressed.

Blanche was, herself, a woman of eminent, though not always gentle, virtues. Her mother, Eleanor of England, queen of Castile, and her sister, Uraça, queen of Portugal, were reverenced for their goodness. Two of the eleven children of Blanche left the name of saints : Louis IX., one of the best and greatest of French kings, and the pious and humble Isabel.

Blanche of Castile was a noble woman : she once said to St. Louis : " I love you, but I would rather behold you dead at my feet than see you commit one mortal sin." These words, uttered by a mother who loved him with the most impassioned tenderness, produced on Louis a horror of sin which nothing could ever efface. To every royal and manly virtue he united a severe purity rarely displayed on the throne. Isabel was worthy to be the daughter of this illustrious woman, and the sister of this good king. She lived in retirement at the court of her brother, showing no inclination either for the cloister or for the married state. Blanche and Louis wished her to contract some powerful alliance, and the pope strongly urged her to comply with this reasonable request ; but Isabel defended her freedom with mingled humility, firmness, and good sense. She dwelt in such forcible language on the miseries of unhappy princesses sent into exile, and sacrificed to state policy, that her relatives, who loved her tenderly, at length gave up the point.

Blanche had given her daughter a religious and learned education ; and Isabel attained so perfect a knowledge of the Latin language, that she often corrected the compositions of her chaplains. Her great delight was to remain in her closet reading the holy Scriptures, or some book of devotion, whilst the princesses of the royal family and their ladies shared in the amusements of the court. To please her mother, she sometimes appeared in those festivities ; but although she

had, like Blanche, inherited the memorable beauty of Eleanor
of Guyenne, their maternal ancestress, the young princess
took no pleasure in adorning her person : it was very reluctantly that she allowed her attendants to dress her hair ;
which, like her mother's, was of extraordinary length and
beauty. Some of those women, who already revered her as
a holy being, carefully preserved the hair which they combed
out of the head of their mistress ; Isabel, perceiving this,
asked to know the reason. "Madam," answered one of the
women, " we keep it to make relics of it, for the time when
you shall have become a saint." Isabel laughed very much
on hearing this.

Charity to the poor was her favorite virtue. Her brother
Louis one day found her spinning wool for a cap; he asked
her to give it to him, saying, he should wear it for her sake.
"This," answered Isabel, " is the first work of the kind that
I have spun ; I therefore owe it to Jesus Christ, to whom all
my first fruits are due." Jesus Christ, in the pious phrase-
ology of the age, meant the poor. The cap was given to an
old woman, from whom two of the attendants of Isabel
bought it, to keep it as a token of the charity of their young
mistress. Louis, much pleased with the answer of his sister,
hoped that she would at least give him the second fruits of
her industry ; she promised to do so, as soon as the first cap
was finished. The days of Isabel were devoted to such
labors : she also practised the more difficult charity of attending on the sick, with whatever infectious and repulsive
diseases they might be afflicted. She ultimately founded a
monastery of poor Clares near Paris, to which she retired ;
and where she died, without having taken the vows, in
1269. She was canonized in 1521.

Her sister-in-law, the good and amiable Margueritte of
Provence, the worthy wife of St. Louis, was a saint herself
in all save the name. She is celebrated for her conjugal
love, and her heroism in misfortune ; but her own humility,
and the jealousy of her mother-in-law, have rendered her
private life obscure : we know her through what she underwent, not through what she did. Historians agree in praising the faultless beauty of her character.

In the following age lived St. Hedwiges of Hungary ;
descended through her father from Blanche of Castile, and

through one of her maternal ancestors from the same royal family of Hungary which had already produced so many eminent women. Hedwiges was elected queen of Poland in her thirteenth year. The Polish magnates who chose her for their sovereign, exacted that she should marry Jagellon, duke of Lithuania. She complied, and sacrificed her own inclination, in favor of an Austrian prince, to the good of her kingdom and the extension of her religion ; for on his marriage with Hedwiges, Jagellon received baptism, and afterwards labored with her to spread Christianity amongst his subjects. Hedwiges was both a great and a good sovereign : she sold her jewels to relieve the poor, and to complete the buildings of the university at Cracow. There is a little anecdote which paints her under a very charming aspect. Some poor peasants came to her in tears, complaining that the servants of the king had carried off their cattle ; Hedwiges went to her husband and obtained instant redress. "The cattle have been restored to them," said the queen, "but who shall give them back their tears?" Only a woman, and perhaps, we may add, only a Christian woman, could have said this. Hedwiges died in 1399, in her twenty-eighth year. She left a memory deeply venerated in Poland, and the name of having been the most beautiful and accomplished princess of her age.

We have occasionally alluded in the preceding pages to the convents of the poor Clares, where Cunegondes of Hungary, Isabel of France, and Elizabeth of Portugal, retired. This order was then recently established ; but neither caprice nor the love of novelty had dictated the choice of these princesses.

For several ages monastic establishments had progressed : sovereigns had endowed and erected magnificent abbeys ; great lords and ladies had enriched them with ample revenues ; and the pious, high and low, had brought offerings more or less costly, to their shrines. Abbots and abbesses lived with the state of princes : they had lands and vassals ; they could raise levies and make war on their neighbors ; in short, they exercised the great and almost irresponsible power vested in them as feudal lords. But precisely as they reached this state of temporal prosperity, some fervent and ascetic spirits began to remember that the monastic state was prop-

erly a state of penance, mortification, and gospel poverty.
Then arose the austere orders of the Franciscans, Domini-
cans, Augustines, and Carmelites. These mendicant and
preaching friars were meanly clad and poorly lodged ; they
refused to possess domains or revenues : they lived partly on
alms, partly on their own industry ; they went about preaching with great fervor ; they were learned, humble, and
pious ; and the contrast which their simple mode of existence offered to the luxurious life of the other religious orders,
secured them universal pre-eminence ; until they too forgot,
with time, the strictness and poverty enjoined by their original founders.

It was in the thirteenth century that St. Francis of Assissi,
one of the most eminent and extraordinary men of his age,
founded the great order of the Franciscans. His work
would not have been complete had it not included women.
He did not at first think of them ; they came to him ; his
peculiar character, his boundless charity, his humility, the
fervor of his devotion, impressed both their imagination and
their heart.

At the time when the religious fame of the saint began to
spread in Italy, there dwelt in his native town of Assissi (so
called from the stony hill of Assi on which it is built), a noble knight named Favorino Sciffo ; who, with his wife Hortulana, held the first rank in the place. They had three
daughters, Clare, Agnes, and Beatrice. Clare was charitable and devout : she disliked the thought of marriage, and,
wishing to leave the world, applied to Francis for advice.,
He strengthened her in her resolve ; she left her home one
evening in the spring of the year 1212, and went out of town
to the Portiuncula, where Francis and his brethren resided.
The friars received her at the door of the church with lighted
tapers, singing the hymn, Veni Creator. Clare entered the
church, and before the altar of the Virgin put off her sump-
tuous garments for a robe of sackcloth tied round her with a
cord. Francis cut off her hair and placed her in a Benedictine nunnery : she was then eighteen.

Her parents and friends, exasperated at the step she had
taken, came to draw her from her retreat. They attempted
to use force ; Clare passionately clung to the altar and held
it fast, though their violence was such that they dragged

down the cloths with which it was covered. She remonstrated with them, and, uncovering her head, showed them her shorn locks; declaring that she was now the bride of heaven, and would never own a mortal spouse. They reproached her—for this was her chief offence—that she disgraced her family by embracing a rule so mean as that of the mendicant friars; but she bore their insults with patience. At length they left her.

Soon after this, Clare was joined by her sister Agnes, a girl of fourteen. Twelve men succeeded in entering the convent and attempted to carry her off: they struck her, and dragged her by the hair along the pavement of the church. "Help me, dear sister," she cried, addressing Clare, who prayed, prostrate and weeping : "Help me, nor let me be taken from the Lord Jesus Christ." The men finding it impossible to conquer the resistance of this young girl, ended by retiring. Soon after this, Agnes took the habit, and went to live with her sister in a mean house of Assissi. They were joined by their mother Hortulana, who had become a widow; and sixteen noble ladies followed their example.

The order of the poor Clares spread rapidly. They practised austerities hitherto unknown amongst women, and made it their fundamental rule never to possess any thing. A large fortune devolved on Clare by the death of her father; but she would not bestow the least part of it on her monastery, and distributed it amongst the poor. When Pope Innocent IV. visited her, she requested him to confirm to her order the singular privilege of perpetual poverty. He promised to do so, declaring, at the same time, that no such demand had ever before been addressed to the apostolic see. Pope Gregory IX. vainly endeavored to persuade Clare to accept a yearly revenue, which he offered to settle on her monastery of St. Damian's. "If your vow prevents you," he said, "I will release you from it." "Holy father," answered Clare, "I have no wish to be released from amongst the followers of Christ."

She died in 1253, poor as she had lived. The pope and the whole sacred college assisted at her funeral.

5*

CHAPTER VIII.

Catherine of Sienna—Catherine of Sweden.

Dominic, the contemporary and friend of Francis of As-sissium, established a female religious order, which was afterwards known as the third order of St. Dominic. It enjoined few austerities, but great regularity. Some of the members were nuns, took the vows, and resided in cloisters; others were women who lived in their own houses, but who devoted themselves to works of mercy, and especially to serve the poor in hospitals. It was this order which St. Catherine of Sienna joined, in the second age of its estab-lishment.

Catherine is one of the many instances of the democratic power inherent to Christianity. The purity and holiness of her life alone raised this young and obscure nun to a position so high, that she became a negotiator between contending States, a support to the Church in her peril, and the con-templated ambassadress of a pope to a great queen. These honors have induced some of the biographers of Catherine to derive her origin from one of those Italian families of illustrious citizens who vied in power and magnificence with the princes of other lands; but the plain truth is, that her ancestry was obscure, and that her father, Jacopo Benincasa, was no more than a prosperous dyer of Sienna.

Both Jacopo and his wife Lapa loved Catherine more than their other children. She was beautiful, highly gifted, and devout beyond her years. Her parents treated her with marked indulgence until she had reached her twelfth year; they then wished her to marry, but Catherine unexpectedly declared that she had solemnly vowed to know no other spouse than Christ. Lapa was greatly incensed : to divert the thoughts of her daughter from the religious state, she deprived her of the little room to which she was in the habit of retiring for meditation and solitude, and gave her all the drudgery of the house to perform. Catherine bore with great patience the anger of her parents, the insults of her jealous sisters, the humiliation of the menial tasks set to her, and the loss of her dear little room. She at length supplied its place by making, as she said herself, a cell and oratory in her heart, so calm and secure that, in the midst of the most distracting occupations, she could ever retire to it, and rest in peace within the shadow of her own thoughts.

A temper so resolute, and a mind that could so early exercise the philosophic power of abstraction from external occupations, were not of the order that is controlled or influenced easily. We find, accordingly, that all the time this domestic persecution lasted, but one compliance was wrung from Catherine: her sisters prevailed on her to assume a dress somewhat more elegant and becoming than that which she usually wore. This momentary indulgence of feminine vanity was the great sin of Catherine's youth. It is easy to smile at so much rigidity: but to the pure nothing is light; and to all, any deviation from their own principles of right and wrong ought to seem a sin.

The parents of Catherine, seeing there was no chance of succeeding with their inflexible daughter, at length gave up the point, and allowed her to resume her former mode of life. She practised great austerities, relieved the poor, and visited the prisoners and the sick. Many severe illnesses, aggravated by the remedies the physicians prescribed to her, tormented her for some years: she bore her sufferings with exemplary patience.

In the year 1365, Catherine, who was then eighteen, received the habit of the third order of St. Dominic, in a nunnery of Sienna. She suffered much from those spiritual troubles which seem to exceed all others in bitterness, but she never relaxed from her charitable pursuits: people often met her in the streets of Sienna bending beneath the weight of the corn, wine, oil, and other provisions which she was carrying to the poor. She practised, to its fullest extent, the heroic charity of the good Elizabeth of Hungary. An old leprous woman named Tocca, had, by order of the magistrates of Sienna, been sent out from the hospital into the city. The entreaties of Catherine obtained her readmittance into the hospital, where she promised to attend on her; she accordingly visited Tocca twice a day until her death, when she laid her out with her own hands. The only return she ever received for so much goodness was the most bitter abuse the tongue of old Tocca could bestow on her, and which Catherine endured with true Christian patience. In another case, that of a woman whose cancer she dressed, Catherine fared no better: this woman, abetted by a sister of the convent, invented and spread calumnious reports against the reputation of her benefactress. Lapa, on learning this, angrily forbade her daughter to attend any longer this ungrateful wretch; but Catherine, with that excess of charity which makes it a sort of passion, threw herself at her mother's feet, and would not rise until she had wrung from her the permission of continuing her generous task. So much patience and goodness at length touched the two sinners, they implored the forgiveness of Catherine, and retracted those slanders which originated in their own mean jealousy of her virtues.

Catherine possessed a gift which does not, like charity, depend on the will and holiness of those who own it—the gift of eloquence : the young nun of St. Dominic, who tended the leprous and the sick, could speak so as to move the hearts of worldly men, and soften into penitence blaspheming sinners. Factions ran high in the republican cities of Italy ; long and sanguinary feuds divided the chief families of every State, and Sienna had her share of the universal strife. The persuasive eloquence of Catherine in reconciling recent or hereditary enemies became celebrated in her native city : when her arguments failed, she prayed.

A powerful citizen of Sienna named Nanni, distinguished for the relentless bitterness of his animosities, was urged by a certain religious man to go and see the saint. He long refused to do so, and when he ended by consenting, he solemnly declared before going that nothing Catherine might say should induce him ever to forgive his enemies. All her remonstrances having failed in producing the least effect, Catherine began to pray that God would touch the unforgiving sinner. Nanni wished to leave the place, but a force he could not withstand had already seized his heart; he threw himself at the feet of Catherine, and promised with tears to obey her. " My dear brother," she gently said, " I spoke to thee, and thou wouldst not hear me; I spoke to God, and he did not despise my prayer. Do penance, lest tribulation should befall thee."

In the year 1374, when pestilence laid waste Sienna and the surrounding country, Catherine displayed her apostolic zeal: she tended the infected with all the assiduity and tenderness of a woman, and exhorted them in strains so fervent and moving, that they touched the most hardened. Her fame spread, and thousands flocked from remote parts of Italy to hear her. "I myself," writes her friend, Raymond of Capua, "have sometimes seen more than a thousand persons of either sex, who had never before left their hills unless to see and hear this virgin, held the wonder of her age."

So powerful were her exhortations, that Raymond of Capua and another priest were specially appointed by the pope to hear the confessions of those whom Catherine had converted. They were often thus engaged for the whole of the day and of the night without being able to break their fast: nothing but the example of zeal and energy which Catherine gave them could have enabled them to bear so much fatigue.

By command of her superiors, and at the earnest request of the citizens of Pisa, Catherine undertook a journey to that city in the year 1375. The superior of a convent near it immediately begged that she would come and address his monks; which she did, we are told, with surprising wisdom and eloquence. Catherine was still at Pisa when the great league of the Italian States was formed against the Holy See: Florence was at the head of the movement. By her prayers, letters, and entreaties, Catherine contributed to preserve Arezzo, Lucca, and Sienna to the cause of the pope. With a sorrowful heart she prophesied, it is said, that the troubles of the Church were only commencing, and foretold the great schism which took place three years later.

The diocese of Florence having been laid under an interdict, the citizens thought proper, for a time at least, to retrace the course they had adopted. The magistrates sent to Sienna to beg that Catherine would become their mediatrix with the Holy See; she willingly consented, and immediately went to Florence. She was met outside the city by the priors or chiefs of the magistrates, who agreed to leave to her the management of the whole affair, and said that ambassadors should follow her to Avignon, and ratify whatever terms she might have made. Relying on these promises, Catherine proceeded to Avignon, which she reached in June of the year 1376.

The pope and the cardinals received her with the greatest distinction. In reference to the matter which had brought her, Gregory XI., after conferring with her, went so far as to say, "I desire nothing but peace: I put the affair entirely into your hands; only, I recommend to you the honor of the Church." Spite of this apparent good-will on either side, the negotiation failed as soon as the Florentine ambassadors reached Avignon.

The journey of Catherine was not, however, wholly unproductive of good. In leaving Italy for the French city, where the bishops of the Roman Church had chosen their abode for the last seventy-four years, Catherine had at heart a project dear to her national feelings—the return of the pope to the great city, which he and his predecessors had deserted for a foreign home; and which, irritated at such treatment, now openly threatened a schism. Gregory had indeed taken a secret vow to return to Rome, but foreseeing much opposition to his project, and not knowing how to execute it, he consulted the saint: she is said to have answered, "Fulfil what you have promised to God." Whatever may be the truth of this, it is acknowledged that she persuaded the pope to leave Avignon: he did so in the month of September, shortly after her departure: he overtook her at Genoa, where she had been detained by the illness of her attendants, on whom she waited herself, with the zeal she had not ceased to evince in such tasks.

She was soon again in her convent at Sienna, caring for the poor and the sick, converting sinners, and reconciling enemies. Wherever she went, she spread her own holiness and peace; for there was that in her presence which, according to Pius II., her fellow-citizen, made those who approached her leave her better than when they came.

Virtues so eminent, joined to an influence seldom exercised by, and distinctions rarely bestowed on, a woman, were of a nature to create envy. Whilst Catherine was at Avignon, three prelates one day asked the pope what was his opinion of this young girl; he answered briefly, that she was a person of great prudence and rare sanctity. They wished to know whether they might visit her; he consented, assuring them they would not be disappointed. They went forthwith; said they were sent by the pope, and asked if it were really true that the republic of Florence had intrusted her with so great a negotiation. Without waiting for an answer, the prelates reprimanded her for her temerity in presuming to accept an office of this importance. A witness of this interview assures us that their words were sharp, and that their tone was bitter and scornful; Catherine, on the contrary, was calm, modest, and respectful. From political, the conversation took a theological turn: the prelates pressed the young nun with difficult questions, in the hope of finding her at fault; but her answers proved a spirit so enlightened, and a doctrine so pure, that they were compelled to confess themselves conquered. A similar triumph awaited Catherine in her native city, where certain Italian doctors came to expose her ignorance, and after conferring with her, departed, ashamed and astonished.

Gregory had kept his promise : he was at Rome; but Catherine, whose heart bled at the distracted state of her native land, wrote to him, earnestly imploring him to contribute to the peace of Italy. The pope bade her go to Florence, which was again at war with the Holy See. In the midst of the factions, murders, and confiscations which disgraced the turbulent city, Catherine, though she was often personally menaced, showed the most undaunted spirit. She sought to moderate the zeal of the partisans of the pope; yet their excesses were unjustly attributed to her : the populace asked for her death by fire or sword; and her own friends were so much terrified at the fury her name excited, that they would no longer receive or shelter her in their houses. A large body of people, learning that she had retired to a certain garden, went to seek her there with drawn swords, and crying out aloud, "Where is that accursed Catherine?" She came forth to meet them with untroubled aspect, and said, "If I be her whom you seek, here I am. Do that which the Lord will permit; but in his name I forbid you to harm those that are with me." The chief of the insurgents, putting his sword into the scabbard, said, "Retire, and save your life by flight." "No, I will not retire," replied the courageous woman; "if by shedding my blood

I can promote peace, why should I fly, now that the honor of Christ, and the peace of his spouse, are in peril?" Her spirit and dignity saved her: the crowd departed, and left Catherine unhurt. She consented to leave Florence for a while; but she remained in the vicinity of the city until peace was concluded.

This did not happen until the year 1378. Gregory had died; Urban VI. sat in the chair of St. Peter. His pontificate was marked by the fatal schism Catherine had foretold. Urban, though legitimately elected, was disowned by several cardinals, whom his harsh temper had alienated; and who, after electing the anti-pope, Clement VII., retired with him to Avignon. Catherine wrote to them, pathetically exhorting them to retract their error. She likewise addressed Urban, strongly advising him to modify that harsh temper to which he owed some of his misfortunes. Urban had the good sense and policy to heed this advice; he wrote to Catherine to come to Rome. She modestly objected, that so many journeys were not advantageous to a virgin; but when the pope insisted, she complied with his request. Her discourse comforted him so much, that he desired her to speak in the presence of the whole sacred college; Catherine did so, with much grace, modesty, and success. When she had ceased, the pope, turning towards the cardinals, emphatically said, "Here, my brethren, is what should make us blush: the courage of a maiden reproves us." Much more he added in the same strain, greatly praising the faith of the young nun.

The value Urban set on her zeal and talents, is proved by the fact that he intended sending her to Joan, queen of Sicily, who had sided with Clement. The project being attended with great personal peril, was abandoned; to the regret of Catherine. She wrote to Joan, likewise to the kings of France and Hungary, exhorting them to renounce the schism. In this contemplated embassy Catherine was to have had a companion; like her, a woman, a nun, and a saint: the beautiful Catherine of Sweden, daughter of St. Bridget, through whom she descended from the royal Swedish line, and from one of the ancient Gothic kings. Both mother and daughter left their home in Sweden, to undertake a pilgrimage to Holy Land. It was on returning from this long and fatiguing journey that Bridget died at Rome; whence Catherine conveyed her remains to the monastery of Vatzen, in Sweden. Before her death Bridget wrote to Pope Gregory XI., entreating him to leave Avignon for Rome; a step to which, as we have seen, he was strongly and successfully exhorted by Catherine of Sienna.

In the year 1375 Catherine of Sweden came to Rome to procure the canonization of her pious mother; and it was during her sojourn in the capital of the Christian world that Urban VI. designated her as a fit person to share the mission of Catherine of Sienna. To two women, one scarcely forty, the other several years younger, one a princess, the other a dyer's daughter, was to have been confided a task in which the peace of Christendom and the honor of the Church were engaged. Catherine of Sweden died in 1381; and, like her, Catherine of Sienna did not long survive this intended distinction. Worn-out by the infirmities which had early afflicted her, she died at Rome on the 29th of April, 1380, in the thirty-third year of her age. She was canonized in 1461; but long before this her remains were held as relics, and her mother, Lapa, who reached the age of ninety, was always venerated as the mother of a saint. In the Strada dell Oca of the city of Sienna stood the house where Catherine was born; it was converted into an oratory, which still exists. Her cell was shown to Evelyn when he visited Sienna in 1645, and he records that the door of deal wood was half cut out into chips, by the many devout persons who came to visit the spot once hallowed by her presence.

CHAPTER IX.

Catherine of Genoa—Teresa of Avila.

THE charity of Catherine of Sienna shone forth in her namesake, Catherine of Genoa, in the succeeding age; whilst more than her enthusiasm and genius revived in the great St. Teresa of the sixteenth century.

Catherine Fieschi was born at Genoa in 1447. She belonged to one of the first families of that illustrious city, and was married in her sixteenth year to Julian, of the noble house of Adorno. Julian was an ill-tempered profligate, who squandered the fortune of his wife, and rendered her very unhappy for ten years. Her patient virtues at length brought him to a sense of his errors; and soon afterwards he died, in sentiments of great penitence.

In early youth Catherine had ardently desired to enter the religious state; but her short stature and delicate health had caused her parents to refuse their consent, and in obedience to their wish she had contracted her unhappy marriage. She was now at liberty to dispose of herself as she thought fit; and, as she desired to unite the contemplative and active duties of religion, she entered the great hospital of Genoa; where she lived in a state of ecstatic piety, even whilst she was daily recalled to earth by the tasks most painful and repugnant to human nature. It was long before Catherine could conquer her natural reluctance to the self-imposed duties she had sought; but she persevered, and ended by winning a complete victory over her feelings.

Her charity was not confined within the hospital where she lived: she went out to seek the sick poor of the city, and attended on lepers and similarly afflicted persons, whom no one else would touch. To deny herself, and to accomplish in all things the will of God, was her object in life. She had taken as her motto that petition of our Lord's prayer, "Thy will be done on earth as it is in heaven," and she remained true to it throughout. She died in 1510, in the sixty-third year of her age, in that hospital where she had spent the greatest portion of her life; and which she preferred to the marble palaces of Genoa. She wrote and left a few treatises, so mystical that they have caused her doctrine to be censured. But, whatever the theological opinions of Catherine may have been, her life was as beautiful and pure in spirit as she was in aspect. An ancient portrait represents her wearing the veil of a nun, and half bending in an attitude of prayer: there is great beauty in the clear Italian profile as well as in the rapt glance of adoration.

Not less humble, though far more celebrated, is St. Teresa of Avila. Her name is imperfectly known in this country; but on the Continent it has been held high in popular veneration for nearly three centuries.

Bossuet bowed before the authority of her writings; Fleury quoted them with the decrees of the Council of Trent; and men of modern France have devoted their leisure to the translation of those mystical productions, of which the original manuscripts were preciously kept locked in the royal palace of the Escurial, whilst a haughty Spanish monarch carried the key on his person. Convents of the austere order, which she reformed, rise in every Catholic land; stately churches have been erected under the invocation of her gentle name; humble engravings and high works of art have alike perpetuated the image of a handsome dark-eyed Spaniard, clad in the brown robe of the Carmelite nun, and bearing with modest mien the symbolic pen; which, save in this illustrious instance, the artist gives to none but the fathers and doctors of the Church.

To attain this extraordinary distinction, which she never sought—for she was humble to a fault—Teresa of Avila had nothing, save the power of her genius, and of a love in which the passion of the southern blended with the tender purity of the woman.

St. Teresa was born on the 28th of March, 1515, in Avila, an episcopal town of Old Castile. Her father, Don Alfonso Sanchez, of Cepeda, was a gentleman of good family, a devout Christian, and a man of unsullied honor. His second wife, Beatrice Ahumada, mother of the saint, was eminent for her virtues and great beauty. They reared their children with much care, and brought them up as became their rank and strict piety. When Teresa was about six or seven years of age, she gave all the money she had to the poor, and delighted much in reading the lives of the saints with her little brother Rodriguez. The legends of the martyrs—of their brief torments and eternity of bliss—fired her imagination. "Forever! to see God forever!" the children exclaimed to one another, awed and amazed. At length a strange project occurred-to them : they took a little supply of provisions, and stealthily leaving their father's home, set out for the land of the Moors ; where they hoped to be speedily put to death for the faith. They were quickly missed, and over-taken on the bridge of the Adaja by their uncle ; who asked where they were going, and why they had thrown their mother into so much alarm. They confessed their design : but Rodriguez threw the whole blame on his sister Teresa, who was then seven years old. Being thus disappointed of martyrdom, they turned hermits, and built themselves in the garden frail retreats, which the first stormy gust shattered and overthrew.

The mother of Teresa lived in great retirement, for she was almost always ill, and died in the prime of her years and beauty. Her only pleasure in this languishing condition, was to read those voluminous romances of love and knight-errantry, which, at a later period, perished beneath the keen and fatal mirth of Cervantes. She neglected none of her household duties ; but when every task was done, she loved to sit and while away, with the lays of poets and the tra-ditionary tales of ancient troubadours, a solitude rendered more wearisome by disease. The austere Don Alfonso, of Cepeda, greatly disapproved of this ; and he felt still more displeased, when he saw that his children shared the passion of their mother. Teresa exceeded the rest in her ardor, and read by stealth the romances her father held idle and per-nicious. She who had wept over the lives of the saints, and been fired with emulation by the legends of the martyrs, now placed her whole delight in Amadis de Gaul, and sat up at night to read in the mirror of chivalry the deeds of the twelve peers of mighty Charlemagne.

The greatest portion of her time was devoted to the read-ing of romances, old or new. Her chief pleasure was to procure some work which she had not yet read, and which she immediately perused with extreme avidity. All these tales of gallant knights, fair ladies, stirring deeds, and marvellous adventures, so charmed her ardent imagination, that she at length resolved to compose one herself. What the romance was like, and how far it shared in that genius which her later works display, posterity will never know : the tale remained unfinished, and was committed to the flames in a fit of penitent sorrow. But before this revulsion of feeling took place, vanity and the love of the world had entered the heart of Teresa. She began to perceive that she was beautiful; to adorn her hair; to take great care of her hands; to dress with elegance; and to use rich perfumes and the choicest scents. The death of her mother, whom she lost when she was in her twelfth year, gave her more liberty. Her father, like a true Spaniard, allowed no men, save his own nephews, to enter his house and see his daughters.

These young men were somewhat older than Teresa, and were very fond of their handsome cousin. They spoke to her freely of their flirtations, of the failure and success of their adventures; and she heard them with that eagerness with which, in every age, youth has listened to the narrative of tales of love. The society of a female relative, of frivolous mind and imprudent conduct, proved still more injurious to Teresa; but though her piety suffered, her pride and sense of womanly honor protected her more than her father's vigilance. Bitter as she is in her self-accusations concerning this part of her life, she acknowledges that so great was her dread of shame, that nothing earthly could have led her into sin.

Don Alfonso of Cepeda felt greatly dissatisfied with the acquaintances his favorite daughter had formed; but not knowing how to forbid his house to his nearest relatives, he resolved to place Teresa for some time in a convent of Avila.

Here the heart of Teresa underwent a great change. She would have devoted herself to God, but that she felt terrified at the idea of a perpetual engagement. She remained in a state of indecision for some years, suffering much from troubles of the spirit and the flesh; for she had inherited her mother's beauty and ill health. The epistles of St. Jerome to Eustochium strengthened her resolve; but she did not yet dare to declare it openly. Her reason is characteristic : " I was so much attached to every thing that concerns honor, that nothing, I thought, could make me relinquish a

resolve I had once announced." At length Teresa broke
this last barrier between herself and liberty, and told her
father that her vocation led her to the cloister. He opposed
the project; for he loved her with infinite tenderness. Teresa
perceiving that he would never give his consent, left his
house one morning, and repaired to the Carmelite convent
which stood without the walls of Avila. She has herself
recorded, in forcible language, the bitterness of this self-
imposed sacrifice :—" I think I may say, that had I been on
the point of giving up the ghost, I could not have suffered
more than I did on leaving my father's house. It seemed to
me as if all my bones were being riven and taken asunder,
because my love for God was not strong enough to overcome entirely that which I felt for my father and my kindred.". None suspected the internal conflict which rose to
its height when she took the habit ; all admired her joy and
serenity, whilst she endured the greatest agony of spirit ;
but the excess of the sacrifice wrought its own cure, and
once it was accomplished her sorrow vanished, and was
changed into perfect gladness.

Teresa was then in her twentieth year. She had embraced her new mode of life with all the fervor of her nature.
There were moments of enthusiasm when the world she had
forsaken seemed to lie at her feet, and she knew not how to
repress the outpourings of her joy. This great ardor gradually cooled. A mysterious illness consumed the years of
her youth, rendered her a cripple for some time, reduced
her to the verge of death, and threw her into a four days'
lethargy ; during which her grave was dug, and but for her
father's vigilant love, would have received her. She showed
great patience and resignation ; but she declares that her
heart was lukewarm, that prayer wearied her inexpressibly,
and that she now placed her whole delight in innocent but
worldly conversations held at the grating of the convent : for
those things were tolerated in the order, once most austere,
but at that time greatly relaxed from its original spirit.
Eighteen years were thus spent in alternations of disease,
infidelity, and fits of devotion.

Teresa ever looked back to this period of her life with
remorse ; yet so pure was her conduct, so fervent in the eyes
of the world her piety, that she was already revered as a

saint. She hated untruth, or the least dissimulation, with the warmth of an honest spirit; and so tender was her charity, that she would never suffer a word of detraction to be uttered in her presence : wherever she was, people knew their fair name to be safe. Her greatest fault—a gentle fault—was excess of human love : she yielded and required too much. She says herself, with perfect simplicity, "So soon as I knew that a person whom I esteemed and loved had an affection for me, my thoughts were with that person every hour in the day. I kept remembering those good qualities which I had noticed, and placed all my joy in mutual converse."

This last tie with earth had to be broken. Creatures no longer replaced the Creator in the heart of the saint. She raised her soul to God, and devoted herself to the reformation of her order : a mighty task, which filled with toil and trouble the remaining years of her life.

She lived to see established and flourishing sixteen convents of nuns and fourteen of friars, all obeying her reformed rule, and most of them founded by her ; spite of the innumerable obstacles which the slander of the envious, the lukewarmness of her order, and the little sympathy of civil and ecclesiastical authorities constantly raised against her. With few protectors, no money of her own, and ill health to contend with, Teresa yet travelled over Spain, and founded religious houses in Medina, Toledo, Salamanca, Valladolid, Segovia, Granada, and Seville, besides many other places of note. The difficulties were great ; but her ardent faith never forsook her. In one of her earlier undertakings, she had, as she tells us herself, neither house nor money to begin with. A convent had to be founded, and there was none to do it save "a poor Carmelite nun, amply provided with letters patent and good wishes, but without means to fulfil them, and without aid, save that of God, to look to." But with the faith and ardor of the Carmelite nun, this was more than enough. She attempted and succeeded. When Teresa founded the Carmelite convent of Toledo, she had only four ducats to begin with. Some one objected to the smallness of the sum ; the saint cheerfully replied, "Teresa and this money are indeed nothing ; but God, Teresa, and four ducats can accomplish the thing." A house, after some difficulty,

was procured, and a friend came to say that Teresa and her
nuns could remove their furniture into it as soon as they
wished. "Indeed," answered Teresa, "that will soon be
done ; for, up to the present, our furniture consists in a
blanket and two straw mattresses." Straw for the nuns to
sleep on, was one of the first necessaries Teresa provided
when she opened a monastery. The trouble and fatigue
which she underwent in founding these religious houses are
thus summed up in the interesting work entitled her Foundations ; and in which she relates to her spiritual daughters,
in a strain of tender familiarity, the many obstacles she overcame.

"Ye have seen, O my daughters! part of the labors I
have undergone, and which, in my opinion, have been the
least. 'I could not, without wearying you, have recorded
them all, and told you how great were the fatigues which
we underwent in rain and snow, with great trouble through
the losing of our way and my want of health ; for sundry
times have I been beset with a violent fever, and many other
ills, inward and outward. . . . . When God gave me health,
I bore corporal labors with joy ; but it was no little trouble
to adapt myself to the various tempers of the people amongst
whom we went ; and above all, to part from my daughters
and sisters, when I was obliged to leave them in order to go
elsewhere. The tenderness with which I love them is so
great, that I may truly say these partings were not the least
of my crosses ; especially when I remembered that I should
see them no more."

The love of God sustained her ; for, in her pure yet fervent heart, that love was the disinterested adoration which
is not induced by the hope of reward or the dread of punishment. In a sonnet of almost impassioned tenderness, she
protests to Him who died upon the cross, that her love
springs neither from hope of heaven nor from terror of hell.
Great as it was, this fervor was by no means the only characteristic of St. Teresa ; her works display judgment and good
sense, with great shrewdness of observation, whenever she is
called upon to advise and direct. Her instructions for the
government of religious communities prove her to have been
—what she was according to all contemporary accounts—a
woman of rare tact and prudence ; well skilled in the difficult

art of living in peace with tempers the most opposed, and knowing how to win the love of those whom she governed with the absolute power of religious rule. Her virtues were great, but she never fell into singularity; which was, indeed, quite foreign to her frank temper. Those whom the renown of her sanctity had awed and kept away, were surprised to find a handsome woman of cheerful and pleasant aspect, both shrewd and sensible.

She professed great respect for genius and learning ; and advised her nuns to consult the learned in their spiritual troubles, emphatically declaring that the spirit of darkness feared them. The learned, in her opinion, did not need to be deeply devout in order to enlighten the pious in their difficulties. She thought, very justly, that habits of examination and inquiry must lead, even unconsciously, to the knowledge of truth. The practice of submitting to the spiritual guidance of an ignorant director she strongly reproved, and frankly declared that she had never been able to submit to it. In the same spirit, the first requisite she looked to in the nuns she received under her rule, was not so much fervent piety as good sense. "A sensible nun," she said, " will perceive that which is good, attach herself to it because she knows it to be good ; and, even though her own progress should not be great, she will be very useful to the rest, chiefly by good counsel ; and at least she will trouble none : but I cannot see of what use she who wants sense can be, whereas I can very well perceive that she can do much mischief."

After many years of weary toil, she who ardently deplored the length of life, was at last called to her much desired rest. Teresa was returning from founding a convent at Burgos, to Avila, where she was prioress, when the Duchess of Alva sent for her. Although she was then very ill, she complied with the lady's request, and conversed with her for several hours ; then went to her convent in the town with a strong presentiment of her approaching death. Her illness was brief, and her departure joyful. Her confessor asked if she did not desire to be buried in her own convent at Avila, the first she had founded in the place of her birth. She merely answered : " Have I any thing mine in this world ? or will not they afford me here a little earth ?" She

calmly expired at nine o'clock in the evening, on the fourth
of October, 1582, being then in the sixty-seventh year of her
age. She was canonized in 1621.

The great labors of Teresa of Avila in the reformation of
the Carmelite order, entitled her to a high place in Church
history; but it is not to them she owes her widely spread
fame : from that fame she shrank, with exaggerated humility.
But for the command of her spiritual advisers, Teresa would
never have written those works which have won for her the
singular distinction of being ranked by two popes—Gregory
XV. and Urban VIII.—amongst the doctors of the Church;
an honor bestowed on no other woman.

It is difficult to speak of works so mystical as those of
St. Teresa. Few read them, and still fewer can understand
them, so as to value them rightly. Their theme is that
intense contemplation which it requires a long course of self-
discipline to attain, and the love which a soul weaned from
the world may feel for its God. To turn to them with a
mind worn and wearied by worldly tasks and cares, is not to
do them justice; they require to be read with something of
the absorbed and yet fervent mood in which they were
written. Yet even the indifferent and the cold cannot but
perceive some of the merits which have rendered St. Teresa
celebrated. Apart from her subtle and mystical flights
concerning the degrees of prayer—and even leaving aside
the visions of heaven and hell and the mysterious revelations
of the spiritual world, where she had placed her home—
Teresa wrote much, which, in a literary point of view merely,
would repay perusal. Her style, besides great freshness and
felicity, has all the breadth and warmth of genius.

Her whole works are pervaded by a strain of romance and
a sentiment of old Castilian honor, betraying the strong impressions she received from the chivalrous stories she loved
in her youth. The soul, she tells us, is like a bird that longs
to wing its ardent flight towards its native heaven; like a
valiant captain, who cannot rest content with unfolding the
standard of the cross of Jesus Christ, but who, after signal-
izing himself by his courage and fidelity, plants the banner
on a high turret, whence, fearless and triumphant, he beholds
at his feet others engaged in those perils he longs to brave
anew for the glory of his divine Master.

But the most interesting feature of those works is, that they portray Teresa as none else can portray her. She has written the story of her own life—of her inward struggles, backslidings, visions, and fervent repentance—with a frankness and simplicity that render it little inferior to the Confessions of St. Augustine. Even in those works in which she speaks least of herself, we see her thoroughly : she betrays unconsciously a certain greatness and magnanimity, which rank her amongst those souls she herself termed " generous and right royal."

At a time when the power of spiritual agencies was admitted as an article of faith, and dreaded with servile terror; when Ignatius of Loyola strove against the spirits of darkness in the grotto of Manreza, and Luther hurled his inkstand at the archfiend himself; the Carmelite nun wrote, with a fervent daring which modern skepticism will scarcely appreciate : " It has happened to me to think, what can I apprehend, and who shall make me fear ? My only desire is to serve God. I seek but to please him : to fulfil his will is my joy, my rest, and my happiness. If the Lord be almighty, if the demons be his slaves, as I know by faith, what evil can those unhappy spirits work unto me, being, as I am, a servant of the sovereign Master ? Why, then, should I fear, even though all hell were let loose against me ? I then took a cross, and not doubting but I could subdue the spirits of darkness, I said : ' Come all, I fear ye not ; and being only an humble servant of the Almighty God, I wish to see what harm ye can do me ?' " The faith and love which rendered her thus daring, breathed in all her thoughts, actions, and words. Love, such as few mortals have felt it, dwelt in her heart, and gave her feelings and answers, which, in Catholic countries, have long been traditional. We will conclude with one the most celebrated and the best. Being once questioned concerning the torments of the damned, Teresa thought it sufficient to reply : " They do not love."

CHAPTER X.

Decline of the Religious Spirit—Genovefa Malatesta—Paula Malatesta—
Cecilia Gonzaga—Lucia of Marny—Women of the House of Gonzaga—
Cassandra Fedele—Vicentina Lomelino—Isabella of Castile—Beatrix
Galindo—Mary of Escobar—Mary and Catherine of Aragon—Eliza-
beth of York—Margaret Beaufort—Margaret Roper—Anne Askew—
Lady Jane Grey—Lady Mildred Burleigh—Margaret of Lorraine.—
Margaret Paleologue—Frances of Amboise—Joan of Valois—Claude—
Elizabeth of Austria—Louise of Vaudemont.

As we pass the limit generally assigned to the middle
ages, a great change occurs. That strongly marked indi-
viduality which sometimes fell into exaggeration, but which
also often led to noble feelings and great deeds, declines, and
gives place to a calmer mood and a more uniform spirit.
An inquiring skepticism was abroad : learning had progressed, but piety had grown more weak. The good themselves
had no longer the early ardor of faith, and their historians
had lost the frankness and naïveté of the primitive biographers. This is very apparent in the sixteenth century. The
pious and the good are not less numerous, but they are more
worldly. That age of queens, who governed men with
manly genius and policy, or who charmed them as the perfect embodiment of female wit, seduction, and grace,—of
studious ladies, to whom the pages of Plato were more dear
than the joyous tumult of the chase, offers only one really
striking religious character—Teresa of Avila, a nun, and by
no means learned. She alone had that ardent and ever active spirit without which religion is too much a matter of
form, and which, reviving in the following age under a more
practical and modern aspect, gave to Christianity some of
the most noble women it has yet known.

From the close of the fourteenth century to the opening
of the seventeenth, extends a long series of queens, princesses, and noble ladies, who were no doubt very generous
and amiable women, but in whom we must not hope to find
the charity of Elizabeth of Hungary, or the fervor and eloquence of Catherine of Sienna. It was not in vain that their
lives were spent amidst the tumult of great enterprises,
religious changes, and civil wars which marked those stirring

times; too actively good for their names to be omitted here, they were not so exclusively devoted to piety and good deeds as to justify more than a brief notice to each.

In Italy, ladies of the houses of Malatesta and Gonzaga united, through several generations, a sincere piety to great learning and accomplishments. In the fourteenth century, Genovefa Malatesta was celebrated for the purity of her life, and the great attractions of her wit and conversation. The most eminent personages of the times held themselves honored by her acquaintance.

In the following age, Paula Malatesta, wife of Francis of Gonzaga, first Marquess of Mantua, was held to be the most beautiful woman in all Italy, where so many women are beautiful. We are told that she was still more eminent for learning and piety than for loveliness. She would never adorn her person, but spent in erecting and repairing churches, in feeding the poor, and portioning young girls, the sums which other ladies bestowed on dress and jewels. She reared her daughter Cecilia in the love of piety and learning, until she became, like her, one of the most charitable and accomplished women of her age. Cecilia died in a convent, where she had taken the vows with the sanction of her mother, but in opposition to the wishes of her family.

Similar virtues distinguished, in the succeeding age, the blessed Lucia of Marny, wife of the Count of Milan. Her alms were most extensive: not only her revenues, but her jewels, plate, and linen, were bestowed on the poor; and in a great dearth, the good countess made bread for them herself.

In the sixteenth century, Lucretia, Eleonora, and Isabella of Gonzaga, rendered themselves remarkable for many virtues, but chiefly for conjugal love. In the same age lived Julia Gonzaga, the widowed Countess of Fondi; the renown of whose excellence and singular beauty so enamored Soliman II., that he sent Barbarossa to carry her off. She escaped this fate by taking refuge in the mountains, amongst the banditti.

To Italy, that land which has never yet failed in either the great or the good, also belonged, in the latter part of the fifteenth century, Cassandra Fedele. This learned Venetian lady was deeply versed in Greek, Latin, philosophy, history, and theology. She pronounced a Latin harangue in the presence of the Doge and Senate of Venice; she taught publicly in the celebrated university of Padua, and maintained against its most learned and eminent men, a thesis on theology, and another on philosophy, with great honor to herself. She also excelled in music, and sang exquisitely. Louis XII., king of France, Ferdinand of Aragon, his wife Isabella of Castile, and the Popes Julius II. and Leo X., gave her many tokens of their admiration, which was shared by all Italy. These honors never affected the modest Cassandra: after the death of her husband in 1521, she entered the hospital of St. Dominic in Venice, of which she became superior, and where she died at an advanced age.

Vicentina Lomelino of Genoa was likewise a woman of eminent virtue. She was married and had eleven children; yet she knew how to unite the performance of every domestic duty with unwearied charity. The chief objects of her pity were unhappy women who had fallen into sin, and young girls exposed to temptation; she provided the former with honest means of earning a livelihood, and to the latter gave marriage portions. Vicentina died in 1605, after founding the order of the Annonciadés.

We cannot pass over the name of Isabella, the celebrated queen of Castile; but though this good and pious sovereign lacked none of the virtues which become a woman, it is chiefly as a queen that she must be held great and worthy of admiration. To her other virtues she united charity. Her governess, Beatrix Galindo, was both learned and munificent. She founded a hospital in Madrid, which took the name of *Latina,* that had been bestowed on herself on account of her perfect knowledge of the Latin tongue. Amongst the contemporary benefactors of humanity we must also include another Spaniard: Mary of Escobar, who introduced wheat into the newly discovered land of Peru.

Two daughters of Isabella showed themselves worthy of their noble mother: Mary, queen of Portugal, where she became eminent for a charity that was not confined to her own subjects; and the good and unhappy Catherine of Aragon, queen of England, whose virtues wrung a reluctant testimony from Henry VIII. when in the very act of seeking the divorce which broke her heart, and made him enter on a career of sensuality and crime.

The predecessor of Catherine, Elizabeth of York, wife of Henry VII., was also a queen of great piety and virtues: she is best described by her early adopted motto: "Humble and reverent." Her mother-in-law, Margaret Beaufort, was learned, pious, and charitable: she kept twelve poor persons in her house, and waited on them herself in their sickness and death. She was a liberal patroness of learning, and to her munificence Christ's College and St. John's College, Cambridge, owe their existence.

In this age, England could also boast of Margaret Roper, the pious and devoted daughter of the illustrious Sir Thomas More. The same tyrannical monarch who sent More to the scaffold as too rigid a Catholic, consigned his Protestant subjects to the fires of Smithfield, by means of that statute termed "bloody;" and which inevitably condemned the professors of the ancient and of the new creed: every one, in short, who did not adopt the religious tenets of the king. Thus died the pious and unhappy Anne Askew, persecuted by her husband and friends for having embraced the new faith; and burned alive in the twenty-sixth year of her age, for having denied transubstantiation. The popular story that she was tortured previously to her death, and that the chancellor with his own hands stretched her on the rack, seems unworthy of credit.*

A few years later, perished Lady Jane Grey; by far the most touching and popular victim of her hard-hearted cousin. Her youth, her innocence, her learning, her piety, her tragic fate, the courage with which she met her death, are scarcely paralleled in history. "She had," says Dr. Fuller, "the innocency of childhood, the beauty of youth, the solidity of middle, the gravity of old age, and all at eighteen: the birth of a princess, the learning of a clerk, the life of a saint, yet the death of a malefactor for her parents' offences."

The learning of Lady Jane Grey was remarkable, but not singular: the sixteenth century was eminently the age of learned women. The three daughters of Sir Thomas More, and the four daughters of Sir Anthony Cooke, acquired a celebrity which was not confined to England, but had spread

* See Jardine's Reading on the use of Torture.

far amongst the learned of foreign lands. To this day, the names of Margaret Roper, Elizabeth Dancy, Cecilia Heron, Anna Bacon, the mother of the celebrated Francis Bacon, Elizabeth Russell, Katherine Killigrew, and Mildred Burleigh, are remembered with honor.

The charity of Lady Burleigh is worthy of record. She was the eldest daughter of Sir Anthony Cooke, who bestowed great pains on her education. Mildred was well skilled in Greek and Latin, and especially in the former language. She was of a serious and devout turn of mind, and delighted in reading the works of Basil the Great, of St. Cyril, St. Chrysostom, St. Gregory of Nazianzen, and other fathers, in original Greek. In the year 1546, Mildred, who was then twenty, was married to William Cecil, afterwards Lord Burleigh, lord high treasurer of England, and privy councillor to Queen Elizabeth. Through every change of favorites, the talents and integrity of Burleigh secured the good-will and esteem of his capricious mistress. His influence over her councils remained great to the last; and the history of her reign is the history of his life. With this eminent, though not amiable statesman, Mildred lived very happily for forty-three years. Five days after her death Lord Burleigh wrote a "Meditation," in which he records the virtues of her whom he had lost. We give it here in his own language:

"There is no cogitation to be used with an intent to recover that which never can be had again; that is, to have my dear wife to live again in her mortal body, which is separated from the soul, and resteth in the earth, dead, and the soul taken up to heaven, and there to remain, in the fruition of blessedness unspeakable, until the resurrection of all flesh, when, by the almighty power of God (who made all things of nothing), her body shall be raised up, and joined with her soul, in an everlasting, unspeakable joy, such as no tongue can express, nor heart can conceive. Therefore, my cogitations ought to be occupied in these things following:

"I ought to thank Almighty God for his favor in permitting her to have lived so many years together with me, and to have given her grace to have had the true knowledge of her salvation by the death of his son Jesus, opened to her by the knowledge of the Gospel, whereof she was a professor from her youth.

"I ought to comfort myself with the remembrance of her many virtues and godly actions, wherein she continued all her life, and especially that she did of late years sundry charitable deeds, whereof she determined to have no outward knowledge whilst she lived, insomuch as when I had some little understanding thereof, and asked her wherein she had disposed any charitable gifts, according to her often wishing that she were able to do some special act for maintenance of learning and relief of the poor, she would always only show herself rather desirous so to do, than ever confess any such act, as since her death is manifestly known now to me, and confessed by sundry good men, whose names and ministry she secretly used, that she did charge them most strictly, that whilst she lived they should never declare the same to me, nor to any other; and so now have I seen her earnest writings to that purpose, of her own hand.

"The particulars of many of these hereafter do follow, which I, with mine own handwriting, recite for my comfort in the memory thereof, with assurance that God hath accepted the same in such favorable sort, as she findeth now the fruits thereof in heaven.

"About — years since, she caused exhibitions to be secretly given by the hands of the master of St. John's in Cambridge, for the maintenance of two scholars for a perpetuity whereof to continue.

"She did cause some lands to be purchased in the name of the dean of Westminster, who also, in his own name too, did assure the same to that college, for a perpetual maintenance of the said two scholars in that college; all which was done without any signification of her act, or charge to any manner of her person, but only of the dean, and one William Walter of Wimbleton, whose advice was used for the writing of the purchase and assurance.

"She also did, with the privity of the deans of Powles and Westminster, and of Mr. Alderly, being free of the haberdashers in London, give to the company of the said haberdashers a good sum of money; whereby is provided, that every two years there is lent to six poor men of certain special occupations, as smiths, carpenters, weavers, and such

6*

like, in Romford in Essex, twenty pounds apiece; in the whole, one hundred and twenty pounds. And in Cheshunt and Wooltham, to other six like persons, twenty marks apiece; in the whole, fourscore pounds. Which relief, by way of loan, is to continue. By the same means is provided for twenty poor people in Cheshunt, the first Sunday of every month, a mess of meat, in flesh, bread, and money for drink. And likewise is provided four marks yearly, for four sermons, to be preached quarterly, by one of the preachers of St. John's College. And these contributions have been made a long time, whilst she lived, by some of my servants, without giving me knowledge thereof; though, indeed, I had cause to think that she did sometimes bestow such kind of alms, but not that I knew of any order taken for continuance thereof; for she would rather commonly use speeches with me, how she was disposed to give all that she could to some such uses, if she could devise to have the same faithfully performed after her life, whereof she always pretended many doubts. And for what she used the advice of the deans of Powles and Westminster, and would have her actions kept secret, she forced upon them some small pieces of plate, to be used in their chambers as remembrances of her good-will for their pains. She did also, four times in the year, send to all the prisons in London money to buy bread, cheese, and drink, commonly for four hundred persons, and many times more, without knowledge from whom the same came.

"She did likewise, sundry times in the year, send shirts and smocks to the poor people, both in London and at Cheshunt.

"She also gave a sum of money to the master of St. John's College, to procure to have fires in the hall of that college upon all Sundays and holidays betwixt the feast of All Saints and Candlemas, when there were no ordinary fires of the charge of the college.

"She gave also a sum of money secretly towards a building for a new way at Cambridge to the common school. She also provided a great number of books, whereof she gave some to the University of Cambridge—namely, the great Bible in Hebrew, and four other tongues; and to the College of St. John's very many books in Greek, of divinity

and physic, and of other sciences. The like she did to
Christ's Church, and St. John's College in Oxford. The
like she did to the College of Westminster.

"She did also yearly provide wool and flax, and did distribute it to women in Cheshunt parish, willing them to work
the same into yarn, and to bring it to her to see their manner
of working; and, for the most part, she gave to them the
stuff by way of alms. Some time she caused the same to
be wrought into cloth, and gave it to the poor, paying first
for the spinning more than it was worth.

"Not long afore her death, she caused secretly to be
bought a large quantity of wheat and rye, to be disposed
amongst the poor in time of dearth, which remained unspent
at her death; but the same confessed by such as provided
it secretly, and therefore in conscience to be so distributed
according to her mind.

April 9th, 1589. Written at Collings' Lodge, by
me in sorrow, W. B."

The same virtues and the same generous spirit shone
forth in many ladies, sovereign, or simply noble, of other
lands. Anne, queen of Hungary, in her own right; Anne
of Austria, queen of Spain; and another Anne of Austria,
queen of Poland, were remarkable for their piety and
charity.

Margaret of Lorraine, duchess of Alençon, governed her
little dominions after the death of her husband with great
moderation and wisdom. She paid all the debts of the late
duke, amounting to a hundred thousand crowns; she married her son to the only sister of Francis the First, king of
France, and her daughter to the Marquis of Montferrat, one
of the most powerful princes in Italy; she ruled her household with strict economy, yet lived in a style that became a
princess; her ladies were celebrated for their virtue, her
officers for their integrity and honor. In the same wise
spirit did this good princess govern her subjects, who loved
and revered her as their mother. To crown her many virtues, Margaret was pious and charitable: her alms were
great, and always well bestowed. Through her aid and
exertions, many unhappy women left the ways of sin, and
returned to a pure life. When her children needed her no

longer, Margaret, who had remained in the world for their
sakes, retired to a convent of poor Clares; where she died,
in 1521, in odor of sanctity.

Her granddaughter, Margaret Paleologue, the beautiful
Duchess of Mantua, remained a widow in her youth, governed her dominions with vigor and justice, and died revered
by all for the great purity and charity which had adorned
her life.

Frances of Amboise, duchess of Brittany, is one of the
women whose virtues may be held worthy of remembrance
in the fifteenth century. Her early piety; her patience under the cruel treatment which she endured from a jealous
husband; and, above all, her charity, have often been commemorated. Even as a child, she was in the habit of giving
away to the poor her food and her garments, sooner than
not give. This irresistible tendency to charity influenced her
devotion. On every Christmas morning a poor child was
brought to her; she clad him in new garments, and then
said, in the joy and simplicity of her heart, " This little one
shall be to us this year even as the child Jesus."

Peter, the husband of Frances, became duke of Brittany
in 1450. He had then long ceased ill-using his wife, and he
even gave her a large share in his counsels. One of the first
acts of his parliament was to frame an edict for new taxes:
Frances opposed the measure, and said to him in plain language, " that the intent of those who had given him this
piece of advice, was not to fill his coffers, but to feather
their nest at the expense of the people; of which the affection is better to the prince than any other treasure." Her
wise counsel prevailed; the edict was not published, and the
people, who soon knew this, covered their good duchess
with blessings.

Peter died in his youth, and many afflictions beset his
widow. Arthur, who succeeded him, took offence at the
privacy in which Frances lived. He deprived her of her
revenues, seized her jewels, and caused her furniture to be
sold; saying ironically, " that a widow needed not so much
wealth, and a nun had no business to have a cabinet so rich
in jewels." Frances bore this persecution with great patience; when her maidens murmured indignantly, she said
to them, " how easily you are disturbed! God had lent us

these things, he takes them away; shall we then say aught against his goodness ? No, no, my daughters ! his holy will be done, and his name be blessed forever." Death prevented the duke from carrying his ill-usage to greater lengths. No sooner did Frances hear of his illness, than she constituted herself his nurse : she was by him when he expired ; she laid him out with her own hands, and buried him at her own expense.

The successor of Arthur caused the property of Frances to be restored to her, and treated her with marked respect. Other troubles were, however, in store for the young widow. She had promised her late husband never to marry again, and after his death she had taken a solemn vow to that effect. Louis XI., king of France, was extremely anxious to marry her to his brother-in-law, the Duke of Savoy, and her relatives pressed her to give her consent to this illustrious alliance. Frances refused to do so. An attempt to carry her off by force was made in open day in the streets of Nantes : but the citizens rose unanimously in her defence, and escorted her to her house, which they guarded, until she assured them that the danger was over, and that they might disperse. After a long persecution, which her firmness rendered unavailing, Frances was at length allowed to retire to a Carmelite monastery which she had founded. Her death was worthy of her life : a contagious disease having made its appearance amongst the nuns, Frances, who was then prioress, insisted on being the only one to attend on her spiritual daughters. She died, victim of her charity, towards the close of the year 1485, in the fifty-eighth year of her age.

In the early part of the following century died Joan of Valois, the pious daughter of Louis XI., and the unhappy wife of Louis XII., who had married her against his own inclination, whilst he was still Duke of Orleans. Joan thus early became a victim of that stern policy to which Frances of Brittany had resolutely refused to submit. She was good and gentle, but plain and deformed. Notwithstanding her devoted attachment, she never succeeded in winning the affections of her husband : he treated her with marked neglect : indeed her own father disliked her, and spoke with contempt and aversion of the poor girl, whose personal disgrace was held a reproach to the royal blood.

.The conjugal love.of Joan is celebrated. When the re-bellion of her husband endangered his life in the following reign, he owed his safety, and finally his freedom, to the impassioned entreaties of Joan. No sooner, however, had the death of his brother-in-law, Charles VIII., called Louis to the throne, than he divorced the woman to whom he was. so deeply indebted. The resignation with which Joan bore this disgrace touched him : he gave her ample revenues, which she spent in deeds of piety and mercy.

Her successor on the throne, the handsome Anne of Brit-tany, was one of the most charitable of French queens. Her daughter Claude, first wife of Francis the First, died in her youth, deeply regretted. Her confessors unanimously declared that one mortal sin had never stained her pure life; and the people called her "the good queen;" a name which all her successors, save the two Medici, might have received with equal propriety.

A few pages must be devoted to Elizabeth of Austria, wife of Charles IX., whose name is so fatally connected with one of the darkest pages in the history of his country. The too faithful disciple of a perfidious mother, the monarch who lured his subjects to their destruction—who planned and commanded the massacre of the St. Bartholomew, who fired from the windows of his palace on the fleeing Huguenots; and who, ever after haunted by spectres of blood, died in the prime of youth—is remembered only for his crimes. The very excess of his remorse proves him to have been worthy of a less guilty destiny. Charles had all the elegant and cultivated tastes of the Valois race; he prided himself on being the friend of the poet Ronsard, and wrote in his praise fine verses, full of generous and manly eloquence. To have had a name like that of his ancestor Francis the First —not unstained by error, but at least not darkened by crime —Charles needed but a mother like Louisa of Savoy, a woman still in her failings, instead of that wily and cruel Catherine of Medici, the evil genius of her four ill-fated sons.

History has blended the sins and the fame of Catherine and of Charles: it has arraigned them before its tribunal side by side, and not unjustly; but it has left too much in the shade his pure and pious wife, Elizabeth of Austria, grand-daughter of Charles the Fifth of Spain. To those who.

have read in contemporary memoirs the little that is known
of her, she will ever seem to stand by her husband, like
heavenly mercy pleading for earthly guilt.

In the year 1570, Elizabeth, then sixteen years old, was
granted in marriage to King Charles IX., who had not long
passed his twentieth year. "My daughter," said her father,
the emperor Maximilian II., as they parted, "you are going
to be queen of the fairest, most powerful, and greatest of
kingdoms, for which I hold you happy; but happier far it
would be to find it as secure and flourishing as it was of
yore. But you will find it strangely troubled and divided;
for if the king, your husband, holds great part of it, the
lords and princes of the religion (the Huguenots) have all
the rest." Elizabeth was met at Mezières by the king and
all the royal family, and crowned at Paris in the following
year.

The young queen was not beautiful; but her figure, though
she was not above the middle size, was perfect. Her face
was fair, mild, and somewhat pale. Her Spanish blood betrayed itself in the silent gravity of her bearing, still more
than by the Spanish language, which she preferred and
mostly used. She spoke little; and not even by an over-
hasty word did she once offend any of those around her.
"She was very devout," says Brantôme, "but not at all
bigoted." Spite of his infidelities, which she bore with exemplary patience, Charles loved his wife at heart, and respected even more than he loved her: he called her "My
Saint," but unfortunately gave her no influence. There was
room for no other woman's power in a mind ruled by the
imperious Catherine.

The contrast of their tempers contributed to render their
marriage happy: Charles was warm and hasty, Elizabeth
was calm and temperate; but a still better reason was, that,
though so quiet outwardly, the young queen loved her husband with a passion full of tenderness. The ignorance of
state affairs, in which she was purposely kept, by no means
grieved her. Like Elizabeth of Hungary, her patroness, she
had taken as her share of royalty the relief of the poor, and
the visiting of prisons and hospitals: she dressed more simply than any court lady, and all the money she spared was
spent in charity. Her charity, like every thing in her, was

simple and free from ostentation; whilst her women thought her fast asleep, the queen was kneeling in her bed, and praying or reading books of devotion, often for hours. She was greatly disconcerted on being once detected by an inquisitive attendant, and thought to conceal her pious exercises more carefully for the future; but the light of the little lamp which she kept by her, betrayed her, by casting her shadow on the closed curtains.

On the fatal night of the St. Bartholomew, Elizabeth prayed as usual, and slept in peaceful ignorance. When she awoke in the morning, she was told of what had happened. "Alas!" she suddenly exclaimed, "does the king my husband know of it?"

"Yes, madam," was the answer, "for it is he has commanded it."

"Oh, my God!" cried Elizabeth, "what is this? And what counsellors are they who could give him such advice? My God, I beseech thee to forgive him; for if thou hast not mercy on him, I greatly fear this sin will not be forgiven him." With this she asked for her prayer-book, and, with eyes full of tears, knelt and prayed for her guilty husband. The king, who, without the poor excuse of fanaticism, had stained his reign with so great a crime, survived the dark deed but two years. The grief of Elizabeth, as she witnessed his slow decay and harrowing remorse, was silent and deep. She would sit in his room—not by his bed, but a little apart, where she might see him unobserved—and there, without speaking, as her habit was, she would gaze on him so fixedly, "that she seemed," says Brantôme, "to be brooding over him in her heart." Stealthy tears sometimes trickled down her cheek; she then looked aside or feigned to want her handkerchief, thinking that none of those present would guess the truth; but by this attempt at concealment, she only excited in the hearts of the beholders greater pity for a love and sorrow so deep that they shrank from every eye. When she left the sick-room, it was to pray and weep alone.

Charles died on the 31st of May, 1574. On his death-bed he tenderly commended Elizabeth to his brother-in-law, Henry of Navarre, afterwards Henry IV. They had but one child, a daughter; who died a few years later, and was excluded from the succession to the crown by the Salic law.

One of the ladies of Elizabeth thought fit to condole with her on this subject: "At least, madam," she said, "if God had given you a son instead of a daughter, you would now be queen-mother of the king, and be so much the more powerful and great." "Alas!" answered the gentle Elizabeth, "do not hold me any such discourse. Has not France misfortunes enough already, without my presenting her with another to complete her ruin? If I had a son, how many divisions, troubles, and seditions, would have arisen for the possession of the regency during his infancy and minority! There would have been more wars than ever; for every one would have tried to rob and despoil the poor child; as would have been done with the late king, my husband, but for his mother and faithful servants. And for having conceived and brought him forth, should not I, miserable woman, have been the cause of all this, and have been cursed a thousand times by the people, whose voice is the voice of God? Well content, therefore, am I with the child God has given me."

Elizabeth after a while returned to Vienna, where her brother Rodolph II. then reigned. She built the monastery of St. Clare, in which she resided without taking the vows. The remaining years of her life were devoted to pious exercises, deeds of charity, and literary pursuits. According to the articles of her marriage, she possessed the revenues of the dukedoms of Berry and Bourbonnais, and of the counties of Forez and March. She confided the administration of this wide property to persons of known integrity and virtue; and expressly desired that no judicial offices should be sold, but that they should be bestowed on worthy individuals. By far the greater portion of her French revenue was spent in the provinces from which it came. For some time, half of it went to her sister-in-law Margaret of Valois, the improvident wife of Henry IV. Elizabeth divided in three parts what remained of her income: one part was for the poor; with another she portioned young girls; the third was for her own personal expenses. She died on the 22d of January, 1592, deeply regretted by her fellow-citizens, and no less so by her former subjects, who had preserved a lively remembrance of her many virtues. To the last she tenderly cherished the memory of Charles IX., and would never hear

of a second marriage. Her relative Philip II. of Spain vainly
endeavored to change her resolve. On learning her death,
the Empress of Austria exclaimed : "The best amongst us
is gone."

Some years before her death, the place Elizabeth had once
held in France had been filled by a woman of charity as great,
although her piety was not quite so enlightened : the beautiful Louise of Lorraine Vaudemont. Like her predecessor,
she was remarkable for her modesty in the midst of a dissolute court, for great charity to the poor, and for the ardent
love she bore to an unfaithful husband. She died in 1601,
after filling her life with good deeds.

PERIOD THE THIRD.

THE SEVENTEENTH CENTURY.

CHAPTER XI.

The Women of the Seventeenth Century.—Madame de Chantal.

THE religious women of the seventeenth century bear the mark of their age—earnestness. In England, Germany, and France, we may trace in them, whether Protestant or Catholic, the same high and austere character. They are not always liberal or tolerant; but they are, at least, ever earnest. Though we might wish for a spirit less unbending, we may seek in vain for a belief more firm, for a charity more fervent and yet so essentially practical. Too much of puritanic severity may be laid to their charge, but none can say that they were not deep in their feelings and in their faith.

The share of France alone in this gallery of serious female portraits is sufficiently extensive and remarkable to have suggested to one of the most celebrated of modern French writers, Victor Cousin, the project of writing their history. The plan has been laid aside, or, at least, confined to a few striking sketches; but it shows how much the truth and earnestness of these women could impress a philosophic mind, in many respects opposed to the opinions which guided their lives.

The earliest, and, perhaps, the most eminent of these women, is Madame de Chantal. She was the friend of two great saints, a saint herself, and the ancestress of a woman to whom witty and charming letters have given more fame than Madame de Chantal earned by a long life of piety and charitable deeds.

At the time of the massacre of St. Bartholomew and the wars of the League, there lived in the ancient town of Dijon a president of the parliament of Burgundy, named Benigne Fremiot. His nobility was only that "*noblesse de robe*," on which the courtly aristocracy affected to look down; but he stood high in the province, where his worth and virtue were acknowledged by men of all parties. His opinions were strong without fanaticism, and ever tempered by a sense of justice most becoming in a magistrate. He was a faithful adherent of Henry IV., the Protestant king; an enemy of the League, and yet a staunch Catholic. Though he took no share in the persecutions directed against the Huguenots, he detested their religious opinions, and ruled his own in a spirit of devout obedience to the Church.

This gentleman was married to a lady of good family, who had already given him one daughter, when a second was born to him on the twenty-third of January of the year 1572. This was the festival of St. John the Almoner, so called on account of his great charity to the poor; and after him the child was named Jane. Madame Fremiot bore her husband a son, afterwards Archbishop of Bourges; she then died, when Jane was only eighteen months old. President Benigne Fremiot proved a kind and attentive father. To preserve his children from the doctrines of Luther or Calvin, he instructed them carefully in the points contested between Catholics and Protestants. Little Jane relished such teaching exceedingly; for she was a precocious child, deeply impressed with a sense of religion, and ardent and impetuous in her faith.

She was about five years of age when her father and a Protestant gentleman engaged, in her presence, in a discussion concerning transubstantiation. Jane broke from her nurse to argue with the Huguenot, who kindly dropped some sweetmeats in her apron in order to pacify her; but she threw them into the fire, passionately exclaiming, "Even thus shall all heretics burn in the fire of hell, because they do not believe what our Lord has said!"

This intemperate zeal might have degenerated into bigoted intolerance, but for the indulgence her father inculcated, and which her own goodness of heart led her to feel. An incident of her youth proves, however, that she could never grow reconciled to the new doctrines. Her eldest sister was married, and Jane went to spend some time with her. A

Huguenot gentleman of rank and wealth fell in love with Mademoiselle Fremiot, paid his addresses to her, and passed himself off as a Catholic. She discovered the cheat, and rejected him indignantly. Her sister and brother-in-law vainly sought to shake her resolve ; Jane emphatically declared, " I would sooner choose a perpetual prison than the dwelling of a Huguenot, and rather endure a thousand deaths, one after the other, than bind myself by marriage to an enemy of the Church."

She might have added, that the man who could thus attempt to deceive her, had become unworthy of her respect and confidence. She endured with great firmness and constancy the persecution her relatives inflicted on her, in consequence of this refusal ; until her father fortunately recalled her to his house. Jane wished to enter a cloister ; but to this Monsieur Fremiot would not consent ; " Christian virgins," he said, "should remain in the world, and edify it with their virtues." Jane dutifully yielded, and left the choice of a husband to the president, who married her, in her twentieth year, to the Baron de Chantal, a distinguished officer, high in the favor of Henry IV., rich and noble, and no more than twenty-seven years of age.

A few days after the ceremony had been solemnized, the baron took his bride to his seat at Bourbilly. As a proof of his confidence, he insisted on giving up to her the management of all his property. She shrank from so heavy a responsibility; which would not, she conceived, leave her sufficient time for her devotions ; but M. de Chantal very sensibly objected, that piety was not incompatible with the daily tasks of life : he quoted the case of his own mother, a lady of many virtues, reared in a court, and who had yet found it possible to become the most notable woman in the province. Madame de Chantal promised to comply with her husband's wishes ; and by her prudence, economy, and good management, justified the trust he had placed in her household virtues.

She rose with dawn, and had finished her devotions, and ordered her household affairs, by the time her husband was up. She give little time to dress, and only wore plain-camelot. Prayer, work, the lives of the saints or French history, her husband, her family, and the poor, absorbed all the thoughts of the pious lady. Her great anxiety was to keep her little household pure and religious. On her arrival at Bourbilly she had found a few profane books—most probably romances—with which M. de Chantal amused his leisure : she remorselessly consigned them to the flames ; and such works never again entered the old mansion whilst she was its mistress. There was a chapel in the château ; yet every Sunday Madame de Chantal resorted to the parish church, in order to share in the devotions of her husband's vassals. They needed not this proof of friendly sympathy to love and respect their lady : in all their troubles and distresses they appealed to her. M. de Chantal, though kind-hearted, was passionate and proud. The temper of his wife was still warmer, especially where her religious feelings or affections were concerned ; but she had long exercised the virtue of self-control, and with all who approached her, she was the gentlest of human beings. She made it her task to soothe her husband's anger when it had been roused by vassal or servant : he allowed himself to be pacified, but not without some reluctance. "If I am too quick," he said, "you are too charitable." It often happened that, in a fit of choler, the baron would consign some offending vassal to the prison of Bourbilly ; and thus practically remind the little realm over which he ruled, of the power vested in him by feudal law. The dungeons of Bourbilly were damp and unwholesome : the kind-hearted baroness secretly delivered the captive, made him sleep in one of the baron's excellent beds, and early in the morning placed him once more under bolt and bar ; then about the time of her husband's rising, she would enter his room, greet him cheerfully, and having put him into a good temper, gently coax him out of the freedom of the unlucky prisoner.

Her goodness to the vassals who lived on the domain of Bourbilly was not confined to these acts of kindness : she relieved their wants with boundless charity—for charity was, and ever remained, her favorite virtue. She often said : "I can with more confidence ask of the Lord to grant me my necessities, when for love of him I have bestowed alms on the poor." A famine desolated the country around her : she opened her stores to the indigent, and daily gave bread and soup to all those who asked. They came in great numbers—often from a distance. Madame de Chantal presided over the distribution herself; and to render it more orderly, made those who entered by a front gate leave by a back door. Many took advantage of this to walk round the château, and coming in again, to claim a second portion; Madame de Chantal perceived the cheat, but would neither notice nor resent it. To those who remonstrated with her on the subject, she said that her inward reflections were: " My God, am I not a beggar at the gates of thy mercy ? Should I like to be refused a second or third request ? A thousand times hast thou borne with mine importunity, why then should I not endure that of thy creatures ?" Whilst this hard time lasted, poor families, too proud to beg, were relieved privately by Madame de Chantal.

Such were the tasks in which she delighted ; and which were her only pleasures when, as often happened, her husband was away at court, or with the army. It was only to please him that she dressed or saw company ; in his absence she lived retired, and wore the most homely garments. If any one chanced to ask her for the reason of this, or remonstrated with her, she warmly replied, " Speak not of this to me : the eyes I must please are a hundred leagues off." She loved her husband tenderly, almost passionately ; for it was not in her nature to love by halves. When he was at Bourbilly, prayer was too often neglected ; and she confessed, with penitent sorrow, that he rivalled God in her heart. His affection for her was great : he loved her as an amiable, attractive woman, and respected her as a saint. Her example influenced him so much, that he at length spoke of retiring wholly from court, and fixing his residence at Bourbilly. Whilst cherishing that project, he fell ill. Madame de Chantal attended him devotedly ; his recovery was slow ; and as she sat by his bedside, the baron and his wife discoursed together of religion and death. He wished her to enter into the agreement that, should one happen to survive the other, that one should embrace a religious life. Devout as she was, Madame de Chantal would not hear of this : for she said that it implied a separation, of which she could not endure to think. The baron at length fully recovered, but he did not seem much more cheerful. He told his wife that, in a recent dream, he had seen himself clad in a crimson garment, which he took as a sign that he should be badly wounded. Madame de Chantal had a free, generous spirit, wholly removed from superstition, even in that superstitious age. She laughed at her husband's fears, and gayly said, "I might as well think that I am going to become a widow, for the other night I dreamed that a long crape veil enveloped me from head to foot."

A few days after this, the Baron de Chantal went out shooting with one of his friends. He wore a fawn-colored habit: his friend, seeing him moving through the bushes, mistook him for a deer, fired and wounded him mortally. Madame de Chantal, though recently confined of her last child, was soon on the spot. She found a doctor doing for him all his art could do. "You *must* cure him!" she exclaimed in the passion of her woe. She offered to Heaven all she had that was precious—her children and her wealth, for that one life; but the sacrifice was not accepted: M. de Chantal survived this sad accident nine days. He died like a Christian: his chief anxiety was to console his wife, and the unhappy man who had caused his death. He repeatedly declared that he forgave him freely, and caused this pardon to be recorded in the registers of the parish church, in order to secure him from any annoyance or trouble. In the same noble and generous spirit, Madame de Chantal afterwards became godmother to the child of the man who had made her a widow.

She was in her twenty-eighth year when this sad event happened. She had already lost two children; but four, one son and three daughters, remained to her. Her grief, though tempered by resignation, was great, and she took a solemn vow never again to marry. She distributed her rich garments amongst the poor, and resolved that henceforth the labor of her hands should be devoted to them and to the Church. Prayers, alms, and her children, divided her life. Her old longing for the cloister returned to her, and but for her children, she afterwards said that she thought she should have gone and buried herself in Holy Land. This confession shows that her ardent religious feelings were much in need of wise control. Her widowhood was a time of great tribulation. She was peacefully residing with her father at Dijon, when her father-in-law, M. de Chantal, then seventy-

five years of age, wrote to her that, if she did not come to
live with him, he would marry again, and disinherit her
children.

Madame de Chantal complied with this peremptory request, and went with her children to Montelon, the seat of
their grandfather, near Autun. She might have lived there
happily enough, had not her father-in-law been provided
with a shrewish housekeeper; who had ruled his establishment despotically for many years, and now beheld with
displeasure the presence of one whose near relationship and
rank threatened to interfere with her own authority. Madame de Chantal, who quickly saw that her father-in-law's
interests were not always cared for by the woman in whom
he trusted implicitly, did indeed attempt to interfere; but
love of peace induced her to relinquish the attempt. The
authority of the housekeeper prevailed to that degree, that
Madame de Chantal had not the liberty to give away a glass
of water without her knowledge and sanction. She bore
this tyranny with heroic and silent patience : years elapsed
before her father learned indirectly how much she had suffered at Montelon. The only place in the whole house
which she claimed and owned, was a little room where she
kept the medicines and unguents she gave away to the
poor; and the only vengeance she exercised against the
woman who daily insulted and tormented her, was to rear,
instruct, and attend her five children with her own. She
washed, combed, and dressed them daily; and in reply to
the objection which was once made to her, that it was degrading to perform these offices for children of a rank so
mean, she merely said, " Have not they been redeemed, as
well as my own children, by the blood of Jesus Christ?"

Madame de Chantal had, like the saint whose name had
been given her at her birth, the passion of charity. The luxuries of her rank pained her; she could not bear to touch
dainty food whilst the poor were starving. A confidential
attendant served her at dinner, and, whenever some choice
bit of fowl or game was placed before her mistress, took
away the plate, for a purpose which she alone knew. Madame
de Chantal gave away not only the food from her plate; she
gave away every thing it was hers to bestow, even to a ring
from her finger, once that she had no money about her. It

7

is recorded of her, that she never refused alms asked for the
love of God. Had her charity been confined to mere almsgiving, it would have been of little worth; but it extended
much further. On the afternoons of Sundays and holidays,
she went forth, a little after dinner, to visit the sick and poor
of her parish, undeterred by summer heats or wintry cold.
Two of her women generally accompanied her. She cheered
them on with gay and pleasant discourse, and often said to
them as they went along: "We are going on a pilgrimage
to Calvary, or to the Olive Mount, or to the Holy Sepulchre."
Her faith had all the imaginative fervor of her character;
she loved to visit and serve the poor, not merely because of
the tenderness and compassion of her heart, but because the
words of the Gospel, "I was an hungered, and ye gave me
meat: I was thirsty, and ye gave me drink: I was a stranger,
and ye took me in:"—"Naked, and ye clothed me. I was
sick, and ye visited me: I was in prison, and ye came unto
me," were to her a strict and literal truth. She confessed
that the most tedious day was that on which she found no
fitting opportunity of exercising charity. Those days were
few in her sanctified life: seldom did there pass one of
which some hours had not been devoted to the sick poor in
their own homes; she dressed their wounds, cleaned them,
made their beds, gave them clothes, which she kept in readi-
ness, took home their linen, boiled it, to free it from vermin
and other impurities, mended it, and then returned it to
them. All the neighboring sick were known to her; for she
had requested that, so soon as a poor person fell ill, she might
be informed of it. She visited and assisted them, and was
often present at their agony: when they were dead, she
washed and laid them out. She esteemed this mournful
office so great a privilege, that she claimed it as a sort of reward for the care she took of the sick and ailing. Whenever
a death occurred in her absence, Madame de Chantal was
promptly acquainted with the fact: the villagers would not,
through respect, lay out the deceased. "It was a right,"
they said, "which belonged to Madame."

Cavillers who thought fit to censure this excessive charity
were not wanted: Madame de Chantal was plainly told that
her duty was to stay with her aged father-in-law, and not to
desert him for the poor. She modestly replied, that she only

gave to the poor those hours which her father-in-law did
not need from her: "Besides," she added, "has he not
many servants to attend on him? whereas the poor of Jesus
Christ will have none, if I forsake them." She spoke the
literal truth; for she was indeed the only hope of those who,
but for her, must have perished irretrievably. She had requested that the forsaken poor—and in those times there
were many such, who were often left to die in a ditch, or by
the hedges on the road-side—might be brought to her; and
the peasants on her father-in-law's domain readily obeyed.
One amongst the rest, returning from Autun, found, lying at
the foot of a hedge, a lad afflicted with leprosy, whom he
brought to Madame de Chantal. She received him with
great joy, and placed him in the bed which she kept ever
ready for such guests. The unfortunate leper was in an
awful state. Madame de Chantal cut off his hair, burned it
herself, and would allow no one else to touch it; she dressed
his sores with her own hands, and attended on him daily.
He was half-starved when brought to her, and required to
be fed slowly, and to receive only a little at a time; she
visited him several times in the course of the day, to give
him his food and attend on him. It sometimes happened
that, being detained by her father-in-law, she could not
come; she then sent one of her attendants in her stead.
The woman, who had not the ardent charity of her mistress,
fulfilled the task with a sense of disgust which she did not
care to conceal: she laid down the food near the leper, and
then hastened out of the room. Once, on seeing this, he
burst into tears, and said: "When madame comes, she does
not stop her nose; she sits down by me, and speaks to me of
my salvation; but when she cannot come, every one else forsakes me." He lingered a few months, at the end of which
death released him from his misery. For several nights before
he died, Madame de Chantal sat up by him, exhorting and
consoling him to the last. As he was on the point of expiring,
he turned towards her, and, clasping his hands, asked her
to grant him her blessing. She embraced him tenderly, and
said: "Go, my child, confide in God; for angels will bear
thee, like Lazarus, to the place of thy rest." He died almost
in her arms; she washed and laid him out herself, spite of
the remonstrances of a haughty relative, who could not

comprehend that a lady of her rank should stoop to such offices.

Not long after this, Madame de Chantal took in an unfortunate woman, whose face was eaten away by a frightful cancer. She was the wife of one of the villagers, whose horror of her condition made him inhumanly turn her out of his house. Madame de Chantal kept her until her death, and she lived nearly four years. The details connected with the state and sufferings of this poor creature, display the charity of Madame de Chantal as something almost beyond humanity : but we will not sicken the reader by dwelling on them, as some of her zealous biographers have done. The woman was succeeded by an old man, covered with ulcers, and who lived ten months; indeed the room set apart for such afflicted guests was seldom or never empty.

In the year 1606, Madame de Chantal went to her château of Bourbilly for the gathering in of her vintage. Other cares soon absorbed her. She found her vassals afflicted with a fatal dysentery, and she devoted herself to them with the passion she carried into every thing she did. She rose with dawn, visited the nearest houses, returned to mass and breakfast, and then went forth again afternoon and evening. After her last visit, she still found time and energy for business. It was she who managed the estate and property of her children; and the task was never neglected. When it was over, she retired to rest; but she was often called up before morning, to spend the rest of the night by the bedside of the dying. The dysentery lasted seven weeks; during that time, it is computed that Madame de Chantal laid out from two to five corpses daily; at length she fell ill, literally from fatigue. Her friend St. Francis of Sales wrote her a letter of amicable reproof, warning her not to yield too much to the promptings " of that strong heart of hers, which loved and willed mightily." -

The friendship between the Bishop of Geneva and Madame de Chantal had begun two years before this, in 1604, when she went to Dijon for the purpose of hearing him preach. Francis of Sales was then near forty. The eldest son of a noble family of Savoy, he had, nevertheless, consecrated himself to God in his youth. Poor as was his bishopric, since Geneva had exchanged the yoke of Catholic prelates for that of Calvin and his successors, he refused to leave it or his limited flock for a wealthier income and a wider sway. But though he chose to remain buried in Savoy, his fame was great : he was celebrated both for the sanctity of his life and the force of his eloquence. Thousands hung on the words which fell from his lips, and went away with the love of God in their hearts. Holiness and genius were in him aided by many natural advantages, which gave more power to the man and the orator. His voice was harmonious, his address dignified and easy. He was eminently handsome ; sweetness and fire blended in his countenance, and expressed the contrasts of his character ; an ardent temper, and too great a tendency to human love, were the faults against which he struggled, until he finally subdued the earthly part, and kept of both failings whatever they had of divine.

In his enthusiasm, warmth of heart, and boundless charity, Francis of Sales strongly resembled Madame de Chantal : but in his experience of spiritual things, in wisdom, prudence, and discretion, he surpassed her greatly. Their friendship was sudden, yet lasting. A mystical explanation of this fact is given in their respective biographies ; but nothing supernatural is needed to account for the mutual attraction of characters so congenial. The devout attention with which Madame de Chantal listened to him as he preached, drew the attention of Francis of Sales, and made him inquire of her brother, the Archbishop of Bourges, " the name of that widow who listened so attentively to the word of the Gospel."

Their friendship was strengthened by sad circumstances, but too frequent in religious biography. Good, pious, and charitable as she was, Madame de Chantal was not happy : her soul was obscured by doubts, scruples, and fears, which often rendered existence a torment. An ignorant and despotic clergyman, under whose spiritual guidance she had placed herself in the hope of relief, only increased her distress. Francis of Sales delivered her from this thraldom ; his generous spirit was above the narrow doubts and fears which pervert religion from her true aim, the raising of the soul to God. By his indulgence, charity, and perfect knowledge of the heart, he dispelled the gloomy despondency of Madame de Chantal ; she rejoiced in her liberty, and revered her deliverer as an angel. There were, indeed, many relapses, many faintings of the heart and dismal fears; but there was also knowledge with which to strive, and courage that taught her to endure. When her spirit was most oppressed, she could not help saying, " O Lord, take this cup from me;" but no sooner were the words uttered, than she longed to drain to the very dregs the cup she had rejected. " Be merciful, O God!" she exclaimed, with returning courage, "and take not this cup away until I have quaffed it." It were difficult to express more forcibly the mingled fear and daring of an ardent heart.

The influence of Francis of Sales over Madame de Chantal was great; and some traits of her life prove that it was much needed. Being persecuted by her family to marry again, she not only refused to do so, but, in a fit of fervor, branded the name of Jesus on her side, over her heart, with a red-hot iron. It was from this exaggeration of devotion, into which she often fell, that Francis of Sales, the most moderate and prudent of men, sought to cure her. He also attempted to eradicate some little inconsistencies which he perceived in her life: for instance, she was in the habit of praying for several hours of the night, during which one of her women sat up waiting for her. " Our devotion," said Francis of Sales, " should never be inconvenient to others." She took the hint, and acted upon it so effectually, that her servants observed, " Madame prays always, yet is never troublesome to anybody." This great friendship had lasted nearly six years, when the Bishop of Geneva induced Madame de Chantal to take a step which exposed her to the severe censure of the world ; and which her biographers are evidently at some trouble to explain. Francis of Sales had long wished to establish a religious order, mild in rule, but evangelic in spirit, to which ladies of feeble health, and unable to bear austerities, might be admitted. He purposed calling it the Order of the Visitation of the Virgin Mary ; and intended its members to visit the sick and the afflicted, as Mary visited her cousin Elizabeth. They were to reside under the same roof, but neither to take the vow of poverty, nor to be cloistered like nuns of the stricter orders ; practical charity was to be their great aim. This order evidently resembles that which St. Vincent of Paul established, in the course of the same century, under the name of Sisters of Charity.

Madame de Chantal had often expressed to her friend her passionate desire of entering some religious community, and thus fulfilling the early aspiration of her youth. He objected to her, that she could not desert her young children, and forbade her to think of any thing of the kind whilst they needed her care. But when he thought that she could conscientiously do so, he suggested that she should become one of the community he meant to found, in his native town of Annecy in Savoy. She embraced the proposal with joy, but soon felt strangely perplexed, not knowing how to break the news to her family.

Madame de Chantal was then in her thirty-eighth year. She had lost one of her youngest daughters, and married the eldest to M. de Thorens, the nephew of Francis of Sales. Her son was fifteen years old; and in those times the sons of the nobility were launched into the world, far from the control of pious provincial mothers, at an age still earlier. The licentious Rabutin, relative of Madame de Chantal, the young Marquis de Grignan, one of her descendants, entered the army at twelve, and commanded regiments at seventeen, within the same century. Her strongest tie was therefore with her father and her father-in-law, both very aged. They gave their consent to her project, but with the deepest reluctance, and raised numerous objections, which Madame de Chantal overruled. The education of her son, she said, no longer needed her presence: the guardianship of her father would suffice until he entered the world; her married daughter would, on the contrary, be much benefited by her sojourn at Annecy, as she was still very young, and required the advice and direction of a mother. Her youngest daughter she proposed taking with her, and keeping under her own care, until she married her in a manner befitting her rank: in short, she prevailed.

Only the fervor of religious enthusiasm could enable a woman, whose heart was all charity and tenderness, to go through the parting, which her early biographers have related as taking place, between herself and her kindred at Dijon, where all her family had gathered to bid her a solemn adieu. She knelt at the feet of her father, and, not without tears, besought him to bless her, and take care of her son. For some time both wept in silence; at length the president said,—" Oh, my God! it belongs not to me to oppose your designs. It will cost me my life. To you, O Lord, I offer this dear child ; receive her, and be you my comfort." He raised and blessed her as he spoke. Madame de Chantal was a kind mother, full of tenderness ; her children loved her passionately, and none loved her better than the young son she was going to leave, in order to become the help and comforter of strangers. He cast himself at her feet, he twined his arms around her neck, and entreated her not to go ; seeing, at length, that his prayers would not avail, he laid himself down on the threshold of the door, and said,—" I cannot detain you ; but if go you must, pass, then, over the body of your child." She stepped over him, then returned weeping. A clergyman, tutor to her son, thought he saw her constancy waver, and reproved her. Her answer, " I am a mother," might have softened a harder heart.

The parting was over ; the gates of Dijon were passed ; and the consciousness that her intended sacrifice was fulfilled, gave Madame de Chantal something like serenity of mind. Her journey was a progress of charity. She entered Annecy on Palm Sunday, 1610, and was received by Francis of Sales, who came to meet her, with twenty-five persons of distinction. After settling her married daughter, Madame de Thorens, in her abode, she laid the foundation of the new institute on Trinity Sunday. Two ladies took the habit with her, and were soon afterwards joined by ten more. The little community devoted themselves to deeds of charity ; and in these their superior gave them the example of all that the most fervent heart could conceive or accomplish. She took the solemn vow of doing not merely that which was good, but that which was most excellent ; and religiously was the vow fulfilled. The sisters of the Visitation daily went forth to visit and relieve the poor. So intense was the gratification Madame de Chantal found in the practice of charity, that she conceived herself bound to abstain from it occasionally, through a spirit of mortification. For three or four months she daily attended a poor paralytic woman afflicted with dysentery, and took home her linen to wash. The stench in this unfortunate woman's abode was so great, that Madame de Chantal often said to the nun who accompanied her : " I think you had better turn your head away ; for my part, I am accustomed to this." A woman of dissolute life, and a recital of whose infirmities has for once been spared to us by the zealous biographers of Madame de Chantal, fell ill at Annecy. The person who was commissioned to inform the superior of the Visitation of such cases, mentioned this; adding, however, " But it is not very likely that you will go and serve this abandoned creature who has sinned so much." " Our Lord came for sinners, and not for the just," warmly answered Madame de Chantal. She went to see her immediately ; and, as we are told, cured both body and soul. A poor strange woman,—perchance a sinner, too, but one assuredly whom the merciful Jesus would not have rejected,— was taken with the pains of labor in the course of her wanderings; she sought and found refuge in a stable, where she gave birth to her child. Madame de Chantal walked a considerable distance in order to visit her; she knelt down by the poor creature, took the child, baptized it, and cared for its mother until she was able to leave the place and proceed on her journey. All the time she was engaged in her pious office, Madame de Chantal confessed that she thought of the infant Jesus in the stable of Bethlehem. Here lay the secret of all she did : the presence of God in her heart. A nun, who beheld with ever-renewing admiration the marvellous charity of her superior towards beings of repulsive and disgusting aspect, once asked her how she could do so much for such miserable outcast creatures : " Because I do not see them, but Jesus Christ in them," was the fervent reply.

A year after she had founded the Visitation, a great affliction befell Madame de Chantal : her father died at Dijon. Her soul was torn with remorse : she had forsaken him in his old age, when the sacrifice of a year would have made him happy, and would surely not have been accounted as a sin by the merciful God who commanded filial love and reverence. It was long before she recovered this blow. Fortunately for her peace of mind, her absence did not prove injurious to her son : she visited him often, superintended his education, and finally saw him united to the young and amiable Mademoiselle de Coulanges. Her youngest daughter was in like manner happily married to the Count of Tonlonjon. The establishment of her children left Madame de Chantal free to devote herself to the extension of the order of the Visitation. It

7*

spread rapidly, although Francis of Sales was, against his own judgment, induced to make several important changes, which wholly altered its original aim: for instance, the nuns were cloistered, and no longer able to visit the sick and the poor: they relieved them by their alms; but the most generous attribute of charity, sympathy, could no longer exist. The labors of Madame de Chántal were great, and she had ample opportunities of proving her patience, self-denial, and humility: but charity to the poor, her most beautiful and congenial virtue, no longer had the same scope.

Her patience under the many afflictions with which it pleased God to visit her, was deep and touching. She was destined to survive almost all her kindred and her friends. She lost her father and father-in-law; M. de Thorens and his wife, her eldest daughter, within a short space of one another. Her only son, the Baron de Chantal, was killed fighting against the Huguenots, in the isle of Rhé. He left a widow and an only child, then a few months old; that child afterwards became Madame de Sévigné. The gay, brilliant, and worldly lady was born and bred in that old château of Bourbilly, where her pious grandmother had burned romances and relieved the poor. The fatal end of M. de Chantal was followed within a few years by that, no less premature, of his younger sister and her husband. Scarcely had Madame de Chantal received the news, when a messenger entered the parlor of the convent, and informed her that the widow of her son had followed him to the grave. She had loved her daughter-in-law very tenderly, and turning pale, she exclaimed: "Why, how many deaths!" but checking this expression of regret, she clasped her hands and added: "Should I not rather say, how many pilgrims hastening on to their eternal dwelling!"

Her brother, and the first companions of her religious life, likewise preceded her to that dwelling towards which ever tended the desires of her heart. But perhaps the heaviest loss of all was that of Francis of Sales, her much loved friend. Parted as they were, often for years, by their different tasks, their hearts were never asunder. A strong and pure friendship between man and woman ought to need neither apology nor explanation: rare it may be, but none can say that it is impossible. The purity of the tie which united Madame de

Chantal and the Bishop of Geneva cannot be doubted; but it has been said and written, for party purposes, that the affection which she felt for her religious director was a feeling more deep and tender than mere friendship. We think that her life and character protest eloquently against such an assumption. The woman who could brand the name of Jesus on her heart, who triumphed over maternal affection,— the strongest and most passionate feeling of her sex,—because she thought herself called away by the voice of God, was not a woman whom the love of mortal man could move.

The sudden and unexpected death of her friend was a severe trial, but she bore it with Christian fortitude. It was her habit, when suddenly afflicted, to offer up her heart to God, saying: "Destroy, cut, burn whatever opposes your holy will." As she held the letter containing the news which she suspected and dreaded, her heart began to beat: she read it kneeling, weeping much, but resigned. St. Francis of Sales died in 1622; Madame de Chantal survived him nineteen years. One of her cherished tasks was to collect materials for his life. At length she too was called away. Journeying from her convent in Paris to that of Annecy, she was taken ill with inflammation of the lungs, in the convent of Moulins. She died there, in a room whence Madame de Sévigné—whom the nuns of the Visitation called their living relic—dated one of her pleasant letters. In her last moments, Madame de Chantal requested that the death of St. Monica, as related in the Confessions of St. Augustine, might be read to her. After receiving the last sacraments of the Church, she expired peacefully on the 13th of December, 1641, being then sixty-nine years of age. In 1751 she was canonized by Pope Benedict XIV.

The character of Madame de Chantal needs few comments: her life and actions paint her as she was, with her faults and her virtues. Her piety was ardent and enthusiastic to the last. Being asked in her old age, and whilst laboring under great bodily infirmities, if the early fervor of her spirit had not cooled, she warmly answered: "I feel it as strong to act towards God as it was twenty-five years ago." This ardor might occasionally lead her into exaggeration, but it was not superstitious. A nun under her control thought, or pretended to think, that she was possessed with evil spirits, which only relics could chase away. Madame de Chantal took a piece of wood, wrapped it up in a paper, and used it as a relic, when the fit of supposed possession was at its height. It ceased immediately; the nun declared that the spirits had fled; upon which Madame de Chantal calmly informed her of the truth. No more was heard about spirits.

She was herself too thoroughly practical in her faith to place much value on that elevation of spirit which is the delight, but by no means the aim, of religion. A lady once wrote her a long account of the graces with which she was favored by Heaven. Madame de Chantal wrote back: "You have sent me the leaves of the tree; send me likewise some of its fruit, that I may judge of it." Humility was one of the virtues which she inculcated on others, and practised herself with exact fidelity. The reputation of saint which she had acquired, the respect paid to her by queens and great ladies, grieved her sincerely. The world she had hoped to forget, and by which she had remained unheeded as wife and widow, sought and revered the nun in her retreat. But, pure and holy as was the life she there led, we confess that, for our part, we prefer the charitable lady of Bourbilly and Montelon to the sister and superior of the Visitation.

CHAPTER XII.

State of France—St. Vincent of Paul—Mademoiselle Legras—Sisters of Charity—Madame de Goussault and the Association—The Foundlings—The General Hospital.

INDIVIDUAL instances of great Christian virtues, like that of Madame de Chantal, did not prevent the moral state of France from being any thing but pure. The opening of the seventeenth century found her exhausted by the civil and religious dissensions of the preceding age. The nobles were turbulent and immoral; the people wretched and ignorant; the clergy profligate and despised: things had come to such a pass that the name of priest was both a by-word and a reproach.

Such was the state of the nation when a poor priest, of

humble parentage, but filled with the love and zeal of God, first began to devote his long life to the instruction of the poor, the reformation of the priesthood, and to the relief of human misery under every shape, from the innocent and forsaken child to the outcasts of society—galley-slaves. This apostolic man, St. Vincent of Paul, one of the greatest saints of Christianity, was powerfully aided in all his enterprises by women of admirable charity. If they owed much to his spiritual guidance, he owed no less to their womanly tenderness and enthusiasm. He made himself the advocate of foundlings, and great ladies pledged their family plate to give those forsaken creatures a home. He asked "for servants for the poor," and peasant girls answered the appeal; and under that humble name became the first "sisters of charity."

. This admirable order began very simply. Vincent never proceeded from foregone conclusions or fixed designs; he took things as he found them, and made the commonest events the germ of his greatest achievements. Whilst he was at Chatillon, in Bresse, in the year 1617, a lady requested him to recommend to the charity of his congregation a poor family, lying ill in a farm without the town. He did so, but the effect surpassed his desire: he perceived that the sick family had received too much at once, and would probably fall back into their former state ere long; when, pity being exhausted, no one would care for them. This inconvenience, which always attends ill-regulated charity, induced him to establish a sisterhood of prudent and charitable ladies, willing to devote a portion of their time and substance to the task of visiting and relieving the poor. He found many such, and drew up a few simple regulations for their use. This sisterhood proved most beneficial, and spread all over France. When Vincent returned to Paris, and found himself engaged in other far more important labors, he felt the want of a zealous and intelligent person to whom he could confide the difficult task of visiting the various places where the sisterhood had been established, and of seeing that the members remained faithful to the spirit of their institute. Such a person he found in Mademoiselle Legras, a wealthy widow, who, through the influence of a friend, obtained his counsel as her confessor; for in that age of directors, when the excess of priestly influence finally justified the Tartuffe of Molière, Vin-

cent of Paul showed a most determined aversion to the delicate task of directing the conscience of great ladies. The exception which he made in favor of Mademoiselle Legras proved
the source of infinite good.

Though now reduced to the rank of a bourgeoise, Mademoiselle Legras was noble by birth. Her maiden name was
Louise de Marillac; she was born in the year 1591, and married in her twenty-second year to Antoine Legras, secretary
of Mary of Medici. Her husband not being of ancient descent, she had no claim to the title of Madame, and was simply called Mademoiselle. This aristocratic distinction still
existed in France in the eighteenth century; though it was
by no means so rigorously observed as in the preceding age.
Mademoiselle Legras became a widow in the year 1625; and
she resolved to devote herself wholly to the service of God.
From her youth she had been of a serious and philosophic
turn of mind—so much so, that her father gave her a classical education, as the only one worthy of her gravity and intellect. But her soul went beyond the things human learning professes to teach: she longed to enter a religious order;
and would have done so, but that her health proved too delicate for the austerities of the cloister. Even in the world she
led a life of retirement, charity, and self-denial; and from the
first years of her marriage she belonged to the poor and to
the sick of her parish. She visited them in their illnesses—
gave them medicines and relief—attended on them—made
their beds—consoled or exhorted the sorrow-stricken or the
dying—and shrank from no task, not even from the laying
out of the dead. In the fervor of her zeal, Mademoiselle Legras wished, in placing herself under the spiritual guidance
of Vincent, to take a vow of devoting herself henceforth to
the poor; but, with his cautious dislike of any thing resem-
bling precipitation, he forbade her to do so for four years;
during which he put her zeal and charity to repeated trials.

In the year 1627, Vincent proposed to Mademoiselle Legras to visit the charitable sisterhoods which he had established in the country. She eagerly consented, and accompanied by several ladies of equal zeal and piety, she undertook
every summer a task which her delicate health rendered extremely fatiguing. She went over the dioceses of Soissons,
Paris, Beauvais, Meaux, Senlis, Chartres, and Chalons, in

Champagne. On arriving in a village, she collected the women who composed the charitable sisterhood, and gave them the instructions which they often required. She exhorted them to persevere in an office so holy in the sight of God, increased their numbers, taught them by her own example not to shrink from attending the sick in their most desperate diseases, and gave them money, linen, and medicines. Her next care was to ascertain the state of education: to collect young girls together and instruct them; and if the village possessed no schoolmistress, to send for one, and form her to her task by daily examples and judicious precepts. All this Mademoiselle Legras did not, as a task, but with zeal and fervor; cheerfully submitting to every personal inconvenience, living poorly, and sleeping on the worst beds—not because it was a matter of absolute necessity, but because she could not find it in her heart to preach patience to the poor, whilst surrounded by all the luxurious comforts of wealth. The good she thus accomplished was surprising: everywhere her arrival was hailed as a blessing; and when she left, whole towns and villages followed her with benedictions and regrets. She spent the winter in Paris, and was then as eager in the practice of good deeds, as if the summer had been devoted to pleasure. Vincent was often obliged to moderate her zeal, and conjure her to spare her health. Her heroic ardor shrank from nothing: she once attended on a sick girl lying ill with the plague, and issued unharmed from the trial.

Seventeen years had elapsed since the establishment of the first sisterhood in Chatillon, when Vincent perceived with regret that these charitable associations were no longer animated by their original spirit. The greatest ladies in France had indeed become members; some through piety, some because it was the fashion: but they did more harm than good. The husbands of these ladies objected to have their wives exposed to the danger of breathing impure air, and of bringing home the contagion of disease; their own zeal flagged: they hired servants to fill their places; the sick were neglected, and the sisterhood, in Paris especially, daily declined. Vincent thought the mischief lay in the choice of the servants. He reflected that many poor and pious girls, who wished not to marry, and yet were too poor to enter convents, might, for the love of God, far more than for the sake of salary, under-

take to attend on the sick poor, and gladly fill the places left
vacant by the caprice and repugnance of wealthier ladies.
The plan was tried, but answered indifferently. Those "servants of the poor," as they were called, were often unsuited
to their task : above all, they wanted the unity which springs
from a common spirit, and gives association its mighty power.
Still Vincent was not discouraged. In the year 1633 he found
three or four girls whose solid piety promised well. He
placed them under the guidance of Mademoiselle Legras, who
kept them for some time in her house, and then sent them
forth on their arduous labors. Their modesty and zeal, the
purity of their life, the fervor of their piety, edified the parishes to which they had been sent. Their numbers increased
rapidly. Vincent still gave them their original name : the
people called them sisters of charity. St. Vincent of Paul
had never thought of founding a religious order ; but when
he saw that the thing was in some sort done, that the new
order had won both the faith and the affections of the people,
he sought to establish it on a secure foundation, and favored
its increase. Mademoiselle Legras and her disciples took the
vows, which sanctified their duties, but could scarcely add to
the ardent zeal with which they fulfilled them.

Thus simply began one of the noblest associations in which
human beings have ever united for the glory of God and the
service of men. It spread with extraordinary rapidity over
all France, and soon extended to foreign countries : Italy,
Spain, the Netherlands, Poland, America, and even the In-
dies, had their servants of the poor. In the following century the Sisters of Charity had no less than thirty-four separate
establishments in Paris alone. Neither St. Vincent nor Mademoiselle Legras knew the great things they were preparing ;
and, however much we may and must admire their charity,
we cannot give them the glory of a vast design. Providence
worked in them ; they knew it, and that others should know
and feel it too, is not more than their deep and unfeigned humility would have wished.

Vincent and Mademoiselle Legras had at first intended the
sisters to visit and attend the parish poor only ; but, with
time, they very wisely extended this original design, and gave
them a wider sphere of action. The Sisters of Charity successively undertook the instruction of poor children, the care

of the hospital sick, and the rearing of foundlings. Their founder even sent them among prisoners and galley-slaves. They remained foreign to no deed of mercy, however hard of accomplishment or repugnant to the delicacy of woman it might be.

The regulations which St. Vincent drew up for their conduct breathe the most admirable spirit, and are fraught with prudence and wisdom. The Sisters of Charity take the vows of chastity, obedience, and poverty, after a probation of five years; but their vows are for one year only, so that they may always possess the merit of liberty. They renew them every year, on the 25th of March; this being the anniversary of the day when Mademoiselle Legras first took hers. They cannot do so without the permission of their superior, who sometimes inflicts a delay, as the severest punishment in her power. Few sisters have ever sought or wished to re-enter the world; and, though exposed to all its temptations, no cloistered nuns surpass them in the exact and faithful observance of the rules of their order.

In the instructions which he addressed to them, their founder, reminding them of the dangers to which they were exposed, begged them to consider reserve and purity as their most essential virtues; not only because those virtues were excellent in themselves, but because the least suspicion on their morals would render their most fervent charity ineffectual, and bring down contempt and dishonor on the religion they served. He thus contrasted, in earnest and vivid language, their condition with that of other nuns: "Your monasteries are the houses of the sick; your cell is a hired room; your cloister, the streets of the city or the wards of the hospitals. Let obedience be your solitude, the fear of God your grating, and a strict and holy modesty your only veil."

Neither the fasts, vigils, nor other austerities of the cloister were prescribed to the Sisters of Charity. To rise winter and summer at four in the morning, to pray twice a day, live with the greatest frugality, drink wine in illness only, attend on the sick even in their most disgusting and painful illnesses, watch the whole night long by the bed of the dying, think it nothing to be immured within the walls of a hospital, and breathe air tainted by disease; to shrink not from sickness, fatigue, danger, or death: these, and these only, are the mortifications which he prescribed to the Sisters of Charity.

A devotedness so heroic and so pure filled every one with admiration and respect; but none held those feelings more deeply than Vincent of Paul himself. He could not mention the name of his spiritual daughters without much emotion; and he felt so confident of a special protection of God in their favor, that he sent them on perilous errands through Germany and Poland, without seeming to think that they could be molested. A striking testimony of his respect for those admirable women, as well as of the spirit by which they were animated, will be found in his address to the congregation of priests over whom he presided. In the year 1658, the queen-regent, Anne of Austria, asked for a few Sisters of Charity to be sent to the wounded soldiers at Calais. The four strongest of the sisterhood went: two soon died of fatigue. It was to this event that Vincent alluded in one of the spiritual conferences which his simple and manly eloquence had rendered so celebrated. "I recommend to your prayers," said he, "the Sisters of Charity whom we sent to Calais to assist the poor wounded soldiers. Four went, and two, the strongest, have sunk beneath the burden. Imagine, gentlemen, what four poor girls can do for five or six hundred sick and wounded soldiers! Is not this affecting? Do not you consider it an action of great merit before God, that women should thus go with so much courage and resolution among soldiers, to relieve them in their necessities? That they should go and expose themselves to so much fatigue, and even to disease and death, for the sake of those who exposed themselves to the perils of war for the good of the State? We thus see how these poor women are filled with zeal for the glory of God, and for the assistance of their fellow-creatures. The queen has done us the honor to write and ask us for more sisters to be sent to Calais, and four are going away to-day for that purpose. One of them, about fifty years old, came to see me last Friday at the Hôtel Dieu, where I then was. She said that, having learned how two of her sisters had died at Calais, she came to offer herself to go and fill their places, if I thought fit to allow it. 'Sister,' I replied, 'I shall think about it.' She called here yesterday to learn my answer. See, my brethren, the courage of these women, thus to offer themselves like victims, ready to yield up their lives for the love of Jesus Christ and the good of their neighbor. Is not this admirable? Indeed I know not what to say, unless that they will judge me on the great day of the Lord. Yea, they will be our judges, unless we are ready like them to expose our lives for the love of God."

The first Sisters of Charity belonged to the condition of domestic servants; but when with time many highly born and wealthy ladies asked to enter the order, it was not thought expedient to deprive them of the opportunity of making so noble a sacrifice: one which had the power of exciting the admiration of Voltaire himself. "Perhaps," once wrote he who scoffed at every thing, "there is nothing greater on earth than the sacrifice which a delicate sex makes of beauty, youth, and often of high birth, to relieve in hospitals that gathering of human miseries of which the sight is so humiliating to pride and so revolting to our delicacy." "Do you, then, think," exclaims an eloquent Christian, commenting on this passage, "that these asylums are inaccessible to the cares, the weariness, and the agitations which beset the human heart? Do you think that that heart which wearies of pleasures never wearies of sacrifice? Do you think that when these angels of mercy pass through the gloomy wards, and remember that, instead of the calm and pleasant existence which a word would restore, instead of the family which recalls them, they must dress the wounds of strangers, listen to their last gasps, and lay out unknown dead, not for a week, for a month, but for thirty years—nay, forever: do you think, I say, that their courage has never almost failed them? Would you know what sustained them then? question them." Question them! there is no need. There is and can be but one explanation of a sacrifice so heroic and so enduring—the pure and holy love of God.

When the great storm of the first French Revolution shattered the cloisters, which had been hallowed by the veneration and love of so many generations, and scattered their inmates over the land, none ventured to pass the same sentence on the Sisters of Charity: their services, it was found, could not be dispensed with. An infuriate Paris mob did indeed scourge these women, whose purity and holiness ought to have placed them beyond the reach of outrage:

but this act was only the act of individuals, not that of the nation.

The same spirit still prevails in France: the insults of the ignorant and the rude are more than counterbalanced by the love and veneration of the greater number. The Sisters of Charity, servants of the poor, are more numerous and more respected than any similar order. These true daughters of St. Vincent of Paul still labor in the spirit of their illustrious father, and wear the now odd-looking costume of the seventeenth century: a dark-gray petticoat and jacket with loose sleeves, a coarse blue apron, and a large starched cap of spotless whiteness, but more quaint than becoming, are the attire of women who often descend from the noblest blood in France; and of whom many cannot quite conceal beneath their uncouth habiliments features of exquisite loveliness, and that innate elegance which bespeaks habits both delicate and refined.

In the year which followed the institution of the Sisters of Charity, Madame de Goussault, a young, wealthy, and beautiful widow, who was in the habit of visiting the great hospital of the Hôtel Dieu, ended by being much impressed with the many deficiencies and abuses of this establishment. She represented to Vincent all the good that an association of visiting ladies could effect with regard to the spiritual and temporal welfare of the sick. Several meetings on this subject were held at the house of Madame de Goussault; the result was an association, of which she was named president, and which consisted of ladies, great according to the world, but far more illustrious by their piety and charity. This humane thought of one woman produced results of paramount importance: the association thus established became the firmest support of all the philanthropic undertakings of the apostle of the age. The General Hospital of Paris, that of St. Reine, the Foundling Asylum, several establishments for virtuous girls in distress, missionary expeditions, and the redemption of many Christian captives, had their origin in the pious association of a few women. St. Vincent of Paul knew well all he owed to woman, and showed how much he anticipated from her charity, when he attempted one of his most arduous enterprises—one which will ever be connected with his name in France—the succor of the foundling.

It is now difficult to believe in the pitiable condition of the foundling children of those days: we may know that such things have been; but it seems incredible still. Those innocent creatures, the offspring of vice, but not the less children of God, were daily found exposed in public places, and at the doors of churches. The commissary of police caused them to be removed, and taken to a widow residing in the Rue St. Landry; who, with the aid of two servants, undertook to rear them. She was badly paid, and by far the larger number of her little charges pined away and died of want. Tired of their cries, the servants frequently silenced them with perfidious cordials, that led to a lethargic slumber ending in death; those who survived, were given away to whosoever cared to have them, and not unfrequently sold for a few coins. Some took and bought them from mere pity; but it was not always so: many, we are told, were purchased to suck the milk of diseased women, thus finding death in the very source of life; some to be substituted for children of rank who had died inopportunely; others, unhappy victims of a cruel superstition, were murdered to forward magical operations, or to give their blood to those unnatural baths in which old age sought to renew the freshness and vigor of youth.

It was this evil, so great, so deeply rooted, and so extensive, that St. Vincent of Paul, one of the poorest men of his times, attempted to remedy. In the year 1638, he requested the ladies of the association to visit the house of the widow of St. Landry. They did so, and were horror-struck at what they saw; unable, however, to adopt all the children, they resolved to take twelve, who were not selected—they had not the courage to choose—but drawn by lots. Mademoiselle Legras, and several of the sisters, undertook to rear them in a house which was hired for that purpose. To these twelve children the ladies gradually added others, according to their means; the difference between those whom they had taken away and those whom they had left with the widow was too striking not to fill them with pity; but to take all was not in their power, until the year 1640, when the queen-regent obtained from the king a yearly grant of twelve thousand francs. The ladies of the association then undertook to rear all the children at their cost; the expense exceeded forty thousand francs a year—a large sum for the times—especially as it was given by a limited number of married women, rich, indeed, but not sole mistresses of their wealth. Kind as were these ladies, it is evident that, but for the zeal and energetic charity of Vincent, they never would have done so much. A few extracts from the journal, kept by the Sisters of Charity, who reared the children, will serve to show both the goodness of this excellent man, and the simple and tender feelings of his spiritual daughters.

"January the twenty-second.—M. Vincent came at eleven in the evening, and brought us two children. One may be about six days old; the other is older. The poor little things cried. Madame, the superior, has confided them to nurses.

"January the twenty-sixth.—Poor M. Vincent is perished with cold. He brings us a child: this one is already weaned. My God! how hard must be the heart that could thus abandon a poor little creature!

"February the sixth.—The air is very keen. M. Vincent has come to visit our community. The holy man is always on foot: the superior wished him to rest; but he ran immediately to his little children. It is a wonder to hear his gentle words and beautiful consolations; those little creatures love him like their father."

There is an anecdote, that whilst carrying a child to the sisters in the middle of the night, the saint was once stopped by theives; but when he showed his burden, and uttered his name—and who then did not know the name of Monsieur Vincent?—they let him go free, with many a blessing on that charity and holiness which were not unknown even in the haunts of crime.

Some years had thus elapsed, when the ladies of the association, perceiving that the number of the foundlings, and consequently the expense, yearly increased, began to feel alarmed at the heavy burden which rested upon them. The troubled state of the times, reverses of fortune, and the calls of the world, operated upon them so far that they declared the undertaking must be relinquished. Vincent begged of them first to hold a general meeting, and then to decide on what was to be done. The meeting took place. Mademoiselle Legras, and Madame de Miramion, a young and beautiful widow, of eminent piety, whose name will be found fur-

ther on, were amongst the ladies present. Vincent opened
the deliberations. He confessed that the ladies were free:
they had contracted no engagement; and if they wished to
abandon the foundlings, they could do so: on the other hand,
he represented to them how much good they had done, how
many children they had saved from death, and how some of
those children were already beginning to earn an honest livelihood. Warming as he proceeded, and unable to restrain his
deep emotion, which betrayed itself by sighs and broken
accents, the good man concluded with the following touch of
homely eloquence: "And now, ladies," said he, "pity and
charity have made you adopt these little creatures as your
children. Ye have been their mothers according to grace,
since their mothers according to the flesh abandoned them:
see now whether ye also will abandon them. Be no longer
their mothers—be their judges: their life and death are in
your hands. I shall take the votes; it is time to pronounce
their sentence, and to know if you will have no more mercy
for them. They will live if you continue your charitable
care; but, on the contrary, they will surely die if you abandon them: past experience is there, you cannot doubt the
result."

The ladies did not answer: sobs and tears impeded speech.
The appeal made to their womanly feelings, the tender art
with which the saint made them the judges of innocent and
defenceless creatures, more eloquent in their silence than he
could be in his pleading, had not been lost. They began by
giving all the gold and silver in their possession, and ended
by protesting that, happen what might, no matter at what
cost, they would never abandon the poor children they had
adopted. They kept their promise; some had to redeem it
by pledging their plate: one lady alone gave twenty thousand francs. The efforts of the association were finally
crowned with success; and two asylums, enriched by the
gifts and legacies of liberal and pious persons, were opened
in Paris to the foundlings, whose home had once been the
house of the widow of St. Landry.

Good deeds are prolific. The association of ladies who
had shrunk from the Foundling Asylum, now astonished
Vincent by proposing a far greater and more expensive
undertaking: that of a General Hospital for all the mendi-

cant poor of Paris. In the year 1653, they submitted the
project to him, in one of their assemblies. He was startled,
and raised some objections; but one of the ladies promised
fifty thousand francs, and another offered a yearly income of
three thousand. The king, pleased with the project, agreed
to give the grounds and buildings of the Salpétrière. Many
munificent persons contributed largely to the funds; and at
the end of three years—during which the charitable ladies
had to struggle against the keen ridicule of opinion, and the
more serious obstacles raised by authority to thwart their
design—the General Hospital was opened to five thousand
beggars, on the 7th of March, 1657. This establishment,
which still exists, effected what had baffled the efforts of
Henry IV. and his successor: it succeeded in banishing
mendicity from Paris.

Five years after this, Mademoiselle Legras died, in the
seventy-first year of her age. She had taken an active share
in all the generous enterprises of the association. Of her
private life and feelings little is known; but that little is
enough: she was the first Sister of Charity. And a boundless charity did indeed dwell in the heart of her, who was
heard to say of the poor, whose sister and servant she had
chosen to be, "They are our brothers, and our masters!"
She requested that no epitaph might be engraved on her
tombstone—nothing but a small cross, with the words,
"*Spes mei.*" The request was obeyed.

CHAPTER XIII.

Madame de Miramion.

AMONGST the ladies from whom the pathetic appeal of
St. Vincent of Paul drew the promise of continued support
to the Foundling Asylum, was Madame de Miramion, whose
boundless charity gives her a high rank among the most
eminent Christian women of her age. Beautiful and wealthy,
severe to herself, but gentle to others, she was eminently a

woman of faith and good works; a serene purity of soul
marks her whole existence, from her earliest years to her
sanctified death.

Her maiden name was Marie Bonneau de Rubelle: she
was born on the second of November, 1629. She lost her
mother when about nine years of age, and fell ill with grief.
Her father confided her to the contrary influences of a pious
governess who constantly spoke to her of God, and of a gay
aunt who took her to balls and plays. The teaching of the
governess proved the most acceptable; Marie closed her
eyes at the play, and kept her thoughts fixed upon death in
the midst of the dance. Her delight was to hold communion
with God through prayer, and serve him in the persons of
the poor and the sick. Her aunt once gave a great ball,
and vainly looked for her niece to begin the dance. Servants
were sent for her everywhere, fruitlessly; at length they
found her in a retired part of the house, by the dying bed
of a man-servant who lay expiring in fearful convulsions.
Marie was then twelve years of age. This one incident is a
key to her whole existence. Young, rich, handsome, and
summoned by all the pomps and alluring vanities of the
world, the call fell on her ear unheeded. The promises of
the Gospel led her along another path, and summoned her
to a holier destiny.

Her father died when she was about fourteen. With a
prudence and wisdom above her years, Mademoiselle de
Rubelle undertook to superintend the education of her
younger brothers, and rendered herself the real head of the
family. In May, 1645, not being yet sixteen, she married
M. de Miramion, of the family of Beauharnois. The extreme
seriousness and rigid piety of his bride annoyed M. de Miramion. " I renounced cards, dancing, and the theatre," she
records in the brief memoirs of her life, written at the request of her confessor, " which caused a good deal of surprise. . . . Our only discussions were on the subject of my
refusing amusements." But persuasion was amongst the
gifts of Madame de Miramion: she soon won over her husband " to live like a Christian," as she expresses it; adding
immediately afterwards, " We never spoke together of any
thing save death." Strange and gloomy ideal of a Christian
life and marriage.

8

Madame de Miramion had scarcely been six months a wife when she became a widow, on the eve of her sixteenth birthday. Spite of her Christian stoicism, she confesses that grief brought her to the very verge of death. A few months after the decease of her husband she gave birth to her only child, a daughter. The young widow lived in great retirement for two years. She was resolved not to marry again, and said so; but fortune-hunters were irresistibly attracted by a widow of eighteen, well born, still beautiful, spite of the small-pox, and wealthy.

Bussy de Rabutin, the bold, satirical, and licentious cousin of Madame de Sévigné, heard of Madame de Miramion, and resolved that the wealthy widow should help to repair his broken fortunes. He saw her twice in church, was pleased with her modest beauty, and resolved to carry her off and force her into a marriage; to which he concluded that so gentle a woman would easily submit. His personal vanity—and he was perhaps the vainest man of his times—strengthened him in this conviction. In his memoirs, Bussy declares that he was deceived into the belief that Madame de Miramion wished him to carry her off, and makes light of the whole affair. The abduction of heiresses, maids, or widows, was a commom practice of the age. Dubois, valet-de-chambre of Louis XIV., records in his memoirs how Mademoiselle de la Tessònière was forcibly taken from her mother's carriage by M. de Fontenaille, who performed the exploit on horseback in company of five or six friends. This careful ravisher had provided himself with a soft pillow on which he placed the lady before him, then galloped off, spite of her screams and entreaties; but having missed his way, and perceiving that it would not be in his power to keep her, he returned her unharmed to her friends on the following day.

Madame de Miramion had spent the summer of the year 1648 in a country house lying within a short distance of Paris. She received several warnings, which she disregarded, having no knowledge of Bussy de Rabutin's passion for her wealth and person: for that his attempt was not dictated by mere interest, seems to be an acknowledged fact. At an early hour on a fine August morning, Madame de Miramion, accompanied by her mother-in-law, two female attendants, and an old squire, left Issy in an open carriage, in order to

pay her devotions at the shrine on Mount Valerian. They
were within a quarter of a league of the mount, when twenty
men on horseback suddenly arrested them, changed the
horses, and compelled the carriage to take another route.
Madame de Miramion called out for aid; but the spot was
lonely, and none heard her cries; the carriage went fast,
and had soon entered the depths of the forest of Livry.
The road, or rather path, along which they went, was so
narrow that the horsemen, unable to ride on either side,
were compelled to precede and follow the carriage. Madame de Miramion leaped out and ran away, through thorns
and briers, which tore her face and hands; but seeing that
her ravishers had perceived her flight and were pursuing
her, and fearing they might compel her to ride on horseback
for greater security, she retraced her steps and lightly leaped back again into the carriage. It stopped ere long, to set
down the elder Madame de Miramion, her attendant, and
the old squire; and her own attendant and a footman, who
declared he would not leave his mistress, alone remained
with the young widow. Her ravishers offered her food,
which she refused.

They resumed their journey, changing horses from time to
time. Whenever they passed through towns and villages,
Madame de Miramion renewed her cries for aid, and threw
money to all the people she saw. Her escort declared she
was a poor mad lady whom they were taking away by order
of the court; her dishevelled hair, disordered coif and kerchief, and the blood on her face and hands, seemed to confirm the truth of the story. On the evening of the following
day they reached the castle of Launai; no modern château,
but a real relic of feudal ages, with walls of massy strength,
a dark and narrow court, and old draw-bridges, that were
lowered one by one with great clanking of chains, for Madame
de Miramion to pass, and quickly raised again as soon as the
carriage had been admitted. She peremptorily refused to
alight; when a gentleman, whom his attire showed to be a
knight of Malta, approached, and sought to persuade her to
enter the house.

"Is it by your orders that I have been carried away?"
asked Madame de Miramion.

"No, madame," he replied very respectfully, "it is by the

order of Monsieur Bussy de Rabutin, who has assured us that he had obtained your consent."

. "Then he has spoken falsely," she indignantly exclaimed.

."Madame," returned the knight, "we are here two hundred gentlemen, friends of Monsieur de Bussy; but if he has deceived us, be assured that we shall take your part against him, and set you at liberty.".

The noble mien and respectful bearing of this gentleman produced some effect on Madame de Miramion; she consented, on his word, to alight, and enter a low, damp room on the ground-floor. A fire was lit for her, and she sat down on the cushions of her own carriage. Two loaded pistols were lying on a table; she seized them eagerly; food was brought her—she would not touch it, and vehemently asked for death or freedom. Several persons came to intimidate or lure her into compliance: she heard them with disdain. Bussy de Rabutin himself appeared not: the unexpected resistance of Madame de Miramion enraged and mortified him. "I thought to find a lamb, and I have got a lioness!" he exclaimed, in his anger. After some hesitation, he at length sent the knight of Malta to assure her that he did not mean to detain her against her will, and to beg that she would hear him for a few moments. He did not venture to appear alone before her, but entered the room accompanied by a dozen of friends; and the bold profligate, renowned for his daring and his wit, stood suddenly disconcerted in the presence of a woman of nineteen. On perceiving him, Madame de Miramion rose, and exclaimed: "I vow by the living God, my Creator and yours, that I will never be your wife." The passion with which she uttered this solemn protest, made her fall back almost senseless on the cushions. A doctor who was present felt her pulse; which was so low, that he thought her dying; for forty hours she had not tasted food. Alarmed at the possibility of her death, and rendered still further uneasy by the tidings that six hundred armed men from Sens were coming to besiege the castle, and deliver Madame de Miramion, M. de Bussy swore to set her at liberty; but in the mean time he entreated her to take some refreshment. "When the horses are saddled, and I am in my carriage, I shall eat,". replied Madame de Miramion. Her

wish was immediately obeyed, and she consented to take two
fresh eggs.

At length she was free; the carriage left the castle, and
set out for Sens. The knight of Malta accompanied Madame
de Miramion to within a hundred yards of the town, endeav-
oring to excuse M. de Bussy. When he rode away, the
coachman and postillion, alarmed at their share in this business, unharnessed the horses and went off; leaving Madame
de Miramion and her two attendants to proceed on foot to
Sens. They found the gates shut, and were told that the
whole town was arming, by command of the queen, in order
to deliver a lady who had been carried off. "Alas! I am
that lady," replied Madame de Miramion. She entered an
inn, and being no longer sustained by the spirit of resistance
which had till then upheld her, she became so ill that she
had to be carried back to Paris on a litter. On the prayer
of his patron, the Prince of Condé, she forgave her persecutor; but stipulated that he should never appear before her:
a condition which he faithfully observed for thirty-six years.
When that length of time had elapsed, he solicited her influence in favor of a law-suit of his, then pending. She consented to see and hear him, and promised to serve, as far as
her power extended, the man whose cupidity and passion had
brought her to the verge of death.

When Madame de Miramion recovered, several other attempts to carry her off were made. They failed; but
frightened her so much, that she well-nigh resolved to marry
again, in order to secure a protector. She contented herself, however, with retiring into various convents: she thus
resided for some time with Mademoiselle Legras and the Sisters of Charity. It was in their house that she privately consecrated herself to God, and resolved to divide her life between the education of her daughter and the care of the poor.
"I am so comfortable, and the poor are so wretched," she
often observed. Forsaken children interested her deeply.
She hired a house, filled it with twenty poor orphan girls,
fed and clothed them, paid mistresses to instruct them, and
frequently left her own home to go and teach them herself;
sharing their meals, and sitting amongst them like a mother
with her children. Her mornings were devoted to the relief
and visiting of the poor in their own homes; her afternoons

to the hospitals. She had a natural repugnance to the sight of those ills and sufferings of humanity which she daily witnessed ; yet spite of those feelings, she once compelled herself to attend, until she finally cured her, a poor girl so sadly afflicted with the scald, that no one else would even so much as touch her. To these habitual tasks, Madame de Miramion added frequent missions in the country, to instruct peasant women, and establish schoolmistresses in the villages. Resolves written in her own hand, and found amongst her papers after her death, show the spirit which animated her. "To think of putting my temporal affairs in good order ; to write down every thing ; settle with my daughter's guardian ; pay all ; retrench something ; be very economical. To spend as little as I can on myself and my daughter ; to give the rest of my income to the poor ; to give three thousand francs a year from my daughter's property to the poor ; to exhort my brothers to give to them also. . . . . To receive contradictions, contempt, and grief, with joy ; to thank God for these things, and beseech him to continue and increase them ; to be quite satisfied under them, *and grasp at humiliation like a treasure.* To love a hidden life, known to none save God ; and whatever is done, to do it for him alone."

She who, in the fervor of her faith, spoke thus of "grasping at humiliation like a treasure," had yet enough human weakness to suffer keenly from the raillery of the light and worldly-minded ; whose life and pleasures she renounced, in order to acquire a practical knowledge of medicine, and even, spite of ridicule, to bleed the sick.

The office of treasurer to her parish gave her abundant opportunities of doing good, as the civil wars of the Fronde had filled Paris with poor. Thanks to her zeal and excellent management, two thousand indigent persons received soup daily. She often deprived herself of the innocent gratification of presiding over the distribution. "When I serve the poor," she said, "I have no merit : I am rewarded by the pleasure it gives me." But misery increased so rapidly around her, that her income, though large, no longer sufficed to the wants of her charity. She sold her pearl necklace for twenty-four thousand francs. "God-inspired me well," she observed to her confessor ; "I got rid of an occasion of vanity, and at the same time found the means of assisting many poor creatures." Her plate was disposed of in the same manner, for the same purpose, in the following year. This ardent charity did not always meet with due gratitude. "How much trouble you take to oblige ungrateful people!" once observed a lady to her. "I have received more from God," replied Madame de Miramion, "than those people have received from me. He therefore gives me a great proof of his mercy, in affording me those opportunities of satisfying his justice." This mortified spirit, the result of will more than inclination, did not render Madame de Miramion quite dead to the vanities of life. She loved elegance, and once indulged her taste by causing her room to be newly furnished, and hung with black and white velvet. A single remark made by one of her friends, " that this magnificence was scarcely needed in the room of a Christian widow," sufficed to make her renounce this last lingering affection for the luxuries she had relinquished. At the age of twenty, Madame de Miramion had cut her hair short, and given up laces, silk, and colored garments; wearing only plain woollen stuffs of gray or black hue: we have already seen the use to which she put her jewels. A dangerous illness interrupted those tasks of charity, and induced her to write thus to her daughter:

"I pray to God to give you his holy benediction. My last words to you are: love God with your whole heart, and serve him faithfully; love and assist the poor; walk in the path of the Gospel. Let that be your rule; keep it inviolate. Renounce the vanities of the world: God is not there. Confide in him; he will care for you. . . . Adieu, my dear, and more than very dear daughter. I leave you God for a father: you are well thus, and to him I abandon you. Choose to die sooner than to offend him. Pray, and cause prayers to be offered up, for me. Farewell once more! but only for a little while, since we shall meet before God. Your mother and best friend."

Madame de Miramion recovered, but was afflicted with a painful cancer. She brought up her daughter in the spirit which had dictated this letter: with the tenderness of a mother, and the faith of a Christian. The health of her only child was so delicate, that almost every year some severe illness brought her to the point of death. Madame de

Miramion adopted every human remedy, then offered her up to God, saying: "If she is not to live and die a Christian, take her from me, Lord." She educated her in her own principles and habits; took her with her everywhere; taught her to give alms, to instruct poor children, and visit hospitals. "The road of the hospitals leads to heaven," she often remarked. She made her learn dancing, for the sake of the elegance it imparts to the carriage; and once took her to a ball, that she might know what sort of a thing it was, and learn to despise it. She urged her not merely to shun evil, but to do good; to be modest in her dress, moderate in following the fashions, neither to adopt extremes nor to censure those who did; above all, to love the poor. She once brought her two skirts, saying: "Choose one of them; if you take the least handsome of the two, you will have four pistoles remaining to give to the poor." The austere lessons thus inculcated were not distasteful to Mademoiselle de Miramion, because they were never compulsory. From her twelfth year her mother treated her like a sister: never reprimanded her without giving her motives for so doing, and listened impartially to her remonstrances and justification. "If my reasons are better than yours," she said, "you will yield to them; but if yours are the best, I shall give in." In this friendly spirit, mother and daughter discussed together the various offers of marriage which the latter received; until both decided in favor of M. de Nemond, an honorable magistrate. An act of Christian charity signalized their marriage: a thousand louis, instead of being spent on jewels, were given to the poor. Madame de Miramion had stipulated that her daughter should be allowed to govern and spend her own property. She presented her with an account-book, and the first article of expense set down was the wide and paramount one of charity.

Madame de Miramion now thought that her part with active life was done. She longed for the silence and repose of a cloistered solitude, and spoke of retiring to some provincial convent of the austere Carmelite order. All her spiritual advisers, who knew how admirably adapted she was for the practice of the highest religious duties, opposed the project so strongly, that she relinquished it; and thus added another act of self-denial to the many sacrifices of her pure life. She resumed and extended all her tasks of charity, contributed largely to foreign missions, and for six months fed at her own expense poor nuns, whose convents had been ruined by the war. Grieved at the sight of all the abandoned women who then filled Paris with profligacy, Madame de Miramion attempted to reform them. With the permission of the magistrates, she shut up seven or eight of those unhappy creatures in a house hired by her for that purpose, and placed two discreet women over them. Madame de Miramion often visited them herself, spoke to them of God, and endeavored to warn them from vice, by promises of liberty, and a more honorable livelihood. Most of these women listened to her arguments, and turned away from evil. The success of this little establishment, which lasted two years, induced Madame de Miramion to attempt on a larger scale, and at public cost, what she had effected from her own private resources. Three ladies of great liberality and charity, Madame d'Aiguillon, niece of Cardinal Richelieu, Madame de Farinvilliers, and Madame de Traversai, to whom she suggested this project, met to consider it. They admired it extremely, but thought it too difficult of accomplishment, and declined interfering. As they came to this decision, Madame de Miramion entered the room where they sat. She belonged to those ardent spirits to whom the word "impossible" only imparts new zeal; and she spoke in favor of her design with so much force, conviction, and eloquence, that she carried away the hearts of the three ladies. When, at the conclusion of her brief address, she declared that she would give for her part, besides her time and labor, ten thousand francs to the new establishment, each of the ladies protested that she would give an equal sum. A contract was passed; the house was built; Madame de Miramion drew up the regulations, and assumed the fatiguing task of governing this establishment: it rapidly improved and extended under her judicious rule, and was afterwards well known under the name of Sainte Pélagie.

In the year 1662, the price of corn was so high that the General Hospital of Paris, established by the ladies of the association, was on the verge of ruin. Madame de Miramion applied to Madame Martinozzi, the illustrious Princess of Conti. She painted to her the wants of the hospital in a

8*

strain so pathetic, that the princess presented her with the magnificent gift of a hundred thousand francs. In the course of the same year, this admirable woman, who had not yet reached her twentieth year, sold all her pearls and jewels for the sum of forty thousand crowns, which she caused to be distributed amongst the starving poor of Berry, Champagne, and Picardy. At the time that she thus exerted herself in favor of the General Hospital, Madame de Miramion was engaged in active and daily duties, which might have been supposed sufficient to engross her whole attention. For several years she had cherished the project of establishing, not a religious order, but a community or association of twelve women, who would undertake to devote themselves to the education of poor children, and the attendance of the sick and the wounded. After the marriage of her daughter, she went, in 1661, to reside in a house of the Faubourg St. Antoine, where five or six pious women shared her zeal and good works. This little community ultimately joined that of St. Genovefa, similar in its spirit and obligations. Madame de Miramion relinquished, with the joy of a lowly heart, the opportunity of spiritual pride and vain-glory which the establishment of a religious order always affords; but, spite of her humility, the sisters, whom she supported for nine years at her sole expense, were always called by the people, up to the first French Revolution, by the name of "Miramionnes."

Under the guidance of this zealous superior, the Miramionnes, or daughters of St. Genovefa, fulfilled with admirable charity the duties of their institute. In the year 1673, troops quartered in the town of Melun introduced a contagious disease, so rapid and fatal, that upwards of a hundred persons died daily. All intercourse with the neighboring towns was interdicted; and the terror in Melun was so great that the sick were thrust out of doors to die in the streets. Priests forsook their flocks, nuns left their convents, and the magistrates and civil officers of the town were on the point of deserting the place; when Madame de Miramion arrived on the spot, accompanied by surgeons and several sisters. She began by assembling the magistrates: a step which her well-known virtue far more than her rank authorized. Her exhortations and unshrinking courage shamed them from their fears. A house was turned into a hospital; the sick, no longer left to perish in the streets, were conveyed to it; and Madame de Miramion and her sisters entered it immediately. The priests and nuns who still remained in the town, ashamed to see a few women usurp the Christian charity they were bound to exert, endeavored by tardy zeal to repair the disgrace of previous indifference. The contagion lasted two months; when it was over, Madame de Miramion returned to Paris overpowered with fatigue; yet, when she learned on her arrival that a similar calamity afflicted the town of Senlis, it required the express prohibition of her religious superiors to prevent her from going to it immediately, so ardent was the zeal of her charity.

Indeed, Madame de Miramion may be described as ever on the watch for doing good: this was both the aim and passion of her life. Thus the immodest language of a few idle girls, whom she overheard as she was returning home one evening, suggested to her the excellent project of workrooms, with mistresses to instruct and superintend girls who were ignorant and idle, but willing to learn and work. The plan was tried, and succeeded admirably; young girls came to those rooms in the morning, worked all day, received their dinner, and were paid for their work at the end of every week. At a period when commercial industry was so imperfectly developed, there was much in this idea. In the year 1694, corn became extremely dear: the hardship, of course, fell most heavily on the poor. Madame de Miramion used her influence with Madame de Maintenon and the king to induce them to cause a large quantity of rice to be brought to Paris, and either given away or sold very cheap. She herself made for her establishment six thousand distributions of soup three times a week. It not unfrequently happened, that those whom she thus relieved acknowledged her charity by coarse abuse; which she bore, and exhorted her sisters to bear, with heroic patience. "Courage, sisters!" she said, "the more you receive contradictions from men, the more does your merit before God increase. Let them speak, and do you continue to serve them; your patience will prevail in the end." She spoke truly: many of those who had insulted her most grossly, repented their ingratitude, and came to ask her forgiveness.

In consequence of the scarcity which prevailed, the funds

of the General Hospital became so low, that the administrators resolved to expel all the women of dissolute life it contained. The prospect of the vice and misery into which these poor creatures must inevitably fall again, greatly distressed Madame de Miramion. She proved to the administrators that the seven hundred women—there were no less—could be kept for forty thousand francs a year. They granted the fact, but objected that they had not this sum; she immediately undertook to procure it. Madame de Maintenon gave her twenty-five thousand francs; she obtained several large sums from various noblemen; the rest she had to ask for in different quarters—an ungracious task, which subjected her to cold looks and slights, which she felt keenly. "Indeed!" she observed to the sister who accompanied her, "one must love God to do this." In less than a week she had obtained upwards of fifty thousand francs, a sum which sufficed to keep the women for two years; for, time being granted, some found husbands, others work or situations; and few ultimately remained in the hospital.

The last year of this noble life, filled with good deeds, had now come. Madame de Miramion, though ill herself, went to comfort and assist a dying friend, the Princess of Guise. She came home extremely fatigued, on the 18th of March, 1696, and fell ill the following morning. She submitted to the prescriptions of her medical attendants with docility, but without faith in their efficacy. She suffered acutely; but nothing could exceed the serenity of her last moments. She gathered around her the little sisterhood over which she had presided for so many years, and gave them her last advice. Scarcely had she concluded, when a sister belonging to a community of Paris, which she loved greatly, entered the room, and said abruptly: "Madame, our community would much like to have your heart when you are dead." Madame de Miramion smiled at the request, and pointing to the sisterhood around her, replied, "My heart belongs to my daughters." Her weakness increasing, the prayers of the dying were read to her. Her niece, who was then bending over her, heard her saying in a low tone: "My God, I accept death, and the destruction of this my body: be it reduced to dust, be it the food of the worm. And thou, my soul, go forth, and unite thyself to thy God!" Two days more she lingered, then died on the 24th of March, 1696, in the sixty-seventh year of her age. No one wept around her death-bed; but the house was besieged by carriages and anxious crowds. When the tidings of her death reached the street, the people broke open the doors to see their benefactress once more. They found her lying on the bed, where she had expired without effort or convulsion: her eyes had closed of themselves; her features were serene. She remained thus for two days, exposed to public veneration.

Madame de Miramion had requested to be buried like a sister of St. Genovefa, and the wish was obeyed. Six poor men bore her coffin to the parish churchyard; thirty sisters carrying lighted tapers followed; then came eighty young girls from the work-rooms she had established, fol-lowed by three hundred children educated by the Mira-mionnes; and the superior of the General Hospital, accom-panied by those women whom Madame de Miramion had recently saved from misery and vice. Her own relatives closed the funeral train, which was followed by an immense crowd. The church where the last rites were performed was bare of drapery, and imperfectly lighted: the simplicity and poverty which she had ever loved in life, accompanied her in death.

Thus lived, and passed away from life, a woman whom birth, beauty, and talents of no mean order, would have fitted for a far more brilliant destiny in the eyes of the world, but a far lower one before God. She, too, might have shone in the polite circles of the Sévignés, the Cou-langes, and the Cornuels; and who would have reproached her for the poor unassisted; for orphan children in ignorance, for abandoned women left to vice, for the sick allowed to die in the streets; whilst, surrounded by all the elegant comforts of a luxurious home, she discussed court scandal, or indulged in the seducing charm of refined and intellectual society? She chose another lot—not without effort; for by nature she was proud, wilful, attached to the refinements of social life, and averse to the sight of poverty and disease. She subdued desire and conquered aversion, until she be-came what is here imperfectly recorded.

We have chiefly spoken of those good deeds which she planned and executed herself; but no task of charity was foreign to her mission. On the express request of the Bishop of Angers, she once undertook to restore peace and order in a religious community; and where all his pastoral authority had failed, her gentleness and conciliatory spirit succeeded. She took an active share in the establishment of the Foundling Asylum and of the General Hospital. The association, directed by St. Vincent of Paul, had the highest respect for her character and talents; and no important resolution was ever taken without her approval. So great was the esteem in which she was held, that when the supe- rior of the General Hospital was compelled, by the infirmi- ties of age, to relinquish her post in the year 1687, Madame de Miramion was requested to instruct her successor in all the duties of her office: an arduous task, which she accepted and fulfilled in a manner that displayed her great adminis- trative talents. But her chief characteristic, after all, was her ardent love of the poor: their welfare was ever upper- most in her thoughts; her property was a trust which she held for them. When her solicitor once informed her, with evident dismay, that she had sustained a heavy loss: "Do not pity *me*," she replied, "pity the poor.".

The name of Madame de Miramion does not often occur in contemporary works; but it is ever accompanied with praise. Madame de Sévigné records in one of her letters, that she "honored with her presence" Racine's tragedy of Esther, performed at St. Cyr. This was probably an act of deference to her munificent friend, Madame de Maintenon; with whom, as well as with the king, she possessed, accord- ing to St. Simon and Dangeau, unlimited influence. "The king," declares the latter, "never refused her any thing." Her influence over the haughty Madame de Montespan had not been less great: it was Madame de Miramion, the pious and the pure, who consoled the royal favorite for the loss of her lover, and finally induced her to leave the court. She was revered even by those who knew her little: and in the world she was little known. On learning her death, Madame de Sévigné wrote off, in her graphic way, "The loss of Madame de Miramion, that mother of the Church, is a public loss."

The Miramionnes gave their name to the Quay of St. Bernard, where they resided until the revolution of 1793.

They daily received and attended the poor, whom they also provided with valuable medicines, originally invented by Madame de Miramion; and of which the receipts still exist. We have several times alluded to her administrative talents; the proof of them, as well as the highest praise they can receive, lies in the fact, that the rules which she laid down, and the principles on which she proceeded, are the acknowledged models on which establishments similar to those she guided have since then been conducted in France.

CHAPTER XIV.

Charity of the Women of the Seventeenth Century in France—Madeleine du Bois—Noble Ladies visit the Hospitals—Martha d'Oraison—Madame de la Sablière—Mademoiselle de Melun—Madame Héliot—Madame de St. Beuve—Madame de Magnelai—Madame de St. Pol—Madame de Neuvillette—Madame de Ranfaing—Madame de Combé—Madame d'Aiguillon—The Princess Palatine—Madame de Longueville—Jeanne Biscot.

OUR limits will not allow us to mention at length all the French ladies who, in this memorable age, rivalled the zeal and virtues of those whom we have already specified. There are actions, however, which must be recorded; and names that cannot be passed over in silence.

In the year 1631, the price of bread rose, and the poor of Paris suffered much. Madeleine du Bois, prioress of a convent of Carmelite nuns, not only increased the quantity of bread which the monastery was in the habit of giving to the poor, but expressly ordered that no one should be sent away from the gates of the convent unrelieved; the consequence was, that no less than four hundred poor persons were daily assisted. Amongst the applicants for the bounty of the Carmelite nuns were some English scholars, who, but for this timely aid, must have died of hunger.

Whilst some thus extended their charity beyond the limits of the cloister, others found in hospitals arduous tasks for the present, and a home where they forgot the misfortunes or errors of the past. St. Vincent of Paul and the

Sisters of Charity had raised high in public estimation the
practice of visiting hospitals. When Evelyn visited Paris,
in 1644, he beheld with surprise "how decently and chris-
tianly the sick people in the Charité were attended, even to
delicacy;" and he records that "he had seen them served
by noble persons, men and women." This was no uncommon fact: the gay and imperious queen-regent, Anne of
Austria, had certain days set apart for that purpose. She
always wore a mask, in order to remain unknown. Her
niece and successor, the pious Marie-Thérèse, was often seen
attending on the sick of the hospital of St. Germains. Some
ladies, as we have already said, made these dismal abodes
their home.

On the 30th of May, 1627, Martha d'Oraison, widow of
the Baron d'Allemagne, died in the Hôtel-Dieu of Paris, in
odor of sanctity. Fifteen years before this her husband had
perished on the ramparts of Aix, in Provence, in a terrible
duel, memorable even in the annals of those sanguinary conflicts : by mutual agreement the combatants were fastened to
one another, the left arm of one being firmly tied to the left
arm of his foe, whilst the right hands of both wielded the
deadly knife—the only weapon which, it seems, could assuage
their fierce thirst of vengeance. Both perished in this mortal embrace of an unrelenting hatred.

From that day Martha d'Oraison forsook the world : the
widow of the vindictive lord made herself the nurse and servant of his poorest vassals, and took up her abode in the home
of the indigent sick of Paris. As if to atone for the unhal-
lowed death of her husband, or to triumph in herself over
those passions through which he had perished, she cast away
from her the opinion of the world, and devoted herself, in her
youth, to a destiny far more austere and cheerless than that
of any cloistered nun.

Towards the close of the same century there died, in another hospital of Paris, engaged in the same cares, another
and very different woman—Madame de la Sablière. The
constant friend of La Fontaine, the charming bourgeoise who
deprived Mademoiselle de Montpensier of the Duke of Lau-
zun, the handsome and witty woman whose delightful society
often kept the most agreeable noblemen from appearing at
court, retired heart-broken to the Incurables, when her lover,

La Fare, forsook her, after a long and constant passion. She had placed her happiness in forbidden love ; she now tasted all its bitterness. Too humble to give to God, amongst pure virgins and holy widows, a life which she had sullied with earthly passions, she devoted herself to him through her suffering brethren.

Mademoiselle de Melun is another of these generous women ; with this difference, that neither sin nor sorrow led her to charity. Her parents, William of Melun, Prince of Epinoy, and Ernestine of Aremberg, were still more eminent for piety and charity than for their high rank and ancient birth. Mademoiselle de Melun was their second daughter, and she inherited all their virtues : for twenty-two years that she was canoness at Mons, she was the friend of the distressed, the instructor of the ignorant, and the nurse of the sick. She also established a sisterhood of ladies, who met every week to share with her these charitable labors. The princess of Epinoy retired to Abbeville, in Picardy, after the death of her husband. Mademoiselle de Melun joined her, and was soon engaged in her favorite tasks. On one occasion she attended on five individuals attacked with a contagious disease ; no remonstrances could deter her from risking her life in the service of those for whom Jesus Christ had died.

After overcoming great difficulties, and spending considerable sums, Mademoiselle de Melun succeeded in establishing the Hospital of Baugé. She entered it in order to devote herself entirely to the sick, but took no vows ; she thus remained free to dispose of her wealth. The poor came to her from every part, drawn by the renown of her boundless charity ; and to assist them she gladly deprived herself of luxuries, of comforts, nay, of the most necessary things : she endured cold, hunger, and every inconvenience, for the gratification of the passion of her life. Her garments, of the coarsest gray cloth, were threadbare, rent, and covered with darns and patches ; to please her friends, she would sometimes cause new clothes to be made for herself, but scarcely had she begun to wear them when she gave them away.

For thirty years did this daughter of an ancient race make the Hospital of Baugé her home. Her daily and self-appointed tasks were to rise between three and four in the morning, to ring the bell that called up the sisters, take lights to their rooms in the winter, make the fires, sweep the wards, and make the beds of the sick ; on whom she also attended in the course of the day. She felt for this last office a natural repugnance, which she heroically conquered : yet, often overpowered by disgust, and by the foul exhalations around her, she fainted away in the performance of her painful task. She died in the home she had chosen, on the 13th of August, of the year 1679.

Other ladies practised, in the world, virtues as great, and a charity no less heroic. Madame Héliot devoted herself to the sick poor, though in the married state and surrounded by all the pleasures of life. The young and beautiful Madame de St. Beuve remained a widow in early youth, and rendered herself eminent by the constant practice of charity. A girl of abandoned conduct having shown signs of repentance, received from her a hundred louis, to encourage her in keeping her good resolves. Another time, having nothing else left, for she almost reduced herself to poverty, she presented a poor man with a valuable piece of plate. She was in the habit of saying that her greatest satisfaction was to know, on awaking in the morning, that she would be able to give away something on that day : she accordingly employed several trustworthy persons, in Paris and its vicinity, to discover fit objects of charity for her to assist.

The Marchioness of Magnelai, of the illustrious house of Gondi, consecrated herself to God and the poor, on losing both her husband and her son. She deprived herself of every luxury, and would have parted with her carriage had she not needed it ; for she was almost always out on some charitable errand, visiting the poor in their houses, in hospitals, or in prisons. In vain her attendants remonstrated with her, and begged that she would not go into places whence she seldom issued with unsullied garments : she only laughed, and told them she liked it. So great and entire was her self-denial, that when her brothers, the Dukes of Retz, who loved her very tenderly, wished to dine with her, she frankly told them, " they must bring both provisions and servants, as she had a large family of her own to keep, and could not afford to entertain company."

A similar domestic affliction led Madame de St. Pol to equal devotedness ; with this difference, that, not satisfied

with what she could do at home, she travelled in search of
the poor and afflicted.   When strangers enter a city, they
ask to behold whatever it holds worthy of note ; the charitable widow had but one question, " Who is there here I can
relieve ?"

The Baroness of Neuvillette devoted herself especially to
prisoners, to galley-slaves, and to the painful task of consoling the condemned in their last hours.   The poor were not
less dear to her :. for their sakes she stripped herself of almost
all she had.   And so perfect and lively was her faith, so
thoroughly did she consider in them the Saviour whom
she served, that she would never give them cast-off garments or broken victuals : clothes which had never been
worn, food which none had touched, or money, were her
gifts to the poor—a rare and touching instance of delicate
feeling.

That nobler charity, which does not confine itself to mere
physical distress, but knows how to minister to the spiritual
wants of sinners, was exercised in the same age by Mary
Elizabeth de Ranfaing, foundress of the Institute of our Lady
of Refuge.   She was born in 1592, and was married young
to a brutal and profligate gentleman named Du Bois.   She
became a widow in 1616 ; she had three children, and little
wealth ; prudence as well as devotion induced her to lead a
retired life.   Her beauty inspired a neighboring doctor with
a passion which he sought to gratify by making her take a
philter.   His guilty superstition failed in its object ; but
caused him, and a servant by whom he had been abetted, to
be burned alive for magic in 1622.

This event alarmed Madame de Ranfaing.   She wished to
retire to a monastery, partly for protection ; but not being
able to do so, she received penitent girls into her house.   The
Bishop of Toul suggested to her the propriety of extending
this meritorious task, by founding a religious order, specially
devoted to reclaiming erring women ; and on the 1st of
January, 1631, Madame de Ranfaing, her three daughters,
and seven of the penitent women, took the veil.   The order
rapidly spread over Lorraine, Burgundy, and the southern
provinces of France.   The foundress died in 1649, in odor
of sanctity.

A similar labor was achieved by Mary Magdalen of Combé,

a Dutchwoman; who, though alone in France, and scarcely
able to speak the language, yet found means to open a religious asylum for penitent girls of dissolute lives. We know
little of this lady, excepting her good works.

Her maiden name was de Cyz; she was born at Leyden,
of noble parents, in the year 1656, and married, at the age
of nineteen, to Adrian of Combé, a wealthy gentleman of
violent temper and confirmed libertinism. They lived very
unhappily together, and separated at the end of eighteen
months. A year afterwards, Madame de Combé became a
widow. She was still young, attractive, and amiable; but,
disgusted with her experience of marriage, she refused every
offer, and came to France with her sister and brother-in-law.
She fell ill in Paris, and suddenly abjured the Calvinist faith,
in which she had been brought up. Renounced by her
family, she soon found herself alone in a foreign land; where
she might have died of want, but for the charity of strangers.
La Bermondière, parish priest of St. Sulpice, procured her a
small pension.

Madame de Combé sold her rich garments, assumed a
coarse woollen robe, and for some time lived alone; giving
herself up to fasts and austerities more extraordinary than
commendable. This excess of zeal found a worthier channel
in the establishment above alluded to; which at first consisted of only a few girls; but subsequently became a large
and celebrated house, known under the gentle name of "Asylum of the Good Shepherd." Madame de Combé began her
undertaking more rich in faith than in worldly means. A
charitable lady, hearing of her design, gave her two hundred
francs to hire a house; in which she did not establish herself
without obstacle: several libertine young men threatened to
set fire to it; but the lieutenant of police, La Reynie, fortunately took Madame de Combé, and the penitent girls she
had gathered around her, under his special protection. For
two years these poor women, whose number daily increased,
were supported, partly by their own limited earnings, partly
by charitable donations. In 1688, the king granted them a
sum of money and a larger house. They were already
seventy in number: "And if a hundred were to come," exclaimed their devoted friend and superior, strong in that faith
which only rises higher with obstacles, "I feel I could not

refuse them." "Will you always find, at the right moment, the money wherewith to supply so many wants?" once asked a lady, startled by her daring trust in Providence. Madame de Combé smiled, and replied, "Ask the sea if it will ever want water? Do you not know," she added, more gravely, "that the mercies of God are inexhaustible?"

Houses similar to that of Paris were soon established in Orleans, Angers, Troyes, Toulouse, Amiens, Nantes, and several other places. Madame de Combé had one great, and yet simple rule, which guided her in the difficult task of first winning, and then governing, women long abandoned to vice —the rule of gentleness: "Let not those sinners who are forcibly taken from evil be brought here," she remarked: "the house of the Good Shepherd is only for those who embrace virtue freely."

The days of this gentle and amiable being were abridged by a painful illness, which rendered the last two years of her life a slow agony. She endured pain with admirable patience. "How do you feel?" once asked one of the sisters, addressing her. "Very well, daughter," she answered. "Mother," resumed the sister, "how can you say so, being in the state in which you now are?" "Because, to be as God wishes us to be, is to be well," was the calm reply. In this entire resignation to the Divine will, the pious woman, who had not turned away in the pride of her purity from her poor erring sisters, gave up her soul to God on the 16th of June, 1692, in the thirty-sixth year of her age. She was buried, as she had requested, amongst the poor of the parish. Establishments similar to that which she founded now exist in almost every land of Europe.

A faith as frank and daring took Margueritte Bourgeois to Canada, to instruct the Indian women in the truths of the Gospel. She devoted her lifetime to this arduous task.

Although their charity was not quite so remarkable, we should not be justified in omitting the names of several great and titled ladies who lived in those times. The generosity of the Princess of Conti has already been mentioned in the preceding chapter. The liberality of Madame d'Aiguillon, the favorite niece of Richelieu, is likewise worthy of record. She had the lofty spirit of her uncle, without his vindictiveness and pride. She placed herself under the spiritual guidance of St. Vincent of Paul, and devoted her immense wealth to religious and charitable purposes. She endowed hospitals, redeemed Christian captives in Africa, and erected, at her expense, the Hôtel Dieu of Quebec. She died in 1675, worthy of the funeral eulogy which Fléchier pronounced over her remains. Bossuet has likewise commemorated the piety and charity of Anne of Gonzaga, Princess Palatine; who had been a gay, worldly woman, and had taken a great share in the Fronde. Like her, the beautiful Duchess of Longueville, once celebrated for her romantic adventures, became eminent for the exalted piety of her later years.

Whilst nobly born ladies devoted themselves in Paris to every task of Christian charity, a young bourgeoise of Artois did not remain behind them in either self-denial or persevering goodness. The province of Artois, and its capital Arras, then belonged to the Spanish kings, in right of their descent from the celebrated dukes of Burgundy; and were accordingly the chief seat of the war between France and Spain. Here Condé and Turenne won their great victories, and fought with or against one another; and here, too, the country laid waste by the sword, pestilence, and famine—with miserable peasants flocking into the towns for refuge, sick and wounded soldiers left to die on the bare earth, and wandering widows and orphans—attested the eternal miseries of those wars, which make men famous, and win their name a place in history.

In those times, so disastrous for Artois, the inhabitants of Arras often beheld in their streets a young and handsome girl, simply attired in a black woollen robe. Ever bent on some errand of mercy, she fearlessly sought out dissolute women in their darkest haunts; and, to relieve the peasants dying on dunghills in the streets, or the sick soldiers in hospitals, she daily braved the terror of pestilence. This courageous maiden, well worthy of being named the Heroine of Charity,* was Jeanne Biscot, the youngest daughter of a wealthy and respected citizen of Arras. Jeanne was, as we have said, handsome; tall, graceful, with regular features, a transparent complexion, and an expression both fervent and serene. Being, moreover, of a rich and honorable family,

---

* Her biography has been published under this title.

she possessed all the advantages which attach the soul to the world; but her soul ever remained firmly fixed on Him to whose service she had consecrated herself so exclusively, that, in her fourteenth year, she took the vow of never marrying. From early youth unto the grave, Jeanne carried one fervent maxim in her heart—a maxim which was still more deeply impressed in her actions: "All for God."

This great love once outstripped the bounds of reason. In the village of Merville, the dreary devotion of some gloomy recluse of a past age had established a sort of living tomb close by the church. Here human beings had immured themselves of old; and here, too, Jeanne seriously contemplated retiring, in order to forget the world, and live entirely to God. This is the one weak point of her life: the one moment when judgment swerved; when the devotion of imagination prevailed over that of the heart. We have recorded it, because it is well to know the weaknesses and delusions which beset the good, even in their most earnest aspirations towards that ideal aim of all great souls, the perfecting of humanity. Humility saved Jeanne from this act of folly. She would not act without consulting two persons, in whose wisdom and piety she had great faith: a Capuchin monk and a Jesuit. Both remonstrated so forcibly with her, and condemned this project in terms so strong, that Jeanne gave it up; and, in compliance with their advice, resolved to devote herself to the active duties of Christian charity. She could do so freely: her parents, pious and charitable people, in the general sense of the words, respected the more ardent piety and less restricted charity of their youngest daughter; and her own time and their wealth were both at her disposal.

After the death of his wife, the father of Jeanne yielded to her the sole administration of his business and property, in the year 1636; and, though he knew her intention of remaining single, he gave her a dowry equal to that of her married sister. Her time was thus more restricted, but her means to do good increased, and were used to their fullest extent. Opportunity did not fail her. In that same year the chances of war caused a large number of poor German women to be thrown on the charity of Arras; and their position was the more distressing that they knew not a word of

French. Jeanne could not understand their language; but she needed not this to pity and relieve their misery. She hired a house, placed them in it, procured them every assistance, and rested not until, at the end of five months, she had put them in a way to earn their bread. In this good work, as in most of her other undertakings, she was chief, but not alone.; several pious and charitable ladies of Arras gave freely their time and money to forward her generous design: not the less praise is due to her with whom it originated.

One good deed interfered not with another. Whilst she provided for the fate of the poor German women, Jeanne, filled with concern at the large number of orphans the war had made, and especially at the peculiar dangers to which the girls were exposed, resolved to open to them a place of refuge. A house belonging to her father was devoted to that purpose, and received seven young girls. The home duties of Jeanne did not allow her to tend and instruct them herself, but she placed a respectable woman at the head of this little establishment, which filled so rapidly that the aid and superintendence of a second person soon became necessary. The house which she had thus opened to deserted orphans, received from Jeanne the pious and tender name of Holy Family.

The war had driven within the walls of Arras a great number of peasants, young and old: Some were half dead with want; others were badly wounded, or had their limbs frozen with the cold; many were afflicted with skin diseases, and lay in the streets on heaps of dung, listless and unheeded. Jeanne placed as many of the younger ones as she could in a house, attended them and dressed their wounds herself, and kept them until they were well; then, having clothed and partly instructed them, she placed them in apprenticeship, and received in their stead the older peasants, who needed longer and more attentive care: those for whom she could find no room were taken home to her father's house. In the mean while she did not forget her younger protegés. They required to be fed, and their masters had to be paid: her active zeal saw to all their wants. Many kind persons of the town agreed to give them food, if they would come and look for it when their work was over. Jeanne undertook to provide them with places to sleep in, and to get their linen washed and kept in repair.

In the year 1640, Jeanne Biscot displayed a charity not less touching, and still more heroic. Louis XIII. wished to wrest the province of Artois from Spain, who resolved to defend it vigorously. An army of German soldiers encamped beneath the walls of Arras ; and dysentery broke out amongst them, which, with want, made many victims. Every morning, those who had perished in the night were found at the gates, or beneath the walls of the town, lying as they had died, without religious consolation or human aid.

It was not in the heart of Jeanne to see such things unmoved ; and she imparted her zeal to her married sister, and several other ladies. They divided the town and its vicinity into districts, and every evening, when household tasks were over, each went forth to visit and relieve the sick soldiers belonging to the quarter she had undertaken to attend. These ladies stooped to every office : they took large pans of broth to the sick, lint and unguents to the wounded, and bundles of straw to those whose bed was the bare earth. Their labors were carried on until a late hour of the night; when they had done, they met at the house of Jeanne Biscot, and there concerted the tasks of the morrow. And all this was done cheerfully, without excess of zeal or vain-glory, after every other duty had been performed, and at an hour when few were likely to heed or praise them.

Disease made rapid progress, and Arras became a vast hospital : but neither Jeanne nor her brave companions showed signs of drawing back. They hired two houses, which they furnished, and where they placed the sick soldiers ; but, to the task of attending on them, was now added that of collecting funds, to enable them to carry on these two establishments. The times were hard, and the hearts of men were not open to the calls of charity ; but few gave, and that little was given reluctantly. The sick were badly lodged, and the sight of their sufferings grieved Jeanne to the heart. Accompanied by her friends, she went to the municipal authorities of Arras, and requested them to give her a large building formerly destined to receive poor travellers, but no longer used for this purpose. The request was granted, after many difficulties ; but no sooner was it known to the neighboring inhabitants that a hospital was going to exist in their vicinity, than they raised a great outcry, and loaded Jeanne and her friends with abuse. Jeanne bore this very patiently; but she was not to be moved from her purpose: in a few hours the place was ready, and the sick soldiers were removed to their new home. For nine months the heroic women continued their arduous labors; they attended on the sick, laid out the dead, and bore them to the grave; fearing not fatigue, danger, or the mockery of the selfish and worldly, in the performance of their self-imposed duties. Further trials awaited them: the plague broke forth in their hospital. The magistrates of Arras immediately ordered all the sick to be removed to a marshy place beyond the town, where miserable sheds had been prepared for their reception. Here they lay forsaken by all, save those whose fervent zeal no danger could cool.

Labors so great did not seem sufficiently constant to the ardent soul of Jeanne. She had lost her father, and since his death had resided in the orphan asylum she had established. After entertaining and relinquishing a project of joining the missionaries in Canada, she decided on remaining at home, and devoting herself to the children she had adopted. Her unceasing charity had considerably restricted her means; yet she resolved to consolidate what was as yet only temporary, and to perpetuate a passing good, by founding a religious community. After numerous difficulties she succeeded. Civil and ecclesiastical authority sanctioned her project, and she procured a house which had formerly belonged to a sisterhood of St. Agnes, dispersed by the troubles of the times. It opened on the 7th of December, 1645. Five ladies of Arras were the companions of Jeanne Biscot, and a few afflicted orphan girls, whom she had found in the streets, her guests. The sisters of St. Agnes, for thus they were called, took the vows of chastity, obedience, and poverty; Jeanne was their superior, and laid down the simple regulations of their institution. During the space of forty-five years, the sisters received and educated six hundred and eighty-six orphan girls, besides a great number of out-door pupils, for whose daily instruction they received no remuneration: they gave them a plain education, taught them to make lace, and kept them until they were old enough to earn their bread.

This establishment was supported by voluntary contributions, and by such trifling sums as the orphans could earn.

When Jeanne perceived the establishment of Arras to be in a prosperous condition, she resolved to open a similar one at Douay. Her sisters and adopted children, fearing lest they should lose her, earnestly begged of her to relinquish this design; but after a severe illness, in 1660, which she attributed to divine displeasure, and considered the just punishment of her lukewarmness, Jeanne could no longer be deterred from her project. She was then in her fifty-ninth year, still weak from recent illness, and exhausted by the fatigues of a life filled with good works; she had little or no money, and but few protectors: nothing, however, dismayed or deterred her. Several journeys to Douay being necessary, she took them on foot, in the depth of winter, when snow and rain had rendered the roads almost impassable. On her arrival at Douay, she first settled every thing relative to the business which had brought her; and it was sometimes one in the afternoon before she broke her fast. A younger sister who accompanied her often observed, in a tone of remonstrance, " How tired you are, mother !" " All for God, my poor child ; all for God," cheerfully replied Jeanne. The obstacles against which Jeanne had to contend at Douay, though not so great as those which had beset her in Arras, were sufficient to try her patience and her faith. There already existed in the former place a sisterhood of St. Agnes, devoted to the education of youth ; and with a jealousy of which conventual history offers but too many instances, they decried Jeanne and her attempt. They were joined by a schoolmistress, who was at the head of an establishment for female orphans, and whose office had been offered to Jeanne by the mayor of Douay. Jeanne Biscot soothed the ruffled temper of the sisters of St. Agnes, by assuring them, with equal simplicity and truth, that she could not interfere with their establishment, since she was as exclusively devoted to the children of the poor as they were to those of the rich. To the schoolmistress she said nothing, but she refused to supplant her: an instance of generosity which changed an enemy into a friend. After some other difficulties, she succeeded in opening a house at Douay. Her severest trial was to leave the sisters and children of the house of Arras; who wept bitterly as they saw her depart. She promised to come back to them some day; but events interfered and prevented her return: her time was brief, and she saw them no more.

- Jeanne was loved, not merely because she was good, but because she knew how to love. If some poor orphan, covered with rags and vermin, was brought to her, she kissed and welcomed her, with as much tenderness as a mother whose child was lost, and who rejoices because it is found. She always urged on the sisters the duty of respecting the children confided to their care. " With what inward and outward respect must we not attend on those children," she often said, " when we consider the image of Jesus behind those disfigured faces and torn garments!" Her gentleness towards her adopted children was extreme: she would never allow them to be treated with severity; she attended them in their illnesses, and mourned for their death, with so much of a mother's human love, as to excite the surprise of those around her. But love was indeed the atmosphere in which she breathed and lived: her countenance lit up when she spoke of it to her sisters, often with so much warmth and emotion as to be unable to proceed. Her faith was that of a child in its persistent simplicity. When she was seeking to establish her house at Douay, a Capuchin monk represented to her the difficulties raised by the magistrates, and declared that the project must be abandoned. " Reverend father," quietly replied Jeanne, " we will let them get over this, and pray of God to accomplish his holy will." She answered in the same spirit to all those who gave her similar advice—" God will take his own time: the business is his." Her trust was firm and boundless.

She would never receive among her orphans the children of parents in easy circumstances: no offers or entreaties could induce her to do what she averred would take the blessing of God from the house. In the same disinterested and evangelic spirit, she refused the portion which a rich young girl wanted to bring with her on entering the sisterhood. Jeanne declared that she dreaded wealth much more than poverty for her institution. A modest simplicity marked every thing in the house she governed: the chapel was almost without ornament. " It will be more agreeable to God," she said,

" if we nourish and preserve his living temples—human creatures—than if we spend to adorn this, his material temple."
She was extremely sparing in those expenses that only related
to herself, but would never allow the sisters or the children
to want for any thing. " When all our money is gone," she
cheerfully remarked, " we shall pledge or sell what we have :
ay, even to our chalice ; and then I shall bless God." She
kept no accounts of receipt or expense ; and a wooden bowl
held all the money of the house : there she placed whatever
she received, and thence she took forth whatever she needed.
Providence seemed to justify her trust : whilst she lived, that
bowl was never found empty. The care of two establishments could not absorb the zeal and charity of Jeanne Biscot : she reclaimed dissolute women from vice, and relieved
the sufferings of the poor. In the year 1654, after the siege
of Arras by Condé, she once more gave an example of that
heroic charity which she had displayed in 1636 and 1640.
Again, but assisted this time by her sisters, she attended the
sick soldiers, and laid out and buried the dead. The fervor
of the sisters of St. Agnes equalled that of their mother,
Jeanne, who led them to toil and danger with her favorite
and noble watchword, well worthy of a true servant of Christ
—" All for God."

Exhausted by so many labors, little suited to her naturally
delicate health, Jeanne became infirm before her time, and
fell into a languishing state. On her death-bed she recommended three things to her sisters : " To fulfil her intentions ;
never to abandon charity towards the poor ; and to live in
peace and unity." She then gave them her blessing, and
bade them farewell. They asked where she would like to be
buried. " No matter where ; in the parish," she calmly answered. The superior of the house of Arras being present,
ventured to observe : " Mother, we should like to have you at
Arras with us." " Where you like," replied Jeanne : these
were her last words. Her spirit passed away so gently that
her death was scarcely perceived. She died on the 27th of
June, 1664, in the sixty-third year of her age. The useful
establishment which she founded still exists in her native city,
under the name of the House of St. Agnes. Of all the charitable women of France in that age, Jeanne Biscot is one of
the least known, though surely not one of the least eminent.

We have passed over in silence, though not without regret, the names of Marie-Angélique Arnauld, Catherine her sister, Angélique her niece; of Jacqueline, worthy sister of the illustrious Pascal, and other ladies of the Port-Royal. There is something truly impressive in the austere and energetic character of these gifted women; but to speak of them properly, it would be necessary to enter into the narrative of a tedious and now well-nigh forgotten controversy. We have not undertaken a history of opinions, but one of actions; and we could not mention the Port-Royal ladies without also mentioning the other women who, before that time or since, have taken an active share in religious quarrels: which Heaven forbid!

One of the fathers said of the early Christians, "They knew not how to dispute, but they knew how to die." In the same spirit we may say of the women whose names are recorded in these pages—"They are not mentioned here for their learning in theology or their skill in discussion. They practised the Gospel in the simplicity of their hearts. They might have been found weak in controversy, but none can say that they knew not how to live."

CHAPTER XV.

Magdalen of Pazzi—Helena Cornaro—Elizabeth of Bohemia—The Empress Eleanor.

The ascetic and yet practical spirit of the religious portion of the seventeenth century was not less characteristically displayed in other Christian lands. St. Magdalen of Pazzi, a native of Florence, and a relative of the Medici, was, in the fervor of her devotion, another St. Teresa, whose order she embraced. Her life was spent in the obscurity of a Carmelite cloister; but her last words deserve to be recorded: "I leave this world," she said, "without ever having been able to understand how it is possible that a creature should consent to offend God, and to commit a single sin against its Creator."

The self-imposed sacrifice of Helena Cornaro is likewise worthy of mention. This learned lady, daughter of a procurator of St. Mark, was born in Venice, in the year 1646. She died in 1684, at the age of thirty-eight, and was held to be a prodigy of learning and virtue. Besides her own language, she knew Spanish, French, Latin, Greek, ancient and modern, Hebrew, and the Arabic languages. She sang and played exquisitely, and could speak with judgment and eloquence on philosophy, mathematics, astronomy, music, and theology. But this singular amount of learning could not impair her natural modesty. She was devout, and in principle shunned distinctions flattering to her vanity. She consecrated herself to God in her youth; when her parents wished her to marry, she told them of her vow. They obtained a dispensation from the pope, and showed it to her; she fainted on seeing it, but refused to avail herself of her liberty. Indeed, all her parents could obtain from her was, that she should remain in their house, where she led the life of a recluse. To gratify their parental pride, she reluctantly consented to leave her retirement and appear in the university of Padua, where she received the degrees. In the acts of the university occurs the following entry: "We, sitting in the tribunal of the university of Padua, acknowledge that the noble maiden Helena-Lucretia-Cornaro is so well versed in sciences and belles-lettres as to deserve a place amongst the doctors of this university; and for this do we receive her mistress of liberal arts, and acknowledge her as such, in the name of the Father, the Son, and the Holy Ghost. Done at Padua, on the 25th of June of the year 1678, in the cathedral church of the same city, because the halls of the college could not hold the vast concourse of persons present." It is said that, but for the opposition of the archbishop of Padua, the dignity of doctor of divinity would likewise have been conferred on Helena Cornaro.

This illustrious Venetian is a striking but not solitary instance of a noble and gifted mind early consecrated to God. Elizabeth of England, queen of Bohemia, celebrated for her romantic adventures and misfortunes, had three daughters—Sophia, ancestress of the royal family of England; Louisa, eminent for her skill in painting, and who became abbess of the Catholic convent of Maubuisson in France; and Eliza-

beth, who was likewise abbess, but of the German and
Protestant community of Herworden. Elizabeth was grave
and learned. Her grandmother Juliana, by whom she had
been brought up, had given her some of her own seriousness
and asceticism. The misfortunes of her family, the death of
her father, and of her elder brother, Henry Frederick, saddened her youth. She rejoiced when the alliances proposed
for her failed, and did not conceal that a solitary life was the
object of her ambition. She distinguished herself as abbess
of Herworden, by the rare virtue of tolerance on religious
opinions. She was the friend and disciple of Descartes; who
dedicated one of his works to her, and declared that of all his
readers she understood him best. William Penn visited her,
and was favorably impressed by her religious feelings. Piety,
good deeds, and science, filled her life; which closed in 1680,
in the sixty-first year of her age.

Three years before this, a princess, by no means so learned
as Elizabeth, but more ardent, though not more sincere, in
her piety, had become empress of Germany. It was on the
13th of December of the year 1677, that the Emperor
Leopold I. of Austria solemnly espoused, as his second wife,
Eleanor, daughter of the Duke of Neubourg. Leopold was
then near forty, his bride was scarcely twenty-two. Eleanor
had no claim to beauty; but she was a fine girl, with a cheerful, animated face, a generous heart, an ardent and passionate
temper, unbroken health, and nerves of iron. She could
carry weights from which men shrank; and walked at a pace
that left delicate court ladies far behind. Her spirit was
prompt and energetic; it ever rose equal to her sorrows and
calamities, and these were great. No shock could affect her
courage: a thunderbolt once fell on the table at which she
sat, and she remained undaunted and unmoved.

In person and temper Leopold nowise resembled the high-
spirited girl he had taken to wife: he was a mild, pusillani-
mous little man, of insignificant aspect. He had indeed
inherited the grave mien and projecting nether lip which the
daughter of Charles the Bold brought into the house of
Austria; but he lacked the fiery and magnificent spirit of his
Burgundian ancestors. A flowing peruke, black garments,
with a scarlet plume to his hat, and scarlet stockings, were
his invariable attire; but neither costume, nor all the formal-

ity of Spanish etiquette, to which he rigidly adhered, could give him the dignity of imperial rank. His subjects loved and admired him very little; and history has not much to say of him: save that he was good-natured and conscientious, but without either talent or courage; that in foreign policy he was baffled by Louis XIV.; that at home he knew not how to stand and fall with his people; that he fled to Linz in dismay when Vienna was besieged by the Turks, and left his capital to be delivered by John Sobieski, the brave king of Poland. In two points only—charity to the poor and piety to God—did Leopold resemble his bride: but there was a passion and enthusiasm in her religion, which never discomposed the devotion of the apathetic emperor. Eleanor had been reared in a convent of barefooted Carmelite nuns, who followed the austere rule reformed by St. Teresa; and the ardent faith of the patroness of the place seemed to have come down to the young princess. Her governess, and the other women appointed to watch over her, missed her one day; for some time they looked for her in vain; at length they found her kneeling, and all in tears, at the foot of a crucifix. They asked to know the cause of her weeping, and the child replied: "I weep because I see my Saviour naked and bleeding, whilst I behold myself magnificently clad, and nursed in luxury and delight."

The education which Eleanor received in the convent was strictly classical; and she learned to mingle something of the stoical severity of heathen times with Christian tenderness: she was harsh to herself, gentle to others. When she returned to her father's palace, and could obtain the permission of her mother, the duchess—a cold, hard woman, who ever treated her with formal severity—she spent all her leisure and money in visiting and relieving the sick and the poor: the most wretched were those whom she loved best. "We are all Christians," she would say: "all redeemed by the blood of Jesus Christ; and if we live well, shall not the same heaven receive us?" She loved to mingle on earth with those whom she hoped to meet, in the presence of God. Closely veiled, and followed by a solitary servant, she would steal out and visit some church of the city, merely to be able to kneel, unknown and unheeded, with the crowd of worshippers. Of all the formal amusements of her father's

9*

court, but one, the chase, had the power to charm Eleanor: she delighted, not without lingering scruples, in riding fearless and foremost in a gallant train of hunters and noble ladies; but plays and every thing of the sort she held in utter horror. The stately pageantry of rank allured her not; and the news that her sovereign had chosen her to share his throne filled her with dismay. She had set her heart on becoming a barefooted Carmelite: the brown gown of St. Teresa's nuns was more precious in her sight than the robes of an empress. With a touch of worldly feeling, which by no means takes away from her sincerity, she also reflected that the wife of Leopold could no longer follow the chase on horseback, but must ride in a state-carriage. Unable to think of any other expedient by which to break off the marriage, she resolutely exposed herself to the ardent heat of a summer noonday sun; hoping to acquire such a complexion as might unfit her for an imperial bride. The experiment failed: Eleanor neither got a brain fever, nor injured the bloom of her cheek; she submitted to her destiny, and became empress of Austria.

The marriage, thus reluctantly entered upon, proved singularly happy. Eleanor placed her whole study in rendering herself agreeable to her husband; in obeying him even in things most repugnant to her, and in sacrificing her own inclination to his. He esteemed and loved her greatly: it was to her that he intrusted the task of translating the cipher dispatches of his foreign ambassadors; and she devoted whole nights to this labor. "God," he would often say, "gave me this holy wife to console me through the unhappy years of my reign." If Eleanor could have imparted to her husband some of her own courageous spirit, it would have been well for him: but she had made it her rule and duty to obey, not to advise.

They had been married six years, when Vienna underwent her memorable siege. Alarmed at the news of the approach of the Turks, Leopold fled with his wife and children: they left Vienna in the evening, by stealth; and took their way to Linz, protected by the Danube. Such was the haste and terror of their flight, that they were compelled to spend the first night in a peasant's hut. Eleanor, though far advanced in pregnancy, maintained an undaunted and cheerful bearing. Her husband left her at Linz; and on the day of his departure she gave birth to a daughter; whom, with the stoic self-denial of her character, she would neither see nor embrace until he returned, several weeks later, with the tidings that the empire was saved.

On the 12th of June, 1683, an army of two hundred thousand Turks, headed by the ambitious and warlike grand vizier, Kara Mustapha, had crossed the bridge of Esseck. Pillaging villages, and leading away women and children into captivity on their way, they had advanced unresisted, until they reached the walls of deserted Vienna. For well-nigh two months, the besieged citizens withstood the assaults, springing of mines, and cannonading of their fierce enemy. As they began to despair of succor, and thought themselves abandoned to their fate, the Christian army, led by John Sobieski, appeared on the brow of the Kalen hill. On the 12th of September the battle was fought: it was brief, but decisive. Two hundred thousand Turks were routed by forty thousand Christians. The timely aid of the brave Polish king had saved the city.

Before a hundred years had elapsed from the triumphant day when Turkish hordes fled in dismay, leaving beneath the walls of Vienna their camp, gardens, tents, arms, standards, baths, rare animals, and countless luxuries—when the delivered citizens hailed Sobieski with tears and acclamations; when Te Deums were sung in the old cathedral of St. Stephen, and every eye turned on John III. of Poland, as the priest read at the altar, "There was a man sent from God whose name was John"—a grand-daughter of Leopold and Eleanor helped to subdue and divide the brave nation, the bulwark of Christendom, whose king had saved the throne of her ancestors, and the very walls of the city where she reigned.

The love of Eleanor for her husband originally sprang from duty, but time gave it the depth and tenderness of heartfelt passion. Its force was well proved during the tedious illness which closed the life of Leopold in 1705. She remained in his room to the last, a devoted and un-wearied nurse: jealous in her affection, she would let no hand save her own touch or serve him. Fatigue brought on erysipelas and sciatica, but she would never once undress in order to take a more refreshing rest than the two hours' slumber she allowed herself at night. She knew her sorrow to be useless to him whom she loved, and she stoically suppressed every sign of grief : when his last agony began, she upheld his dying head. He expired on the kind heart where, in trouble or disease, he had ever found consolation and repose. When all was over, Eleanor rose, kissed the cold hands of her husband, retired to the next room, and, for the first time in her life, gave way to a passionate sorrow that would not be controlled.

This grief was long and touching. What though he—loss of whom inspired it—was weak and commonplace : love is not always to be judged by the object loved. Its beauty and holiness lie in the hearts that feel it ; and the widowed empress had loved her husband with the mingled tenderness and passion of her nature. She wore mourning for him the whole of her lifetime, and never heard his name mentioned but her eyes filled with tears. For two years she daily prayed two hours for the repose of his soul. The entreaties of her doctor and confessor induced her to relinquish this practice ; but she did so on condition that, as the hour which had seen Leopold expire returned, one of her attendants should come and whisper in her ear, " This is the time when your husband died." It was not that she feared forgetting one whose memory was ever in her thoughts ; but, with the fond superstition of the heart, she could not endure to spend in mirth, or at least in momentary oblivion, the moment that had divided them on earth.

Though good and charitable during her husband's lifetime, it was chiefly after his death that Eleanor became that without which her name would not be mentioned here—the mother of the poor. If ever woman deserved that title, it was the widowed Empress of Austria. Several hours a day were devoted to prayer ; the rest of her time belonged to the poor. In purses hanging from her girdle, she carried about with her various articles of work for them, and in one or another of which she was perpetually engaged. She worked alone in her room, in the presence of company, out walking, in going to church or in coming back : not a moment was lost ; her hands at length became coarse and hard, like those of a common work-woman, with this constant toil. The meanest and poorest had free access to her person; and they found her patient of hearing, and liberal in her gifts. But there is no good without its attendant evil. Every time Eleanor left the palace she was surrounded by a host of importunate mendicants, who allowed her not one moment's peace; they pressed around her, pulled her garments, and almost snatched the alms out of her hands; but the good empress remained calm and gentle in the midst of her unruly children. Sometimes, indeed, she left the palace by stealth, without her usual suite; and, conscious of her weakness, without money: but she was soon recognized and beset; and then, unable to resist the pleadings of her kind heart, she would borrow money to give away to the miserable objects around her. Impostors often mingled with the real poor: she knew it, yet could not find it in her heart to punish all for the sins of a few. "Alas!" she said to those who remonstrated with her, "I cannot know the real poor from the false; but God can, and He lets His sun shine alike on the wicked and on the just."

Eleanor by no means confined her charity to this public and indiscriminate almsgiving. Almost the whole of her ample revenues went privately to the poor of every rank, sect, or nation. She kept a secret list of those whom decent pride would not allow to beg; and not until after her death did they know the kind hand which had paid their debts, sent gifts often amounting to several thousand florins, or procured the government office that had suddenly placed them beyond want. This was not all: girls, young and poor, were portioned and saved from ruin; the sick in the hospitals, the guilty in the prisons, received her bounty. Her alms extended to Constantinople, and penetrated into the depths of Palestine and Syria, where they reached poor Christians, captives in the land of their redemption.

To effect all this there was but one way—self-denial. The luxuries, and many of the comforts of life, were strictly relinquished by Eleanor; her apartment was simple—almost bare; her garments were of the coarsest cloth; she pieced and mended them with her own hands, and never discarded them until thoroughly worn out. On state days she wore a

few jewels of great value, which she had kept merely to
serve as tokens of her rank. When her conduct was censured, as it often was, Eleanor calmly replied, " This is
strange. If I, were richly clad, if I spent large sums on
pleasures, luxuries, and things of price, no one would have a
word to say against it. Why then should I be reproached
with my charities, the fruits of my savings, often of the work
of mine own hands ? They are my delight, my pleasure, my
jewels." In urgent cases, when her own resources were
exhausted, the empress applied to her son Joseph I. ; and
when able to do so, he granted her large sums, saying, that
such expenses impoverished not the imperial treasury : but
this was the exception, not the rule. Her own revenues
were the only certain source whence flowed her extensive
charities. Her steward, through whose hands the greater
portion of the money passed for twenty years, could not help
frequently expressing his wonder that any income should resist expenses seemingly boundless ; yet, when the empress
died, contrary to his expectation and that of the whole court,
she left not one debt behind her.

Eleanor was naturally generous : to give was to her a
pleasure. But she was not naturally gentle; her temper
was impatient and passionate ; yet she subdued it down to
a mild patience that seemed without limit. Her usual court
was a set of unfortunate and needy applicants, who solicited
her aid or interference ; and not one of whom was dismissed
unheard : she read their endless petitions and memorials,
pouring in upon her day after day, and submitted them to
her son whenever they seemed worthy of his attention. The
ministers grumbled, and often thwarted her requests : her
majesty's demands, they said, were without end : she wanted to please everybody, and her imprudent charity was sufficient to exhaust the treasury. They went so far as to hint
that she lessened the dignity of her rank by thus exposing
herself to the chance of a refusal. " I know my duty," she
answered ; " do yours. God, who sees my heart, will at
least accept my will to do well."

The empress was often deceived and imposed upon ; but
she was at least kind without weakness: if she could not
grant a request, she said so at once. Some peasants from
Bohemia came to Vienna to complain of an officer, whom

they accused of harshness. Eleanor ascertained that their complaint was not justified. She was going to sit down to dinner, but would not eat until she had sent them word that she could give them no aid; but to soften the disappointment, she paid their expenses home. When the cause was just, nothing could exceed her zeal. Oppressed widows and orphans applied to her as to their natural advocate: she gave them advice, protection, and carried them triumphantly through every difficulty. But at length it came to pass that the burden grew too heavy: Eleanor no longer found it possible to read and answer the innumerable petitions which her well-known goodness caused to be addressed to her. Two officers of the household accepted the task, and were soon heartily sorry for having done so: their houses, they said, were like hospitals; petitioners filled their staircases day and night. They could scarcely eat or sleep in peace; and yet they satisfied no one: noise, murmuring, and often insult, were the rewards they reaped. They therefore besought her majesty not to be displeased if they relinquished so unpleasant an office. Eleanor endeavored to dissuade them from doing so: she spoke eloquently of the merit they might acquire in the sight of God by perseverance; but seeing that they remained unconvinced, she bowed her head, and meekly said: "Be it so. If the daytime is insufficient to the labor, I will gladly devote to it part of the night: it will only be a little sleep lost." On hearing her speak so, both officers, touched to the heart, withdrew their refusal; and, though with deep reluctance, resumed their wearisome duty.

Eleanor was a kind mistress, and in her household she was loved and respected, from her maids of honor, whom she treated as her own daughters, down to the meanest servants: they found her punctual and liberal; her economy was never at their expense; far from it: when she knew the salary of some to be insufficient to the wants of a large family, she added to it privately; in order to spare their pride, and to create no feelings of envy in their companions. When they were ill she visited them, cheered them with pleasant discourse, and served them with her own hands. To tend the sick, especially the poor, was one of the most heartfelt pleasures of the good empress: she visited the hospitals of Vienna with her daughters and ladies. After the exertion of a few hours, they were obliged to sit down and rest; but she went about as light and active as ever, carrying burdens of thirty or forty pounds' weight. All the hospitals on her way to Neustadt, Baden, and Eisenstadt, were equally familiar to her. She visited the poorest cottages, and, apart from the gifts she left behind her, rendered her visits pleasant to the inmates by her never-failing cheerfulness and kindness of heart.

It was thus, filling her life with good deeds, that Eleanor progressed towards the grave. She had a consciousness of her approaching end; being asked to pray that her son might have an heir, she replied: " I have a long journey to prepare for." In the year preceding her death, a young girl of modest and engaging aspect asked to be admitted into her household. The empress looked at her attentively: " Verily," she said, " this young girl pleases me much; but, my child," she added, after a pause, " I cannot comply with your wish. I will not deceive you by granting that which you should relinquish at my death; it will happen shortly." The empress then seemed in perfect health. The ladies who heard her speak thus began to weep. She chid them gently: " What!" she said, " you weep! Should you not rather rejoice with me, since after so many storms I touch the port." She gave other intimations of the same feeling to some nuns whom she loved: on leaving their convent for Vienna, she bade them a last farewell, kissed them every one, and told them they should see her no more, as Leopold was calling her to heaven. " My sixty-fifth birth-day will be my last," she said on another occasion.

Eleanor spoke but too truly. She was born on the sixth of January, of the year 1655; and on the first day of the year 1720 she was found lying in her room wholly unconscious. She never recovered the use of speech, and died January 19th, after silently blessing her family. The news of her illness filled the churches of Vienna with supplicants, praying, as they said, for their mother. Her funeral was extremely plain: she had expressly directed in her will that her body should neither be stripped nor embalmed. It was, according to an ancient custom, robed in white garments and exposed for three days to public veneration; then, in obedience to her wish, placed in a coffin of wood, with this epitaph of her own framing : " Here lies Eleanor Magdalen Teresa, a poor sinner."

We have little more to say of this good woman : for good she was, spite of some faults of judgment. We have not shocked the reader with her penance, hair shirts, and iron chains—austerities in which, spite of her religious advisers, she indulged to excess. She said that her passions were strong and fierce, and needed to be so used. Her temper was certainly violent, but she kept it under exact control : even when the eye kindled, and the cheek flushed, the lips uttered no ungentle word. There was a tone of exaggeration in her whole character ; but it was sincere, and led to much that was noble. Her soul was magnanimous : she hated flatterers and flattery, and freely forgave injuries. On the death of her son Joseph, she became regent for a while. Here was an opportunity of punishing those who had ventured, even in her presence, to call her humility meanness, and to say " that her piety consisted in showing herself in the streets and churches of Vienna." Eleanor disdained to take advantage of her power, and said quietly to her ladies : " I care not for those little things." She did well to be indifferent to the opinion of her contemporaries, for it was not always favorable to her ; as we can learn, from the little touch of ridicule with which she is mentioned by gay Lady Mary Wortley Montagu : " I had an audience next day of the empress mother, a princess of great virtue and goodness, but who piques herself too much on a violent devotion. She is perpetually performing extraordinary acts of penance, without ever having done any thing to deserve them." Of her boundless charity Lady Montagu does not speak, and probably did not know. The humility of Eleanor led her to conceal her best actions, and often, too, her best feelings. After her death, the following written prayer was found amongst her papers : "The only boon I ask of thee, oh my God ! is to use me wholly for the service of the poor of Jesus Christ. Let thy love towards us, miserable mortals, be the rule of our charity."

She was faithful to this self-imposed teaching : her mercy, like that of her divine model, was infinite. She once caught a thief in the act of stealing a silver lamp from a church, where she had gone early one morning to clean the sacred vases—a task dear to her pious heart. On seeing her, he let

the lamp fall, and the oil was spilled on the pavement.
"Poor wretch," she cried, "escape quickly." The oil betrayed what had happened, but the empress would never
give the least indication concerning the sacrilegious thief.
We have already said enough of her tenderness to the poor.
Her early inclination had been towards the cloister: when
she became a widow, the temptation of a calm and happy
retreat amongst the daughters of her beloved St. Teresa was
great. She sacrificed it to the good she knew she might do
in the world: a mother forsakes not her children; and she
remained with hers, watchful and tender to the last. In her
apartment there was found an unfinished garment destined
for some poor person. Death had interrupted the task, and
compelled her to leave behind this eloquent though involun-
tary memorial of her own goodness.

CHAPTER XVI.

The Women of England during the Seventeenth Century—Lady Alice
Lucy—Lady Falkland—Lady Vere—Lady Langham—Lady Armyne
—The Countess of Pembroke.

FREQUENTLY, whilst collecting materials for this work, have
I had cause to regret that the lives of the good have been so
briefly and imperfectly written, whilst of the profligate or
notorious more than enough was known. This remark applies especially to the women of England during the seventeenth century.

Mrs. Hutchinson and Lady Fanshawe wrote their own memoirs; Lady Rachel Russel is known by her letters; and
Evelyn has recorded the virtues of his attached friend, Mrs.
Godolphin: but these are exceptions. Whilst we learn more
than is needful of the mistresses and favorites of a licentious
king, funeral sermons are almost the only authorities that
give us an imperfect knowledge of purer characters.

There are three lives extant of Madame de Chantal; the
Abbé de Choisy has left a good biography of his cousin,
Madame de Miramion; and even humble Jeanne Biscot has

found her historian. Their English contemporaries have been less fortunate : their memory has been dismissed with vague and commonplace eulogy, and, beyond the fact that they were good, we know little or nothing of many save the names which they bore.

These imperfect records afford us, however, glimpses of many gentle and charming natures, for which we might vainly seek elsewhere. Every one has heard of Charlecote Hall, celebrated for once belonging to that Sir Thomas Lucy, who punished young Shakspeare for deer-stealing. Many have made the old Elizabethan mansion the goal of a poetical pilgrimage : amongst the rest Geoffrey Crayon, who has lingered with evident partiality in his description of a spot still haunted by the name of Shakspeare. The gateway flanked with towers, the courtyard and its flower-beds, the portal with carved armorial bearings, the ancient park, the Avon winding through, with "large herds of deer feeding or reposing upon its borders, and swans sailing majestically upon its bosom," were held objects of interest, and worthy of record.

The old mansion has faithfully preserved the memory of the poet and of his persecutor ; but it has found nothing to tell concerning one of its former mistresses, a good and charitable lady, Alice Lucy, who dwelt within its walls some two hundred years ago. "A great number," writes her quaint old biographer, "she relieved at her gates, and gave her charge to her porter, that when there came any that were very aged, or that complained of great losses in those dismal times of civil wars, especially if they seemed honest, that he should come and certify her of it, that she might enlarge her charity to such ; which if he had neglected at any time to do, and she had known of it, probably she would have been as much displeased with him as once she was with another of her servants for neglecting a command which she had given him, in reference to the refreshment of some poor. '

" In those times of scarcity, every week she sent many loaves of bread to many neighbor towns ; she caused her own corn to be sold in the markets, as it were, by retail, in such small quantities as might not exceed the poor's abilities to purchase. She allowed certain meals in her house to certain poor neighbors, whose empty bellies were discernible in their

pale faces; and when hereby they had recovered their former complexion, and received, as it were, a new life by her
means, she with joy professed that the sight of such an alteration in them did her as much good as any thing which she
herself had eaten. .

"She continually employed many poor old men and women in such works as were fit and suitable to their skill and
strength. When the physician came at any time to her
house, she used to make inquiry whether any were sick in
the town, that if any were, they might partake of the same
benefit with herself; but at all times, when any wanted
health, she presently had intelligence of it, and most cheerfully communicated whatsoever she conceived conducible to
their recovery, having not only great store of cordials and re-
storatives always by her, but great skill and judgment in the
application of them."

Thus far, and no more, are we told : the good deeds of the
charitable lady of Charlecote Hall have won her no place
among the celebrated of her sex.   With the humility of true
virtue, she strictly forbade any eulogy to be inscribed on the
stately monument which she had erected to the memory of
her husband, by whose side she was laid, in the year 1648:
Her age is not mentioned ; but she had been thirty years a
wife, and some years a widow.   She died after a fortnight's
illness: her health had always been bad ; but she was of
those whom a generous spirit leads onwards, who need not
health or strength to fulfil the active duties of life.

The charity extended by Lady Alice Lucy to the poor suf-
ferers of those long civil wars which distracted England, was
freely exercised by another generous woman of those times—
the widow of Falkland.   The interest which attaches to this
excellent lady is still further heightened by that which lingers around the name of her husband.

The gloom of civil war was already spreading over the
land : king and Parliament were at issue, Royalist and Puritan, each prepared for the approaching contest, when Lucius
Cary, Viscount Falkland, took his seat in that celebrated assembly which met on the third of November, of the year
1640 ; and which, under the name of the Long Parliament,
was destined to act so important a part in English history.

Viscount Falkland was then in his thirtieth year.   His con-

temporaries have united 'in representing him as one of the
most amiable and accomplished men of the age in which he
lived. Loyalty induced him to side with the king; but he
shared neither the errors nor the hopes of the court party.
Though he fought bravely in the royal ranks, the woes of his
country were not forgotten in the excitement of war. After
sitting among his friends in long dejected silence, he would
often exclaim, with deep sighs, "Peace, peace!" and passionately declare, "that the very agony of the war, and the view
of the calamities and desolation of the kingdom did and must
endure, took his sleep from him, and would shortly break his
heart." He was not to die thus: on the morning of the battle of Newbury he had a strong presentiment of his death; it
was fulfilled: he fell among the first, and thus accomplished
his brief and pure career. A gentleman, a poet, a scholar,
above all, a man of high principle and chivalrous honor, he
needed but what fate gave him—a premature and glorious
death—to possess all the attributes of a hero of romance.

Viscount Falkland perished in his thirty-fourth year; he
left several children and a young widow—the Lady Lettice
Morison, whom he had not married for either rank or wealth,
but for the singular virtues which he perceived in her. They
were devotedly attached to one another, and in the bitterness
of her grief for the loss of her husband, which was followed
by that of a beloved son, Viscountess Falkland warned young
wives and mothers not to place too much of their affection in
earthly beings. "Oh! I have had my portion of these very
comforts with the first—no one woman more," she sadly exclaimed; "but there is no lasting, no true pleasure in them."
Such language from one who had been a loved and happy
wife, and who was still a happy mother, sounds harsh; but
they who know the exquisite sorrow of losing objects too
much loved, have a right to speak thus: warnings like these
come from the heart that has overflowed, rarely from the indifferent and the cold; who offer not to others the advice
which they themselves have never needed.

The whole life of this amiable woman shows how far removed she was from indifference or religious severity. From
her youth, she united the piety that worships to the charity
that loves to bestow. She often importuned her parents for
money to put in the purse she had worked for her own alms:

she was eager to have it full, and still more eager to empty it
quickly. Her will to do good kept pace with her means:
whilst her husband drew to his seat at Great Tew, near Oxford, the learned and literary men of the neighboring university, the viscountess fed and clothed the poor under his roof
and at his gates.

"For the poor at home, and for strangers at the door,"
writes her friend, the Reverend John Duncan, in a letter addressed to her mother, "she was very charitable, in feeding
the hungry and refreshing the faint and weak, and for clothing the naked: in some extremities you should see this lady
herself go up and down the house, and beg garments from
her servants' backs (whom she requited soon after with new),
that the poor might not go naked or cold from her door. . . . .
When it was objected that many idle and wicked people
were, by this course of charity, relieved at her house, her answer was, 'I know not their hearts, and in their outward carriage and speech they all appear to me good and virtuous;
and I had rather relieve five unworthy vagrants, than that one
member of Christ should go empty away.' And for harbor-
ing strangers, the many inconveniences ordinarily ensuing
upon it could not deter her from it: sometimes for some
weeks together they were entertained by her. And since
her death I hear of plentiful relief, here at London and at
Oxford, sent privately to prisons and needy persons, with a
strict charge that it should not be known from whence it
came."

Her charity extended beyond this: many of her poorer
neighbors, too old or too young to labor, were wholly supported by her. She erected a school, where poor children
were taught to read and work. She was anxious that no
man, woman, or child near her should want employment;
and, regarding more the benefit of others than her own private interest, she held that to be the best management of her
estate which provided most labor for the poor. Infectious
diseases were then one of the scourges of England; she provided herself with antidotes, cordials, and various medicines,
which she distributed gratuitously on her estate. Though
well versed, like most ladies of her age, in leechcraft, Lady
Falkland was cautious in exercising her skill. As soon as
she learned that any of her poor neighbors were sick, she pro-

vided them with nurses and physicians, and visited them day
after day. She loved to sit in their homely cottages, to become as one of them, and read to them from those volumes
whose pious lore had so often soothed her own bodily sufferings and heart sorrows. "This honorable lady," observes
the writer already quoted, "hath been observed sitting in a
cottage waiting the sick woman's leisure, till the slumbers and
fits were over, that she might read again to her, and finish
the work she had begun. And of late, when she could not
do this good office in her own person (she growing sickly and
weak), yet she would do it still by proxy; for some of her
friends or servants were deputed by her to go to the sick,
with her books too daily, and now and then most of her family—who were fit for such an employment—were sent abroad
on this errand." Life and health were already failing; but
not so her earnest desire to do good. Hitherto she had bestowed only the superfluity of her revenue, and now this superfluity was all which she kept for herself; the rest she gave
away. Extreme simplicity marked her attire after the death
of her husband, and her household expenses were moderate:
she preferred feeding the poor, and educating their children,
to the idle satisfaction of being attended by pages and gentlewomen. Her mind, decisive and practical, led her to cher-
ish projects of general utility; she intended establishing in
her parish, schools and manufactures. A still more cherished
and congenial plan, was that of founding places of education
for young gentlewomen, and of retirement for widows, in several parts of the kingdom; hoping that religion and learning
might thus flourish more in her own sex. The troubled state
of the times, and the brevity of her life, prevented these plans
from being carried into effect. Grief, great in spite of all her
resignation, and a religious melancholy, which her life of active piety could not always allay, clouded her latter days.
Wearied of this world, and of all that bound her to it, she
contemplated retiring to a small house and garden close by
her mansion, and thought there to spend her time with a book,
a wheel, and a maid or two. Death early relieved her from
a life which had become painfully wearisome: she survived
her husband a few years, and died in the thirty-fifth year of
her age. The melancholy of Lady Falkland was most probably a disease; her natural temper appears to have been both

firm and ardent : she was born passionate, and the meekness which charmed all who approached her had cost her many a severe struggle. Not satisfied with requesting her servants to forgive her the sharp words which occasionally escaped her, she often asked for the same forgiveness when she had manifested no anger outwardly. She explained this to them with Christian simplicity : "Somewhat I felt within myself too like anger against you, though I suppressed it as soon as I could." Her love of peace was great ; she valued it the more highly that she had found it so difficult to acquire. She suffered herself to be defrauded sooner than she would allow an unwilling debtor to be prosecuted : "Peace," she said, "is equivalent to the sum detained." She not only valued it for herself, but strenuously endeavored to establish it among others. A contention arose amongst her neighbors concerning the choice of a parish officer ; she restored quietness by hiring one at her own expense. But this prudent gentleness never interfered with matters of principle : she firmly refused to contribute to the support of the Parliament forces ; and allowed her property to be seized, until the king himself granted an indulgence to the oppressed members of his party. Another anecdote illustrative of her delicacy and conscientiousness has been preserved. In her absence from home the sutlers of the army came to her house, and took away provisions, paying the highest price. On returning, Lady Falkland found that they had given her servant too much ; she anxiously caused them to be searched for throughout the whole army, and did not rest satisfied until the overplus amount was restored to them.

A last trait, far more worthy of her and of her noble disposition, will suffice. Learning once that the royal army had made many prisoners who were in a state of great need, she consulted with a friend what means she should adopt to relieve them. "Do you not fear," was the answer, "that such an act will, in the minds of many, raise doubts concerning your loyalty to his majesty ?" With the mingled pride and humility of her character, the widow of Falkland unhesitatingly replied : "No man will suspect my loyalty because I relieve these prisoners, who would not also suspect my Christianity if he should see me relieve a needy Turk or Jew. However, I had rather be misunderstood—if this my secret alms should be known—than that any of mine enemies—the worst of them—should perish for want of my aid."

In those trying times also lived the Lady Mary Vere, under whose care the Parliament placed the younger children of Charles I. She was twice married : to Mr. Hobby, by whom she had two sons; and to Sir Horace Vere, whom she survived. She was of the family of the Tracies, in Gloucestershire, where she was born, in 1581. She died in 1671, at the age of ninety. A firm faith in God was the groundwork of this lady's character. She lost her two sons; one at fourteen, the other at twenty-three; and she survived her second husband thirty-six years. Many trials saddened her long life ; but her trust was never shaken : she chose and kept as her motto, which was found written by her in the front of most of the books in her closet, " God will provide." God did provide, and carried her safely through those stormy times.

Unhappiness in married life was not amongst the troubles of Lady Vere : her second husband, the gallant Sir Horace Vere, was worthy of her. In the year 1628 we find Archbishop Usher writing to the Lady Mary : "The thing that I have most admired in your noble lord, is, that such lowliness of mind, and such a high pitch of a brave spirit, should be yoked together, and lodged in one breast. And, on the other side, when I reflect upon you, methinks I understand that saying of the apostle better than I did, ' that as the man is the image and glory of God, so the woman is the glory of the man.' And, to your comfort, let me add this, that if I have any insight in things of this nature, or have any judgment to discern of spirits, I have clearly beheld engraven in your soul, *the image and superscription of my God.*"

" Her charity," writes W. Gurnall, "was as fruit dropping all the year long." The poor, the hungry, the sick, the wounded, received money, food, medicines, or salves, according to their wants. Her servants had orders to acquaint her with cases of distress ; and if they failed in this duty, the anger of Lady Vere was great. " It fell out," writes her biographer, "that an honest, poor neighbor died before she knew of his sickness; for which, being troubled, she asked her servant that attended her whether he had wanted in his sickness : adding, " I tell you I had rather part with my gown from my back, than that the poor should want !"

10

But there was no ostentation in this goodness: Lady Vere always thought that she had done nothing. "She did not give her charity, as some throw their money into a basin at a collection, so as that it might ring again; but it fell like oil into a vessel, without any noise." Even as her virtues, was her long life: silent, peaceful, and crowned with Christian humility.

To the same period belong the names—and, alas! little more than the names—of Susannah, countess of Suffolk; Lady Reynell; Elizabeth, countess of Bridgewater; Lady Elizabeth Brooke, charitable and learned in divinity; and Lady Elizabeth Langham, a daughter of the house of Hastings: on which its women were to confer no small religious distinction, in the following age. Lady Langham was daughter of the sixth Earl of Huntingdon. Her marriage with Sir James Langham was somewhat unequal; but if he alluded to this circumstance, she interrupted him, to declare herself satisfied with the state of life into which it had brought her. She was naturally humble and modest; and, even in her youth, she showed herself reserved and silent. A lady once said of her, "that she believed this lady had the least account to give, for words, of any that ever she knew." Her piety partook of her character: it was more to be divined than seen; but, like all centred feelings, it was full and ardent. A little before her marriage she fell ill, and was overheard exclaiming, in an impassioned tone, "Oh! that I could do the whole will of God!"

Her marriage with Sir James Langham afforded her the opportunity of displaying her amiable qualities. Her husband had several children by a first wife; and not only did she treat them so tenderly that they might have been thought her own, but she paid marked respect to the memory of her predecessor; "praising, and seeking to imitate the good she had heard of her."

Her authority was always tempered with gentleness: she was once heard telling a child, "that if she did not do such a thing she would not love her;" but, thinking the sentence too severe, she retracted it, saying, "Alas! God deals not so with us, notwithstanding our continual disobedience." This amiable woman died of the small-pox in 1664. Seeing the grief of her husband, she said to him, "We came not into the world together, nor can we expect to go out of it together; yet it is a great satisfaction to me that I am going thither, whither, after a while, you shall follow me." Her secret and extensive charity was revealed by the crowds of sorrowing poor who followed her to the grave. The same modest reserve did not allow her to display all that she owed to an excellent education: Latin, French, and Italian, ranked amongst her acquirements.

In these times, also, lived the good Lady Frances Hobart, eldest daughter of the Earl of Bridgewater, and wife of Sir John Hobart, of Norfolk, who called her "my dear saint." We will not speak of her domestic virtues, though they were great; or, if we mention her economy, let it be to record that, after her husband's death, she could not be persuaded to wear a silk gown, preferring to spend the money in charity. When her liberality exceeded her means, as was often the case, she said, "that it was but wearing a gown two or three months longer." The fourth part of her income was spent in good works. She lodged and relieved strangers, and her coach was oftener seen waiting for her at the doors of the poor than at those of the great. Her physician, the food from her table, the money from her purse, were not her own, but belonged to whomsoever needed them. She died in 1664, in the sixty-first year of her age. Humble to the last, she desired that the friend who was to preach her funeral sermon should abstain from all praise of "a vile sinful creature."

We cannot pass in silence the liberal zeal of the pious and learned Lady Armyne, who died, past eighty, in 1675. She gave devout books to those whose necessities she relieved, and spent large sums annually for the conversion of Indians in New England. By the Act of Uniformity, passed in 1660, under Charles II., non-conforming ministers were ejected from their livings; and many who had large families were utterly ruined. Lady Armyne shared their opinions and came to their aid. "Some few days after," writes Samuel Clarke, "she came to Mr. Edm. Calamy, and brought him £500 (at which time I also was with him), to be distributed among the most indigent and necessitous." By her will, Lady Armyne left £40 per annum to be distributed in charity for four-score and nineteen years.

Peculiar as she was in many respects, we should not feel justified in not mentioning the eccentric but benevolent Countess of Pembroke. She is justly celebrated for one of the most spirited and laconic letters woman ever wrote. Sir Joseph Williamson, secretary to Charles II., having presumed to name a candidate to her for the borough of Appleby, the dowager countess answered in the following style :

" I have been bullied by a usurper, I have been neglected by a court, but I will not be dictated to by a subject; your man shan't stand.

"ANNE DORSET, PEMBROKE AND MONTGOMERY."

We give this well-known letter, because it has become identified with the name of Anne Clifford : but it only displays one side, and that not the most amiable, of her character. The Countess of Pembroke was something besides a proud, independent lady, not to be insulted with impunity : she was one of the most handsome and accomplished women of her age; benevolent, liberal, dauntless in her faith, great in charity.

Anne Clifford was born in Skipton Castle, in 1590, and was the daughter and sole heir of the adventurous Earl of Cumberland, by his wife Margaret. Her parents lived unhappily together; although it has been said of her mother, that "she was a woman fit to pleasure the communion of saints." Their daughter could not boast of much conjugal felicity. She was, however, twice married : in 1609, to Richard, earl of Dorset, who died in 1624 ; and, six years after his death, to the degenerate nephew of Sir Philip Sydney, the Earl of Pembroke, a vicious and ignorant man, who rendered his wife extremely unhappy. He died in 1649, leaving the Countess of Pembroke free, and mistress of an immense fortune.

The noble use which Anne Clifford made of her wealth entitles her memory to honor, and will give her name a place wherever the charity of woman is recorded. One of her first acts was to repair the ruined castles and strongholds of her family. Her friends advised her not to do so, as Cromwell might cause them to be destroyed again. She answered, "Let him destroy my castles if he will; he shall find that as often as he levels I will rebuild them, while he leaves me a shilling in my purse." Besides her six castles, the Countess of Pembroke rebuilt seven churches which had fallen to ruin in the wars. Prudence and economy enabled her to be liberal: she spent little on herself, and lived more plainly and was more simply attired than her own servants. Bishop Rainbow, speaking of her virtues as a mistress, illustrates her self-denial in the following quaint style: " Yet here I may be bold to tell you something to wonder at; that she much neglected and treated very harshly one servant, a very ancient one, who served her from her cradle—from her birth—very faithfully, according to her mind; which ill-usage, therefore, her menial servants, as well as her friends and children, much repined at. And who this servant was, I have named before: *it was her body ;* who, as I said, was a servant most obsequious to her mind, and served her fourscore years."

The active countess never tarried long in one place, but visited her different castles in turns. Wherever she went, she practised a liberal and judicious charity, that endeared her to her tenants and servants. Her bounty was not confined to them : during the civil wars, she allowed £40 a year to distressed clergymen who had been obliged to leave England ; and when she learned that ready money would be more useful to them than an annuity, she sent them the munificent sum of a thousand pounds. Although she had been persecuted by the puritan party, as a zealous member of the Church of England, the Countess of Pembroke did not afterwards exclude dissenters from a share in her charity.

On the 23d of April, 1651, she laid the first stone of a hospital for twelve poor women, called "sisters" and their "mother;" she often went to dine with them, and invited them to her table. When her married daughters came to visit her, she admonished them to pay first a visit to these poor women, and take " the blessing of the poor, the almswomen's blessing by the way." Another of her charitable actions was to repair and restore an almshouse at Bearmky, which had been built and endowed by her good mother, the Countess of Cumberland—" that blessed saint," as Anne Clifford ever called her.

Filial piety and charity are touchingly blended in the

monument known as the "Countess's Pillar," which stands on the side of the road between Penrith and Appleby. It supports a sun-dial for the use of travellers, and bears the following inscription:

"This pillar was erected in 1656, by Anne, countess dowager of Pembroke, &c., for a memorial of her last parting, in this place, with her good and pious mother, Margaret, countess dowager of Cumberland, on the second of April, 1616; in memory whereof she hath left an annuity of four pounds to be distributed to the poor of the parish of Brougham, every second day of April forever, upon the stone table placed hard by. Laus Deo."

This simple record of filial love and human sorrow, is thus mentioned by Rogers, in lines which, though well known, may yet be quoted here:

> "Hast thou, through Eden's wild-wood vales, pursued
> Each mountain scene, magnificently rude,
> Nor with attention's lifted eye, revered
> That modest stone by pious Pembroke reared,
> Which still records, beyond the pencil's power,
> The silent sorrows of a parting hour?"

Mrs. Hemans, in her "Records of Woman," has not failed to introduce a subject so congenial to her womanly genius.

Anne Clifford died in 1675, at the age of eighty-five. She was buried at Appleby, beneath the splendid monument which she had herself erected. A long epitaph records the ancient origin of "the Baronesse of Clifford, Westmoreland, and Vesey; High Sheriffesse of the county of Westmoreland, and of the Honor of Skipton Castle." The titles which she acquired by marriage, and the illustrious alliances of her two daughters, have not been omitted; but the little stone pillar standing modestly by the beaten path, with its sun-dial for the traveller, its table for the poor, and its inscription for the thoughtful to read slowly ere they pass by, is more noble than the stately monument with all its titles; and will live longer in the memory of men, hallowed as it is by the love of two human beings, by Christian charity, and by the lays of poets.

CHAPTER XVII.

Mary, Countess of Warwick—Mrs. Godolphin.

It is recorded of Richard Boyle, first Earl of Cork, that he went from England to Ireland with the munificent sum of £27 3s. in his pocket, and died master of more than twelve thousand acres of Irish land : it had been originally procured by the cheap process of confiscation ; and being both uncertain of tenure and difficult of keeping, was readily sold by the English owners to English adventurers who chose to buy.

The Earl of Cork left fifteen children, prosperous like himself ; amongst the rest the celebrated philosopher and man of science, Robert Boyle. His daughters married English noblemen of high rank and great wealth : Mary, the seventh, born in 1624, became Countess of Warwick at an early age. She was witty and amiable ; she loved the world and its pleasures, without excess ; but enough to make her dread entering a family so rigid as that of her husband. Her new relations succeeded, however, in rendering religion more attractive to her than she had anticipated ; and afflictions, the nature of which we are not told, contributed to chasten her heart. She learned to love the retirement in which she henceforth spent her life, and to abstain without regret from the idle and worldly diversions of which the loss had once seemed so severe.

Prayer and daily meditation were her chief delights : prayer she emphatically called " heart's-ease." Such she had ever found it ; and the serenity it gave to her mind revealed itself in her charming countenance, alike expressive of gentleness and benevolence. Few persons were so well fitted as the Countess of Warwick for accomplishing the excellent purpose which she entertained ; and which is thus expressed by her biographer and friend, Dr. Anthony Walker : " She avowedly designed to represent religion as amiable and taking, and free from vulgar prejudice, as possibly she might ; not so as might affright and scare men from it, but that it might allure them, and insinuate itself into their love and liking: to this end she was affable, familiar, pleasant, and of a free and agreeable conversation: not sour, reserved, morose, sad, dejected, melancholy, which presents religion most disadvantageously. She was naturally of the sweetest temper in the world."

Honor, as it is understood by men in its old chivalrous meaning—a virtue women are not sufficiently taught to esteem in themselves—characterized this amiable lady. Her word, once passed, was inviolable; untruth she abhorred; and, with mingled pride and humility, gave this testimony of herself to her husband: "You know I dare not, I will not lie." A falsehood was, in her eyes, the most unpardonable fault a servant can commit: "Tell me the truth," she often observed, "and I can forgive you any thing." A striking proof of the regard she had for truth, and of the value she set on her name for veracity, is afforded by an anecdote which we owe to Dr. Anthony Walker: to whom, indeed, we are indebted for almost all that is known of this excellent woman. A month before her death, being then in perfect health, she decided on altering her will. For the legacies in money which she had before awarded to persons of high rank, she resolved to substitute valuable gifts; which she also determined to select so as to render them most acceptable; but this she thought to put later in a codicil. The only name which she inserted in her new will was that of her sister-in-law, the Countess of Scarsdale; to whom she had formerly bequeathed a sum of money, instead of which she now left her a set of silver sconces which adorned her own chamber. Dr. Walker asked to know the reason of this exception; the countess gave him the following reply: "Because she is the only person living to whom I ever intimated being in my will; and I would not die and have it found otherwise, and so be under the suspicion of having told a lie, or dying with a lie in my mouth." Although we are simply told that the Countess of Warwick was an excellent wife, mother, and mistress, it is easy to believe so, from what we know of her character. The high esteem of the earl for her was expressed by his often declaring, "That he had rather have her with five thousand pounds than any woman living with twenty." When they lost their only son, he forgot his own poignant grief in the anticipation of hers. "It would kill his wife,

which was," he said, "more to him than a hundred sons."
The countess was too practical a Christian not to bear the
shock with more resignation than her husband expected.
She survived him as well as her son, and was supported
through both trials by the calm fortitude of religion.   As a
testimony of his affection and respect, the Earl of Warwick
left her sole executrix, and bequeathed to her his estate for
her lifetime.   When she had faithfully acquitted herself of
her trust, and came into possession of this large property, the
countess made true what a great personage was reputed to
have said concerning this matter: "The Earl of Warwick has
given all his estate to pious uses."   Indeed, with her usual
frankness, the good countess had declared to a friend, "I
would not accept or be encumbered with the greatest estate
in England, if it should be offered me, clogged with this condition, not to do good to others with it."   Of her charity, her
most eminent virtue, we have not yet spoken: let it be
expressed in those words which were found written with her
own hand, amongst her favorite maxims, original and select:
"It is a great honor to be almoner to the King of Heaven."
How highly she valued that honor, her whole life showed
most faithfully.   In her husband's lifetime, having then a
separate allowance, she inquired of her friend, Dr. Walker,
how much it would be proper for her to give to the poor;
he made an evasive reply: "But she," to quote his own
words, "persisting to urge a more particular answer as to
herself, what would be fit and becoming for her to do, I, not
being ignorant of her circumstances (I must bear my own
shame in acknowledging the straitness of my own heart),
told her, I supposed a seventh part. But before I could
suggest the reason, she preventingly replied, she would never
give less than the third part; and she kept her resolution to
the full, and with advantage, laying aside constantly the
third part for charitable uses, and would sometimes borrow
of that which remained to add to it, but never default from
that to serve her own occasions, though sometimes pressing
enough."

That she was often charitable beyond her power, and
spent her revenues in advance to assist the poor, was well
known; and she was designated as "the lady that would
borrow money to give away." She visited the indigent in
10*

their distress and sickness, provided them with medicine, and sent them physicians. The most miserable were in great numbers relieved at her gates; not only with fragments and broken meat, but with provisions especially provided for the poor. The kind countess, anxious that no sense of discomfort should accompany the receipt of her bounty, caused a convenient house to be built for them close by her London residence—a similar one already existed at Leez—to shelter them from rain and heat whilst they received their dole. Her thoughtful charity did not forsake them whenever she chanced to go to town with her family: twice a week beef and bread were provided for the poor of four parishes adjacent to her country seat; and, by her will, she caused this allowance to be continued for three months after her decease. Her liberality was not confined to these acts of kindness: with mingled secrecy and delicacy she assisted the distressed of every condition. Poor foreigners, fled on account of their religion; young scholars, the expenses of whose education at the universities she wholly or partly paid; children, whom she not only sent to school, but provided with books and clothing: and this not merely in her own neighborhood, but as far as Wales. Ministers, both conformists and non-conformists, whose necessities she relieved, had far more occasion to bless her goodness, than the poor fed at her gates. She was often deceived, but would never allow herself to be discouraged: she declared that she would rather assist ten undeserving objects, than allow one that really needed aid to depart unrelieved. In the practice of these Christian virtues she spent her life; yet she failed in none of the duties of her high rank. Even after the death of her husband she lived up to her station, because she knew that he would have wished her to do so; at the same time she showed herself more careful of the estate which she was to transmit to another, than if it had been her own absolutely. Her courtesy and hospitality increased its value by raising the rent of houses near hers; and she was acknowledged to be an excellent landlady and mistress. The only two faults laid to her charge were worthy of her—excess of charity, and absence of anger. We shall not seek to justify her from such sins.

We have told the little that is known of her life and character; her death alone remains. In the month of March of the year 1678, she was taken with a slight indisposition, which seemed to afford no ground for serious apprehension. "On Friday, the 12th of April," says her biographer, "she rose with good strength, and after sitting up some time, being laid upon her bed, discoursing cheerfully and piously, one of the last sentences she spake was this, turning back the curtain with her hand—'Well, ladies, if I were one hour in heaven, I would not be again with you, as well as I love you.'"

After the departure of a lady who had called to pay her a visit, she rose, was seated on a chair, and requested that one of the two clergymen, who then happened to be staying in the house, should come and pray with her. He readily complied: whilst all the persons present knelt, the countess remained sitting, on account of her weakness, and holding an orange in her hand to refresh herself with its reviving scent. Almost in the beginning of the prayer the countess was heard to sigh deeply: the circumstance was not heeded, until a lady kneeling by her chair looked up and saw her pale and inanimate, with her hand hanging down. She started up in alarm; aid was quickly applied, but in vain: her pulse had already ceased to beat. She had died, as she had often wished to die—in the very act of prayer.

In the course of the same year, died the amiable and much loved friend of Evelyn—Mrs. Godolphin. The readers of this accomplished man's delightful Diary have long been familiar with the few though interesting passages in which she is mentioned, and to which her life—written by him, and published a few years ago—has given still further interest.

Evelyn relates, in his pleasant way, how he long remained indifferent to the attractions and virtues of Mrs. Margaret Blagge; who, being then unmarried, was maid of honor to the Duchess of York, and after her death to the queen. His wife, and some friends who knew her well, strove to persuade him that, though she had lived at court from her twelfth year, she was a very charming and virtuous person; he did not deny the fact, "but to believe there were many saints in that country, he was not much inclined:" an incredulity amply justified by the memoirs which remain of those licentious times. It was not until Evelyn was in some sort compelled

. to renew acquaintance with Mrs. Blagge at Whitehall, that he discovered his mistake; and then beheld with admiration "that so young, so elegant, so charming a wit and beauty, should preserve so much virtue in a place where it neither naturally grew, nor was much cultivated."

Acquaintance, for having been so long neglected, only ripened the more rapidly into friendship. The singular and unaffected piety of the young maid of honor touched the good Evelyn to the heart: "What a new thing is this," he said to himself; "I think Paula and Eustochium are come from Bethlehem to Whitehall." It was not long after this, that, in a conversation, which Evelyn has very agreeably related, Mrs. Blagge, whom he had found somewhat pensive, indirectly solicited his friendship, with a mixture of frankness and finesse, that proved she had not lived at court in vain. Half in jest and half in earnest, she even drew up, signed and dated, a compact "of inviolable friendship," not the less sincere for being a little sentimental; and earnestly entreated Evelyn, whose years warranted the request, to consider her henceforth as his child. He agreed, with some emotion, to do so; and until her premature death, six years later, faithfully kept his promise of paternal affection. The first dawn of their friendship appears by this entry in his Diary: "31st July (1672), I entertained the maids of honor (among whom there was one I infinitely esteemed for her many and extraordinary virtues) at a comedy this afternoon." Mrs. Blagge is here indicated, though not mentioned; in later entries she is termed "my dear friend, Mrs. Blagge."

When their friendship began, Margaret Blagge was near twenty. The loyalty and worth of her father—who lived to see the restoration of the king, for whose father he had bravely fought—procured for his orphan daughters the doubtful advantage of becoming maids of honor in a most profligate court. Margaret Blagge entered the household of Anne Hyde, duchess of York, at twelve years of age; and in that difficult post, as well as in that of maid of honor to Catherine of Braganza, wife of Charles II., she behaved with a modesty and propriety rare then and at any time. Her diary contains some curious entries, concerning the rule of life she found it necessary to observe: "When I go into the withdrawing room," she writes, "let me consider what my

calling is: to entertain the ladies, not to talk foolishly to
men: more especially the king." She seems, indeed, to have
been much on her guard against the last-named personage;
for further on she observes, " Be sure never to talk to the
king."

Never did more discreet and pious maid of honor adorn a
profligate court. Modest in her bearing; devout to austerity
in prayer, fasting, and vigil; yet free from ostentation; de-
tached from the world and its pleasures; cheerful, obliging;
prudent, and wise; she united to the innocence and gentle
ardor of youth, virtues which are seldom possessed before
maturity of years brings judgment. The proof that her religion was not mere lip-worship, but sprang from her heart,
may be found in her extensive charities: " than which I know
no greater mark of a consummate Christian," writes Evelyn.
She gave much of her time and industry to " working for
poor people, cutting out and making waistcoats and other
necessary coverings, which she constantly distributed amongst
them, like another Dorcas." She diligently sought out and
visited the poor in " hospitals, humble cells, and cottages."
Her friend records that he often accompanied her on such
errands of mercy to obscure places of the town, or to lonely
dwellings in the outskirts. He dwells with admiration on
the patience and charity with which she administered to the
sick, condescending to the meanest offices; and how, sitting
by them for whole afternoons, she instructed them with that
insinuating grace which charmed all who knew her. A poor
and good widow assisted her in her charities, and especially
in the difficult task of finding out worthy objects: it was
through her that Mrs. Blagge distributed weekly pensions,
looked after orphan children, put them to school, and paid
the debts of poor prisoners. Her income, which was not
large, was spent thus; and when Evelyn accused her of profusion, she only smiled. He confesses, that though he knew
of twenty-three indigent persons whom Mrs. Blagge " clad at
one time," this was only a very inconsiderable portion of her
charity; which she strove to keep secret, by walking out
alone and on foot, in the midst of winter, when the weather
was such that a servant would not have been sent out, in order to minister privately to poor creatures for whom she alone
cared.

To these tasks did Margaret Blagge devote herself in the bloom of youth, and beauty, and surrounded by pleasures which have had power to charm the senses and the heart of the wisest. The contrast between the mode of life to which her post called her, and that to which inclination led her, is affectingly described by Evelyn. "Often have I known her privately slip away, and break from the gay and public company, the greatest entertainments, and greatest persons too of the court, to make a step to some miserable, poor, sick creature, whilst those she quitted have wondered why she went from the conversation; and more they would, had they seen how the scene was changed from a kingly palace to some mean cottage, from the company of princes to poor necessitous wretches, when by-and-by she would return as cheerful, and in good-humor, as if she had been about some worldly concern, and excuse her absence in the most innocent manner imaginable. Never must I forget the innocent pleasure she took in doing charities. 'Twas one day that I was with her, when seeing a poor creature on the streets, 'Now,' says she to me, 'how will I make that miserable wretch rejoice!' upon which she sent him ten times more than I am confident he ever could expect. This she spake, not as boasting, but so as one might perceive her very soul lifted up in secret joy, to consider how the miserable man would be made happy with the surprise."

In order to assist the poor more freely, Mrs. Blagge restricted her own expenses. Few things pained her more than money ill-spent; she could not always refuse to play at cards, but the money which she won was devoted to charity, and that which she lost bitterly regretted: as is testified by the following entry in her diary:

"June the 2d.

"I will never play this half-year, but at threepenny ombre, and then with one at halves. I will not; I do not vow, but I will not do it. What! loose money at cards, yet not give the poor! 'Tis robbing God, misspending time, and misemploying my talents—three great sins. Three pounds would have kept three people from starving a month: well, I will not play."

Although she filled every duty of her place with propriety and grace, Mrs. Blagge could not be said to be suited to it; or rather, it was not suited to her. She wearied of tasks that brought no satisfaction in their accomplishment: of the monotonous round of pleasures that gave her no amusement, and to which she secretly objected. She at length obtained the permission of retiring from court; and her joy to leave it was such, that, on entering her apartment, she knelt and gave thanks to God, for thus mercifully calling her away from the land of her exile and bondage. Her eyes sparkled, her cheeks were flushed; and, as she entered the carriage that bore her away, she could scarcely contain her joy.

On thus leaving court, Mrs. Blagge went to reside with her friend Lady Berkeley, from whose house she afterwards contemplated retiring to a remote country home, where she intended leading the meditative and lonely life of the widows and virgins of the primitive Church; a design from which the arguments of Evelyn contributed to divert her: we say contributed, because there was, at that very time, a feeling in her heart which pleaded more powerfully than all his arguments against a life of ascetic solitude.

Margaret Blagge was still very young when her beauty began to attract attention at court. Amongst her admirers was a silent and serious gentleman, of ancient family, but no great wealth: Sidney Godolphin, the future minister and earl. He proved the favored suitor. Absence, sickness, and time, had no power over an attachment to which the limited means of the lovers raised serious obstacles for upwards of nine years. When she left court, Mrs. Blagge began to consider whether, the difficulties to her union with Mr. Godolphin being such, it would not be better, in every respect, to relinquish the alliance: she protested that she did not intend to love him less, but she confessed that she thought a life of solitude would give her greater and better opportunities of serving God. Had she been a Catholic, Mrs. Blagge would assuredly have entered a convent: her whole feelings, her whole soul, tended towards a calm retreat, where she might worship God, free from the snares which will beset the purest life. She termed the nunneries which she saw in France, "holy institutions;" "if they are abused," she continued, writing to Evelyn, "'tis not their fault: what is not per-

verted?" She exalted the excellence of the single state, its
purity, its detachment from undue cares and affections; and
at the very time that she spoke so, her heart was torn and
divided. She now found it hard to leave him whom she
loved, for pious exercises and holy duties; what then would
it be to leave him forever? The greatness of the sacrifice
alternately allured and deterred her.

"The Lord help me, dear friend," she wrote to Evelyn,
"I know not what to determine: sometimes I think one
thing, sometimes another; one day I fancy no life so pure as
the unmarried, another day I think it less exemplary, and
that the married life has more opportunity of exercising charity; and then again, that 'tis full of solicitude and worldliness, so as what I shall do I know not." The strength of the
conflict reveals itself better in the impassioned language of
another letter: "Much afflicted, and in great agony, was
your poor friend this day, to think of the love of the holy
Jesus, and yet be so little able to make him any return. For
with what fervor have I protested against all affections to the
things of this world: resigned them all, without exception;
when, the first moment I am tried, I shrink away, and am
passionately fond of the creature, and forgetful of the Creator. This, when I considered, I fell on my knees, and, with
many tears, begged of God to assist me with his grace, and
banish from me all concern but that of heavenly things, and
wholly to possess my heart himself, and either relieve me in
this conflict, now so long sustained, or continue to me strength
to resist it, still fearing, if the combat cease not in time, I
should repine for being put upon so hard a duty. But then
again, when I call to mind the grace of self-denial, the honors
of suffering for my Saviour, the reward proposed for those
that conquer, the delights I shall conceive in seeing and en-
joying him, the happiness of the life above, I that am thus
feeble, thus fearful, call (out of exercise of his grace) yea, for
tribulation, for persecution, for contradictions, and for every
thing agreeable to the spirit, and displeasing to the flesh."

Hard, however, are these sacrifices of human to divine love.
In the very midst of her triumph, Margaret Blagge sorrowfully exclaims, "Happy, ah! happy are you, my friend, that
are past that mighty love to the creature." The event proved
that she had over-estimated her own strength; for on the

16th of May, of the year 1675, she was privately married, in the Temple Church, to Sidney Godolphin.

Somewhat unkindly, it must be confessed, Evelyn was not so much as made acquainted with this circumstance : she who had called him her father, and entreated him to consider her his child ; who had confided to him the most secret thoughts and desires of her heart ; who had requested his advice on that very step which she now took, did not request him to sanction it with his presence. The secretive temper of her bridegroom overruled her own wishes : her regret and penitence for having, for the first time, prevaricated with her old friend, were so great, that Evelyn, though hurt at heart, thought himself bound to check their expression.

Upwards of a year elapsed before Mr. and Mrs. Godolphin could declare their marriage. At length they did so ; and a passage from one of the letters which Mrs. Godolphin addressed to her friend, shows, in a very pleasing light, her mode of life, and the happiness she found in this new state. " Lord, when I this day considered my happiness, in having so perfect health of body, cheerfulness of mind, no disturbance from without, nor grief within, my time my own, my house quiet and pretty, all manner of conveniences for serving God, in public and private, how happy in my friends, husband, relations, servants, credit, and none to wait or attend on, but my dear and beloved God, from whom I receive all this, what a melting joy ran through me at the thoughts of all these mercies, and how did I think myself obliged to go to the foot of my Redeemer, and acknowledge my own unworthiness of his favor ; but then what words was I to make use of ?—truly, at first, of none at all ; but a devout silence did speak for me. But after that I poured out my prayers, and was in amazement that there should be such a sin as ingratitude in the world, and that any should neglect this great duty. But why do I say all this to you, my friend ? Truly that out of the abundance of the heart the mouth speaketh, and I am still so full of it, that I cannot forbear expressing my thoughts to you."

We think we may venture to say, that if no more were known of Mrs. Godolphin's life and character than this fragment of a letter, written nearly two centuries ago, we should still be able to pronounce her a good and generous woman.

The blessings of life are not always bestowed on the good; but only the good know how to be happy, for to them alone are the excellence and purity of God's gifts fully revealed.

But one blessing—a child—had been denied to Mrs. Godolphin: it was granted at the cost of her life. The event is thus narrated in Evelyn's Diary, 3d September (1678): " I went to London to dine with Mrs. Godolphin, and found her in labor: she was brought to bed of a son, who was baptized in the chamber by the name of Francis."

"8th. Whilst I was at church, came a letter from Mr. Godolphin, that my dear friend his lady was exceedingly ill, and desiring my prayers and assistance. My wife and I took boat immediately and went to Whitehall, where, to my inexpressible sorrow, I found she had been attacked with the new fever then reigning this excessive hot autumn, and which was so violent that it was not thought she could last many hours." Remedies were applied, but only seemed to aggravate the disease; on the morning of the following day, Mrs. Godolphin, exhausted by her sufferings, and also perhaps by the violence of the remedies, gently expired, with her hand in that of her old friend. She was scarcely twenty-six, and had been married three years. Her husband, struck with unspeakable affliction, fell down as dead. His sorrow was long and enduring: he never married again.

On Evelyn, who had loved her as his own child, devolved the sad duty of superintending her funeral; for she had requested to be buried in Cornwall with her husband's friends, and in the spot where she knew that he was to be laid one day. Her wishes were fulfilled: speaking of his part in this matter, Evelyn writes: " Having closed the eyes, and dropped a tear on the cheek of my dear departed friend, lovely even in death, I caused her corpse to be embalmed and wrapped in lead, a plate of brass soldered thereon, with an inscription, and other circumstances due to her worth, with as much diligence and care as my grieved heart would permit me; I then retired home for two days, which were spent in solitude and sad reflection."

They " had prayed, visited the sick and miserable, received, read, discoursed, and communicated in all holy offices together;" and there is, in such friendships, a love that not even death can sever. In memorial of the virtues of her

whom he had known and loved; Evelyn wrote her life.
Alliances between the two families perpetuated the memory
of their affection ; uniting in the holy ties of blood and kindred, those whose ancestors and relatives had freely contracted the not less sacred bond of inviolable friendship.

CHAPTER XVIII.

Lady Mainard—Margaret Baxter—Elizabeth Burnet—Lady Neville—
Elizabeth Bury—Catherine Bovey—Lettice Pigot—Mary Astell—Lady
Rachel Russel.

THE friendship of Thomas Kenn, bishop of Bath and
Wells, for the good Lady Mainard, has left us the only record
we possess of that lady's life and character. She was, he
tells us, a royalist by birth and opinion ; and in the civil
wars she relieved liberally the suffering members of her
party ; but after the Restoration, she lived like a recluse at
the profligate courts of Charles II. and his successor. The
bishop, who knew her well, and for many years, did not
think that she had ever fallen into one mortal sin ; and he
praises the fervor of her devotion, the purity of her life, and,
above all, her disinterestedness and liberal charity. She desired not riches for herself, or, what is more rare, for her
children ; she shunned them as " dangerous things, which did
only clog and press down our souls to this earth." Her
means were moderate, but her charity was great. Besides
the extensive relief which she privately afforded to the
needy, she had made herself " the common physician of her
sick neighbors, and would often, with her own hands, dress
their most loathsome sores, and sometimes keep them in her
family ; and would give them both diet and lodging, till
they were cured, and then clothe them and send them home,
to give God thanks for their recovery ; and if they died, her
charity accompanied them sometimes to the very grave, and
she took care even of their burial."
Like another Paula, this Christian mother would not allow
over-anxiety for her children to interfere with the relief she
afforded to the poor : she thought that alms and the poor's

prayers would bring in a greater blessing to them than thousands a year. "Look abroad now in the world," exclaims Bishop Kenn, "and see how rarely you shall meet with a charity like that of this gracious woman, who, next to her own flesh and blood, was tender of the poor, and thought an alms as much due to them as portions to her children." To crown her virtues, she was a most indulgent mistress, and treated her servants like one who was always mindful "that she herself had a Master in heaven." This amiable, though little known woman, died in the year 1682.

Contemporary writers have extolled the piety and virtues of ladies now scarcely remembered. Anne Killigrew, the poetess, praised by Dryden, died in the flower of her age; worthy, it is said, of the laudatory epitaph inscribed on her tombstone. The learning and piety of Anne Baynard drew no less admiration; the names of Lady Grace Gethin, Lady Halket, Lady Masham, and of Susannah Hopton, eminent for her charity, are still remembered in religious biography.

Among these memorials of the good and pious women of the seventeenth century, there is one to which the generous character of the heroine, the name of the writer, and the grave and solemn tone of the composition, give peculiar interest: we allude to the life of Margaret Baxter, written by her husband, the celebrated non-conformist divine.

Richard Baxter has delineated the character of the woman whom he loved—and who shared his sufferings, his prison, and his labors—with much delicacy, power, and eloquence. The affection of an earnest soul that can feel passion, but that never sinks into weakness, appears in every page. Few have read without some emotion the sad and humble deprecation in the opening: "Reader, while I give thee but the truth, forgive the effects of age, weakness, and grief. As the man is, such will be his thoughts and works." And who, after perusing this life of a wife written by her husband, sees no beauty in the proud confession with which it closes: "Perhaps love and grief may make me speak more than many will think fit. But though some passion blind the judgment, some doth but excite it to duty; and God made it to that end; *and I will not be judged by any that never felt the like.*" He might have added, that not only those who had never loved, but those who had not had such a woman to love, were unfit to judge him. It may sometimes happen that unworthy objects inspire devoted passions; but can such feelings ever equal, in force and intensity, the love which a noble being awakens in a generous heart?

The life, character, and writings of Richard Baxter are well known: his strength of principle, his moderation, his earnestness and fervor, have secured the admiration and respect of posterity. He belonged to those whom sufferings have no power to embitter, and whom their own wrongs cannot render partisans: a rare class at any time, and certainly very rare in the political and religious excitement of the seventeenth century.

In France and in England that century was characterized by a struggle between the principles of worldliness and devotion, which is indeed of every age, but which was then stronger than it has been since, and more relentless in England than elsewhere. The memoirs, plays, and various writings of the times, paint two worlds, between which yawns an impassable abyss. For where shall we find a link between the false glitter, the impious wit, the extravagance, the gross profligacy of the court, and the gloom, the rigidity, the enthusiasm of the morose Puritans in their austere homes? Divided by a deep hatred, as much as by the difference of their tempers and inclinations, they were pitiless in their mutual reprobation: their censure was scorn, and scorn is cruel. Their life was a perpetual warfare: the worldly called their enemy hypocrisy—the devout named him Satan.

Yet, in the midst of all this strife, so little favorable to charity, did virtue and gentle piety assert their rights in many good and amiable beings; and of these Margaret Baxter, though fervent and enthusiastic, was assuredly one. In her were blended qualities the most opposed—ardor and gentleness, timidity and courage. Her character, though frank and firm, was like her theological belief, full of nice and subtle distinctions; above which it often rose. The portrait traced by her husband looks true; and though in some points contradictory, it may not be less real for this. The two principles which divided the age—worldliness and devotion—also divided her life.

When Richard Baxter, "son of a mean freeholder," and Margaret Charlton, daughter of Francis Charlton, justice of the peace, first met in Kidderminster, there seemed little chance of their future union. Difference of rank, age, and temper divided them. Baxter was nearly fifty, and had long given up all thoughts of marriage; and Margaret Charlton, then little past twenty, was "glittering herself in costly apparel, and delighting in her romances;" for, as we are informed before this, "in her vain youth, pride and romances, and company suitable thereto, did take her up; and an imprudent, rigid governess, that her mother had set over her in her absence, had done her hurt by poisoning her with ill thoughts of strictness in religion." When the young and gay Margaret came to Kidderminster to see her mother, "she had," we are told, "great aversion to the poverty and strictness" of Richard Baxter's flock. She continued in this mood until a strange and sudden change came over her: the doctrine of conversion, as preached by Baxter, was received in her heart as the seal on wax. For a long time, being naturally of a secretive temper, she would not confess the alteration. The house in which she then resided was large, and the middle part had been ruined in the civil wars; she chose a closet at the further end, where she retired whenever her soul was troubled, and prayed aloud. Without her knowledge, some listened to these secret outpourings of her heart, and declared that never from any person had they heard such devout prayers. Thus, and to the great joy of her relatives, was discovered the change from worldliness and religious indifference to faith and its fervent aspirations, which Margaret continued to conceal from those most near to her. She might have many motives for doing so. Richard Baxter has not exactly said that his eloquence had wrought the change; but it is certain that it was so; and, though he has not confessed it, it is not doubtful that human feelings, in which he had a part, accompanied the agitation inseparable from so great an alteration in the heart of Margaret Charlton. She herself wrote about this time, analyzing her feelings, as was her habit: "How hard it is to keep our hearts in going too far, even in honest affections, towards the creature, while we are so backward to love God, who should have all the heart, and soul, and might! Too strong love to any, though it be good in the kind, may yet be sinful and hurtful in the degree. 1. It will turn too many of your thoughts from God, and they will be too often running after the beloved creature. 2. And by this exercise of thoughts and affections on the creature, it may divert and cool your love of God, which will not be kept up unless our thoughts be kept more to him ; yea, though it be for his sake that you love them. . 3. It will increase your suffering, by interesting you in all the dangers and troubles of those whom you overlove."

But when did reason wholly prevail over the feelings that sway the heart and become its very life ? : This dreary triumph was not reserved to Margaret Charlton : it was, indeed, most difficult to contend against her passion. When she sank into a decline, from which her recovery was not expected, the prayers and fasts of one already too dear, were offered up in her behalf. She recovered in a manner esteemed miraculous ; but remained oppressed with a strange sadness, that was partly the result of temperament.

Whatever suspicions might have been entertained of the truth, the announcement of her marriage with Baxter created some surprise, which was, indeed, warranted by her youth, wealth, and superior rank. He gives on this subject the following imperfect explanation : " The unsuitableness of our age, and my former known purpose against marriage, and against the conveniency of ministers' marriage, who have no sort of necessity, made our marriage the matter of much public talk and wonder. And the true opening of her case and mine, and the many strange occurrences which brought it to pass, would take away the wonder of her friends and mine that knew us, and the notice of it would much conduce to the understanding of some other passages of our lives. Yet wise friends by whom I am advised, think it better to omit such personal particularities, at least at this time. Both in her case and mine there was much extraordinary, which it doth not much concern the world to be acquainted with. From the first thoughts of it, many changes and stoppages intervened, and long delays, till I was silenced and ejected with many hundreds more ; and so, being separated from my old pastoral charge, which was enough to take up all my time and labor, some of my dissuading reasons were then over. And at last, on September the 10th, 1662, we were married in Bennet Fink Church, by Mr. Samuel Clark, having before been contracted by Mr. Simeon Ash, both in the presence of Mr. Ashunt and Mrs. Ash."

Margaret Baxter was then twenty-three, her husband was forty-seven ; but difference of age, which had not prevented love, could prove no bar to married happiness. Baxter acknowledges with much simplicity, that "when they were married, her sadness and melancholy vanished." They never returned, in spite of all the toil and care to which this union led. Though one of the most moderate of nonconformists, Baxter was bitterly persecuted: sudden and frequent removals, heavy losses, and finally prison, entered into his lot. His wife bore every thing with courage and love; and wherever they went, endeared herself to all, by her amiable temper and abundant charity. Too firm and ardent in her faith to shrink from persecution, she labored to extend her husband's ministry, and shared his prison as she had shared his home: when he was carried to the common jail, she cheerfully accompanied him, and brought her best bed with her.

The record which Richard Baxter has left of his wife's efforts in what she esteemed the cause of truth, shows her to have possessed a mind of singular energy and resources, as well as a zealous and indefatigable temper. She spent much to establish places of nonconformist worship, and had the ignorant children of St. James's taught at her expense. She ended by exhausting her means; and on this subject her husband observes: "I take it yet for a greater part of her charity, that when her own estate proved much too short to maintain her in the exercise of such good works as she was devoted to, she at length refused not to accept with thanks the liberality of others, and to live partly on charity, that she might exercise charity to them that could not so easily get it from others as we could do." For one of her naturally proud temper, this was, indeed, no slight concession made to charity. Baxter confesses that "her expectations of liberality to the poor from others were too high, and her displeasure too great towards them that denied: whereupon, when she saw a worthy person in debt, or prison, or great want, she would promise to gather them such a sum; and sometimes she was put to pay most of it herself. But a fortnight or month before she died, she promised to get twenty pounds towards the relief of one of known name and worth, and could get but eight pounds, and somewhat over of it, and paid all the rest herself."

"Her judgment was, that we ought to give, more or less, to every one that asketh, if we have it; and that neighborhood, and notice and asking, next to known indigence and great worth, are the marks by which to know to whom God would have us give. I thought that, besides these, we must exercise prudence in discerning the degrees of need and worth. But she practised as she thought, and especially to those imprisoned for debt, and blamed me if I denied any one."

"Alas! I know many poor widows, and others, who think they have now lost a mother, and are left desolate, whom I could wish some that are able would help, instead of the help they have lost."

So sincere, indeed, was the charity of Margaret Baxter, that, besides the presents she accepted, she borrowed to extend her alms; and at her death, there still remained some of these debts of mercy unpaid. She had always been delicate; and a brief illness carried her off in June, 1681, in the forty-second year of her age.

The grief of her husband was deep. They had been married nineteen years, and had spent that time in untroubled union, peace, and love. The aid which, in all his worldly afflictions, and often too in spiritual difficulties, he had derived from her, is gratefully and touchingly acknowledged by Richard Baxter. Although he speaks of her "weak and too passionate nature," he has drawn in her a woman of no ordinary character and acquirements. Quick, sensitive, gentle,—too ardent, perhaps, in the good at which she herself aimed or expected from others, too intense in her affections and desires,—she was yet of a lofty and generous nature. Though she was far from acting hastily, and was all for prudence and deliberation, calmness was the virtue, or rather the state of mind she most needed. She felt it herself, for she had a morbid apprehension of madness, to which some members of her family had been subject. Her own understanding was unusually firm and clear; but, as her husband confesses, "like the treble strings of a lute, strained up to the highest —sweet, but in continual danger." Her fears were partly realized, for she died in a state of delirium; yet even then her thoughts were all fixed on God.

The natural reluctance of Baxter to record charities in the merit of which he shared, has prevented him from giving a detailed account of the good deeds with which his wife filled her life; yet she was undoubtedly one of the most charitable women of England during this age: remarkable not only for the amount she gave, but also for the spirit in which it was given.

Charity is also to be found in the opposite ranks. The wife of Richard Baxter was not, indeed, equalled by the wife of Gilbert Burnet; but the virtues of the latter, though mild and modest, are worthy of record. The meddling and officious Bishop of Salisbury is celebrated for his conjugal good fortune : the animosity of his opponents, the sarcasms of Swift or Dryden, could not reach him there. He married three times, and well, in every sense of the word. His first wife was Lady Margaret Kennedy, daughter of the Earl of Cassilis. He was a widower when he retired to Holland on the accession of James II. His matrimonial good fortune still attended him; he contracted a second marriage with Mrs. Mary Scott, a lady of Scottish descent, wealthy and highly connected. She died of the small-pox, in time to make room for her successor, Mrs. Berkeley, a widow lady of great piety and virtue, literary, rich, and, if we may trust her portraits, sufficiently handsome.

This last marriage took place about the year 1699. Mrs. Berkeley was then thirty-eight, and had been nearly seven years a widow. She was scarcely seventeen when Dr. Fell, bishop of Oxford, procured her marriage with his ward, Robert Berkeley of Spetchley, in Worcestershire. So great an opinion had the prelate of her worth, that he declared the greatest obligation his ward had ever received from him was his marriage with Miss Elizabeth Blake.

The young bride entered her new family under circumstances very delicate at all times, but still more so in an age more remarkable for strong religious feeling than for tolerance. Her husband was, like herself, a Protestant ; but his mother, "a woman of good life," was a zealous Catholic. This latter circumstance, joined to the influence which she possessed over her son; the fear young Mrs. Berkeley had of seeing her husband change his creed, her wish to keep him faithful to it, her reluctance to engage in religious discussions, and her earnest desire to remain at peace where peace was an especial duty, rendered her position one of great difficulty. Young as she was, she behaved with a prudence and discretion that won the good opinion of those whose religious opinions were most opposed to her own.

Mrs. Berkeley did not feel, however, very secure of her husband's constancy ; for on the accession of James II., she induced him to visit Holland, in order to keep out of the reach of temptation. They travelled over the seventeen provinces, and were especially well received in those that professed the Catholic faith, and where Mr. Berkeley had relatives. Of his wife, it was said in private letters : " If she were of the Catholic Church, her piety and virtue are great enough to entitle her to the character of a saint."

They settled at the Hague, where they remained until the Revolution called the Prince of Orange to the throne. They then returned to England, residing at Spetchley. Dr. Stillingfleet, bishop of Worcester, was so much charmed with Mrs. Berkeley, that he often said of her : " he knew not a more considerable woman in England than she was." His successor, Dr. William Lloyd, and Dr. Talbot, bishop of Durham, likewise held her in great esteem. In 1693 Mr. Berkeley died ; his widow remained mistress of an ample fortune, which she devoted almost entirely to deeds of charity. She likewise put into execution the benevolent intentions of her late husband, who had left a considerable sum to erect a hospital at Worcester, and continued the poor-schools which she had established during his lifetime.

When nearly seven years had elapsed, Mrs. Berkeley married the Bishop of Salisbury. His object was to secure a companion for himself, and a mother for his children. He certainly had no views on her property, since he wished it to remain wholly at her disposal, both during her lifetime and after her death ; and he even desired that she would continue to devote it entirely to charitable uses. Mrs. Burnet refused to do so : she allowed a moderate sum for her board ; the rest was for the poor. Her personal expenses seldom went beyond the one-fifth of her income, and were oftener within it ; when they exceeded these moderate limits, she felt as uncomfortable as others after having been too generous or prodigal. " The being rich in good works," writes one of her biographers, " was visibly the greatest design of her whole life, and that which she most of all delighted in."

Upwards of a hundred children were taught at her expense, in and about Worcester and Salisbury. Notwithstanding her little leisure, she found time to engage in the composition of a religious work, entitled " A Method of Devotion," once highly popular. Though Mrs. Burnet could not exactly be termed learned, she was certainly intellectual, as well as good. Her conversation is described as very cheerful and attractive ;

for, like most persons whose piety is practical, and not confined to points of doctrine, she was not gloomy or morose;
but, by the aspect which she gave it, recommended religion
to the world.

The beauty of her character, which was especially visible
in private life, secured to Mrs. Burnet the affection of her husband and of his children: she treated them as her own, and
they loved and respected her as their mother. It was a due
sense of her worth, and not conjugal weakness, that induced
Burnet to leave, by his will, more power to his wife over his
children than natural mothers are often allowed. Mrs. Burnet did not live to enjoy this proof of esteem; for, though
eighteen years younger than her husband, she was the first
to die. Fasting, watching, and other religious austerities, had
weakened her constitution, which was naturally delicate. She
began to decline in 1707, and died of a pleuritic fever in the
early part of the following year. She was buried at Spetchley, beside her first husband, according to a promise which
she had formerly made to him; and not, as she said in her
will, "out of any want of respect or kindness to her present
husband, who had, by his great kindness and confidence, deserved from her all the gratitude and acknowledgments of
love and respect she could testify."

Like Elizabeth Burnet, several women of the seventeenth
century had their lives prolonged into the eighteenth; yet
may be considered as belonging, by their birth and their virtues, to the age they outlived. In 1715 died the good Lady
Katherine Neville, at Auburgh, in Lincolnshire. She was
not only mean in her dress, in order to be able to give more,
but she spent considerable sums yearly in physic for the sick.
Three times a week she relieved the parish poor, and daily
assisted the strangers who applied at the door.

Elizabeth Bury is celebrated no less for learning than for
piety and charity. She was lively and witty in conversation,
and could study the most abstruse, as well as the lightest of
sciences: Anatomy, in which she made great progress, and
divinity, were her favorite pursuits. The whole of her life
seems to have been devoted to learning and good deeds: she
gave much to the French refugees, to the poor, and to charity schools. She greatly approved the setting apart, to pious
and charitable uses, a certain portion of every one's income or
fortune; "for then," she quaintly said, "they will not grudge

to give out of a bag that is no longer their own." This amiable woman was twice married; her second husband, Mr. Bury, was a dissenting minister. After a long illness, and in the seventy-seventh year of her age, she died, with a smile on her lips.

If Catherine Bovey did not possess her learning, she more than rivalled her charity. Young, beautiful, and wealthy, a childless widow of twenty-two, she refused to marry again, in order to devote her riches to works of piety, to divers kinds of charity, to hospitality, and to the encouragement of learning. The charms of her person were celebrated by more than one writer of the times; and Sir Richard Steele, in dedicating to her the Ladies' Library, records the charity which sought out "the fatherless and the widow, the neglected man of merit, the wretch on the sick-bed; in a word, the distressed under all forms." She died at Flaxley, her seat in Gloucestershire. A long epitaph records her virtues in the spot where they were best known, and where all could testify to its truth.

We cannot pass in silence the charity of Mrs. Lettice Pigott, of Doddershall, near Aylesbury, Buckinghamshire. The poor daily besieged her gates, and never departed unrelieved. For thirty years she gave every week, to six indigent poor of her parish, as much good bread and beer as would suffice for several persons; and to this she yearly added a present of linen cloth and money. Her charity lowered the poor-rates of her parish: to which it was not, however, confined.

The means of alms so extensive were not granted to Mary Astell; who deserves, however, to be remembered for the zeal with which, as a writer, she defended her religious opinions, and advocated the rights of her sex. Like Lady Falkland, she wished for colleges and retreats for women. A great lady, convinced by her arguments, was ready to give ten thousand pounds towards this scheme; but Bishop Burnet interfered, with his usual officiousness, and by protesting against this imitation of Catholic nunneries, "utterly frustrated that noble design."

Although Lady Rachel Russell is more celebrated for her conjugal love, her misfortunes, her noble and amiable temper, and her fulfilment of every domestic duty, than for that exclusive devotion to religion and charity, which we have

attempted to commemorate in the preceding pages, we
cannot close this account of Christian women in England,
during the seventeenth century, without at least including
her name. It tells its own touching and well-known story:
it recalls her as her contemporaries beheld her, sitting by
her husband, and taking notes during his trial; consoling
him in his prison, and wearing a calm, almost cheerful mien,
at the very time her heart was breaking with love and grief.
When was a great sorrow so deeply felt, yet so simply
borne, as during the last silent parting witnessed by Burnet;
and which, when she had left him, made Lord William
Russell exclaim, "The bitterness of death is past!"

Affecting as is her story, Lady Rachel Russell owes less
to its touching incidents than to her letters. Their simple
and unconscious pathos has not yet grown old; but their
greatest charm is, that they show her as she was: simple,
good, and earnest, a grace and ornament to the age in which
she lived.

Of that age we do not wish to say too much—to represent it as better than it was; yet a great age it will assuredly
be thought in history: the goodness of the good, the bad-
ness of the evil, were both remarkable. But the contrast
is lost here, for we have given only one side of the picture.
We have told of ladies who made themselves the servants
of their vassals; but to show how deep was their humility,
we should have painted, in all their insolence, those who
daily triumphed over the poor. We have related the devotedness of the first Sisters of Charity, but not the bitter
and contemptuous neglect of previous years. To portray
the character of Mrs. Godolphin in all its holy purity,
should we not have delineated the court of Charles II. in
all its profligacy? The age which produced Lady Rachel
Russell, also gave birth to that Countess of Shrewsbury,
who, disguised as a page, is said to have held the bridle of
Buckingham whilst he fought with her hapless husband.

We do not say that these extremes of evil produced the
corresponding extremes of good. But who shall say that
those who had already chosen virtue as their part, found her
not the more lovely for beholding sin in its odiousness; that
their purity, their charity, their faith, were not silent, though
most eloquent protests, against things permitted by man,
but condemned by God?

FOURTH PERIOD.
EIGHTEENTH AND NINETEENTH CENTURIES.

CHAPTER XIX.

Mrs. Elizabeth Rowe—Lady Elizabeth Hastings—Hannah More—
Countess of Huntingdon.

WHATEVER may have been the merits of the eighteenth
century, it cannot be accused of too ardent a zeal for the glory
of God, or of excess of charity for the poor. It was essentially
an intellectual, reasoning age; more philosophic, more enlightened than the seventeenth century, but cold, sceptical, and too
often heartless. The exceptions we shall offer by no means
disprove this general rule. There were then, as there always
will be, good and pious women; but they were comparatively
few. We might, no doubt, have increased the list by including many whose names will not be found here; but their good
works, if they did any, have not been recorded by their biographers, who seem to think that attachment to a certain set of
doctrines was sufficient for both God and man. In the
instances we mean to give, we hope to show that earnestness
of belief by no means need exclude the most liberal charity.

The tyrannic measures which Charles II. was induced to
adopt against the nonconformists, consigned to the jail of
Ilchester, in Somersetshire, Walter Singer, a gentleman of
good family, and a dissenting minister, but neither a native
nor an inhabitant of the place where he was imprisoned. Mrs.
Elizabeth Portness, a pious lady of Ilchester, visited those persons who suffered for conscience sake: an acquaintance thus
began, which ended in marriage when Mr. Singer was released.
They had three daughters, two of whom died young. After
the death of his wife, Mr. Singer removed, from Ilchester to
Frome, in the same county; where he had an estate.

Mr. Singer was firm in his own principles, but tolerant to

those of others. He was on terms of friendship with Lord Weymouth, and was frequently visited by Bishop Kenn. He brought up his children in his own spirit of charity, and the whole life of his daughter·Elizabeth revealed the pure and gentle influence of such teaching. She was the eldest of his three children, and the only one who lived to an advanced age : of her two sisters, she lost one in·childhood; the other, who had a passion for study, and especially for medicine, in which she made considerable proficiency, reached her twentieth year, and died.

Elizabeth was born in 1674. She early displayed a great fondness for books, and a taste for poetry and painting, remarkable in one of her years. She was scarcely twelve when she began to write verses ; at a still earlier age, she made attempts in drawing, and squeezed out the juices of herbs to serve her instead of colors. Mr. Singer procured her a master; and though she never attained any extraordinary proficiency in this delightful art, it was to her a source of constant pleasure during the whole of her long life.

Poetry was, however, the favorite amusement of Elizabeth Singer ; for she does not appear to have ever considered it in any other light. She wrote verses with great facility, but seldom corrected her compositions; to which she attached little value. Poetry was to her an elegant and harmonious expression of thought and feeling ; but she did not seek, and she certainly did not reach, that ideal beauty which is at once the delight and despair of art. Her temper was, however, essentially artistic, warm, and overflowing with life. Her conversation is represented as extremely captivating ; she made many friends, and kept them all.

At the time when her poetic efforts were confined to the circle of home, some verses which she wrote drew the attention of the Weymouth family. She was not then twenty ; but this incident was the origin of a long and pleasant friendship. The honorable Mr. Thynne, son of Lord Weymouth, undertook to teach her the Italian language, in which she made rapid progress. In 1696, being then twenty-two, she published, at the request of her friends, various poems, to which she prefixed the poetical name of Philomela. A paraphrase of the thirty-eighth chapter of Job, written at the suggestion of Bishop Kenn, procured her some reputation.

Literary successes changed nothing in her calm and domestic life : the friendship of the polite and the great, found and left her in her quiet home. The happiness which she thus enjoyed was deep, though peaceful. She loved her father with all the tenderness and reverence due to his virtues ; an extract from a letter shows her feelings : " I have ease and plenty to the extent of my wishes, and can form desires of nothing, but what my father's indulgence would procure ; and I ask nothing of Heaven but the good old man's life. The perfect sanctity of his life, and the benevolence of his temper, make him a refuge to all in distress, to the widow and fatherless ; the people load him with blessings and prayers when he goes abroad, which he never does but to reconcile his neighbors, or to right the injured and oppressed ; the rest of his hours are entirely devoted to his private devotions, and to books, which are his perpetual entertainment." This excellent man, to whose example his daughter was no doubt deeply indebted, died in 1719, in sentiments of great piety. A friend, who witnessed his last hours, observed that he settled his affairs, and took leave of the world, with as much freedom and composure as if he had been setting out on a journey. His great care was to see that the widows and orphans with whose concerns he had been intrusted might not be injured after his death. His cheerfulness and sweetness of temper never forsook him ; but he sometimes felt his pulse, complained that it was still so regular, and smiled with a Christian's triumph at every sign and symptom of approaching death.

His only surviving daughter was already a widow when this event took place. Her charming countenance, agreeable conversation, and gentle temper, had early secured her a sufficient number of admirers ; amongst the rest, Prior, the poet, who answered one of her pastorals in a very tender strain, and wished, it is said, to marry her : but she would not go beyond friendship with him. The young and learned Thomas Rowe was the preferred suitor. They were married in 1710 ; Elizabeth Singer being then thirty-six, her husband but twenty-three. Time, which had not taken from her the simplicity and purity of youth, had left her its freshness and comely aspect : without being a perfect beauty, she was extremely attractive. She had hair of a fine auburn hue ; eyes of a deep grey, inclining to blue, and full of fire ; her complexion was

11*

exquisitely pure ; her voice soft and harmonious. The passion which her husband felt for her was both ardent and sincere ; her gentleness, her compliance with his wishes, the many virtues which he daily witnessed in her life, endeared her to him ; and marriage only increased his affection. They had been united about five years, when a fatal consumption, partly brought on by intense study, carried him off, in the twenty-eighth year of his age. He died, as he had wished to die, in the arms of his wife. She had attended on him during his illness with devoted affection ; and though she survived him many years, she could not, a short time before her own death, hear his name mentioned without shedding fresh tears at the loss it recalled.

It was only to please her husband that Mrs. Rowe had ever lived, even for a time, in London. After his death she indulged her passion for solitude by residing almost entirely at Frome ; where, like her father, she devoted her days to piety, good deeds, and books. She gave little time to dress, none to play or pleasure : her leisure was devoted to literary works of a moral character, and to labors of charity. She was constantly engaged in making garments for the poor ; she did so not only for the natives of the lower Palatinate, when the war drove them from their country, but also for whosoever around her needed such aid. She visited the sick, and instructed poor children ; or caused them to be instructed at her expense. She never went out without being provided with coins of different value, to give away to objects of charity. The first sum of money which she received from a publisher was bestowed on a family in distress, and she once sold a piece of plate for a similar purpose.

She carried her indifference in money matters to an excess ; there was no life she hated so much as the sordid and ungenerous love of gold, and none of which she was less guilty. She let her estates beneath their real value, and would not even allow unwilling tenants to be threatened with the seizure of their goods. But another trait of her character seems to us to paint her in a still more amiable light. Mrs. Rowe did not confine her charity to the miserable : she thought that "it was one of the greatest benefits that could be done to mankind, to free them from the cares and anxieties that attend a narrow fortune ;" and she accordingly made large presents to persons who were not in the extremity of want. There are few, we believe, who are unable to feel the pleasure which attends the relief of great misery; but only the most delicate minds, and the most generous hearts, can experience the peculiar gratification which Mrs. Rowe found in relieving, not mere physical distress, but also those many painful cares which are the torment of poverty, as distinguished from want.

The solitude in which Mrs. Rowe lived did not separate her from many valued friends. Her name occurs frequently in the pleasant letters addressed by the Countess of Hartford to Dr. Isaac Watts; and when this eminent man edited her "Devout Exercises of the Heart," it was to the Countess that he dedicated them. All the poetical ardor which characterized Mrs. Rowe's turn of mind appears in this work; once widely popular, and still read by those who are not tempted to smile at the mysticism of a pure and pious heart. Tenderness and enthusiasm are essential to the religion of woman: that of man is more properly belief; hers is love. We will make no extracts from the Devout Exercises, but we will transcribe from Mrs. Rowe's secret effusions a page which needs no comment.

"I consecrate half of my yearly income to charitable uses; and though by this, according to human appearances, I have reduced myself to some necessity, I cast all my care on that gracious God to whom I am devoted, and to whose truth I subscribe with my hand. I attest his faithfulness, and bring in my testimony to the veracity of his word; I set to my seal that God is true; and O, by the God of truth, I swear, to perform this, and beyond this. . . . . All that I have, beyond the bare convenience and necessity of life, shall surely be the Lord's; and O grant me sufficiency, that I may abound in every good work! O let me be the messenger of consolation to the poor! Here I am, Lord; send me. Let me have the honor to administer to the necessities of my brethren. I am, indeed, unworthy to wipe the feet of the least of the servants of my Lord, much more unworthy of this glorious commission; and yet, O send me, for thy goodness is free. Send whom thou wilt on embassies to kings and rulers of the earth, but let me be a servant to the servants of my Lord. Let me administer to the afflicted members of my exalted and glorious Redeemer. Let this be my lot, and I give the glories of the world to the wind."

This solemn vow, which, as Mrs. Rowe herself expressed it, in another part of her manuscripts, "was not made in an hour of fear and distress, but in the joy and gratitude of her soul," was religiously fulfilled, even when it exposed her to much personal inconvenience. To the end of her life, the poor shared with her in those blessings which she held from the bounty of God.

In 1736, her health began to fail. She prepared herself for death in that cheerful spirit with which she had lived. There seemed, however, no immediate cause for fear. After spending an evening in friendly conversation, she went up to her room; where, shortly afterwards, her servant found her in the agonies of death. She was, according to her request, quietly buried by the side of her father, in their place of worship at Frome. Like him, she was lamented by all those who had known her, and by none more than the poor. Amongst her papers were found several letters addressed to valued friends. They express, in ardent and confident language, the belief that, like the spirit, the affections are immortal. To the end, the religion of Elizabeth Rowe remained a religion of love. To love God and his creatures had been her delight on earth, and she hoped to do both in heaven. As she fervently expresses it, "That benignity, that divine charity, which just warms the soul in these cold regions, will shine with new lustre, and burn with an eternal ardor in the happy seats of peace and love."

A few years later, died another amiable woman, the spirit of whose life and sentiments greatly resemble those of Elizabeth Rowe. Those to whom the English literature of the last century is still familiar and pleasant, will probably remember the charming portrait of a lady, drawn by Congreve, under the name of Aspasia, in one of the most popular works of that time—The Tatler. This "Divine Aspasia" is thus described in the number for the 15th of July, 1709.

"But those ancients would be as much astonished to see in the same age, so illustrious a pattern to all who love things praiseworthy as the divine Aspasia. Methinks I see her now walking in her garden, like our first parent, with unaffected charms, before beauty had spectators, and bearing celestial conscious virtue in her aspect. Her countenance is the lively picture of her mind, which is the seat of honor, truth, compassion, knowledge, and innocence.

There dwells the scorn of vice and pity too.

"In the midst of the most ample fortune, and veneration of all that behold and know her, without the least affectation, she consults retirement, the contemplation of her own being, and that Supreme Power which bestowed it. Without the learning of schools, or knowledge of a long course of arguments, she goes on in a steady course of virtue, and adds to the severity of the last age all the freedom and ease of the present. The language and mien of a court she is possessed of in the highest degree; but the simplicity and humble thoughts of a cottage are her more welcome entertainment. Aspasia is a female philosopher, who does not only live up to the resignation of the most retired lives of the ancient sages, but also the schemes and plans which they thought beautiful though inimitable. This lady is the most exact economist, without appearing busy; the most strictly virtuous, without tasting the praise of it; and shuns applause with as much industry as others do reproach. This character is so particular, that it will be very easily fixed on her only by all that know her, but I dare say she will herself be the last to find it out."

This portrait, which might well be fancied ideal, was nevertheless taken from a living likeness—the Lady Elizabeth Hastings, daughter of Theophilus, seventh Earl of Huntingdon, and then in the twenty-eighth year of her age. She is universally represented as one of the most charming and accomplished women of her times. To her had nature been prodigal of her gifts; she had made her amiable, intellectual, and handsome. For the latter fact we have no better warrant than the impression she produced on those who beheld her: the portraits of Lady Hastings do not give us that mingled sweetness and dignity which was the charm of her countenance; but her biographer avers that none of these likenesses resembled the original. Sir Godfrey Kneller himself was baffled in his attempt to portray her features; and, vain as he was, confessed his failure. Through her mother, Lady Hastings was descended from Sir John Lewis of Ledstone, in Yorkshire, and inherited the greater bulk of his property. The death of her brother added to her wealth, and many gentlemen of the first rank became suitors for the hand of that fair Aspasia; whom, in another number of the Tatler, Steele described as " the first of the beauteous order of love, whose unaffected freedom and conscious innocence give her the attendance of the graces in all her actions." Lady Hastings refused these offers of marriage. Her precise motives for preferring a single life, were not known; but it was supposed that she considered it more in accordance with that religious perfection towards which she aimed; and also, that finding herself mistress of a large estate, she did not wish to lose the power of doing good by resigning it into other hands than her own.

Beneath a gentle exterior, Lady Hastings concealed all the religious severity of the preceding age. She was once induced to read a romance with a young lady less austere than herself, and the remembrance of what she considered a crying error, disturbed her to the end of her life. Her temper naturally led her to delight in seclusion and prayer; she shunned the gaieties of her rank; and, even when her means were still limited, the money at her disposal was almost all devoted to the poor. Her life of active charity did not begin, however, until after the death of her brother, the Earl of Huntingdon. Henceforward she resided almost constantly at Ledstone House. Though her income did not exceed L.3000, with this she performed wonders, and became the hope and stay of all the poor around her seat. Her grounds were kept in exquisite order; yet the persons employed were chiefly weak and aged individuals, fit for no other task; but who received a salary as high as if they had been strong and able-bodied. The rule of Lady Hastings was to give the first place to justice, the second to charity, and the third to generosity. She first attended to her household, to the welfare and comfort of her servants; and in those debts of justice, the very cattle, (which are declared to be a property of mercy,) were not forgotten. The poor had her next care : she assisted them in their own homes, or received them into her house : often in great numbers. Meal, physic, raiment, and money, freely distributed ; yearly allowances ; and large sums bestowed ; debts paid ; poor scholars assisted ; charity schools maintained ; religious societies aided ; churches erected and adorned, attested her unwearied liberality. A spirit of prudence and economy, which never rendered her parsimonious, guided all her actions; but her great secret must have been self-denial. She was frugal to herself that she might be generous to others. She was tender of the honor of her family, and liberal to her poorer relatives. One received L.500 a-year from her; she presented another with L.300 in money. Her generosity was not limited to those whose blood she shared. To a young lady, who had very much impaired her fortune by engaging in the South Sea scheme, she once gave three hundred guineas, (all the money then in her possession,) with a large promise of more. Her learned and pious friend, Mary Astell, she often assisted, and once presented her with fourscore guineas—a circumstance which escaped the knowledge of her biographer, so studious was she in concealing the good which she did.

The life of Lady Hastings, though thus devoted to good deeds, was neither cheerless nor unsociable. She mingled with that world where her personal accomplishments, and, above all, her great talents for conversation, always enabled her to shine; for though her own tastes led her to seek privacy, she would not give any ground of accusation or complaint against her by over austerity: she had, indeed, the rare talent of conciliating the love and esteem of all. The poor blessed her. Robert Nelson, no flatterer of rank, applied to her the following text: "Many daughters have done virtuously, but thou excellest them all;" and Steele and Congreve both wrote in her praise.

A painful close was reserved to a life so noble and so pure. In early life, Lady Elizabeth Hastings had received a contusion upon her right breast; a small inward tumor was the result; it gave her little pain, and was scarcely heeded by her; she thought the less about it that, for many years, it never increased. About twenty months before her death, Lady Hastings found this tumor growing so painful, that she applied for advice to the Rev. Dr. Johnson, eminent for his skill in surgery. He declared there was an absolute necessity for amputation of the affected part. Hitherto Lady Hastings had only been good—now she became heroic. Friends thought it needful to give her encouragement and advice under this trying dispensation: to preach resignation and submission to the will of God. With more emotion than she usually displayed, Lady Hastings observed, "I would not wish to be out of my present situation for all the world; nor would I exchange it for any other at any price."

In the eagerness with which she accepted pain, she showed herself a true and faithful daughter of the crucified Saviour. Her cheerfulness was not once disturbed by the prospect of suffering: she waited the day appointed for the operation with serene composure. Strong persons held her hands while it was performed: but a child might have held her, she was so calm. Not one expression of pain escaped her: one of the persons present averred that she sighed deeply when the operation was over; another eye-witness of this painful scene denied that she had betrayed even this slight token of suffering or relief.

Lady Hastings slowly recovered: her life seemed to be saved; when a sudden relapse, to which no surgeon's skill could now devise a remedy, brought her once more within prospect of death. Her resignation did not forsake her: although her sufferings were so exquisite that she could not even turn in bed, she sedulously concealed them, in order not to afflict her faithful servants. Her cheerfulness and composure of mind seemed beyond the reach of physical pain: she saw her friends, comforted and counselled those who still came to her as to their best adviser, and dictated a great number of letters to the many persons of distinction and piety with whom she held a correspondence. To the last her soul thirsted after deeds of mercy. "Where," would she often say to those about her, "where is there a poor member of Christ whom I can comfort and refresh?" She made large presents to those who solicited her aid: to one gentleman whom she had never seen, of whom she scarcely knew any thing, but who had been recommended to her by a friend, she sent forty guineas, in order to release him from prison.

The devising of her will was her chief task. Being filled with charitable bequests, it gave her infinite trouble; for she had to word it so prudently, and yet so clearly, as to run no risk of being misunderstood: this labor is said to have abridged her life. Resigned as she was to the will of God, she yet longed to live until her charities became established by law. Dr. Johnson's skill prolonged her life a week beyond the legal term: no earthly cares clouded her last moments. Surrounded by her whole household, she received the last offices of the Church of England. The lamp, that was burning low kindled with the last flame : a change came over her countenance, and her eyes lit up as she exclaimed, in broken tones: " Bless me, Lord ! what is it that I see ? Oh ! the greatness of the glory that is revealed in me—that is before me !" A while after she gently fell asleep, and all was over.

She was born on the 19th of April 1682, and died on the 22d of December 1739, in her fifty-seventh year. No opportunity of judging of her intellectual attainments now remains ; for though much of her time was spent in writing, she destroyed what she wrote : her memory owes all to her virtues, nothing to literary fame. She deserved to have it said of her, that " her private and public acts of charity were never exceeded by those of any woman in the kingdom."

A few years after the death of Mrs. Rowe and Lady Elizabeth Hastings, was born a woman whose long life was like theirs to be devoted to tasks of beneficence and piety ; who as an author was to attain considerable repute, and to possess an influence more great and extended than any previous female writer in England.

We allude to Hannah More, last but one of the five daughters of Mr. More, master of a foundation school in the parish of Stapleton, Gloucestershire ; where she was born in 1745. She early displayed a precocious facility for learning, strong religious feeling, and a tendency towards moral teaching, and the inculcation of her own opinions ; which remained her characteristics through life. One of her favorite amusements was to correspond with an imaginary sinner : her letters were full of advice, exhortation, and warning ; his answers overflowed with repentance and promises of reformation. When Mary, the eldest of Mr. More's five daughters, had reached her twenty-first year, she opened a boarding-school in Bristol ; she was assisted by her two sisters, Elizabeth and Sarah, whom she had helped to instruct ; and she took the younger ones, Hannah and Martha, under her care. A degree of affection, rare even amongst kindred, united the five sisters. They never married, and were seldom separated for any length of time ; they all reached a great age, and, with one exception, the order in which they had entered life, was also that of their departure. Mary, the eldest, was the first to go; Hannah, the youngest but one, the last.

Hannah was about twelve when the school was opened. She was then, and remained during her long life, subject to severe attacks of illness; which tended to develope still further the grave and reflective turn of her mind. She studied much, and learned languages with ease; translations from Latin, Spanish, and Italian authors were amongst her first poetical attempts. "The Search after Happiness," a pastoral drama, was her first production of any importance; it is characteristic, that it had in view a moral purpose—to substitute an innocent production for works of injurious tendency, which, in the rage for private dramatic performances, were then placed in the hands of youth.

Hannah More was about seventeen when she became acquainted with a gentleman of property named Turner, the uncle of two pupils in the establishment of her sister. She received from him proposals of marriage, which she first accepted and then declined. The whole affair was fraught with much pain to her, and made her determine never again to contract such an engagement: nothing in after-life could induce her to break this resolve. Whilst her sisters prospered in their school, Hannah continued engaged in those literary pursuits which brought her into so much notice, when she came to London in 1773. She was received with flattering distinction, and soon numbered amongst her friends Dr. Johnson, Sir Joshua Reynolds, Mrs. Montagu, Mrs. Boscawen, David Garrick and his wife; with others then eminent in the world of literature, art, and fashion, but now of less note. The letters which she wrote home at this period of her life are both agreeable and interesting. If we were now sketching, not the quiet history of a few pure and pious women, but the witty and varied social world which reverenced the sententious wisdom of Johnson, and frequented the blue-stocking club of Mrs. Montagu in Portman Square, the letters of Mrs. Hannah More would indeed afford us many curious and pleasant pictures of gaieties grown obsolete, of wit and charms once extolled, now known by hearsay and tradition, and give us an interesting insight into the characteristics of English society during the eighteenth century.

But it will be our task to collect from these letters know-

ledge of a very different nature ; we shall find in them other
records besides those of polite society and its intellectual
pleasures : they tell·in simple language the story of a few
women who undertook to civilize, by religion, districts where
vice, brutal ignorance, and crime, had replaced the fabled
pastoral innocence of poets. These generous women, sisters
according to the blood, and still more according to the
spirit, penetrated into spots where their very lives were not
held safe ; and braved every petty persecution to accomplish
their noble object : time, money, and health were devoted to
the task, and never regretted.

For twenty years Mrs. Hannah More continued to visit
London, and mingle with its fashionable and literary society ;
and it was during this period that she wrote her two trage-
dies and her sacred dramas. But gradually she withdrew
from those fascinating circles ; the death of her attached
friend, Garrick, spared her the pain of giving up her yearly
visits to one to whom she owed much, and whom she both
loved and esteemed.

It was towards the year 1783 that Mrs. Hannah More purchased, near Bristol, a small estate called Cowslip Green, on
which she built a little cottage. About the same time that
she fixed her residence in this quiet place, her sisters retired
to Bath, in easy circumstances : they had honorably conducted, for upwards of thirty years, an excellent establishment,
esteemed one of the best and most prosperous in the west of
England. They now fixed their home at Bath, where they
had a house ; between which and Cowslip Green they henceforth divided their time.

Hannah More had retired from the world in order to lead
a more perfect life in the eyes of God ; and, whilst she
restricted the sphere of her pleasures, to extend that of her
duties. She soon exerted herself with zeal and enthusiasm in
a cause dear and sacred to every generous heart. This was
the time when the energy and eloquence of Wilberforce were
devoted to the abolition of the slave-trade. It is recorded
that, when he was but fourteen years of age, he addressed a
letter to the editor of the York paper, " in condemnation of
the odious traffic in human flesh." His manhood adhered to
the principles of his youth. It lies not within our province to
do more than allude to the long and persevering struggle

which Wilberforce waged against this great iniquity : a struggle crowned with a success so glorious, and in which he was assisted by the most earnest and gifted of his contemporaries. To aid this noble cause, Hannah More wrote her poem of "Slavery." Thus began between them, in mutual sympathy for a long-oppressed race, a friendship that proved both warm and lasting.

The philanthropic exertions of Hannah More in favor of the blacks, did not prevent her from devoting a portion of her time to other literary pursuits. She wrote her "Thoughts on the Manners of the Great," and her "Estimate of the Religion of the Fashionable World;" both of which were very successful. Her chief relaxation from the more serious thoughts and tasks which occupied her, was to embellish and cultivate with her own hands the pleasant garden of Cowslip Green. This innocent indulgence was, however, the source of some self-reproach : to one who esteemed duty the end of every hour of life, it could scarcely be otherwise. A new sphere of usefulness opened before her, and removed these conscientious scruples.

At some distance from Cowslip Green, and in the immediate vicinity of the Mendip Hills, lies the village of Cheddar, a decayed market town of Somersetshire. It was then in a state of barbarous ignorance; which caused Mrs. Hannah More to observe, that "while we were sending missionaries to propagate the Gospel in India, our own villages were in pagan darkness." In more than pagan darkness would have been as correct an expression : there is something noble in the free life of the savage; though he may be criminal and barbarous, he cannot, whilst he breathes the pure air of liberty, be quite degraded. But what condition is that of the peasant who, to physical misery unknown in the savage state, unites the vices of civilisation with few or none of its virtues ! By law, indeed, the spiritual distress of Cheddar and its vicinity was provided for : the vicar of Cheddar resided at Oxford, and received fifty pounds a-year for duties which he never fulfilled; the resident rector of Axbridge "was intoxicated about six times a-week, and very frequently prevented from preaching by two black eyes, honestly acquired by fighting."

Mrs. Hannah More, and her sister Martha, who was then staying with her, resolved to go amongst those heathens of

Christianity, and see what good they could do in a place
where they knew not a single individual; where the literary
fame of one sister was unheard of, and where the station of
both was not likely to possess much influence with the few
wealthy and ignorant farmers whose will was the law of the
place. It possessed no gentry, and of the two thousand
inhabitants by far the greater number were miserably poor.
A clergyman rode over from Wells once every Sunday, to
preach to a congregation of eight persons; and in the whole
village there was but one Bible, and that was used to prop a
flower-pot. Hannah More and her sister began by taking a
lodging in a small public-house; then, after having examined
the state of things, they resolved to open a school. In a
letter written by Mrs. Hannah More to a friend, we find the
following account of this first attempt. "I was told we
should meet with great opposition, if I did not try to propi-
tiate the chief despot of the village, who is very rich and very
brutal; so I ventured to the den of this monster, in a country
as savage as himself. He begged I would not think of
bringing any religion into the country; it made the poor
lazy and useless. In vain I represented to him that they
would be more industrious, as they were better principled, and
that I had no selfish views in what I was doing. He gave
me to understand that he knew the world too well to believe
either the one or the other. I was almost discouraged from
more visits, but I found that friends must be secured at
all events; for if these rich savages set their faces against us,
I saw that nothing but hostilities would ensue; so I made
eleven more of these agreeable visits, and as I improved in
the art of canvassing, had better success. Miss W——
would have been shocked had she seen the petty tyrants
whose insolence I stroked and tamed, the ugly children I
praised, the pointers and spaniels I caressed, the cider I commended, and the wine I swallowed. After these irresistible
flatteries, I enquired of each if he could recommend me a
house, and said that I had a little plan which I hoped would
secure their orchards from being robbed, their rabbits from
being shot, their game from being stolen, and which might
lower the poor-rates. If effect be the best proof of eloquence,
then mine was a good speech, for I gained in time the hearty
concurrence of the whole people, and their promise to discou-

rage or favor the poor as they were attentive or negligent in
sending their children."

A house in which to establish a school was procured, not
without some difficulty. The poor, for whose benefit this was
intended, were almost as difficult to conciliate as the rich;
but patience and perseverance ultimately overcame their prejudices. The school was opened by Hannah More and her
sister one Sunday morning; children attended it, and
received their first lessons in the presence of their parents.
On the Sundays they were taught reading, and received religious instruction; on week-days the girls learned to knit and
sew. The two ladies soon had three hundred children, whom
they placed under the charge of a discreet matron.

Encouraged by success, they resolved to extend the benefits
they had conferred on Cheddar to other places, where it was
fully as much needed. Funds were required, and were liberally supplied by their friends. Thus supported, they set
about establishing schools in the neighboring districts; but
everywhere the farmers opposed them; and when this obstacle was overcome, another no less serious existed in the difficulty of finding proper teachers. Mrs. Hannah More and her
sister had, in the end, to teach the teachers,—a laborious and
fatiguing task.

Near the summit of Mendip there existed two mining villages, noted for the depravity and ignorance of their inhabitants. The ladies were warned that constables would not
venture to execute their office in this wild region, and that by
seeking to penetrate amongst these barbarians, they were only
perilling their own lives, with little chance of doing good.
They persisted; but their reception was not encouraging: the
people thought they wanted to make money by selling their
children as slaves, and that if they were unfortunately allowed
to teach them for seven years, they would indubitably acquire
the right of sending them over the seas. Spite of this unpro-
pitious beginning, they succeeded in securing pupils; their
number ultimately exceeded twelve hundred, and parents
gladly availed themselves of the instruction they had at first
dreaded for their children.

Hannah More has not recorded all the difficulties, and, to a
certain degree, the dangers, which beset her in her efforts at
civilizing rude and degraded peasants; but the little she has

said is significant. In a letter to her friend Wilberforce, from whom she derived both aid and counsel, she thus describes the opening of a school, in a spot more abandoned and depraved than any she had yet visited : "It was an affecting sight ; several of the grown-up youths had been tried at the last assizes—three were the children of a person lately condemned to be hanged—many were thieves !—all ignorant, profane, and vicious beyond relief. Of this banditti we have enlisted one hundred and seventy : and when the clergyman, a hard man, who is also a magistrate, saw these creatures kneeling round us, whom he had seldom seen but to commit or punish in some way, he burst into tears."

The bodily wants of these unhappy people were not forgotten by the benevolent sisters: their purse was ever open in seasons of famine or sickness, and the schoolmistresses whom they appointed were the ministers of physical as well as of spiritual charity. Generally speaking, the schools succeeded, and were attended with the most beneficial results. In one parish so violent a persecution was raised by the clergyman, (who had, however, been the first to invite Mrs. Hannah More,) that she was compelled to relinquish her task. Repeated attacks of ill health, and the infirmities of age, naturally restricted her labours ; but she had the satisfaction of knowing that what she could not always do herself, was done by able assistants : many of whom had been educated in those schools where they now taught in their turn.

In 1802 Mrs. Hannah More removed from Cowslip Green to Barley Wood, where she had erected a mansion large enough for herself and her sisters, who gave up their house at Bath to reside exclusively with her. Here Hannah More, though suffering from ill health, wrote "Cœlebs in Search of a Wife;" "Practical Piety," dedicated to Mrs. Fry ; "Christian Morals ;" "Moral Sketches," &c. She had the sorrow to lose her four sisters one by one : Mary, the eldest, died in 1813, at the advanced age of eighty ; Elizabeth departed in 1816 ; Sarah, who had helped her sister in some of her popular writings, followed her in less than a year ; Martha, the last and the most beloved, the sharer of her labors in the schools, lingered until 1819, when she died in great sufferings. Of the five sisters, but one, a lonely woman of seventy-four, now remained. She bore, without repining, her solitary lot. If literary fame and popularity could console under such painful sorrows, Hannah More need not have felt grief. Her name was known wherever her native language was spoken : the religious and moral aim of her writings had spread them to an extent which is not always granted to genius. Numerous editions of her works, and translations of them in almost every language, showed the value in which they, and the lessons they taught, were held. But her motives for resignation were higher than those which human fame holds out. She survived her sister fourteen years, during which she suffered much from repeated attacks of illness. Her last years were saddened by the ingratitude of her servants, who took advantage of her condition to rob and defraud her. She was compelled to leave Barley Wood, endeared by so many recollections, for Clifton, where she died five years afterwards, in 1833, having then reached the advanced age of eighty-eight.

It is difficult to estimate the influence which, as a popular writer, Hannah More has exercised in this country : it was political, moral, and religious. She met, in many essential points, the spirit of the times in which she lived; she was zealous, earnest, and succeeded. Her temper was more liberal and generous than her principles : she deplored the Catholic Emancipation, and yet, at the time of the Revolution, she had published a book expressly for the benefit of the emigrant priests, and the profits of which amounted to two hundred and forty pounds. In the same spirit, she who had braved so much inconvenience to serve the poor—who had sacrificed time, health, and money to instruct their children—seriously apprehended danger and evil if their education should go beyond the Scriptures : as if the bountiful Creator, who has given the same noble faculties to all his children, had not by this proclaimed the free use of those faculties as their inalienable birthright.

But these and similar mistakes of opinion, too frequent amongst religious persons, and by no means peculiar to Hannah More, need not detract from the praise due to her deeds of mercy. To judge individuals, not by their opinions, but by their actions, may be a commonplace rule enough; but it is the rule of charity, and fit to apply to the dead as well as to the living.

To that eighteenth century, beyond which the life of Hannah

More was prolonged for so many years, also belonged Selina, Countess of Huntingdon, sister-in-law of Lady Elizabeth Hastings; so celebrated for the fervor of her religious opinions, and the zeal with which she labored to extend them. Her private charities are said to have been great; but she is best known as the foundress of a sect which still exists. The disciple of Whitefield and Wesley had inherited all their zeal and enthusiasm : sacrificing the prejudices of birth and rank, she devoted herself, heart and soul, to Methodism. As we do not, however, profess to relate the history of opinions, or of those exertions which are connected with them, we cannot enter into any detail of Lady Huntingdon's labors. She was in earnest, and exerted herself assiduously to establish the points of belief which she thought essential to salvation. She founded and supported a college at Trevecca, in Wales, for the education of ministers. At her death, in 1791, there existed sixty-four chapels which she had founded, and in which were preached the tenets she professed.

From her and those who, like her, thought chiefly of the doctrinal points of the Christian faith, we must turn to those women who felt in their hearts that Christ came on earth not merely to save and atone, but also to do good, and teach us the spirit in which good should be done.

CHAPTER XX.

Rosa Govona—Maria Agnesi—Duchess of Ventadour—Catherine Cahouet—Anne Auverger—Madame de Quatremère.

On the northern side of the Ligurian Apennines, in the basin formed by the Upper Tanaro, extends the district of Mondovi, a province of the Sardinian states. Surrounded by a fertile tract of land, rich in corn, vines, mulberry trees, and cattle, rises the chief town, Mondovi. It is built partly on the bank of the Ellero, partly on a hill which rises above the river. It can boast of a strong castle, several churches and convents, a seminary, a college, various manufactories, and some fifteen thousand inhabitants.

In this quiet place there lived, in the course of the last century, a young orphan girl, of the name of Rosa Govona. She excelled in needle-work, her only means of support; she never cared for pleasure, and thought not of marriage: grave, mild, and silent, she lived alone, in the dignity of labor and the honor of womanhood.

Towards the year 1746, Rosa, being then in her thirtieth year, happened to meet a young girl, an orphan like herself, who was destitute, and without the means of earning a livelihood. The sight grieved her compassionate heart, and shocked her feminine delicacy. She took home the young stranger, and addressing her in language of scriptural simplicity, "Here," said she, pointing to her humble dwelling, " here shalt thou abide with me: thou shalt sleep in my bed; thou shalt drink from my cup, and thou shalt live by the labor of thine own hands." This last clause, comprising independence and self-respect, was one of the most cherished points in the creed of Rosa. Pleased with the docility and industry of her young guest, she conceived the project of a female association, based on the principles of labor and mutual aid. Ere long, the girl of Mondovi was surrounded by a society of young and unprotected single women, who dwelt beneath the same roof, and labored diligently for their livelihood.

This association, being something quite novel in Mondovi, was naturally attacked: the wise derided and censured it; grave imputations were cast on the morals of Rosa and her companions, and libertine young men followed and insulted them whenever they left their home. Their prudent silence, and, above all, their blameless life, at length prevailed over calumny; and they were allowed to live and labor in peace: nay, more, the authorities of Mondovi, seized with a sudden fit of official zeal, repaired their long neglect of an institution reflecting so much honor on the community with which it had originated, by offering Rosa, whose abode had now grown too narrow, a house in the plain of Carcassona. This she readily accepted, and was soon surrounded by seventy young girls. She obtained another and larger house in the plain of Brao; but, extending her views with her means, Rosa no longer confined the labors of her friends to the common tasks of needle-work : the house of Brao became a real factory for the manufacture of woollen stuffs. Nine years had now elapsed since Rosa first took home the orphan girl. She might well have rested satisfied with what she had done; but, consulting only her zeal and anxious wish of spreading the good effects of her system, she set off for Turin in the year 1755.

Rosa Govona entered the capital of Piedmont with no other protection than her own strong faith, and no higher recommendation than the two or three young girls who accompanied her. She simply explained her project, and asked for an asylum. The fathers of the oratory of St. Philip gave her a few rooms "for the love of God," and the military depôt sent her tables and straw mattresses. Rosa and her companions were quite satisfied, and establishing themselves in their new abode, they cheerfully set to work.

The fact became known, and attracted attention. On the suggestion of his financial minister, count of Gregory, Charles Emmanuel III. assigned to Rosa and her companions large buildings, belonging to a religious brotherhood recently suppressed. The house was soon filled with forsaken orphan girls. The king read and approved the judicious rules laid down by Rosa, and ordered the factories of the establishment to be organized and registered, by the magistrates appointed to superintend commercial matters. From that time the Rosinas, as they were called in honor of their foundress, enjoyed the special patronage of the Sardinian government.

Rosa Govona felt deeply grateful for the favor her plans had received from the king. Knowing that the most effectual method of showing her gratitude would be to continue as she had begun, and to contribute to the commercial and moral prosperity of his dominions, she established in Turin two factories; one of cloth for the army, and another of the best silks and ribands. Thanks to her, three hundred women without dowry, without any resource save their own labor, earned an honest and comfortable livelihood, and provided in youth for the wants of their old age. Houses depending on that of Turin were established at Novarra, Fossano, Savigliano, Saluzzo, Chieri, and St. Damian of Asti. Over the entrance of every house which she founded, Rosa caused to be engraved the words she had addressed to her first guest: "'Tu mangerai còl lavoro delle tue mani,"—Thou shalt live by the labor of thine own hands.

Rosa devoted twenty-one years to the task of going over the provinces of Piedmont, and founding asylums for the unprotected and industrious poor of her sex; until, exhausted by her labors, she died at Turin. Her remains were deposited in the chapel of the establishment there: on the simple monument which covers them may still be read the following epitaph: "Here lies Rosa Govona of Mondovi. From her youth she consecrated herself to God. For his glory she founded in her native place, and in other towns, retreats opened to forsaken young girls, so that they might serve God. She gave them excellent regulations; which attach them to piety and labor. During an administration of thirty years, she gave constant proofs of admirable charity and of unshaken firmness. She entered on eternal life on the 28th day of February, of the year 1776, the sixtieth of her age. Grateful daughters have raised this monument to their mother and benefactress."

With this simple, yet touching record of a useful and dignified life, closes all we are told of Rosa Govona. We know more what she did than what she was. She appears to us through her good works: thoughtful, silent, and ever doing: a serious and beneficent apparition. In aspect she was grave, earnest, and resolute. A plain cap, a white kerchief, a cross on her bosom, and a brown robe, constituted the attire of the foundress of the Rosinas. One of her biographers calls her Sister Rosa; but it does not appear that she took any vows, or sought to impose any on her community. The Rosinas are bound by no tie; they can leave their abode, and marry if they wish; but they rarely do so. There will always be a certain number of women whom circumstances or private inclination will cause to remain unmarried. Rosa Govona was one of these; and for them she labored. She wished to save them from vice, idleness, and poverty: to preserve to them unsullied the noblest inheritance of human beings: dignity and self-respect.

According to an interesting account published in Paris a few years ago, the Rosinas are still in a prosperous and happy state. They are admitted from thirteen to twenty; they must be wholly destitute, healthy, active, and both able and willing to work. They are patronized by government, but labor is their only income: all work assiduously, save the old; who are supported by their younger companions. The Turin establishment is the chief and central one; the other houses still exist; with the exception of that which Rosa Govona founded at Novarra. It was closed when this town belonged to the kingdom of Italy; and has not since been re-opened. To preserve the spirit of the modest and retired life which Rosa wished her daughters to lead, no commercial matters are transacted save at the establishment in Turin, which governs the other houses. The labors of the Rosinas are varied and complete: whatever they manufacture, they do with their own hands from beginning to end. They buy the cocoons in spring, and perform every one of the delicate operations which silk undergoes, before it is finally woven into gros-de-naples, levantines, and ribands. Their silks are of the best quality, but plain, in order to avoid the expense and inconvenience of changing their looms with every caprice of fashion. They also fabricate linen; but only a limited number of Rosinas can undergo the fatigue of weaving. In order not to interfere with the silk establishment of Turin, the manufacture of woollen stuffs is now carried on at Chieri. Government buys all the cloth of the army from the Rosinas; they even manufacture all the accessory ornaments, and make up the uniforms, which are cut out for them by tailors. Gold lace, and the rich vestments of priests, are likewise produced by these industrious women, who excel in every female art, and are renowned for their skill in embroidery. The produce of their varied labors is gathered at Turin in a large magazine, and sold there by trustworthy persons. The house of the Rosinas is patronized not only by government, but also by many of the inhabitants and tradespeople of Turin; for there is a general preference in favor of goods excellent in quality, fair in price, and manufactured by the hands of these pure and innocent women. Their profits are moderate, but sufficient. The house in Turin alone spends eighty thousand francs a-year; and it holds three hundred women; of whom fifty, who are either old or infirm, and consequently unable to work, are supported by the rest.

"I visited this remarkable establishment," writes an eye-witness, "thanks to the kindness of the worthy ecclesiastic who administers and directs it. He accompanied me through those wide halls containing so many women animated by the holy ardor of labor. Separated from man, they nevertheless share with him the fatigue to which he was condemned on the day when God sent him forth on earth. They went through their tasks with mild gravity and admirable composure, yet displaying the zeal which a mother might feel in working with her daughters for the good of the common family. Six mistresses and one director (a woman) preside over them, and are frequently visited by the queen, who grants a special protection to these industrious women."

One woman, poor, obscure, and unlearned, but strong in her faith, and, above all, in her love for her orphan sisters, did this.

The learned Maria Gaetana Agnesi is not unworthy of appearing after the noble Piedmontese girl. They were contemporaries; and, much as they differed in other respects, their lives were marked by the same earnest and generous spirit.

Like Helena Cornaro in the preceding age, Maria Agnesi united profound learning to Christian virtues. She was born at Milan in 1718, of rich and noble parents. Her love of study was early developed; she asked to share her brother's Latin lessons, and made such rapid progress, that at nine years of age she composed a Latin discourse in favor of women, which was published. At eleven she began Greek, which she ultimately read fluently, and even spoke with ease; she likewise studied Hebrew, and almost every modern language. At thirteen she translated into Italian, French, German, and Greek, the Latin supplements added by Freinshemius to the history of Quintus Curtius; and in the following year she translated from Italian into Greek "The Spiritual Combat," an ascetic work of Father Lorenzo Scupoli.

The father of Maria Agnesi encouraged her in her studies, and directed them towards mathematics, which he thought best suited to the serious bent of her mind. At fourteen she studied the Elements of Euclid and natural philosophy. She commented on the work of L'Hospital on conic sections; and in 1738, when she had reached her twentieth year, she published one hundred and ninety-one theses, which she had maintained in the preceding year, in the presence of the most distinguished persons of Milan. After ten years of close study, she produced her "Analytical Institutions." This work had great success. If it was not exactly the means of introducing Algebra into Italy, it had, at least, the merit of drawing more attention to that branch of science. In the name of the French Academy, Fontenelle proclaimed it the best work which had yet been written on the subject; and Bossut, who translated it into French, gave a similar judgment. Colson of Cambridge showed his opinion of its value by translating it into English.

Maria Agnesi had dedicated this eminent work to Maria Theresa, who thanked and congratulated her, and sent her a valuable ring and a casket adorned with precious stones. She met with still more gratifying tokens of esteem in her native land : she was received as a member of the Institute of Bologna; Pope Benedict XIV. named her honorary reader to the university of the same city, and gave her the mathematical chair. In Milan, Maria Agnesi was treated with marked respect. The house of her father was the resort of the most learned and distinguished individuals of the whole city : whom she knew how to receive with mingled dignity and grace. She was tall, and of an elegant figure; her hair and eyes were extremely dark, although her complexion was exquisitely fair. Her portraits represent a face beautiful indeed, but, like that of an ancient muse, grave and serene in its very beauty. Such was ʻMaria Agnesi—handsome, honored, celebrated—when she declared to her father that her vocation called her to the cloister : she had lost her mother when she was about eighteen, and since then her religious feelings had gradually increased. Her father entreated her not to leave him; he had married twice since the death of his first wife, but of his twenty-three children Maria was the most beloved : she was the pride of his old age, and the guide and instructress of his large family. His grief at the prospect of losing her was such, that Maria, who loved him tenderly, agreed to remain; but on condition that she might dispense from mingling with society, and be allowed to live in perfect retirement from the world. Agnesi readily consented. His death in 1752, which had been preceded by that of several of his sons, was one of the greatest sorrows Maria had to endure. She persisted, however, in her solitary life, and refused every offer of marriage.

Like Pascal, she gave up science : the severe studies which had so long charmed her were relinquished for the Fathers of the Church. So deep became her knowledge in theology, that

Pozzobonelli, archbishop of Milan, having to pronounce on the orthodoxy of a work which was said to contain some doubtful points of doctrine, referred the matter to the judgment of Maria Agnesi. She acquitted herself of this delicate task with great sagacity and moderation, and saved the author from the persecution with which he was threatened.

The piety of this gifted woman was not confined to theological knowledge. It had that test of true faith, charity. She visited the sick of her parish, and of the great hospital of Milan; she even devoted several retired apartments of her house to infirm women, whom she took under her own care. Her whole income was consecrated to this charitable task; but not deeming this sufficient, she sold her most valuable possessions, amongst the rest the ring and casket sent to her by Maria Theresa, and by means of the sum thus raised, she doubled the number of beds in her domestic hospital. Her own house soon became too small; she took a larger one, filled it with sick, and attended on them with a devoted zeal which the most loathsome and afflicting diseases could not weary or repel.

In the year 1771, Prince Trivulzi founded in Milan a large hospital for aged and infirm individuals of either sex. Pozzobonelli, who was still archbishop of the city, requested Agnesi to undertake the laborious office of governing the female department in the new establishment. She accepted, made the hospital her home, and reduced her expenses in order to be able to assist its inmates from her private resources. For fifteen years Maria Agnesi devoted herself to this heroic task; during which her health, sustained by the energy of her will, did not suffer from her incessant and self-imposed labor. She died on the ninth of January of the year 1799, in the eighty-first year of her age.

We think we may say without exaggeration, that Rosa Govona and Maria Agnesi were amongst the most noble Christian women of their age; not merely because they did much good, but because they did it in a noble spirit: giving up all, and forgetful of self.

This spirit, which had been so remarkable in France during the seventeenth century, seems absent from the eighteenth. We hear of good deeds; but, with a few exceptions, we do not find whole lives devoted to good, like those of Mesdames de Chantal, Miramion, Louise Legras, Jeanne Biscot, and others whom we were compelled to mention more briefly. We cannot make this more apparent than by recording all that we have been able to collect on this subject.

The Duchess of Ventadour, governess of the young Louis XV., displayed great generosity during a period nearly approaching to famine; then no uncommon occurrence amongst the oppressed peasantry of France. She spent her whole revenue in charity, and borrowed eighty thousand francs, to give more away. When her alarmed steward remonstrated, she meekly replied: "Let us give always, and even borrow, while it is necessary to save the poor from death. We shall never want; neither I nor my family: in my station there is no great hardship in trusting to Providence."

Much as we admire the generosity of the duchess, we give more honor to the devotedness of humble Catherine Cahouet. In 1691, she established at Orleans a charity school; her two sisters shared her labors. The clergyman of their parish, anxious to forward this good work, presented Mademoiselles Cahouet with a larger house. Two of his sisters joined them, and no fewer than two hundred poor children were instructed by the five ladies.—They gave books to most, and fed and clothed many at their own expense. For sixty years Catherine Cahouet was at the head of this establishment, and labored as assiduously in her ninety-second year as in her youth. From Advent until Easter she addressed the children on religious subjects for two hours every day. She possessed in a rare degree the art of teaching, and instructed schoolmistresses who were sent to her for that purpose by country clergymen. Her long and useful life closed in 1751.

Two years after the death of Catherine Cahouet, Anne-Marie-Gilbert Auverger was born at Châteaugiron, a little town of Brittany; where she died in her seventeenth year. Within this narrow circle, and these few years, she gathered virtues and good deeds sufficient to adorn a long life. At the age of fifteen, she requested her parents to place her as boarder with the Sisters of Mercy, who attended on the sick of Vitré. They consented, although Anne did not conceal from them that it was her intention eventually to share the life of these devoted women. She remained there a year, seizing every opportunity of entering the wards of the sick, and of serving her apprenticeship, by early inuring herself to the sight of dis-

12*

ease, under its most painful aspects. When she returned to
her home, she earnestly asked to wear plain brown gowns, as
most suitable to her taste, and to her future mode of life.
Some persons found fault with this, as well as with her caps;
which were not becoming, they said, for one so young; Anne
smiled, and answered gaily: "I wish to save up all my charms
for heaven; the fashions here do not please me: I hope to be
better adorned there than you are now." Another class of
censors, shocked at her habitual cheerfulness, told her "she
was very merry for a girl so devout." "Religion is not sad,"
she gently answered; "one cannot but feel happy under the
yoke of so good a master as God."

The young girl served that Master in every action of her
life. After her morning devotions, she daily distributed bread
and work to a great number of poor. The afternoon was
spent in visiting the sick: no weather ever kept her within;
no distance detained her; she visited the most remote cottages; the most loathsome stables, where unhappy peasants,
less cared for than cattle, died of cold and disease. In the
evening Mademoiselle Auverger instructed four children.

The fame of her charity gave her means to effect all this
good; for liberal persons intrusted her with their alms: they
bestowed the money, the young girl gave her active zeal and
every moment of her time. In the year 1769–70, Brittany
suffered much from dearth, severity of weather, and contagious diseases. The Marquess of Châteaugiron, a wealthy and
philanthropic nobleman, made Mademoiselle Auverger his
almoner; she was then little more than sixteen, and personally
unknown to him; but common report had long proclaimed the
young girl the most active and faithful friend of the poor, and
the marquess knew that his alms could not pass through hands
more pure. The zeal of Anne Auverger was not confined to
physical distress: she pitied those who sinned even more than
those who suffered; and her pity was most deep for those of
her own sex who had erred. The pure have always been the
most zealous in their charity to the degraded.

It required, however, some courage to act as Mademoiselle
Auverger acted. She visited several unfortunate girls in their
abode; and, though her affecting remonstrances did not always
prove effectual, she was never once insulted. To arrest evil in
its source,—poverty and idleness,—she gathered together some

poor orphan girls, and placed them in a house; where she kept them, gave them work, and superintended their conduct. One evening, Mademoiselle Auverger was horrified to learn that one of these young girls had been seduced into a house of the worst character. She took no time to reflect or hesitate, but rose, and, followed by a servant, proceeded at once to the house. She entered boldly, upbraided the owners of the shameless abode, and led away her protegée, whom she soon after placed at service in the country.

This incident became known, and her conduct was censured: some friends informed Mademoiselle Auverger that the world did not approve her conduct. She mildly answered, " We must let the world speak: it censures everything which seems to censure its maxims."

Mademoiselle Auverger had not long passed her seventeenth year, when a contagious fever broke out at Châteaugiron. She attended the sick with her usual zeal and fearlessness; but she said to some friends, that God would soon remove her. The prediction was fulfilled: a violent fever carried her away, after an illness of five days. She met her fate with fervent joy. A holy death crowned her brief life, and a few words sum up her eulogy: she had scarcely emerged from the years of childhood when she died; yet she left, and deserved to leave, the name, touching in one so young, of " mother of the poor."

The promise held forth by the youth of Anne Auverger was fulfilled in the life of Anne Bourjet, wife of a respected and well known merchant, Nicholas Quatremère. She was born at Paris in 1732, whilst the shameless libertinism of the late regency still disgraced the capital of France ; and she died there in 1790, on the eve of the revolution by which that profligacy was so fearfully avenged. She filled the interval of her life by the practice of woman's most excellent household virtues, as well as by deeds of the most heroic charity.

Mademoiselle Bourjet belonged to a rich commercial family, and received a good education. She was intelligent, quick in her perceptions, and gentle in her temper; but her ardent piety was apt to lead her into extremes: she had already injured her health by too much fasting. When she was married to M. Quatremère, at the age of eighteen, she found means to reconcile the duties of her new position with those of her religious exercises, and of her almost boundless charity. She had ten children, and her health was delicate; yet every day she went forth on errands of mercy, no matter what the weather might be. She visited the most wretched abodes of Paris, groping up dark and noisome staircases, or climbing up ladders that led to remote garrets, in order to find the poor in all their misery. She relieved the wants of all, good or evil, and extended her bounty to Jew, Protestant, and Catholic alike; no more distinguishing them in her charity, than they are distinguished by the great Father of all.

A woman who devoted herself in youth to such a life, had little to do with the world and its pleasures: the duties of home and the service of the poor filled her days, and satisfied her desires. Tenderly loved by her rich husband, who indulged her in her charity, she still found herself poor; and, in order to be able to give more, imposed upon herself restrictions, which, to her, were no privations. She sold her costly laces, and the greater part of her jewels, dressed with extreme simplicity, had only four or five gowns at a time; and, whilst she limited herself to the most scanty supply of body linen, yearly gave away three or four hundred shirts and chemises to the prisons and hospitals: which she had once been in the habit of visiting constantly, but had ceased to frequent, for the sake of her children.

In the year 1767, Madame Quatremère became one of the "Ladies of Charity" of her parish. Two years afterwards they named her treasurer of the poor: an arduous, but to her congenial, task; in which she displayed so much activity and talent that she was re-elected every three years, until the close of her life. No matter how indisposed she might feel—and her health, as has already been said, was delicate—she never missed being present at the weekly meetings. Her charity was so extensive and well known, that it spared her some trouble: she no longer needed to seek out the poor: they came to her. She received them in her drawing-room, where she sat the greater part of the day, weak and ailing, but ever ready to give aid and consolation. The poor were to her guests and friends: she would never allow them to be turned away from her doors. She gave up to them her arm-chair and the seat of honor, made them sit at her board, and shared with them those gifts which her devout spirit always ascribed to the great bestower of all earthly blessings, God. The hall and staircase of her dwelling, we are told, were never empty; and foundlings were often left there, as to the keeping of an earthly providence. Visiters flocked to her from every part of Paris, and from distant provinces, where the fame of her good deeds had penetrated.

The benevolence of Madame Quatremère was especially displayed after the Hôtel Dieu had been burned down, in 1772, and during the severe winter of 1787. Moral sorrows and destitution had an equal claim on her aid and sympathy. She took into her own house under her own care, poor abandoned girls, redeemed them from vice, fed and clothed them, and either found them situations, or paid their entrance into the asylum of "the Good Shepherd," founded by Madame de Combé, or in "the Penitent Daughters of the Saviour," another institution of the same kind.

It was not exclusively with her own resources, however extensive, that Madame Quatremère could effect so much: charitable persons sent her, from every part of France, large sums, to be applied as she thought proper. Every time Marie Antoinette became a mother, she gave Madame Quatremère six hundred francs for purposes of charity. She also possessed much influence with ministers, church dignitaries, great ladies powerful at court, and even over the celebrated Lenoir, lieutenant of police. The prisons were open to her; as the only use she made of her power was to do good, and liberate poor debtors: often, however, by paying their debts herself.

The arduous labours of a charity so continuous exhausted this heroic woman. She died of an illness brought on by fatigue, on the 16th of March, 1790. An immense crowd followed her to the grave; and the general remark was, that the ceremony resembled more the translation of the relics of a venerated saint, than a common funeral. According to one of her last requests, the poor received on that day four hundred loaves of bread; she also left three thousand francs to the poor of the parish. The Ladies of Charity commemorated her death by a solemn service, at which persons of every rank were present. On leaving the church, the old Maréchal of Mouchy said, "I have come here to pray for her intercession, and not to pray for the repose of her soul:" meaning that he considered her a saint in heaven. Louis XVI. and Marie Antoinette

expressed their regret for the death of this charitable lady ; and
the old Duke of Penthièvre, one of the most virtuous and
benevolent men of his age, wrote to M. Quatrèmere, to condole
with him on the loss he had experienced.

CHAPTER XXI.

Madame Necker—Madame de Fougeret—Madame de Pastoret—
Jeanne de Corbion—Sister Martha.

THAT personal sort of charity which delights in giving, is
that which women practise best, because it is essentially the
charity of feeling. But they are also capable of taking a
higher and more philanthropic aim; and the nearer we
approach our own times, the more does this become apparent.
To our seeming, this utilitarian spirit enhances the merit of
charity, and raises it above mere impulse. We have already
recorded several remarkable instances of it in the past; we
shall also see it faithfully exemplified in the lives of Madame
Necker, Madame de Fougeret, and other generous women.

The wife of the minister on whose sagacity the destinies of
France were long supposed to depend, and the mother of the
illustrious Madame de Staël, had a twofold life and character.
She lived in the world ; she gave dinners to philosophers, she
had friendships with the great : but she ever remained the same
pure and austere daughter of the Protestant minister of Lau-
sanne, whom Necker had married in the days of his obscurity.
Her friend, Lally de Tollendal, compared her to the fountain
Arethusa, whose clear waters preserved their purity in the midst
of the sea.

The whole amount of the good and charitable actions which
adorned her life has not been revealed to us. Madame Necker
was a Christian, and most unassuming in her virtues ; but
though much may be hidden, much is also known. When
Necker became director-general of the finances in 1776, his
wife, who had always possessed great influence over him,
resolved to use that influence for the noblest and most disinterested purposes. She attempted to do away with the lottery ;

and though she failed, her representations induced her husband to impose as many restrictions on it as the nature of his power allowed. She succeeded better when she interfered in the direction of prisons and hospitals. During the five years of her husband's administration, she devoted herself to the amelioration of these places of suffering and punishment; restraining abuses, and introducing important reforms. On retiring from office in 1781, Necker thought himself warranted in closing his Compte Rendu with the following testimony to the virtues of his wife: "Whilst retracing a portion of the charitable tasks prescribed by your majesty, let me be permitted, sire, to allude, without naming her, to a person gifted with singular virtues, and who has materially assisted me in accomplishing the designs of your majesty. Although her name was never uttered to you, in all the vanities of high office, it is right, sire, that you should be aware that it is known and frequently invoked in the most obscure asylums of suffering humanity. It is no doubt most fortunate for a minister of finances to find, in the companion of his life, the assistance he needs for so many details of beneficence and charity, which might otherwise prove too much for his strength and attention. Carried away by the tumult of general affairs,—often obliged to sacrifice the feelings of the private man to the duties of the citizen,—he may well esteem himself happy, when the complaints of poverty and misery can be confided to an enlightened person, who shares the sense of his duties."

In this touching homage we find no mention made of a benevolent and munificent act in which the king had desired to bear a part with Madame Necker—the foundation of the hospital which still bears her name in Paris. A Benedictine convent, situated in the Rue de Sèvres, having been suppressed in 1779, Madame Necker rented the vacant buildings; which she converted into an hospital capable of holding one hundred and twenty persons. Louis XVI. contributed to its support; and in 1782, it held sixty-eight men and sixty women. Madame Necker directed the establishment herself, until the great revolution compelled her and her husband to retire to Coppet. She died there, in 1794, of a painful and lingering disease, which never once impaired her cheerfulness. In her last moments she thanked God "for having placed in her heart an unmoved faith, and given her as her earthly support the man she respected most."

The task of Madame de Fougeret lay in another direction, but was not less useful. This lady was the daughter of a celebrated jurisconsult, and of a woman remarkable for her talents and virtues. She was early married to M. de Fougeret, receiver-general of the finances, and won both esteem and love in the circle in which she moved. She was one of the few women of that age who, to become agreeable, did not forfeit every claim to respect. Her countenance was pleasing and expressive, her discourse elegant, her judgment clear and sound, her temper amiable, her conscience serene, her life innocent and useful.

Her father, M. Dontrémont, had long administered the hospitals of Paris. She often heard him lament the insufficient accommodation of the Foundling Hospital, established by St. Vincent of Paul; as in consequence of this want of room, a heavy mortality prevailed amongst the foundlings. The Sisters of Charity, whom Madame de Fougeret frequently visited, uttered the same complaints: four rows of cradles extended along the great hall; and all the care of the sisters and nurses could not prevent deaths, far above the average, from taking place amongst this great number of children. The reason of this was, the administration could not afford to put out a sufficient number at nurse. Madame de Fougeret accordingly proposed, in 1784, to take a certain number of the children, and confide them to aged unemployed women; who would rear them, on goat's or cow's milk, at a cheaper rate than regular nurses. The suggestion was adopted: a large car, constructed under the direction of Madame de Fougeret, and in which twenty cradles were slung, so as to allow no jolting, conveyed eighty children to her husband's estate, where they were distributed amongst the cottagers. The experiment failed; three-fourths of the children died: a mortality not so heavy as that which prevailed in the Foundling Hospital, but which nevertheless greatly afflicted Madame de Fougeret, and convinced her that another and more efficacious remedy must be adopted.

St. Vincent of Paul had established the Foundling Hospital for illegitimate children; but the times were hard, and it was

a well-known fact, that many infants born in wedlock were
sent and admitted: there was indeed no power to exclude
them. Madame de Fougeret was struck with this circumstance; and she thought that the best remedy for the existing
evil would be to enable poor mothers to rear their children at
home. Too modest to seek for publicity, she solicited the aid
of the Duchess of Cossè, superior of the hospital; and, with
that lady's consent, she issued in her name a simple and affecting circular. Titled and wealthy ladies promptly answered
the appeal; and regulations were drawn up concerning the
quarters of Paris to be visited, and the amount of relief to be
given. A Greek name was proposed for the new institution,
but Madame de Fougeret resisted the suggestion; and it
received the simple, though appropriate, designation of "Maternal Charity." The society began its labors in 1788; Louis
XVI. headed the list of subscribers, and Marie Antoinette
accepted the title of Protectress: she received several times
the ladies who administered the society, and testified her
approbation and esteem, to her who directed its labors under
the modest title of secretary. The first seal of the society
represented Moses saved by the daughter of Pharaoh, and confided to his own mother; and it bore the name of the queen:
but that ill-fated name was soon effaced by the Revolution,
which interrupted the good work in the very midst of its
prosperity.

The ladies who had governed and supported the society were
now dispersed in foreign lands, or had perished on the scaffold.
Madame de Fougeret remained; but she had to struggle against
the indecent innovations which the revolutionary committees
wished to introduce, by voting rewards to the unmarried women who had given citizens to the state. Her arrest closed
the debate; yet so judicious and regular had always been her
proceedings, that, though want of funds interrupted the progress of the Maternal Charity, every one of its engagements
was fulfilled: for it had very properly been made a rule, that
the full amount of money needed for the support of a child
should be ready before the claims of the infant were admitted.
The husband of Madame de Fougeret was arrested with her,
and he died by the guillotine: they had enjoyed together
thirty years of uninterrupted happiness and perfect union.
Her life was spared; but not her property. She had children;

for whose sake she braved the danger which then attended imprudent claims; and her eloquent and energetic remonstrances succeeded in preserving the wreck of M. de Fougeret's former wealth. She retired to the country with her four daughters, their husbands, and children: she was now the head of this large family, and ruled it with prudence and tenderness.

Madame de Fougeret had thus spent a few peaceful years, when tidings reached her in her retreat, that Napoleon, with that enlightened sagacity which characterized his administration, had adopted the Maternal Charity, and declared it an imperial establishment by a decree of the senate. To give it, more lustre, he placed it under the protection of his wife, Marie Louise. No subscriptions under five hundred francs were received; all the ladies of the imperial court were expected to subscribe; and government gave a yearly allowance of five hundred thousand francs. The Maternal Charity was no longer confined to Paris alone: Societies, on the model of the central one, were established in every large town; and the judicious rules which Madame de Fougeret had first laid down now extended over all France. It must not be inferred from this that Napoleon had founded the society anew: Mesdames de Pastoret and de Grivel had for some years given it a second birth. Only a limited number of the members could afford to pay the high subscription of five hundred francs; but as policy far more than charity was the chief motive of the ladies of the imperial court, it was agreed that whilst they gave the money, the original members would give their zeal, time, and experience.

No one seemed to think of Madame de Fougeret; without whom such a society as the Maternal Charity would never have existed. She felt the neglect, and wrote to a friend: " Only one of my daughters has made a fortune; but she has been received at court, and has forgotten her mother." She could not afford to subscribe to the society, and no one suggested that its foundress should be received as an honorary member. The ladies by whom it had been re-established, after the revolutionary storm had abated, were nevertheless on friendly terms with her; and they honored her memory with a tribute of praise, rendered public by the press, when she died at the close of 1813.

When the Bourbons were restored to the throne after the fall of Napoleon, they found the Maternal Charity in a prosperous condition, and showed every inclination to protect a society which had enjoyed the favor of Louis XVI. and of his ill-fated wife : the Duchess of Angoulême accepted the title of protectress, and undertook the duties of president. The society survived the fall of the elder branch, and continued to flourish under the reign of Louis Philippe; and when the report from which the preceding account is extracted was published, it preserved to their families no less than seven hundred children a-year.

In the course of these remarks, the name of Madame de Pastoret has been mentioned—it must not be dismissed without further notice. This lady, who died a few years ago, left the name of having been one of the most handsome, witty, and actively charitable women of France. Married on the memorable day of the taking of the Bastile, she lived for years in constant apprehension of the scaffold. Her husband was compelled to flee ; she remained behind with her child, and was thrown into prison, where, for a year, death daily seemed to await her. Twice her husband returned, but was again forced to leave France; and when calmer days were restored, and the long-divided couple met again, their fortune was well-nigh gone. M. de Pastoret was a practical philosopher, and one of the most benevolent of men. His wife shared his indifference to wealth, his love of the poor, and practised the enlightened charity which guided all his actions. If they could not give much, they understood at least the difficult art of giving well. Besides the Maternal Charity which she mainly contributed to re-establish, Madame de Pastoret opened the first of the Salles d'Asile, now universally adopted in France. She chanced one day in 1801 to visit a poor woman whom she was in the habit of relieving. The woman was out, but her child, whilst alone, had crept out of its cradle, and fallen on the floor ; where it lay, seriously injured, and covered with blood. Madame de Pastoret was much affected at the sight; and she conceived the project of opening a place where poor women could leave their children whilst they were out at work. She supported the expense of the first establishment ; where, under the superintendence of a nun, fifteen children were daily received : the number ultimately increased to thirty.

The biographer of Madame de Pastoret complains that, at the peace of Amiens, Richard Lovell Edgeworth and his daughter came to France, saw Madame de Pastoret, who showed them her salle d'asile, and took away the idea to England; or rather, (for there would be no cause of complaint in this,) that, in consequence of their having borrowed and extended the plan, the merit of originality was ultimately denied to her in her own country. But the idea could and did occur to persons having no mutual intercourse: long before Madame de Pastoret thought of the salles d'asile, they had been established, by the benevolent Pastor Oberlin, in the village of the Ban de la Roche.

To the same period, and rather to the eighteenth century than to this, belong the devoted lives of two generous women—Mademoiselle de Corbion, and an humble lay sister, still remembered in France as Sister Martha. Jeanne de Corbion was born in the little town of St. Brieuc, in 1777. Her earliest thoughts seem to have been thoughts of charity: she once hid a poor child in the house of her parents, and kept him there privately; and she often took off her shoes and her garments to give them to the half-naked children whom she met in her walks. As she grew older, and was allowed more liberty, her great delight was to carry the indigent and the sick any little delicacy placed before her at table. This passion of charity increased with her years: dress and dancing, to both of which she was much addicted, were relinquished, that more time might remain for God and the poor. She rose early; spent two hours in the neighboring church, absorbed in adoration; then visited the poor, assisted them in their wants, or waited on them in their sickness: she made their beds, she swept their rooms, she read to them. In the afternoon, another hour spent in the church again preceded those visits of mercy; in the evening, she collected in her room all the children, rich or poor, whom she could find, and prayed with them. Days begun with God closed worthily in communion with the purity and innocence of childhood.

Of all her self-imposed duties, only one—visiting the prisoners—was somewhat painful: the licentiousness and profanity of their discourse disturbed a mind so pure and serene. Yet the ardent desire of effecting some good sustained her. She endeavored to give the women some religious instruction; and, when she could do so, she made herself the bearer of messages, and the medium of their intercourse with the outward world. Her task was far less painful when, with her friends the Sisters of Charity, she devoted herself to the prisoners of war who chanced to pass through St. Brieuc: she dressed their wounds, and daily brought them linen, bread, meat, wine, and soup. How she procured the means is not known; but it is certain that, within a short space of time, no less than four thousand poor foreigners were thus relieved: the behavior, not always courteous, of the officers and soldiers to whose custody the prisoners were committed, could not deter her. Humility was her favorite virtue; perhaps because her temper, naturally high and somewhat warm, rendered it difficult to practise; and she ended by laying a tax for the poor on all those who persisted in calling her Mademoiselle de Corbion, instead of giving her the plain name of Jeanne.

She was naturally delicate, and there is every reason to believe that she exhausted her youth and strength in labors beyond her powers of endurance. In her last illness, which was languishing and slow, she clung to the feelings which had been the food of her life: she was nearly dying, when, remembering that a prisoner was going to be tried, she requested that some bread and wine might be taken to him in the court; and that, if he were condemned to the pillory, the same sustenance might be repeated. She died at the close of the year 1812; and, strange and sad to record, this pure and pious creature expired in the same terrors of judgment which might beset an abandoned sinner: terrors which not even the exhortations and assurances of the priest who attended her in her last moments could dispel.

The generous charity which Mademoiselle de Corbion displayed in every relation of life, but especially towards prisoners, French or foreign, was surpassed by another woman, of health more robust, though not of a spirit more devoted. Some years before the first French revolution broke out, a peasant girl, named Anne Biget, entered a convent of the order of the Visitation, in her native province of Franche Comté. It is recorded of her, that once meeting, in her childhood, some poor prisoners on the bridge of Besançon, she gave them the cakes she was taking to her sister: this simple act of the child, foreshadowed truly what was to be the life-long task of the woman.

Being only a lay sister, Anne Biget, now called Sister Martha, was not obliged, like the other nuns, to keep within the convent walls; and she often visited the prisons of Besançon. The Revolution, which opened the gates of every convent in France, soon gave her entire liberty of action. Sister Martha was now reduced to the scanty pension of three hundred and thirty-three francs, allowed by government to the nuns, as a compensation for the home of which they had been forcibly deprived : but she also possessed, in Besançon, a small house, where she henceforth took up her abode. The Terror filled the prisons of Besançon with innocent victims of either sex and every age ; Sister Martha, and another nun not less devoted or courageous, visited these unhappy captives, and ministered to their necessities according to their means.

This was not all : to the house of Sister Martha daily resorted aged men and women, children, and sick people. She gave them alms, food, and consolation; she begged for them from house to house; and so true and deep was the respect she inspired, that she seldom asked in vain. Her robust health and native energy enabled her to do more : she took long expeditions of mercy, and was known to the sick peasants of many distant villages; she visited them, prepared their medicines, and prayed by their bed of sickness or death. The hour or the weather could not detain her : she braved alike the burning summer heats or the keen winter winds. This life of toil was also one of daily sacrifice and self-denial : no cheerful fire ever blazed on the lonely hearth of the lay sister; she called this simple luxury a robbery of her poor; and for twelve years, milk and the coarsest bread was the only food she ever tasted.

She adorned her life with heroic actions as well as with good deeds. In the spring of 1805, a hamlet near Besançon took fire, and was half burned down. Sister Martha was promptly on the spot, displaying her usual zeal, courage, and good sense. One of the cottages had taken fire so speedily, that its inmates, a woman and her two children, had not found time to escape; no one attempted to rescue them : Sister Martha implored and threatened uselessly. After vainly offering all she possessed to him who should at least make an effort, the devoted woman entered the burning cottage, and, though not without sustaining severe injuries, saved the three inmates.

Two years after this, as she was gathering medicinal plants on the banks of the Doubs, Sister Martha heard and saw a child falling into the river. She rushed in, seized the boy, and, after a severe and dangerous struggle with the stream, which was already bearing him away, she succeeded in reaching the shore.

In 1809, six hundred Spanish prisoners of war were brought to Besançon : they were in a deplorable state ; wounded, sick, and almost naked. The ingenious charity of Sister Martha provided for their necessities : we are not told how ; but He who fed the hungry multitude gave her means. This noble woman was then sixty-one ; but neither age nor fatigue deterred her : she became the guardian angel of the prisoners ; to whose captivity was added the grief of exile in an unfriendly land. In their wants and troubles they looked to her : she was their deputy, their advocate, the bearer of all their requests or remonstrances to the French military commander of the place. This officer, who esteemed her greatly, said to her one day, " You will be very much grieved, Sister Martha, for your good friends, the Spaniards, are going to leave Besançon." " Yes," simply replied the nun, " but the English prisoners are coming." Surely this is the true spirit of Christ, which forgets the difference of race or creed to remember but the one great and universal brotherhood in God ! The hereditary enemies of her land and faith, the English heretics, were as welcome to Sister Martha as the Catholic Spaniards. The chances of war enabled her to bestow her impartial charity on prisoners of every race ; and travellers have found her name and memory venerated in many a distant land, by those whose captivity she had soothed, and who gratefully acknowledged that, to her care and tenderness, they owed life, and, through life, ultimate liberty and return to their own home.

The devastating warfare which France had carried to every foreign soil, was brought back to her own bosom by allied Europe. New tasks now awaited Sister Martha. She had been seen in the prison, and by the sick-bed of the poor ; she had braved fire and flood in the heroism of her charity ; now

she haunted dreary battle-fields, covered with the dying and
the dead. Frenchmen or foreign foe alike received her care.
More than once she ventured within reach of the guns, to
tend the wounded as they fell. When the combat had
ceased, she went about the country begging for old linen, and
enlisting all the women in the task of making lint; with
which she promptly returned to the temporary hospitals,
established wherever the fighting had been most fatal. It
was whilst thus engaged that Sister Martha met the Duke of
Reggio, in the year 1814. "I have long known you by
name," said he to the nun. "for whenever my soldiers
chanced to be wounded, they immediately exclaimed, 'where
is our good Sister Martha?'" So much was she loved and
respected in the army, that a young deserter was, at her
request, reprieved on his way to the place of execution. This
was a rare instance of condescension and leniency, at a period
when the severity of military law was justified by the well-
nigh desperate position of invaded France.

The peace of 1814 freed Sister Martha from a portion, at
least, of her self-imposed duties: all the military prisoners of
Besançon were set at liberty. Their first spontaneous thought
was to give their good nun a fête; which took place within
those very walls where her presence had so often been to
them the harbinger of hope and peace. Distinctions more
flattering, but not perhaps so grateful to her kind heart, were
subsequently awarded to Sister Martha. Already in 1801,
the Agricultural Society of Besançon had presented her with
a silver medal, bearing the inscription: "A Homage to
Virtue." In 1815, the French minister of war sent her a
cross; the Emperor of Russia forwarded to her a gold medal;
the King of Prussia paid her the same compliment: but with
the medal he sent a hundred pieces of gold, to be distributed
by her in acts of charity; and, in a letter written by one of
his ministers, he warmly thanked her for all the care she had
taken of his wounded and captive subjects. The Emperor of
Austria bestowed on her the medal of civil merit; she also
received a decoration from the King of Spain.

In 1816, Sister Martha took a journey to Paris, in order to
make a collection for her poor, as her own resources were
well-nigh exhausted. She was received with distinction at
court, and in the most fashionable circles; and bore her

honors with great simplicity and composure. She soon
returned to her province, where she spent all the money she
had brought back with her, by assisting no less than two
thousand poor persons daily during the famine of 1817.

Of her further labors we find no record : the last years of
her exemplary life were spent in obscurity. She died in 1824,
in the seventy-sixth year of her age. At the time of her
visits to Paris, a popular portrait of Sister Martha was
engraved from a painting by her nephew, an artist of promise,
who died young. In that portrait she wears the close cap
and plain attire of the peasant women of her province ; but
foreign orders and medals glitter amongst the folds of her
kerchief, and appear there side by side with the humble cross
of the nun. There is goodness and intelligence in the strongly
marked features, which bear the trace and wrinkles of years ;
there is also will, decision, and energy. Even as she seemed
she was : prompt to decide and act, and independent in the
good she did. Her spirit was that of the scriptural woman
whose name she early assumed : of Martha, who could not,
like Mary, sit quietly at the feet of the Lord ; but in whom
the word, though it led not to holy contemplation, produced
the fruitful seed of a life filled with good deeds, and sanctified
by daily obedience to the commands of the Divine Master.

CHAPTER XXII.

Mary Lecsinska, Queen of France.

THE snares, the temptations which beset sovereign rank,
only render more lovely and more pure virtues always attractive. We shall, therefore, give at some length the lives of
three women who reigned in the last century, and one of
whom also belongs to our own times. One married the de-
scendant of an ancient line of kings, and the master of the
fairest realm of Europe ; another was united to a subtle and
daring monarch, whom, as general and as ruler, his contemporaries styled the Great ; the third was wife of a sovereign
whose vast empire extended over three parts of the world,

13

and who, amongst his subjects; numbered men of almost every race. Their names will be found in other works, because they were the consorts of sovereigns so great or powerful; they are here in their own right, because they were meek, good, and lowly.

A court intrigue raised the daughter of Stanislas Lecsinski, the exiled king of Poland, to the throne of France in the year 1725.

Louis XV. was then fifteen, and had been betrothed to a little Spanish princess several years younger than himself. In the event of his dying childless, the crown would have fallen to his heir, the Duke of Orleans, the personal enemy of the Duke of Bourbon, then prime minister. To ward off this danger, the Duke of Bourbon resolved to marry the young monarch to his own sister, Mademoiselle de Vermandois; a beautiful and accomplished princess of the royal blood of France, then residing in the old and celebrated abbey of Fontevrault. He commissioned his mistress, the clever, unprincipled Madame de Prie, to visit his sister in her retreat, and ascertain how far she could answer their purpose, and was likely to enter into their views. Madame de Prie took an assumed name, and framed a pretence to see the princess. She was charmed with her person and her manners, until she unluckily asked to know the opinion entertained in the convent of a certain Marchioness of Prie. "Oh! madam," candidly replied Mademoiselle de Vermandois, "that wicked creature is thought very little of here. How unfortunate it is that my brother should thus keep near him a person who causes him to be universally detested! why does not some kind friend advise him to send her away?"

Madame de Prie subdued her indignation; but, on leaving the convent, she vowed that the haughty princess should never become queen of France. She kept her word; for she was then all powerful over her weak lover. Mademoiselle de Vermandois remained in the abbey of Fontevrault; and when the Spanish Infanta was unceremoniously sent back to her parents, the portionless daughter of a fugitive and dethroned king was chosen to fill her place, and wear the first crown of Europe.

Mary Lecsinska had then reached her twenty-second year. Her stature was short, her features were plain and pale, and

there was nothing in the whole of her unpretending person to
strike or attract the eye; but her manners were simple and
pleasing, and her calm countenance had an expression of mingled delicacy and finesse. Her judgment was quiet and solid;
she spoke little, but well, and with simple grace. Her mind
was subtle and penetrating, without guile; for she was all that
she seemed to be, and much more besides—a modest, unpre-
suming woman, and a saint. Her fervent piety had been pu-
rified and strengthened by misfortunes, which began almost
with her life, and were caused by the struggle between her
father Stanislas and his rival Augustus for the crown of Poland. She was still an infant when Stanislas was obliged to
flee from the kingdom with his wife and child. In the hurry
of escape the future queen of France was forgotten by her
nurse in one of the villages through which they passed; she
was soon missed, and, on being sought for, was found lying in
the manger of a stable. After years of wandering, the exiles
at length found a home in the château of Weissemberg, where
they settled in 1720. For five years Mary Lecsinska lived
there with her parents, in the seclusion and obscurity that
suited their fallen fortunes. It was in this abode that her approaching greatness was first intimated to her by the singular
prediction which all her biographers have faithfully recorded.
She was walking one day in the garden of the château, when
a low, beseeching voice attracted her attention. She looked
up, and through the paling beheld the wan, haggard face of
a beggar woman. Filled with pity, Mary gave her the only
piece of gold she then possessed. In the transport of her gratitude, the woman exclaimed : " God will bless you : you will
become queen of France !"

Never did prediction seem less probable. So little did
Mary hope for a crown, that she had not been far from ac-
cepting the hand of one of her future subjects—the Duke of
Estrées. Six months after the prediction of the beggar woman, Stanislas entered the apartment of his wife and daughter, and addressing them, said, with much emotion : " Let us
kneel and give thanks to God."

" Father !" exclaimed Mary, " are you called back to the
throne of Poland ?"

" No, my child," he replied ; " Heaven is far more favorable to us—You are queen of France ! Be seated," he added,

bringing an arm-chair forward, "and let me be the first to congratulate the queen of France on her accession."

The marriage ceremony was solemnized at Strasbourg on the 14th of August, 1725, the Duke of Orleans personating the King of France ; and a few days later, Mary parted from her parents. The journey of the young queen through her new dominions resembled a triumphant progress ; but she had too much tact to be deceived by flattery, and on the second day we find her writing to her father : " Every one does his best to divinize me : yesterday I was the wonder of the world ; to-day I am a benignant luminary, and to-morrow no doubt I shall be placed above the immortal ones themselves." On the 5th of September, 1725, a second marriage ceremony united Mary Lecsinska and Louis XV. in the chapel of the royal residence of Fontainebleau.

The king was young and very handsome ; too indolent and apathetic, but still blameless in his life. The queen was the first woman whom he loved, and years elapsed before he gave her a rival. Whenever insidious noblemen drew his attention, to any of the beauties of the court, he checked them with the simple and dignified reply : "Do you think her handsomer than the queen ?" A natural sense of diffidence in a position so novel and difficult, induced Mary to write to her father for advice to guide her. He complied with her request, and concluded with the following remarks : " Be such as you have ever been from your earliest years. Attach yourself to the spirit of religion ; unite it to piety, without which it is only a delusion ; unite piety to morality, else you are only superstitious ; and do not separate morality from worship, for otherwise it does not differ from that modern philosophy which only acknowledges virtue and duty to be freed from their yoke."

Mary Lecsinska was worthy of receiving such counsel. Her piety was deep and unaffected. If she strictly exacted all the respect and observance owing to her as queen of France, it was because she felt deeply impressed with the reverence due to the kingly state ; she was wholly free from personal pride, and ever separated herself from the crown she wore. She liked to recall her once lowly condition, and it was to those same courtiers from whom she expected the strictest etiquette, that she once said, on perceiving the Duchess of Estrées at

Versailles; "Do you know that I might have been in that lady's place, and be now curtseying like her to the queen of France." Courtiers sometimes complained of her formality, but the poor ever found her as easy of access as she was free to give : the same woman, lowly of spirit and generous of heart, who bestowed her last piece of gold on the beggar of Weissemberg. She was passing one day through the apartments of Versailles, followed by her usual suite, when a peasant woman approached her, and unceremoniously said : "My good queen, I have come from a great distance to see you. Pray let me enjoy that satisfaction a little at my ease." "Very willingly," replied the queen, stopping short; and she opened the conversation by questioning her visitor concerning her name, birthplace, and family. After answering a few questions in her turn, the queen added : "Have you seen me at your ease ? Can I go, and feel that I leave you satisfied ?". The peasant woman assented, and retired overjoyed at so gracious a reception.

The tastes of Mary Lecsinska were naturally simple : no lady of her court gave less time to the toilette. She had been told, that, to please the king, she should follow the universal custom of wearing rouge ; she conquered her secret repugnance, and complied ; but, through want of habit, she put on her rouge so badly that Louis XV., who had the good taste to detest this meretricious fashion, could not refrain from once telling her, in a jesting way, "that she reminded him of double-faced Janus, and that he admired the pains she took to disfigure herself." From that time Mary rouged no more, and declared that the custom must have been first introduced "by the old and ugly women, anxious to render their daughters as old and ugly as themselves."

The indolence of the king, and the manner in which he forsook the court, often threw on his wife the burden of supporting its state. The disadvantage of her short and slight figure was partly effaced by the ease and dignity of her manners ; and she received the French nobles, foreign ambassadors, and strangers of distinction, with much affability and grace. She dined in public, as was then the custom, and excelled in the difficult art of guiding the conversation ; she strictly discouraged scandal or slander, under their mildest form. "Have we not, perchance, spoken ill of any one ?" was a question which she often asked, with conscientious uneasiness at the close of the discourse. She deserved the more praise for this reserve, that she had naturally a taste and some talent for raillery : M. de Croy, a lame, gouty, white-headed, but still languishing old beau, celebrated for the conquests of his youth, was once aptly defined by her as " the invalid of Cythera."

The goodness of heart and delicacy of feeling which prevented Mary from indulging in repartee, often suggested to her charming sayings, full of grace and finesse. The celebrated Maréchal de Saxe, to whom France then owed her triumphs in war, stood high, spite of his Protestant faith, in the favor of the queen, to whom he paid his court very assiduously every time he came to Versailles. As he once took leave of her on the eve of his departure for the army, Mary assured him that she would pray and cause prayers to be offered up for him. "My prayer to Heaven," answered the maréchal, " would be to die like Turenne, on the battle-field." "Whatever may be the death of the Maréchal de Saxe, he cannot but die covered with glory," graciously replied the queen ; " but how happy I should feel if, at the close of a long and glorious career, he could, like Turenne, sleep in St. Denis !"

Turenne, it is well known, abjured Calvinism, and the queen thus adroitly hinted to the Maréchal de Saxe the propriety of following so great an example, and earning, like Turenne, the privilege of a last resting-place amongst the heroes and monarchs of France. But Maurice de Saxe had neither the policy nor the destiny of Turenne: he died in his bed, and died as he had lived, indifferent to the spirit or practice of religion ; though belonging, outwardly at least, to the Lutheran creed. On learning his death, the queen exclaimed, with equal à-propos and grace, " Alas ! what a pity that we cannot sing a *De Profundis* for a man who has made us sing so many *Te Deums*."

It was one of the favorite maxims of Mary Lecsinska, "That the mercy of kings was to be just, and the justice of queens to be merciful." She accordingly sacrificed a great portion of the day to the wearying task of giving audiences and receiving petitions. When she had leisure, she amused herself with music, painting, and a little printing press, with which she printed short and pious treatises for private distribution. One of the weaknesses of this good princess lay in imagining that she could paint. She once undertook four large Chinese pictures, destined to adorn her private drawing-room. The artist who gave her lessons, designed and painted the figures, leaving the draperies to the queen : he held her palette, and handed her the brush with the red, blue, or green color required, repeating constantly : "A little higher up, madame ; a little lower now ; to the right, if you please ; to the left, madame." In her absence he rectified the mistakes his pupil had committed. Yet so confident did the queen feel that those pictures were the result of her own exertions, that she bequeathed them as such to the Maréchale de Mouchy, who caused to be engraved over the door of the apartment where she kept this legacy of her royal mistress : "The innocent untruth of the good princess."

Mary Lecsinska had conceived much affection for the Duke and Duchess of Luynes ; who were both remarkable for piety and virtue : she called them " her honest people," and often spent her evenings in their society. The duchess sometimes took the friendly liberty of censuring the queen, who never loved her better than when she did so ; and even wished to find the same frankness in her own personal attendants. One evening as she undressed, previously to retiring for the night, she lamented, in the presence of three of her women, the little progress she made in virtue ; and deplored especially her want of Christian charity. Two of the women warmly contradicted her ; but the third declared that the queen was certainly given to injustice and uncharitableness of speech. Mary defended her against her companions, who heard the accusation with indignant surprise, and encouraged her to proceed : " Go on, my good girl," she said, " go on, tell me more ; tell me all."

" Surely," resumed the woman, turning towards the other attendants, " surely you must confess that her majesty is guilty of injustice and uncharitableness of speech whenever she speaks of herself, as she has spoken this evening." They readily assented ; but the humble queen remained more disconcerted than pleased at the adroit flattery she thus received.

Mary Lecsinska was loved in her private circle ; but at court she was only esteemed : notwithstanding the charm of her goodness, courtiers often complained of the queen, and accused her of parsimony. She bore patiently the unjust reproach implied by cold looks and a formal bearing. "It is better," she once remarked, "to listen to those who cry from afar, 'Relieve our misery,' than to heed the voices which whisper in our ear, 'Add to our wealth.' The treasures of the state are not our treasures : we are not free to bestow in arbitrary gifts sums exacted in farthings from the poor and the working man. Courtiers may say : 'Give to us, and reckon not what you give;' but the people say : 'Reckon what we give you.'" The whole conduct of the queen during the forty-three years of her reign, showed how deeply she was impressed with those maxims. " If there were no little ones," she often said, "we should not be great; then let our greatness be but for them." The " little ones" gave their kind-hearted queen many proofs of their confidence in her. The fame of her benevolence and charity penetrated the farthest provinces of France. An aged woman finding herself suddenly destitute, and fearing the approach of winter, which could not but add to her miserable position, resolved to apply to the queen ; she took the road leading to Versailles, and, after a long and fatiguing journey, reached the royal residence. Mary Lecsinska received her with all the familiar kindness we yield to a welcome guest : she gave up to her her own arm-chair, made her take some wine, and sitting down on a low stool by her side, listened patiently to the tedious recital of her troubles, and of the fatigue she had endured during her journey. When the old woman had ceased, she gently consoled her, and promised to provide for her in future.

There are many ways of doing good : it is well to relieve those who apply to us : it is better still to seek them out. Mary Lecsinska liked to speak of herself as if she were the mother of her subjects; and the beauty of her charity was, that it had not only the tenderness, but also the unceasing vigilance of maternal love. Whilst the court was at Marly, she happened, early one morning, to be looking out from her window, when she saw a sister of charity passing by ; she addressed her, and learned that she had come some distance in order to solicit aid for the hospital to which she belonged. "Shall I speak for you to the minister ? " asked the queen. The sister of charity joyfully assented, thanked her, walked away a few steps, then, suddenly coming back, exclaimed :

"May I know the name of the kind lady who honors our poor hospital with her protection ? "

"Hush ! " mysteriously replied Mary Lecsinska; " tell it to no one : it is the queen."

On another occasion she was walking in the gardens of Versailles, when she met a poorly dressed woman holding a can in her hand, carrying a baby in her arms, and followed by several children. The queen questioned her, and learned that she was the wife of a poor mason, to whom she was now taking his soup ; that they had five children, and the man's earnings never exceeded sixpence a-day. The queen wondered, as well she might, how seven persons could live upon this.

"How do you manage to do it, my good creature?" she compassionately asked; " what is your secret? "

"Ah, madame, here is the secret," replied the poor woman, pointing to a key hanging from her girdle, "I lock up the bread, and try to have always some for my husband. If I minded those children, they would eat in a day what must last a whole week."

The eyes of the queen filled with tears ; she slipped ten louis into the hand of the poor mother, and gently said : "Pray, give more bread to your children."

After years of almost unbroken happiness, and during which she gave birth to ten children,—two sons and eight daughters, —Mary Lecsinska had the misfortune of losing the affections of her husband. Admirable as was the spirit of her piety, it often became too narrow and minute in practice; and the austerity and exaggerated scruples of her devotion wearied and estranged Louis XV. The advice of courtiers and the unblushing seductions of women—younger, more beautiful, and, above all, more complaisant and entertaining than the pure and pious queen—did the rest. Her sorrow was deep, but unavailing : she never won back the heart of her husband. At first he took some pains to conceal the truth ; but, ere long, he threw off all disguise, and Madame de Maillé became his acknowledged mistress. Spite of her usual meekness, Mary could not help betraying slight marks of resentment: Madame de Maillé, who belonged to her household, once asked her permission to go to Choisy, where the king then was. "You are the mistress," sharply replied the injured queen ; and none of the courtiers present lost the double meaning the words conveyed.

13*

Madame de Maillé was soon replaced by her intriguing sister, Madame de Vintimille, who died suddenly. A second sister, Madame de Châteauroux, undertook the task of consoling the king, whose dishonoring favor she shared with another of her sisters, Madame de Lauraguais. In the year 1744, Louis XV. fell dangerously ill at Metz; and, rendered penitent by the dread of death, banished his mistress, and publicly implored the forgiveness of his wife. But no sooner had he recovered than he recalled his favorite, and once more neglected the queen. The triumph of Madame de Châteauroux was brief; she died so suddenly that her enemies were accused of having poisoned her. The kind-hearted Mary Lecsinska, who had known and protected her for many years, was painfully affected by her death. She was not free from a superstitious fear of spirits, and on the evening of the royal favorite's decease, she detained one of her attendants by her bedside, because, as she confessed, "she could not help fearing that poor Madame de Châteauroux might come back."

"Madame," replied the woman, with a good deal of naïveté, "if Madame de Châteauroux does come back, depend upon it it is not to your majesty she will pay a visit." The queen laughed, and acknowledged her weakness.

Madame de Pompadour succeeded to Madame de Châteauroux; but she had a longer rule: the king gave her a place in the household of his wife; who felt the insult deeply. M. de Marigny, brother of the favorite, was superintendent of the royal domain, and he frequently offered to the queen, through his sister, the finest fruits and flowers of Trianon and Choisy. One morning the marchioness entered the apartment of Mary Lecsinska holding a large basket filled with flowers. Irritated by her presence, the queen began admiring, with undisguised irony, the beauty of her rival: she praised her charming complexion, fine eyes, and exquisite arms, with that minuteness which is in itself a slight, and at length begged of her to sing; for the admirable voice of Madame de Pompadour was not the least of those many attractions which had seduced Louis XV. The marchioness, who still held the basket of flowers, endeavored to excuse herself; but the queen imprudently ordered her to comply. After a brief pause, the favorite obeyed, and in the presence of all the ladies then assembled round the queen, she sang the triumphant monologue of Armida: "At length he owns my power." The queen felt the taunt, and turned pale. Were we writing a panegyric, we might have omitted this anecdote; we have recorded it to show, that, good and pious as she was, Mary Lecsinska was not always free from the weakness of a woman wounded in her love and pride.

She sought and found consolations more worthy of her character in the practice of her favorite virtues—charity and self-denial. Whilst the mistress of the king exhausted the resources of the state with lavish extravagance, and lived in scandalous luxury, his wife daily sacrificed her most innocent tastes for the sake of the oppressed poor. She was naturally fond of jewellery and rare porcelain; the dealers in those wares, who were allowed to sell and display their goods along the marble staircases, and even in the galleries of Versailles, never failed to attract her attention to their rarest and most costly articles, whenever she passed by their stalls. The queen sometimes paused to look; but she rigidly obeyed the self-imposed law, of never buying anything without having first allowed twenty-four hours to elapse; after that space of time, she seldom yielded to the temptation. "I like it," she once said, speaking of a rich and elegant article of jewellery, "but I cannot judge of it with my eyes of to-day; I must wait for my eyes of to-morrow." On the following day the queen was informed that the jeweller wished to speak to her majesty. "No, not to my Majesty," replied Mary, "but to my caprice: tell him it is gone." She once refused to buy a dress, saying simply, "It is too dear: I have dresses in plenty, and our poor want linen." Her charity was boundless; and when she had no more money, she privately sold her jewels. The misery of the poor had seldom been so great as it was under the reign of Louis XV.; and, when it was most heavy, the queen sold all her jewels, and every article of gold and silver in her possession. She first took, however, the precaution of causing them to be faithfully imitated; and for a whole year she wore mosaic gold and paste diamonds, until she was at length able to supply their place with genuine ornaments. No one ever suspected this pious fraud, which was revealed many years afterwards by one of the attendants of the queen. To do good seemed the sole study of this excellent woman. She kept in her private apartments a depôt of everything human beings could need, from baby-linen to that last garment

—the shroud : all these articles had been manufactured under her own eyes, and many of them by her own hands. This depôt, intended for, and ever open to the needy, included a collection of medicines, to be distributed by a sister of charity to the poor of Versailles. So well was the charitable spirit of the queen known, that whenever an accident occurred in or near the palace, the sufferer, whatever his rank might be, was immediately conveyed to her apartment.

In order to lose no opportunity of extending her charity, Mary Lecsinska employed several trustworthy persons to dispense her alms, and seek out objects worthy of compassion. The person whom she had chosen for this office at Fontainebleau was a plain honest girl of the place, whose abrupt manners and coarse garments excited the merriment of the courtiers. But the queen gaily said to her : "I like you as you are, *ma brillante*; remain so, and laugh at those who laugh at your dress : I find that it becomes you charmingly." *Brillante*, as she was henceforth called at court, complied with the judicious advice. She daily visited the poor, and ascertained their wants, which she faithfully reported to the queen ; and generally concluded in the following unceremonious fashion : "You see, madam, you must give me so much for that poor family, so much for this sick person, and so much more for that other one ; which, being added all together, makes so much." The queen was often imposed upon, and she knew it ; but she always relieved those who publicly implored her assistance. "If I refuse alms to a poor person," she once remarked, "will not all think themselves dispensed from giving him anything?" Thanks to this reasoning, Mary Lecsinska, wherever she went, was followed by a host of beggars : her guards were forbidden to prevent them from approaching her person ; the churches and religious or charitable establishments, which the pious princess frequently visited, were besieged by them : this multitude was popularly known by the significant name of "The Queen's Regiment." The only answer which Mary Lecsinska gave to those who remonstrated with her on the subject of her charitable extravagance was both simple and touching : "Everything that belongs to the mother belongs also to the children."

She who understood so well the force and beauty of maternal love, was destined to become the victim of that feeling :

the deepest which woman knows. Mary Lecsinska had ten
children; she had the misfortune to lose six. Her eldest
daughter, Madame Anne Henriette, died in 1752, at the age
of five-and-twenty. Pious and charitable, like her mother, she
was already known as "the good princess." But the loss
which Mary Lecsinska felt most deeply was that of the dauphin, her only surviving son; who died at the close of the
year 1765. It is difficult to judge of princes who have never
reigned; but, even making every allowance for exaggeration,
the dauphin appears to have been fully worthy of the bitter
regrets which hastened the end of his mother. Two months
after his pious and resigned death, the queen fell into a declining state, from which she never recovered. Her grief was
increased by the loss of her amiable daughter-in-law; who,
though she was the daughter of Augustus, the triumphant
rival of Stanislas, had endeared herself to Mary by her many
admirable virtues. This princess, after showing herself a
model of the purest and most devoted conjugal love, during
the long illness of the dauphin, died of grief occasioned by
his loss. Mary Lecsinska lingered for two years; her meekness and resignation never forsook her; she knew that her
end was approaching; but, good and pious as she was, how
could she dread death? Some time before her decease she
visited the Abbey of St. Denis, as was her custom whenever
she passed by the spot which was to be her last resting-place.
This time she asked to go down into the vault which received
the coffins of the kings and queens of France. "And this,"
said she to the prior who accompanied her, "this is the palace
where you will soon place me! Pray show me the precise
spot that is to be mine?" The monk declined to answer this
painful question; nor could the queen induce him to comply.
But she knew at least that in this vault the place would be;
and kneeling down on the damp flags, surrounded on every
side by the frail remains of so many generations of kings sleeping there with their consorts, Mary Lecsinska humbled her
soul before the eternal majesty of God.

During the whole course of her long and painful illness, the
patient queen uttered no complaint. On being once asked if
she suffered, she replied, "I suffer; but it is not equal to what
was once suffered on Calvary;" and to be for ever reminded
of that divine sacrifice, she caused a crucifix to be placed at

the foot of her couch. Deep as was the sorrow which thus led her to the grave, she forbade herself the luxury of regrets. Once, indeed, she could not help saying to her medical attendants: " Give me back my children if you would cure me."

Whilst she thus mourned for the children God had given and taken away, the sainted woman forgot not those other children of whom Providence had also made her mother; and only two days before her death she still busied herself in making and sewing garments for the poor. But even this last task had to be abandoned: she fell into the dull lethargic slumber of approaching death. The only way to rouse her was to speak to her of God. On the 24th of June, 1768, she rallied a little; and after blessing her four surviving daughters, gave up her pure soul to God, in the sixty-fifth year of her age and the forty-third of her reign.

Few women have fulfilled so well as Mary Lecsinska the duties of the station to which Providence had called her: she never sought to be more than the wife of the king. When she ventured to advise her husband, it was only to urge him to more firmness with his ministers, and to beg of him to shun war for the sake of his people. Her name appears in none of the political intrigues of those times. The only attempt which she made to interfere in state matters was, when the minister Choiseul and Madame de Pompadour undertook to dissolve the order of the Jesuits. The queen begged of Choiseul to stop the proceedings against them. " Your majesty asks me for a miracle," replied the minister. "Then perform that miracle, and be my saint," promptly answered the queen. But Madame de Pompadour decreed the ruin of the Jesuits, and her influence easily triumphed over that of Mary Lecsinska.

The most beautiful feature in the character of this good queen, is her deep sense of the patriarchal character of royalty, and the fidelity with which she carried out this touching and holy feeling. After the death of her father Stanislas, she was pressed, as his only heir, to claim a pension on the duchy of Lorraine, which he had possessed during the latter years of his life. She refused to do so; "Because," as she said, " the burden of this pension would probably fall on the poor people of Lorraine."

Whilst her husband hastened the ruin of France and monarchy, squandering in guilty indulgence the resources of the state, the pure and pious queen sanctified the crown which she wore. His death was hailed as a blessing; the tears and lamentations of a whole nation followed her to the grave.

She had led the life, and left the name of a saint. Soon after her death, one of her daughters, Madame Louise, retired to a Carmelite convent; where she took the vows, and died on the eve of the Revolution. Two of the grand-daughters of Mary Lecsinska were eminent for their piety : Mary Clotildis, queen of Piedmont; and Madame Elizabeth, the sainted sister of Louis XVI.

CHAPTER XXIII.

Elizabeth Christina, Queen of Prussia—Mary Fedorovna, Empress of Russia.

In the same age, two female sovereigns of the north of Europe—Elizabeth Christina, wife of Frederick, styled the Great, and Mary Fedorovna, Empress of Russia—displayed the same self-denial and Christian charity which had distinguished Mary Lecsinska. The destiny of the Queen of Prussia was singular. She was married to one of the most remarkable men of his age; whom she loved tenderly; yet she never lived with him as his wife, and was never heard to complain of this treatment. Frederick, on the other hand, married this amiable princess against his will; and, though she was good and pretty, the circumstances of their union were such as to justify his indifference. That he treated her with coldness, surprised no one; but that, on ascending the throne, he should not divorce her, and yet remain on precisely the same terms with her as before his father's death, was thought singular. Such was his conduct, however, and to this day his motives have remained a matter of doubt. Chivalrous generosity has been ascribed to him by some; others have beheld in this circumstance another proof of that aversion from women attributed to the warlike king : a feeling that rendered the prospect of a second marriage highly distasteful, and which not even the desire of an immediate heir could subdue.

The unhappy youth of Frederick is well known. His brutal and tyrannic father beat, ill-used him, imprisoned him, and would have put him to death if he dared. Frederick wished to marry his cousin Amelia, daughter of George the Second of England; but, to his great disgust, and to that of the whole royal family of Prussia, his father declared that Elizabeth Christina, daughter of the Duke of Brunswick, should be his bride. Frederick submitted with undisguised reluctance.

The state of the court of Prussia has been described, with more freedom than delicacy, by the satirical and gossiping princess, Wilhelmina, margravine of Bareith, and sister of Frederick the Great. The intrigues, animosities, and petty passions to which her royal relatives condescended to stoop, are recorded in her pages with a graphic and merciless pen. She visited Berlin in 1733, as the marriage of her brother was going to take place; and found her mother and sisters highly indignant at the projected alliance, and spitefully venting their anger by abusing their future relative. "She is a perfect fool," said the queen, at supper, in the presence of her son and of the servants: "to whatever you say she answers 'yes,' and 'no,' with a stupid laugh that is enough to make one sick." This gracious account was corroborated by the Princess Charlotte; who added some delicate observations of her own on the person of her brother's intended wife, and emphatically asserted that she was deformed and padded. The poor prince, not much comforted by these remarks, retired immediately after supper; the Margravine of Bareith followed him out: she was his favorite sister, and some confidential talk on the subject of his marriage took place. He confessed that it was extremely disagreeable to him; "but as to the princess," he added, "I do not hate her so much as I pretend to do: I affect to be unable to endure her, that my obedience to the king may appear in a stronger light. She is pretty; her complexion is of lilies and roses; her features are delicate, and her whole face is that of a beautiful person. True, she has no education, and dresses badly; but I flatter myself when she comes here, that you will have the goodness to form her."

The marriage was solemnized at Salzdahl, by the celebrated Mosheim. The margravine thus describes her first interview with her sister-in-law:—"The whole court of Brunswick arrived on the twenty-fourth of June. The king, accompanied

by my brother, the hereditary prince, went on horseback to
meet the princess-royal. The queen, my sisters, and myself,
received her at the door. I shall describe her as she then
appeared, for she is now much altered.

"She was tall, but her figure was not delicate, and she
threw her body forward in an awkward manner. She was of
a dazzling fairness, and it was heightened by the most brilliant
complexion; her eyes were of a pale blue, and gave no great
indication of talent; her mouth was small; her whole features
were pretty, without being beautiful, and the general appearance of her countenance was so charming and infantine, that
one would have supposed it was the head of a child twelve
years old; her hair was light, and curled naturally; but all
these charms were disfigured by her teeth, which were black
and irregular; she was totally without manner, and had no
engaging ways; she had the greatest difficulty in speaking so
as to be understood, and her meaning had always to be divined,
which was the occasion of no small embarrassment."

The princess was seventeen; she was timid, and had an
impediment in her speech; her husband was twenty-one, but
abrupt and soured by the misfortunes of his youth; his reception of her was neither courteous nor encouraging. As she
hesitated in her answer to the compliments of the margravine
of Bareith, her bridegroom, seized with disgust, called her
"fool," and told her to thank his sister. The newly married
couple went to reside at Rheimsberg. As he discovered the
mild virtues of his bride, Frederick softened a little towards
her; he is even said to have allowed her some influence over
him, but, in his latter life, there is nothing to prove, and much
to contradict, such an assertion. So cold and constrained was
their intercourse, during the seven years that elapsed from the
marriage of Frederick to his accession, that, when Frederick-
William died in 1740, every one expected the first act of the
new sovereign would be to repudiate his wife. After compli-
menting the king on his accession, the whole court proceeded
to the apartment of the queen. Whilst they congratulated
her, and addressed her by that title which few thought she
was to retain, the poor princess disguised her secret uneasiness
under the calm and courteous bearing natural to her. In the
very midst of this trying ordeal, the doors of the room flew
open, Frederick entered, and the courtiers fell back on either

side, leaving the passage free. Elizabeth thought that this visit could have but one object—the public intimation of her approaching disgrace. She rose trembling, and was obliged to lean on one of her ladies in order to advance and meet her husband. He took her by the hand, embraced her, and presenting her to the assembled court, simply said, " This is your queen."

No plainer intimation of his intentions was needed. From that hour, Elizabeth Christina was treated with all the homage and respect due to the queen of Prussia. Her husband behaved towards her with a singular mixture of affection, esteem, and indifference; which lasted until his death in 1786. In the first year of his reign, he presented her with the palace of Schönhausen, near Berlin; she spent the summer months there, but resided in the palace of Berlin during the winter. It was she who held the court, and who, on certain days and hours, received ministers, generals, envoys, courtiers, and for-eigners of distinction. A few visits to Charlottenburg varied the monotony of her life. When the king happened to be in the palace at the same time with her (and this never was for more than a few weeks in the year) he sent every morning to inquire after her health, and often accompanied the message with a billet-doux in French prose or verse; to which the queen answered in the same language, of which she was per-fect mistress. He also occasionally dined with her and his brothers on a Sunday; but to this their intercourse was limited. It is recorded, that a family meeting, in 1744, brought him to Schönhausen, and that this was the only time he ever paid the queen a visit there. Whenever he left Pots-dam for Berlin, Elizabeth left her country residence for the capital, where she dined with him and the queen-mother; but he never invited her to Potsdam or Sans-Souci: and, much as she desired to see his favorite residence, she never asked to go. To such a point did she carry her reserve, and perhaps her pride, that she never expressed her feeling on this subject in the presence of any person by whom her wishes might have been conveyed to Frederick.

No fondly beloved or indulged wife could, however, have been more faithfully devoted to her husband than Elizabeth was to the king. She admired him beyond any other human being, and wanted every one to share in her enthusiasm:

whatever he said or did, he could not, in her opinion, but be in the right. In the year 1742, he had given her, as *grande gouvernante*, the widow of Colonel von Camas; a lady for whom he felt the highest regard, who was possessed of extraordinary mental qualifications, and with whom he corresponded until her death in 1766. The chief study of this lady, and of her royal mistress, was to rule the court in the manner that might be most agreeable to the king.

The singular position in which Elizabeth Christina was placed, served to display her patience, prudence, and good sense. She kept within the limits tacitly prescribed by her husband, and never sought to go beyond; her name was never mentioned in any cabal or intrigue; she solicited nothing for herself or for others. Her life was devoted to piety, beneficence, and study: she had received a good education, and liked reading, especially works of a religious character; she had a good library, and loved the society of divines and men of letters. Gellert was her favorite author; she took some pride in being able to say that she was born in the same year with him, and she translated into French his moral lectures, odes, and songs. She also translated into the same language German works of devotion; of which, when printed, she sent a copy to the king. The value which the patron of Voltaire was likely to set on such productions may be easily divined; but, not to be behind her in courtesy, Frederick regularly sent her in return a copy of one of his military or historical works: which were perhaps as much to her taste.

The allowance of Elizabeth was 40,000 dollars a-year; of which 24,000 were spent in charity; but so secret was she in her beneficence, that it long remained unsuspected: like Mary Lecsinska, she allowed herself to be accused of meanness and avarice. She was once asked to purchase a magnificent pearl necklace; she looked at it with evident desire, but after a few moments she said to her women: "Take it away; I shall be able to relieve more than one poor person with the money it would cost." Her household economy was very strict: a merry Frenchman once said: "There is a grand gala at the queen's to-day, for as I went through the palace, I saw an old lamp lighted on the grand staircase;" and her guests often complained that, when she gave suppers, the table was covered with plate instead of dishes.

Until the end of his life Frederick showed evident anxiety for the welfare of his wife; but his personal attentions, such as they were, diminished. He ceased to visit her oftener than once a-year, on her birth-day; which was also the only day on which, to do her honor, he put by his boots and appeared in stockings; he kept a pair of black silk for that especial purpose, but as he disdained to wear garters, they hung in wrinkles down his legs. After talking with the queen, and the other persons present, for about half-an-hour, he retired. During the latter half of his reign, Frederick ceased, however, to speak to the queen: he did not complain of, her, he accused her of nothing, but he did not address her. When he dined with her after the seven years' war, he bowed on entering her apartment, on sitting down at table opposite to her, and on retiring, but never uttered one word. When Elizabeth had an attack of the gout in the year 1770, Frederick, who was dining in her apartments, entered the drawing-room where she sat, went up to her chair, and politely inquired after her health, to the astonishment of every one present: this was sixteen years before the death of the king, and is believed to have been the last time that he addressed her. He continued, however, to give her proofs of attention and respect: in 1778, he presented her with a complete dinner-service, and two tea-services of the finest porcelain. Learning once that she had been suddenly seized with a dangerous illness, he immediately sent a chasseur from Potsdam to the Doctor Muscellius, with the following note in his own hand: "Sir, I learn with extreme grief that her majesty the queen is ill, and that her illness is liable to become serious, and even dangerous, unless immediate remedies are applied to it. I recommend you, in consequence, to see her without delay, and to unite with yourself the two other physicians of Berlin in whose talents and knowledge you have the most confidence, in order to administer to her all the assistance your art is master of. Remember, above all, that it is question here of the person the most necessary to the state, to the poor, and to me."

One of the last attentions paid by the king to his wife was to dine with her on the new year's day of the year 1785; the royal family and many noble guests were present.

On the 17th of August of the year 1786, Frederick the

Great closed his long and brilliant career. By his will he
desired' his successor " to pay the respect due to the widow of
his uncle, and to a princess of distinguished virtue." He
requested him to add ten thousand dollars to her allowance.
" During the whole course of my reign," he added, "she
never caused me the least grief, and her virtues deserve
esteem, devotedness, and homage."

Elizabeth Christina survived her husband eleven years.
She died on the 13th November, 1797, conscious and
resigned, and blessing those who stood around her.

In an interesting work published some years ago by the
Société Montyon et Franklin, we have found an account, furnished by the generous admiration of a Polish refugee, of the
philanthropic labors which filled the life of Mary Fedorovna,
one of the most pious and charitable women who ever wore a
crown. Of herself personally the account says little ; her life
reads not like a biography, but more as a long-list of good
deeds and great designs, nobly conceived and perseveringly
followed out until their final accomplishment. She often
said : " We must work while we can, the time is short ;" and
never was a generous maxim more faithfully fulfilled.

Mary Fedorovna was born Princess of Wurtemberg in
1759. She was married at the age of seventeen to Paul son
of the celebrated Catharine II., empress of Russia. She
became empress in 1796, and widow in 1801. She had ten
children by her husband, and lived to see two of her sons
emperors—Alexander, who succeeded his father, and Nicolas,
the present czar.

On ascending the throne of Russia, Paul I. confided to his
wife the administration of the establishment founded at St.
Petersburg in 1781, for the daughters of the nobility. Her
first act was to give from her privy purse a yearly sum of
15,000 rubles, destined to provide for the poorer young
girls when they left the house, and to reward the services of
governesses and professors. Her next step was to improve
the interior organization, still extremely deficient, and to create a new system of education, the result of her own thought
and observations. She proved so successful in this task, that,
in May, 1797, the emperor gave her the administration of the
foundling hospitals of St. Petersburg and Moscow, and of other
charitable establishments ; which she found on the verge of

ruin, and by her prudent and vigorous management, restored to prosperity : the foundling hospitals, especially, were in a deplorable condition. The empress began by bestowing on them—still from her privy purse—an income of 9000 rubles : then gave all her attention to their financial condition, and to the physical welfare of the children. She considerably lessened the amount of mortality, by adopting the plan so successfully pursued in France, under the name of maternal charity : not considering the edifice in St. Petersburg sufficiently large and salubrious, she induced the emperor to extend it by purchasing the adjoining palace and gardens of a Russian nobleman. Having thus secured the health and well-being of her protegés, Mary Fedorovna next drew up for their particular benefit an excellent plan of education, founded on a great number of private notes, which she had been taking for some years. Facts will show how far she carried her maternal forethought.

The foundlings are put out to nurse amongst peasants : in order to cure them of the rustic habits they thus acquired, the empress created a preparatory school, which they enter on leaving their nurses. The same thoughtful spirit prevailed throughout the whole system of education established by Mary. Her plan does not merely provide for the physical, moral, and intellectual welfare of the foundlings ; it also adapts them to the position they are to fill in life on leaving the hospital. Twelve pupils are received in a gardening school, established at Gatschina, where there is also a school for the blind : their number amounted to fifty in 1827. For those who wished to become tillers of the soil, the empress established several agricultural colonies, remarkable for their excellent organization. Nay, more, wishing those forsaken children to derive help and protection, throughout life, from the establishment which had been the home of their youth, she founded, in 1813, a house of aid for those foundlings, either in or out of the hospital, whose bad health or infirmities prevent them from earning a living ; their claim on the family, bestowed upon them by the charity of the state, is broken only by death.

In 1818, William Allen, the Quaker philanthropist, visited St. Petersburg. He has left in his journal the following interesting account of the " Enfants Trouvés :"—It does not depend upon the crown, but has ample funds of its own, and sometimes even a surplus at the end of the year. The buildings contain three thousand inhabitants. All children are received who are presented for admission; and if the baptismal registers are sent with any of them, and a wish is expressed respecting the religion in which a child is to be brought up, it is educated accordingly; but if not, they are all educated in the Greek Church. This conduct does honor to the tolerant spirit of the directors. From fifteen to twenty infants are received in a day. The apartments, beds, and everything, were clean, and in the nicest order, and perfect tranquillity seemed to reign. The children are instructed in various works of industry, as well as the usual branches of learning, and are kept till they are eighteen years of age. The empress mother has this establishment under her particular care, and visits it constantly without any notice, sometimes early in the morning, sometimes in the evening, and sometimes at noon."

Several large and useful establishments, depending on the foundling hospital, also owe their existence to the empress. In 1797, she founded at her sole expense an institution destined to instruct eighty midwives in their art, and to assist twenty poor women in their lying-in. The philanthropic Demidoff had left a sum of 20,000 rubles to found a school of midwifery at Moscow, but his intention had been frustrated; it was Mary Fedorovna who caused it to be carried into effect in 1821: four years later she added to it a lying-in institution at her sole expense. In the year 1806, she established at Pavlovsk a small school for twelve deaf and dumb pupils, several of whom came from the foundling hospital. This establishment—the first of the kind in Russia—was confided to the direction of a pupil of the celebrated Abbé Sicard. At a later period the empress doubled the number of pupils received, transferred the institution to St. Petersburg, rendered it dependent on the foundling hospital, and admitted twenty children from the institution of Moscow. Notwithstanding all these expenses, the two hospitals were still so wealthy—thanks to the wise administration of their protectress—as to enable her to found from the superfluous funds an hospital for the sick, and an asylum for widows. The hospital was opened in 1803; it contained two hundred and fifty beds in twenty-six airy rooms; and a country house, situated between Peterhoff and Oranien, received the convalescent patients. A similar hospital was founded at Moscow; and each of the two establishments received from the empress a yearly sum of 3000 rubles. To these hospitals she added an asylum for the widows of government officials.

William Allen describes the hospital in St. Petersburg as "a magnificent building, with a portico, supported by lofty columns in the centre. It is open, day and night, to all applicants who bring a passport from the police. There are eight physicians in constant attendance. There is a female superintendent who presides over the nurses, and six of the Veuves de la Charité, who are under a vow to serve the Lord in the persons of the sick, are always there. The vow permits them to retire from the service, if disabled by infirmity, or, in short, when they will. A black board is placed at the head of each bed, on which the patient's name is neatly written in chalk, and the name of the disease in Latin; the latter, suggested by the emperor, is another trait of his delicate and feeling mind. The empress-dowager places large sums of money at the disposal of the senator for the relief of cases of peculiar distress; and when a peasant, who comes from the country for work in the summer, is obliged to resort to this hospital, and he is cured, he is supplied with fur boots and warm clothing to return home. Everything in the power of art to alleviate the miseries of human nature appears to be done here. There is an excellent system of ventilation; the most perfect neatness and order prevail; and, in short, it may be considered as a complete model. I have never seen it equalled anywhere. It seems the work of a most benevolent mind, guided by a superior intellect, and working with unbounded means."

It was in 1814 that Mary Fedorovna instituted "The Widows of Charity." They were chosen from amongst the widows of the two above-mentioned asylums; and, as William Allen stated, they take the vow of attending on the sick, and going wherever the poor and wretched may require their presence. All these establishments owe their existence to Mary Fedorovna, but are dependent on the foundling hospitals. The name of this excellent woman is equally connected with numerous other useful institutions. Thus, in

1798, she founded in Moscow the "Institution of the order of St. Catherine," for sixty of those young girls whose birth does not entitle them to enter the institute of the daughters of the nobility, but whose fathers hold high offices under government. Many Russian nobles contributed largely towards this institution. Soon after it had been opened, the emperor founded at Moscow another establishment—" The Institution of Alexander"—destined to the education of women of the middle class, and likewise intended to serve as a model for the provinces. She also took under her own immediate superintendence an educational establishment for women, founded by government at Odessa.

About ten miles from St. Petersburg, at Alexandroski, she established a large cotton-spinning manufactory, which afforded employment to seven hundred and fifty young people, who were boarded and lodged on the premises. A boarding school, a Sunday school, and a library were attached to this establishment: but the profits not equalling the expenses, there was a deficiency, which the empress had to make up every year. This was the more to be lamented, that the conduct of the individuals for whose benefit this manufactory had been established was in every respect excellent.

During his sojourn in St Petersburg, William Allen had an interview with the empress. He describes her as "a tall, fine figure." Her manner was both graceful and dignified; her countenance announced "a very clever woman." Their conversation was almost entirely on philanthropic subjects. Mary Fedorovna asked his advice on several points, and requested him to visit an institution for orphans, called St. Mary's. He did so, and gives in his journal the following account of what he saw:

"It is maintained entirely at the expense of the empress-dowager, for those children whose parents are artisans. They look healthy, neat and clean. They are taught reading, writing, the French and German languages, useful kinds of needle-work, embroidery, drawing, and knitting. Great pains are taken to find suitable situations for them, when they are of an age to leave the institution, on which they receive one hundred rubles, and a complete set of clothing. They rise at six o'clock all the year round, and, besides having prayers, read every evening in the scriptures. There is no difficulty in pro-

14

curing places for the girls educated there. If some of our
English ladies would imitate this illustrious example, how
much purer pleasure would they receive than from routs and
balls !"

Schools were a subject of deep and lasting interest to the
benevolent empress. In 1772, Demidoff had founded at
Moscow a commercial school, which, through neglect, had
been perverted from its original aim. The empress organized
it anew, and transferred it to St. Petersburg in 1800. In this
school the sons of merchants are received at ten years of age,
and educated free of expense. In the year 1823, the empress,
to commemorate the anniversary of the opening of this establishment, presented it with the sum of three thousand rubles ;
which she repeated yearly, and secured to the house by her
testament. In 1807, the Emperor Alexander placed under
the protection of his mother the house of the orphan daughters
of the military at St. Petersburg. Mary found it on the verge
of ruin, and rapidly restored it to prosperity. In 1820, she
founded at St. Petersburg a school for the daughters of
soldiers. At a later period, two similar schools, for the
daughters of sailors and of soldiers employed in the sea
service, were established at Sebastopol and Nikolaief : all three
received large yearly grants from the empress. In the year
1797, Mary had allotted, from her own resources, a yearly
sum of twenty thousand rubles, to be distributed in small
pensions to the poor widows of soldiers. In 1802, she established at Gatschina a house of aid for eighty old peasants of
her domains ; and founded at Pavlosk an hospital containing
thirty beds ; both establishments were wholly supported at
her cost. Tasks, often laborious, accompanied her own
charities. Thus, in 1808, she undertook to see the legacy
left by M. de Schemeretof, in order to found an asylum for
twenty-four disabled officers, properly applied. After the
campaigns of 1807 and 1812, the empress established, at her
own cost, a temporary division in the hospital, and to which
fifty wounded officers were admitted. In 1812, she opened an
establishment destined to receive the infirm and mutilated
soldiers who had distinguished themselves in the patriotic
defence of their country. In 1816, she undertook to direct
the institution founded at Moscow for the sick, by Prince
Galitzyne, and introduced many useful regulations. In 1821,

she superintended the foundation of an establishment for thirty old officers at Sympheropol. She presented this institution with a thousand rubles a-year, and bequeathed to it landed property to the amount of thirty thousand rubles. On the request of the governor, she undertook, in 1823, to organize and administer an institution destined to aid foreigners, which had been founded at Taganrog by Greek merchants. Besides the eminent services which she rendered to this establishment, the empress granted to it a yearly sum of one thousand rubles.

. With that generous spirit which characterized her so eminently, Mary had founded an asylum, open to the pupils of the various establishments under her protection, in case they should ever fall into want. Another institution of the same kind being found necessary, was endowed by her after the great inundation of 1824.

In 1828, the present emperor Nicholas requested his mother to undertake the general superintendence of all the charitable institutions of St. Petersburg. Mary accepted this task, and accomplished it with equal zeal and sagacity. She frequently visited the institutions confided to her care, studied their necessities, and entered into the most minute details ; and she distinguished herself, during those visits, by the gentle kindness with which she addressed the sick ; the insane interested her deeply ; and they owed to her a separate dwelling, more convenient than that which had hitherto been allotted to them.

. Many useful suggestions on the management of the insane were made by Mrs. Fry, with whom the empress was in correspondence, through Mr. Venning : her letters were, on their receipt, immediately translated, and entered in the journal of the asylum, by order of the empress. One of the suggestions made by Mrs. Fry, "that all, except the violent lunatics, should dine at the table covered with a cloth, and furnished with plates and spoons," was adopted with so good a result, that, on beholding its effects, the delighted Mary Fedorovna exclaimed to Mr. Venning : "This is one of the happiest days of my life !". It was because she placed her happiness in such pure pleasures that this good woman deserved to have it said of her, with truth, that "she did acts of love, with love." When the lunatics were ailing, she visited them, and spoke to

them kindly : she would send an easy-chair to one, nicely
dressed meat to another; and every week, wine, coffee, tea,
sugar, and fruit, were sent by her from the palace for the use
of the insane. During the last seven months of her life, she
visited the asylum no less than fourteen times.

An hospital had long been wanted for the sick of Vasili-
Ostrof. This quarter of St. Petersburgh contains fifty-two
thousand inhabitants ; whom the thawing of the ice excludes,
twice a-year, from intercourse with the rest of the city. In
1828, Mary Fedorovna purchased a large house on the banks
of the Neva, and turned it into an hospital capable of holding
a hundred and sixty sick. Persons of every station were to
be admitted for a trifling sum, and the poor gratuitously.

After the sanguinary campaign of Turkey, the empress
granted, from her privy purse, a sum of fifteen thousand rubles,
to be distributed amongst the soldiers and officers who left
the hospitals and returned to their separate homes. The
letter she wrote on this subject was dated October the 21st,
1828; three days after, she had ceased to live. She closed
her life as she had spent it, with an act of generosity and
munificence worthy of a woman and a sovereign. On learning her death, a young lunatic burst into tears.

We have not interrupted this long list of good deeds by the
private history of Mary Fedorovna : little of it is known ; and
that little is sad. The life spent in such constant devotion to
humanity was obscured by some of its heaviest sorrows.

Young, handsome, and gifted with more than ordinary
talents, Mary was sacrificed at seventeen to that unhappy
Paul the First, whose only excuse lies in his evident insanity.
He was kind to her, and gave her abundant opportunities to
exercise her benevolence; but his cruel and capricious despot-
ism filled her existence with gloom. They chiefly resided at
Gatschina ; where Mary superintended the schools which she
had established for her favorite foundlings ; whilst Paul fortified their residence with jealous care, until a pleasure abode
became converted into a gloomy fortress, with moat and draw-
bridges. Precautions like these have seldom saved tyrants ;
Mikhailofski, though equally fortified, could not protect Paul
against treachery. He was assassinated on the night of the
24th of March, 1801 ; and, on the following morning, the
Countess of Lieven entered the apartment of the empress,

and informed her that her husband had died of apoplexy in
the night. Mary Fedorovna knew the truth but too soon;
and the consciousness that the murderers of her husband were
beyond the reach of retribution added to her grief and horror.
She claimed the throne which his death had left vacant; but
was induced to relinquish her right in favor of Alexander, the
eldest of her ten children. This brief discussion for power did
not affect their mutual harmony.

One of the first acts of Alexander was to aid, by all the
means in his power, the splendid generosity which his mother
had already displayed, in the establishment of charitable and
useful institutions. The happiness which the empress mother
might have enjoyed in such congenial tasks was saddened by
the calamities of the empire; but her greatest sorrow was the
death of Alexander in 1825.

News had come that the emperor was recovering from the
dangerous illness with which he had been seized at Taganrog;
Mary Fedorovna and the other members of the imperial
family were returning thanks in the chapel of the palace,
when the songs of thanksgiving were suddenly interrupted,
and a priest, bearing a cross veiled with crape, advanced
towards the empress. "Man must bow before the decrees of
God," he said. The unhappy mother understood his meaning, and fainted away in the arms of her attendants. The
death of Alexander was quickly followed by that of his widow,
the lovely and amiable Elizabeth; who had written, in the
first burst of her grief, to her mother-in-law, "Our angel is in
heaven, and I linger still on earth." A few months united
her to him whom she mourned so passionately.

The grief of Mary did not prevent her from devoting the
three remaining years of her life to the tasks which had ever
been hers so peculiarly. She distinguished herself to the last
by the boundless charity and unwearied zeal which she had
ever displayed. We need not speak in her praise: her deeds, we
believe, are a sufficient eulogy of her piety and virtue. With
regard to her talents, it requires little discrimination to
perceive that the woman who could found and direct with
success so many different establishments was no ordinary
woman. To govern well is a rare gift: Mary Fedorovna possessed it in no mean degree; and in her, the gift was
strengthened by pure charity and love of God.

CHAPTER XXIV.

The Montyon Prizes.

FROM the benevolent sovereigns who made their high rank subservient to every good and noble object, we must now pass to a series of women poor and lowly; but who, according to their means and power, faithfully followed the generous and self-denying teaching of the Gospel.

A rich and philanthropic Frenchman of the last century, M. de Montyon, left by his will a large capital, of which he directed the interest to be given away, in various sums, to virtuous persons designated by the French Academy. Authentic details concerning the actions of the individuals thus selected—generally without their knowledge—are forwarded to the Academy by the local authorities. The sums given vary from six thousand to five hundred francs, and are called "prizes of virtue."

As rewards of virtue, or promoters of virtuous deeds, these prizes fail: the good have a higher aim than the gifts or praise of men, and the sums bestowed are not such as will ever tempt the cold-hearted to make a speculation of heroism or charity. But another and very important object is attained: home duties heroically fulfilled, life-long devotion to the miseries of the poor, deeds touching and sublime, which might have passed unknown, save within a limited circle, have thus become revealed to all. By far the greater portion of these benefactors of humanity are women, the most poor and obscure of their sex. Setting aside those whom filial piety, friendship, fidelity, or gratitude have distinguished, we find that the number of those whom the purest and most disinterested charity has alone actuated, is still too great for all to be mentioned here. We confess, moreover, that of their lives we know little, and scarcely anything of their characters; save here and there by a few individual touches. We will not, therefore, attempt useless and unreal detail or description, or seek to destroy that strong family likeness which proclaims them sisters in feeling, and daughters of the same faith : we will speak of them. by all that is known of them, save their humble names—their deeds. These deeds are such as may well create wonder and admiration—as may make us ask, what species of human misery the charity of woman has left unrelieved.

Of Catherine Lafage we are told that she visited hospitals, " in order to learn how the Sisters of Charity tended the sick." Of Marie Anne Allardin, a poor widow, with five children, that she once shared with a beggar her last piece of bread. Of Charlotte Pierre, that after devoting herself to a mistress fallen into poverty, and supporting her until her death, she could be charitable from earnings of two francs a-week ; and that of two garments she gave one away to a still poorer woman. Of Marie Goujon, a widow with twelve children, that she adopted, as " her thirteenth child, sent by God," a helpless old woman, upwards of eighty. Of Jeanne Maréchal, midwife, that she devoted herself to the victims of seduction ; opened her house to them, saved them from despair, and procured them honest means of livelihood, when the scorn of the world told them to choose between utter ruin and death.

We should not soon come to an end, were we to mention separately all those maidens, wives, and widows, who took the houseless into their own homes—welcomed them as guests ; who adopted orphans, or the still more unfortunate children forsaken by their parents ; who consecrated themselves to the sick and the indigent ; humble women, who had taken no vows, who obeyed no rule, and were not the less tender sisters of charity, and faithful servants of the poor.

Revolting infirmities, which hardened all hearts save their own—cancers, ulcers, leprosy, the helplessness of utter imbecility, the fury of confirmed madness, never once daunted or deterred them. When pestilence raged around them, and strong men turned cowards, their hearts rose to the intrepidity of heroes : they entered plague-stricken houses, and crossed the threshold that none other dared pass ; they watched night and day by the bed of the sick whom all else shunned ; they laid out and buried the dead which no other hands would touch.

To select instances, where all are equally worthy of record and admiration, is impossible : we will take them as they come. A poor nun, banished from her convent by the French Revolution, was without a home ; Mademoiselle Petit-Jean gave her one, and shared with the stranger an income of fifty pounds. The nun lived twenty-six years ; and her last illness was tedious and expensive ; but the friendly charity of the generous lady remained true to the end : she deprived herself of necessaries in order to procure little comforts for the poor sufferer, and made herself the nurse and servant of her guest.

Marie-Margueritte Montveran, a greengrocer, near Paris, successively received and kept for life three old women : one lived twenty years, another twelve, and the third, a woman of sour and disagreeable temper, seven years. This admirable charity was rivalled and surpassed by a widow named Marie-Madeleine Girard. She had a little income of seven or eight pounds, and on the strength of this worldly wealth, she took into her house several poor women, of whom she knew nothing, save that they were unhappy and needed her aid. In winter she went begging from door to door ; in summer, she gathered dry sticks, and gleaned after the reapers : and all this was not for herself, but for the poor. Every Sunday and holiday she made as plentiful a supply of soup as her means would allow ; then gathering around her a dozen or more poor wretches, she sat down with them, and they all gaily ate together. Some of the instances recorded display a rare and marvellous degree of self-denial.

Fanny Muller was, in the year 1830, servant in a hotel of Paris. Amongst the lodgers of the establishment was an Italian officer, in the service of France, who suffered from a bad wound, which it was Fanny's daily task to dress. She thus contracted a sort of intimacy with him ; and after some time she learned that her master had given his lodger warning to leave. The Italian's last resources were exhausted, and he was now reduced to utter misery. Fanny earned about thirty shillings a month : out of this she had saved a pretty round sum, which she resolved to devote to the poor foreigner. Learning that he was able to give lessons in music, she took a small apartment for him, furnished it, and endeavored to find him pupils. She partly succeeded. The Italian's youthful son was then in London with his mother, and on hearing of

this he came to Paris. Fanny did not complain of the
additional burden ; she continued to aid the father, and bore
the expense of the son's education. The wounded officer
became at length unable to attend any more to his pupils ;
the means of Fanny were exhausted ; but, hoping for happier
days, she borrowed money from some friends. Things, however, went on from bad to worse : the borrowed sums had to
be repaid, and this could not be effected, save by sacrifices
which, in the position of Fanny, were immense ; the money
was paid back for all that.

Fanny Muller had been long betrothed to a young man of
her native place,—she was born in the north of France,—
named Peter Wat. He came to Paris to claim the fulfilment
of her promise ; he had saved up about eighty pounds, and
thought that with this they might enter on wedded life.
Fanny frankly told him the whole story,—how, but for her,
the poor exile must have perished of want ; how his son must
have remained in ignorance. She merely told him this, and
then asked him what she should do now. " As you have
done hitherto," was Peter Wat's reply. He gave her his
two thousand francs, and returned alone to his village.

Years elapsed ; the exile died ; but not a sou of the two
thousand francs remained : the savings of Peter Wat had
been spent on the Italian and his son. For that son, and to
give him an education befitting his original station, Fanny
remained in Paris, and labored assiduously. The youth of
the betrothed had been passed in vain expectation, and hopes
still deferred, when a clergyman, who had known them both
for some years, moved with their patient devotedness, forwarded a notice of these facts to the French Academy, in the
year 1846. The result was a sum of five hundred francs
awarded to Fanny Muller, in order to facilitate her marriage
with the generous and faithful lover of her youth.

The intelligent charity of the following case seems to us
well worthy of attention. In a hamlet of the Lower Alps, a
poor peasant woman gave birth to a deaf and dumb female
child. In the same village resided Thérèse Mélanie Hermitte,
whose parents, formerly well off, had fallen into straitened
circumstances. She induced her father to take into his house
the deaf and dumb child, then eleven years old. Thérèse
knew that the deaf and dumb could be educated, but she

14*

knew no more : signs were her only medium of communication with the child she had adopted ; but she was patient, intelligent, and persevering. In two years the deaf and dumb girl knew how to read and write French. When we consider that Mademoiselle Hermitte did this alone ; that household duties and ill health took much of her time ; it is impossible to admire too much the mingled sagacity and goodness of heart—for both were equally needed—which led to such a result.

Two sisters, Françoise and Catherine les Douillot, poor spinners in Lorraine, gave a touching instance of Christian charity. A poor forsaken old man, above eighty, who had long been in a state of second childhood, sat down one day at the door of their dwelling. They received him as a guest sent by God, and mindful that by hospitality "some have entertained angels unawares."

The old man was foolish ; he would often leave his home, and wander far away into the country, until he became too wearied to return. The sisters then put by their work, pursued the fugitive, and many a time have been seen bringing him back on their shoulders.

Anne Billard, an old dressmaker of Paris, was so wretchedly poor, that she lived for days together on bread so nauseous, that prisoners would have thrown it away with contempt, and on vegetables that were literally the refuse of the streets. Yet, in this abyss of wretchedness and misery, Anne Billard did more in the way of true charity than many a daughter of luxury and wealth. An old governess, who had known better days, became her guest for four years ; then followed an infirm soldier, who had long passed his seventieth year : and after him a poor Polish refugee, whose name Anne Billard never even asked to know. In this manner had been spent the last thirteen years of her life ; when attention was drawn to her. Her unhesitating charity had made her poor, for she might by her industry have placed herself beyond the reach of want ; but, though infirm and old, Anne bore her lot without repining. She sought not praise, and never spoke of the good she had done. Many persons wondered at the excess of her poverty ; but to those who questioned her on this subject she merely replied,—" It is the will of God."

The Sisters of Charity and of St. Joseph have long been in

the habit of devoting.themselves to the duty intimated by the
declaration of the Saviour,—"I was in prison, and ye came
unto me." In Protestant countries, private women have occasionally undertaken. the task .allotted to religious orders in
Catholic lands: England boasts of Mrs. Fry, and of Sarah
Martin. In all these cases,.aid or.consolation to the prisoners
has come from without. Jailers, turnkeys, and their wives, are
inevitably associated with bolts, chains, harshness, and despo-
tism; those are held to be the best whom the daily aspect of
human misery has least hardened. In the year 1833, facts
were proclaimed to the French Academy, which proved that
charity can inhabit every dwelling; that a zeal as tender and
ardent as that of Elizabeth Fry, or a daughter of Vincent of
Paul, may fill the heart of a jailer's wife.

In 1807, a man, named Guiraud, became jailer of the
prison of Florac, in the south of France. He was active and
vigilant, without harshness; he fulfilled every duty of his
place, but he allowed his wife, Suzanne Géral, to soften the
hard fate of the prisoners, by all the means—limited, it is true
—in her power. Madame Guiraud had six children, and the
duties of her own home to attend to; her husband's salary
was small, and she had little enough to bestow; but charity
knows how to find time and means for everything. She did for
the prisoners all that humanity could suggest; she relieved
their wants, and consoled them in their distress. Her duties
became two-fold in 1817; for, as Florac had no hospital, the
sick poor were received into the prison. In 1818, a prisoner
of Milhau was transferred to Florac, who brought the typhus
fever with him. The contagion spread rapidly; fourteen
prisoners lay ill at once; every one fled in terror from the
unhappy outcasts; Suzanne alone deserted them not. Her
husband took the fever; she shared her cares between him,
the fourteen prisoners, and her six children: four of whom
were still extremely young. It is declared and proved, that
for two months Suzanne Guiraud never once went to bed. A
few years later a similar calamity, the fatal result of the introduction of the sick, befell the prison of Florac; and this time
Madame Guiraud was aided in her heroic task by her own
children.

But her life consists not merely of dangers braved in the
cause of humanity. The prisoners are her friends,—her chil-

dren,—for whom she has cared with all the tenderness of a
mother: she has given them her own garments, and distributed amongst them the food she had prepared for her family.
When her own means have failed, she has gone forth in the
town, and begged for them from house to house; seldom to
be refused. There is but one name in Florac for the jailer's
charitable wife: "The Angel of the Prison."

The highest charity is that which bears traces of a design
extending beyond limited or momentary good. The published accounts of the Montyon prizes afford interesting though
brief narratives of permanent benefits effected by women of
limited means, but of fervent faith. A peasant girl named
Claudine Treille, who was upwards of fifty when this century
began, had then devoted herself from early youth to the education of the poor. She held ignorance to be one of their
greatest calamities, and opened a charity school to the children
of her village. Many, detained by their work, were unable to
attend; Claudine went forth to find them in the fields, and
gathering the young shepherd boys around her, she taught
them in the open air, whilst their flocks grazed quietly.

With the same generous forgetfulness of self, Marie Guéry,
a weaver of Yvetot in Normandy, educated, for thirty-five
years, the children of her poor neighbors, and taught them her
trade, free of expense. Mesdemoiselles Lioud, of Annonay in
Provence, two sisters of noble family, united their little property in 1817, in order to found a free school for poor girls:
they endowed it with a yearly sum of 3,200 francs. Thanks
to their excellent management, and to their plan of making
the work of the girls contribute to the support of the younger
ones, the establishment was soon in a thriving condition. A
young relative joined Mesdemoiselles Lioud, and devoted her
life to the same task. The result of their united efforts was,
that in the year 1834 no less than a hundred girls had been
brought up in this charitable institution. Two other sisters,
Mesdemoiselles Garnier, of Croisic in Brittany, were too poor
to found a similar establishment; but, after devoting the little
they possessed to relieve the indigent of their native place,
they opened a school. Their object was to earn a comfortable
living; but they were too charitable to succeed completely.
They taught gratuitously the children of the poor; adopted
two orphans; and a strange woman, afflicted with an incura-

ble disease, whom they kept nine years, helped to absorb the scanty profits of their little school.

In the year 1817, two attached friends, Dorothea Schreiber and Opportuna Vaillant, seamstresses, opened in their own house a little establishment destined to receive twelve poor girls, whom they taught and kept gratuitously. As soon as one of the twelve knew enough, she was replaced by another: the good was always doing, but the burden was never less on the two kind women. Regina Françon of St. Etienne, in the west of France, a working girl, animated with the same womanly and philanthropic spirit, also received in her dwelling orphan girls, whom she brought up in the love of labor. In 1829, Regina Françon had gathered around her eighty young girls ; superintended by mistresses, who gave their aid gratuitously ; for the establishment was self-supporting. The girls were taught to read, write, and sew, and were kept until fully able to earn their living ; they were then placed in good situations, and provided with an outfit of clothes, and money enough to keep them for a month.

The generous devotedness of Mademoiselle Barrau, daughter of an honorable magistrate of Cahors, was no less admirable. Mademoiselle Barrau had inherited some wealth from her father, which soon became the property of the poor : she received in her house penitent girls, whose errors excluded them from society ; she opened a school for female children, whom she instructed herself ; three ladies sharing her labors. Charitable persons gave money ; and in some cases the pupils paid a slight sum, which helped to cover the expenses of the institution. Mademoiselle Barrau was not satisfied with this : she relieved and visited prisoners, the sick, and poor women lying-in. One of her most cherished tasks,—a task exquisitely painful, and through which only heroic charity could carry a woman of gentle and tender feeling,—was to aid and console the condemned in their last hours. One of those wretched creatures evidently heeded little the religious instructions which Mademoiselle Barrau offered to her on her way to the place of execution ; and as she was going to ascend the scaffold, she thus confessed the cause of her inattention : " I could die in peace, if I only thought you would take care of my three daughters." Mademoiselle Barrau did not hesitate to give this last consolation to the wretched mother : she promised to provide for the orphan children, and religiously kept her word. It is gratifying to be able to add, that the excellent conduct of her three protegées never allowed her to repent the generous impulse.

These facts became known through the medium of the French Academy in the year 1830; in the same manner, and at the same time, was revealed the admirable charity of a widow named Margueritte Mayer. She inhabited the town of Béfort, in the department of the Upper Rhine. When this town was besieged, during the wars of Napoleon, Madame Mayer fearlessly followed the sorties of the besieged troops. They went forth to carry fire and slaughter into the ranks of the besiegers; her task was to linger on the field of battle with the wounded, whether friends or foes; to distribute amongst them linen, lint, and refreshment, and to bear them away to places of safety; undeterred by personal danger and the seeming uselessness of her efforts. In everything she displayed the same heroism. A contagious disease desolated the hospitals of Béfort; Madame Mayer devoted herself night and day to the sick. The famine of 1816 and 1817 followed; it found her ready to display the same ardent charity: she created and presided over an assembly of ladies, who undertook to collect and distribute alms whilst the dearth lasted. The presence of soldiers had injured the moral character of Béfort: the place was filled with illegitimate children, the offspring of poverty and vice. Madame Mayer devoted herself to them: by the mere force of kindness she compelled them to gather around her; she freed them from uncleanness and vermin; she fed and clothed them; taught them reading, writing, and the pure precepts of the Gospel; she paid their apprenticeship, and found them work: in short, she did all which could be done to change children of vicious habits and character into honest and useful citizens.

Caroline Berteau of Elbœuf, in Normandy, displayed a charity as ardent and persevering. In 1833 she was fifty-six years of age, and had for twenty-nine years directed, without remuneration, the hospital of Elbœuf. With her this was no nominal task: she attended on the sick, and dressed their sores or wounds, as assiduously as any nurse about the place. In the year 1824 the local authorities of Elbœuf opened an asylum for the aged poor; Mademoiselle Berteau agreed to direct it gratuitously. These labors, though great, did not absorb her entirely. Mademoiselle Berteau is described as poor and unconnected, yet she succeeded in opening an asylum for orphan girls, to which she gave the name of "Providence:" the grateful inhabitants of Elbœuf called it "Providence Berteau." In 1833 this establishment held 150 children, fifty of whom were under eight years of age. The elder children taught the younger ones how to read and write; some were employed in household tasks; others were sent out to visit the sick, and emulate the devoted charity of their benefactress: a charity which seems to know no limit.

In the year 1821 a foreign woman died in the hospital of Elbœuf. She left a boy of seven, whose passionate grief, as his mother's coffin was borne away, broke forth in screams and lamentations. The kindhearted directress adopted him, and replaced the mother he had lost, until he was nineteen years of age. Another poor child afflicted with epilepsy, and with two loathsome diseases besides, whom no one would venture to touch, was likewise adopted by Mademoiselle Berteau. She took him, cured him, and kept him six years. At the time when her name was mentioned in the French Academy, Mademoiselle Berteau had adopted and was supporting five orphan children.

Her charity rose to heroism when the cholera first appeared in Elbœuf. A hundred and fifty patients were successively admitted into the hospital; a hundred and nine left it cured; but three nurses had died of the fatal disease, and none came to replace them. Mademoiselle Berteau did not shrink from the heavy burden cast upon her; her days and nights were devoted to the sick, and whilst she attended on them, her meals were often left untouched. In the midst of all this woe, a consolation remained: the houses next to the dwelling of her orphans suffered heavily from cholera, but not one of the children was so much as attacked. This singular good fortune was generally attributed to the cleanliness and excellent order Mademoiselle Berteau had established.

Towards the year 1820, a young Norman girl of Cancale, named Jeanne Jugan, left her native place, and came to look for a situation in St. Servan; a quiet little town of Brittany, formerly a suburb of rocky and fortified St. Malo. Jeanne found a place in the house of a lady of great charity. Years elapsed, and the lady died ; her heirs came and claimed her property ; Jeanne took, as her inheritance, the good deeds which the death of the charitable lady had left unfulfilled. From that time her life and her energies were devoted to the poor. A blind and aged woman was suddenly left destitute by the death of her sister ; winter was near ; her case seemed desperate ; Jeanne took her home. A faithful servant, who had kept by her masters in good and ill fortune,—who had spent on them her savings of years, and supported them by her labor when all other means failed,—remained alone and infirm in her old age. The masters, to whom she had sacrificed everything, were dead ; she had no home and no friends ; Jeanne took her home. She received so many that her house at length became too small ; she took a larger one, and entered it on the 1st of October, 1841. · Within a month the house was full ; twelve human beings, men and women, were sheltered beneath its roof.

The people of St. Servan had cared very little about Jeanne until then ; but now they began to think and talk of the poor servant girl, who, with means so scanty, had done so much good. A larger house was bought and presented to Jeanne Jugan ; but the gift was accompanied with cautious restrictions and much prudent advice.

" They gave the house, but more they could not engage to do. All the expenses must, of course, rest upon Jeanne ; they therefore advised her not to be in too great a hurry to fill the house."

. The faith of her reply was such as an apostle might have envied : " Give the house," she said ; " if God fills it, will He forsake it ? "·

She entered the house with her twelve guests. She soon had twenty ; and in 1845 the number amounted to sixty-five. Three women of the place had come to share her labors ; a doctor gave his attendance and medicine gratuitously ; in short, St. Servan possessed a real hospital through the persevering charity of a poor servant girl. To enter that hospital no petition is needed, no tedious formalities are exacted. Jeanne Jugan looks out for the sick, and waits not for entreaty to open her doors to the poor.

An old sailor of seventy-two, starving and in rags, lay neglected on a bed of straw, in a damp cellar : Jeanne im-

mediately had him brought home. A poor lame child became
an orphan; no one would have her; Jeanne took her. Two
boys had run away from their miserable home in Lower Brittany; they reached St. Servan as a cold wintry night was
closing in; they went from door to door, seeking an asylum, in
vain. "Take them to Jeanne," said a voice. Jeanne received
and kept them until they could be sent home to their family.
A young girl of fourteen was abandoned by her parents, who
left the town precipitately: Jeanne became her protectress,
and shielded her from ill.

So well was her charity known, that all the poor, the sick,
and the forsaken of the place were brought to her house, as to
their own home. A dissolute woman, wearied of supporting
her aged mother, who was, moreover, afflicted with a horrible
ulcer, brought and laid her down at the door of Jeanne, in
significant silence. Nor was she mistaken in her previsions:
Jeanne took the mother, forsaken by the unnatural child.

But how, it may be asked, does Jeanne Jugan do all this?
It is difficult to do: but charity is ingenious, and faith is not
to be cast down. Jeanne works hard, and when her work no
longer suffices, she goes forth with a large basket: she begs
from door to door; she is eloquent in her pleadings, and the
basket is never empty when she returns.

We will conclude with a name dear and familiar to English
readers,—Louisa Scheppler, the servant and adopted daughter
of the good pastor Oberlin. There are few, we believe, who
do not know how, in the course of the last century, a poor
Protestant clergyman of Alsace succeeded in reclaiming a
wild district, extending on the heights of the Vosges mountains. He found the soil barren, and the inhabitants ignorant
and miserable; he left, at his death, fertile lands, and a popu-
lation far advanced in morality, industry, and civilization. In
the course of his manifold labors, the good pastor was much
assisted by a devoted young girl, named Louisa Scheppler.
She was conductress of one of the infant schools which he
established for those very young children to whom their parents,
engaged in daily labors, could not always attend. The health
of Louisa not agreeing with this occupation, she became servant in the family of the pastor. On the death of Madame
Oberlin, the office of housekeeper devolved on Louisa, who
had then been eight years in the family. After faithfully ful-

filling the duties of her office for nine years, Louisa addressed to her master—whom, like every one in the *Ban de la Roche*, she called "papa"—the following touching letter, written on new-year's-day, 1793.

"Dear and beloved Papa,—Permit me, at the commencement of a new year, to request a favor for which I have long been desirous. As I am now in reality independent, that is to say, having no longer my father nor his debts to attend to, I beseech you, my dear papa, not to refuse me the great favor of making me your adopted daughter. Do not, I entreat you, give me any more wages; for, as you treat me like one of your children in every other respect, I earnestly hope you will do so in this particular also. Little is needful for the support of my person. My shoes, and stockings, and sabots will cost something; but when I want them I can ask you for them, as a child applies to its father. I entreat you, dear papa, to grant me this favor, and condescend to regard me as your most tenderly attached daughter,   "LOUISA SCHEPPLER."

The request was granted: Louisa became the adopted daughter of her master, the sharer of his charitable labors, the stay and consolation of his declining years, saddened by the loss or absence of his own children. After his death, she remained with his son-in-law and successor, continuing her laborious exertions in favor of the inhabitants of the Ban de la Roche. In the year 1829, the French Academy bestowed on her a Montyon prize of five thousand francs, and appointed Cuvier, the eminent naturalist, and one of the most lofty geniuses of this age, to relate the simple story of a life passed in the wild haunts of the Vosges, in diffusing the light, charity, and peace of the Gospel.

CHAPTER XXV.

Elizabeth Fry—Her Youth and first Religious Feelings.

In the year 1780, there resided in a roomy quadrangular house of the parish of St. Clement, in the town of Norwich, a quaker family bearing the ancient name of Gurney. As far

back as the days when William Rufus reigned, the Lords of
Gournay en Brai in Normandy had held fiefs in Norfolk;
and there they-left their name and their descendants to be
perpetuated through many generations. In the latter part of
the seventeenth century, John Gurney, merchant, a younger
son of a younger branch, issued from the old Norman lords,
embraced the tenets of George Fox. John Gurney of Earlham, his great-grandson, inherited his name and his principles.
In 1775 he married Catherine Bell, daughter of a London
merchant, and descended from Robert Barclay, the well-known
apologist of the Quakers.

Mr. and Mrs. John Gurney were thus hereditary members
of the Society of Friends; but their mild and lenient Quakerism was not such as to win the approbation of those who called
themselves "Plain Quakers." They led a pleasant and a very
comfortable life, spending the winter at Norwich, and the
summer in the pretty village of Bramerton. They were both
of a cheerful, sociable disposition, and shrank not from gaiety:
they kept their carriage, saw company, and had friends even
amongst those whose religious principles nominally differed
most from their own; they used neither the plain garb nor the
"thee" and "thou" of Quakers; their daughters sang, and
both sons and daughters learned to dance. In short, like many
members of their sect, John and Catherine Gurney had lost
the fervent spirit of early days; from proselytizing enthusiasts,
they were now become calm, intellectual, amiable, moral, and
somewhat worldly people, who called themselves Quakers, and
attended meeting; but in whom many a zealous brother silently
lamented to see "the marks of wealth and grandeur," which
the devout William Savery of America noted amongst his
English brethren of Norwich.

In 1786, Mr. and Mrs. Gurney removed with their family
to Earlham Hall, an old mansion, irregularly built, but standing fair and venerable in the centre of an ancient park, with a
wide lawn, shady groves, and a dark avenue rising on the
banks of the clear and winding Wensum. Here were born
the last three of their twelve children: it was whilst they still
resided at Norwich, that Mrs. Gurney gave birth to her third
daughter, Elizabeth, on the 21st of May, 1780.

The child was fair, shy, and quiet; her mother called her
"my dove-like Betsy:" her very faults were silent. She

dreaded the dark with the intensity of childhood's fear, and she never spoke of her terrors. She was gentle in look, manner, and speech, but proud, and inexorably obstinate at heart. She yielded to a request; whereas nothing could subdue her tacit revolt against a command, howsoever just. Her abilities were great, though, for a child, peculiar; for they were tact, penetration, and independence of thought. She was weak, sickly, and disliked study, in which she made little progress; indeed, she was thought stupid, and thought herself so. Her pleasure was tranquil and meditative: she loved flowers, shells, and, with her sister Rachel, had a little cabinet, where they placed collections of natural curiosities, and all their childish treasures. Her religious feelings were serious, and somewhat solemn: her whole soul and being were impressed, when in the evening, after hearing her mother read some portion of Scripture and a Psalm, she sat by her awed and silent. That mother, a beautiful and amiable woman, Elizabeth loved with a tenderness verging on passion; but more deep than demonstrative: the thought that she might die and leave her behind, often made her lie awake and weep at night. She seldom left her side, and she watched her sleeping, haunted by a fear that her mother might cease to breathe, and waken no more from that calm slumber which resembled all that she had heard or knew of death. When death did at length remove Mrs. Gurney, the grief of Elizabeth, then twelve years old, was deep and enduring. Thirty-six years later, she felt and wrote that the remembrance of this event was "sad even to the present day." An incident of her childhood is too characteristic to be omitted. She had so great a desire to visit a prison, that her father at last took her to see a bridewell: the impression this sight produced was never effaced.

Years elapsed, and wrought their change on Elizabeth Gurney: the pale, shy child grew up into a tall, slight girl, of elegant figure, and soft, winning aspect, heightened by a profusion of flaxen hair. She had six sisters, who were all attractive, gay, and lively. Elizabeth sang and danced with much spirit, and rode both fearlessly and well: she appeared to peculiar advantage in a certain scarlet riding-habit, and was fond of dress and admiration. Her life was innocent, but her thoughts were gradually settling on the world: ill health was her excuse for not attending meeting; and the excuse was reluctantly abandoned. When she went she seemed restless and uneasy: her heart was not with the grave worship of her brethren. The religious feelings of her childhood, the silent awe felt after the Scripture reading, had faded away: if she still believed, it was vaguely; with that dim belief which lingers in every soul, save the dark and desolate one of the atheist. As she reached her seventeenth year, light began to pierce this gloom: doubts, the forerunners of faith, assailed her. She stood half way between the world and religion—loving the one, called by the other. A generous ambition awoke within her; she felt the want of "a better, a greater stimulus to virtue than she then had, wrapt up in trifles as she was:" she had the wish, but not the power. In the spirit of her sect, she resolved to wait for the workings of her own heart. She refused to read religious books: when the time came, if it was to come, she would take up the New Testament, and shape out her own path.

Her early journals paint very forcibly the state of her mind and feelings at this period. At one time "her mind is in so dark a state that she sees everything through a black medium;" then she longs "for the Prince to come,"* and attributes the desire to pride. She has to struggle against her passions; she would not give them up, but she would keep them silent and subdued. She deplores the evils of a worldly life; the false stimulus which it creates; the pomp, pride, vanity, jealousy, and ambition it fosters; the vacancy of spirit which ultimately compels to fly to novels and scandal as a refuge. These philosophic reflections on the vanity of the world are followed by a characteristic entry: "I met the Prince —it showed me the folly of the world; my mind feels very flat after this storm of pleasure."

Her heart also overflowed with a vague and dreamy tenderness. She loved the luxury of her feelings—"to feel for the sorrows of others—to pour wine and oil into the wounds of the afflicted." The hopes and desires of her years are thus frankly expressed on her seventeenth birthday:

"Monday, 21st.—I am seventeen to-day. Am I a happier or a better creature than I was this time twelvemonths? I

* His Royal Highness William Frederick, afterwards Duke of Gloucester, then quartered at Norwich.

know I am happier; I think I am better. I hope I shall be much better this day year than I am now. I hope to be quite an altered person; to have more knowledge; to have my mind in greater order; and my heart too, that wants to be put in order as much, if not more, than any part of me—it is in such a fly-away state; but I think, if ever it settled on one object, it would never, no, never, fly away any more; it would rest quietly and happily on the heart that was open to receive it."

From such thoughts, Elizabeth sometimes turned towards what is often the secret ambition of youth—self-subjection.

"June 20th.—If I have long to live in this world, may I bear misfortunes with fortitude; do what I can to alleviate the sorrows of others; exert what power I have to increase happiness; try to govern my passions by reason; and strictly adhere to what I think right.

"July 7th.—I have seen several things in myself and others I never before remarked; but I have not tried to improve myself. I have given way to my passions, and let them have command over me. I have known my faults and not corrected them; and now I am determined I will once more try, with redoubled ardor, to overcome my wicked inclinations. I must not flirt, I must not even be out of temper with the children; I must not contradict without a cause; I must not mump when my sisters are liked, and I am not; I must not allow myself to be angry; I must not exaggerate, which I am inclined to do; I must not give way to luxury; I must not be idle in mind; I must try to give way to every good feeling, and overcome every bad. I will see what I can do; if I had but perseverance, I could do all that I wish: I will try. I have lately been too satirical, so as to hurt sometimes: remember it is always a fault to hurt others.

"11th. . . . Company to dinner. I must beware of not being a flirt: it is an abominable character; I hope I shall never be one, and yet I fear I am one now a little. Be careful not to talk at random. Beware, and see how well I can get through this day without one foolish action. If I do pass this day without one foolish action, it is the first I ever passed so. If I pass a day with only a few foolish actions, I may think it a good one."

"August 6th.—I have a cross to-night. I had very much

set my mind on going to the oratorio; the Prince is to be there, and by all accounts it will be quite a grand sight, and there will be the finest music; but if my father does not like me to go, much as I wish it, I will give it up with pleasure, if it be in my power, without a murmur. I went to the oratorio; I enjoyed it, but spoke sadly at random: what a bad habit!"

This is the last time the name of the young Prince, who seems to have exercised no slight fascination on Elizabeth, occurs in the early journals. His image, and all the pleasures and attractions of the world, were slowly fading away before thoughts more solemn and joys more holy. But ere the victory could be won, there was a struggle, sharp though brief, to undergo: the mind of Elizabeth was tossed on a sea of doubts. "She does not know if she shall not soon be rather religious," and then "she fears being religious, in case she should be enthusiastic." One day she writes, "Idle and relaxed in mind, greatly dissipated by hearing the band, &c., &c. Music has a great effect on me: it at times makes me feel almost beside myself."

And then, a few months later, after expressing, in vivid and ardent language, how great is her need of religion, she adds with sudden caution, "But I have the greatest fear of religion, because I never saw a person religious, who was not enthusiastic."

This fear kept her back until she felt herself sinking into a state of mental darkness, from which there seemed no coming into light. She sadly confesses that she has "no real faith in any sort of religion." "I don't feel any real religion," she writes in January, 1798; "I should think those feelings impossible to obtain; for even if I thought all the Bible was true, I do not think I could make myself feel it: I think I never saw any person who appeared so totally destitute of it. I fear I am by degrees falling away from the path of virtue and truth." Two days later, a change has already occurred: "Her mind is in a state of fermentation: she believes she is going to be religious, or some such thing."

The instrument of a change which affected the whole existence of Elizabeth Gurney, was William Savery of America, then on a religious visit to England. He had once been a gay, unbelieving man; he was then a fervent Quaker, enthusiastic, eloquent, yet humble. On the 4th of February, 1798, he preached at the Friends' meeting-house in Norwich. Richenda Gurney thus described the impression he produced on her sister:

"On that day, we, seven sisters, sat as usual in a row under the gallery at meeting. I sat by Betsy. William Savery was there. We liked having yearly meeting friends come to preach; it was a little change. Betsy was generally rather restless at meeting, and on this day I remember her very smart boots were a great amusement to me: they were purple, laced with scarlet.

"At last William Savery began to preach. His voice and manner were arresting, and we all liked the sound; her attention became fixed: at last I saw her begin to weep, and she became a good deal agitated. As soon as meeting was over, I have a remembrance of her making her way to the men's side of the meeting, and, having found my father, she begged him if she might dine with William Savery at the Grove, to which he soon consented, though rather surprised by the request. We went home as usual, and, for a wonder, we wished to go again in the afternoon. I have not the same clear remembrance of this meeting; but the next scene that has fastened itself on my memory is our return home in the carriage. Betsy sat in the middle, and astonished us all by the great feeling she showed. She wept most of the way home. The next morning William Savery came to breakfast, and preached to our dear sister after breakfast, prophesying of the high and important calling she would be led into. What she went through in her own mind, I cannot say, but the results were most powerful and most evident. From that day her love of pleasure and of the world seemed gone."

It seemed, but was not. Nothing of good or evil perishes utterly in a day. Many a conflict did the heart of Elizabeth endure before the final victory was won. The force and depth of her own impressions alarmed her. She dreaded lest what she had felt should wear away. On the evening of that day, to her so eventful, she writes, in the language of mingled doubt and awe:

"My imagination has been worked upon, and I fear all that I have felt will go off. I fear it now, though at first I was frightened, that a plain Quaker should have made so deep an impression upon me; but how truly prejudiced in me to think, that because good came from a Quaker, I should be led away by enthusiasm and folly. I wish the state of enthusiasm I am now in may last, for to-day I have felt *that there is a God*."

For two days she was humbled and subdued. It was as if a refreshing shower from heaven had fallen on her spirit, parched like "earth that had been dried up for ages;" but, alas! she went to Norwich; and though she had "a very serious ride there," yet "meeting, and being looked at, with apparent admiration, by some officers, brought on vanity." She came home "as full of the world as she went to town full of heaven."

The next Sunday found her oppressed with all her old irreligious feeling at meeting. Her mind was naturally inclined to both scepticism and enthusiasm: when she reasoned and argued, faith fled; when she yielded to her feelings, and waited in patient humility, it returned, a willing and welcome guest. Her fidelity was soon put to the test by a visit to London and all its gaieties. Like a novice who leaves her convent before pronouncing the irrevocable vows, in order to partake once more in all the pleasures and vanities she is going to forsake, Elizabeth Gurney beheld what is called the world for a few weeks, to bid it adieu for ever, and bind herself down to the austere faith and habit of her most rigid brethren.

Mr. Gurney took his daughter to London, and left her there under the care of a relation. The first prospect of going had put the mind of the young girl "in a whirl;" but reflection sobered down this mood, and the thought of seeing William Savery and his friends, the plain Quakers, agitated her more than a visit to the capital and a share in all its pleasures. Two days after her arrival, on February 26th, she went to Drury Lane; and for the first time entered the magic circle, where feigned joys, woes, and passions charm the fancy and subdue the heart of the beholder. But the expectations of Elizabeth had been raised too highly for the spell to work: the house she found "grand and dazzling;" for the rest she cared not. The play perhaps was not good: at all events it failed to please her. She saw Miss Decamp, Jack Bannister, Mrs. Jordan, and she wished the performance over. This impression was not removed by other plays and different performers. With her hair dressed, which made her "feel like a monkey," she went

15

to see "Hamlet" and "Bluebeard." She found the acting, music, and scenery perfect, but she still wished the entertainment fairly ended. "I do not like plays," she writes in her diary; "I think them so artificial, that they are to me not interesting, and all seems so—so very far from pure virtue and nature." This indifference to theatrical amusements did not save Elizabeth from a dissipated, worldly frame of mind; which she records, and briefly laments.

"Wednesday, February 28th.—We were out this morning; I felt proud, vain, and silly. In the evening we had a dance.

"March 4th.—I feel uncharitably towards ——, I said uncharitable things of them, and gave way to inclination, for I own I love scandal, though I highly disapprove of it; therefore it is the more commendable if I overcome it.

"5th.—I took a lesson in dancing, and spent the day quietly."

Two days after the dancing lesson, a meeting where Elizabeth heard William Savery preach from a text in Revelations, and pray most eloquently, brought out religious fervour. "Most awfully she felt it," and, as before, fear and doubt blended with her enthusiasm. She wished for the quiet of Earlham; for though plays were not attractive, there were other gaieties which, she confesses, troubled and excited her greatly. The last records of this London visit betray her weakness, and show that, whilst it lasted, she saw something of London society.

"March 26th.—This morning I went to Amelia Opie's, and had a pleasant time. I called on Mrs. Siddons, who was not at home; then on Dr. Batty; then on Mrs. Twiss, who gave me some paint for the evening. I was painted a little. I had my hair dressed, and did look pretty, for me. Mr. Opie, Amelia, and I, went to the opera concert. I own I do love grand company. The Prince of Wales was there; and I must say, I felt more pleasure in looking at him, than in seeing the rest of the company, or hearing the music. I did nothing but admire his royal highness; but I had a very pleasant evening indeed.

"27th, I called with Mrs. H—— and Amelia on Mrs. Inchbald. I like her vastly; she seems so clever and so interesting. I then went to Hampstead, and staid at our cousin Hoar's until the 12th of April. I returned to Clapham. My uncle Barclay, with great begging, took us to the opera. The house is dazzling, the company animating, the music hardly at all so, the dancing delightful. H—— came in, in the middle of the opera; I was charmed to see him—I was most merry—I just saw the Prince of Wales.—Tuesday. My dearest father came to London. We dined at the ——, and went to a rout in the evening.—Friday. I had a pleasant, merry day with Peter Pindar (Dr. Walcot).—Monday. I went with my father and the Barclays to Sir George Staunton's.

"April 16. I arrived at home with my father, after paying a few more visits."

Thirty years later, Elizabeth Gurney, then Mrs. Fry, of European celebrity, reviewed, in serious mood, this period of her youth, "like the casting die of her life," during which she was marvellously "protected," and received striking proof of "the tender mercy of her God." The severest part of the struggle was now over. The thoughts of Elizabeth Gurney daily became more turned towards the austere tenets of her sect; she had for a long time been every night troubled with a strange and bitter dream, of an agitated sea rising against her with waves ready to wash her away: the circumstances might vary; the danger, and its agony of fear, ever recurred. At length, when come to the day of perfect faith, the dream changed: the sea did indeed rise as usual, but she stood safe beyond the reach of its waters; from that night the dream troubled her no more. Elizabeth looked on this as a warning from above, as a type of her future destiny; and, recording it, devoutly hoped "not to be drowned in the ocean of the world, but permitted to mount above its waves, and remain a steady and faithful servant to the God whom she worshipped."

She had always been charitable, for her nature led her to pity and relieve suffering; but now she extended the sphere of her duties. She visited and relieved the poor of Earlham and Norwich, especially the sick; she read the Bible to them, and instructed their children. A school at home, which had begun with one boy, so increased, that she had to receive her pupils in a vacant laundry. She ruled and instructed alone no less than seventy children: a singular instance of that power of tuition and control which she displayed so strikingly in after-life.

A few days spent at Colebrook Dale, with relatives who were plain Quakers and fervent believers, confirmed Elizabeth in this resolve. She gradually gave up dancing and music, which she held to be "the first pleasures in life;" she said "thee" and "thou," and modified her dress until it acquired the strict simplicity of Quaker attire. Her journals reveal, however, how much these sacrifices cost her : what between the love of pleasure and the dread of ridicule, her mind was sorely troubled. Once chancing to meet an old acquaintance, and not knowing how to address him in the plain language, she fairly ran away. It was also painful when asked to sing and dance by her friends, either to do so with a sense of wrong, or to grieve them by a refusal. The struggle was evidently a bitter one; but, in the end, her deep—though, as we think, mistaken—sense of duty, prevailed.

It was not merely because plain Quakers object to music and dancing that Elizabeth abstained from both; she found them exciting, and therefore dangerous. If dancing did indeed make her feel, as she says, vain and disposed to flirt, she did well to relinquish it; but though the excitement which it created was the only objection which she could raise to music, she held it sufficient. If excitement be in itself a sin, then it is wrong for the heart to be raised with some generous emotion : to feel the thrill which is awakened by the sight or sound of the beautiful; to indulge, like David, in the transports of religious fervor, and express them in the ardent and impassioned language of the shepherd boy of Israel.

The excitement of religion is not its noblest part—no more is it so in pleasure or art—but it exists : to deny it, would be useless. Of all the ideas which can absorb a human heart, there is none more exciting than religion : it gives to this life its aim and aspirations, and holds before our gaze the solemn mysteries of a life yet to come. God, futurity, our souls, all that we can conceive of sublime, or awful, or sympathetic, lie comprised in the word. That perfect calmness, which a mistaken idea of religion has caused so many to seek, would be the death of the soul, if it were possible ; but it is not. The Supreme Being alone may unite incessant action to eternal repose ; that repose does not exist even in Nature : she is not always calm and soothing : she has aspects and murmurs more seductive than man's sweetest music, because infinitely more beautiful. We may indeed strive to check the outpourings of the spirit with which we have been gifted, but we can never wholly succeed : if the pleasant and the beautiful are to be set aside, something must take their place. God gave them to us as antidotes against the sordid cares of life : against instincts less noble, and feelings far more selfish. Is our wisdom greater than His ?

But though we cannot help protesting against the strange mistake into which Elizabeth Gurney fell, we must not be misunderstood. When once she thought wrong that which had formerly appeared innocent, she did well to relinquish it utterly ; indeed, no other course was left open to her. It is only fair to state, that she was by no means precipitate : that conscience and judgment, and not those friends, whom in her enthusiasm she calls "superior, fascinating Quakers," guided her in this step ; and that one of her chief reasons for adopting it was, the sincere conviction that " the formation of her mind required the bonds and ties of Quakerism to fit it for immortality." There is a never-failing virtue in sacrifice, howsoever mistaken : that of Elizabeth Gurney was entire and generous —it bore its fruit.

CHAPTER XXVI.

Elizabeth Fry—Her Married Life—Visits to the Prisoners in Newgate.

In 1800 Elizabeth Gurney married Mr. Joseph Fry, and removed from her country home to St. Mildred's Court in the city. She there inhabited the house where her husband and his brother carried on their extensive business. He was, of course, a Quaker ; and, indeed, all his family were so strictly devout that the young bride found herself the "gay, instead of the plain and scrupulous one of the family," as she had been at home.

The first nine years of Mrs. Fry's married life offer few events of importance. The birth of five children, the death of valued friends, household cares and duties, gentle acts of charity—thrown into the shade, but not effaced, by the exer-

tions of later years—belong to this period of her existence.
She was happy, and acknowledged it with a thankful heart.
" Time slips through quickly," she writes on the second anniversary of her marriage, " trials and pleasures, before unknown,
have indeed been felt by me; trials and joys of many kinds.
The love of a husband, the unity experienced, the love of a
child, the maternal feelings, when under subordination, are
real and great sources of enjoyment."

In the spring of 1809 Mr. and Mrs. Fry removed to Plashet,
in Essex. The change from the city to the country was delightful to one who, whilst she cared little for the works of men,
ever keenly enjoyed the exquisite loveliness of Nature. She
promptly established a girls' school on the Lancasterian
system, and distinguished herself by acts of universal charity :
she kept a depôt of calico, flannels, and outer garments, ever
ready for the poor ; a large closet was well stored with medicines for their use; and in the hard winters, soup was boiled
in an out-house, and distributed to hundreds of poor people.
About half a mile from Plashet, there was a little Irish colony
where " Madam Fry" was deservedly beloved and popular.
" It was a pleasant thing to observe the influence obtained by
Mrs. Fry over these wild, but warmhearted people. She had
in her nature a touch of poetry, and a quick sense of the droll ;
the Irish character furnished matter for both. Their powers
of deep love and bitter grief excited her sympathy ; almost
against her judgment, she would grant the linen shirt and the
boughs of evergreen to array the departed, and ornament the
bed of death. She frequently visited Irish Row, never but to
do good or administer consolation. Gathering her garments
round her, she would thread her way through children and
pigs, up broken staircases and by narrow passages, to the
apartments she sought; there she would listen to their tales
of want or woe, or of their difficulties with their children, or of
the evil conduct of their husbands. She persuaded many of
them to adopt more orderly habits, giving little presents of
clothing as encouragements; she induced some to send their
children to school, and, with the consent of the priest, circu-
lated the Bible amongst them. On one occasion, when the
weather was extremely cold, and great distress prevailed, being
at the time too delicate herself to walk, she went alone in the
carriage, literally piled with flannel petticoats for Irish Row ;

the rest of the party walking to meet her, to assist in the delightful task of distribution."*

The gipsies, who yearly visited Plashet on their way to a neighboring fair, were not forgotten by the kind lady. She also did an amount of good, that can scarcely be estimated, by extending vaccination. She was not only successful in performing the operation, an art which she had learned from Dr. Willan, but at intervals "she made a sort of investigation of the state of the parish, with a view to vaccinating the children. The result was, that small-pox was scarcely known in the villages over which her influence extended."

Beautiful and pure as was a life thus spent, happy as she was in many respects, Elizabeth Fry—to whose religious fervor time had only given more strength—was secretly troubled at heart by the thought of work left undone, and of a high destiny unfulfilled. Every one knows, of course, that the Friends do not exclude women from the ministry. Two years before her marriage, at the time when William Savery visited Norwich, there is an indication in the journal of Elizabeth Gurney, that the prospect of "becoming a preacher" had offered itself to her mind. Her sister Richenda mentions how he prophesied "the high and important calling she would be led into." On a solemn evening spent at Colebrook Dale, and when, as Elizabeth expressed it, "her heart began to feel itself silenced before God," Deborah Darby, a minister amongst the Friends, spoke, and addressed part of her discourse to the young girl; who, with awe and wonder, heard herself designated as one that was to become "a light to the blind, speech to the dumb, and feet to the lame." There can be no doubt that these prophecies, founded on a subtle perception of the innate eloquence, zeal, and fervor of the young girl, helped to work their own fulfilment in the woman.

Soon after her marriage, this subject began to haunt her with strange doubts and fears. Was she really called to the ministry? Was it imagination that misled and lured her too far, or lukewarmness and want of zeal that kept her back? The struggle, and to her it was most momentous, lasted ten years.

* Memoir of the Life of Elizabeth Fry.

On the 20th of August 1808, Elizabeth Fry writes thus: "I have been married eight years yesterday; various trials of faith and patience have been permitted me; my course has been very different to what I had expected; instead of being, as I had hoped, a useful instrument in the church militant, here I am a careworn wife and mother, outwardly, nearly devoted to the things of this life." But, after a long conflict against her secret dread, the spell was broken. She poured forth her soul, in thanksgiving and prayer, by the death-bed of her father, and on her return to Plashet she spoke in the meeting, and thus assumed the ministry. This event took place at the close of 1810. Mrs. Fry was naturally a timid, sensitive woman; she found strength in the belief that this work was not " her own doing, nor at her own command." She thought herself called by the Lord, and professed her willingness to follow " in the ways of His requirings, even if they led her into suffering and into death."

Mrs. Fry was soon acknowledged as a minister by the society; she was gifted, eloquent, and, when deeply moved, forgot all dread of man and his presence. Her voice, her manner, arrested attention; her fervor filled with awe, and moved to devotion. The testimony of all who ever heard her is unanimous; and they were not always of her own faith, nor insensible to the strangeness of hearing a woman pray and preach in public.

We have not thought it right to pass over this period of her life hastily. It is not, indeed, to her early doubts and struggles, to her labors in the ministry, that Elizabeth Fry owes her celebrity. Her name is associated with the darkest haunts of wretchedness and crime; with labors, spiritual indeed, but seemingly foreign to a nature so tender and a piety so mystical. But every human being whose story is told, has a right to have the tale related even as it befell. It is not indifferent to know by what steps the gay young girl of Earlham, who danced, who flirted, whom looks of admiration greeted, and who knew it but too well, became a visiter of prisons, and an apostle of light and truth amongst those who lingered there in the darkness of sin. The ways of the human heart, like those of its Creator, are many: it is something to know the path along which, and according to her faith, journeyed a woman like Elizabeth Fry. The spirit which moved her to speak was no transitory enthusiasm. On two solemn and trying occasions—the death of her father, and later, of one of her young children—she shrank not from uttering a fervent thanksgiving for the pure victory won by the departed, in a manner never to be forgotten by those who heard her. And yet her grief was deep; and by the journal, we see how much her heart yearned towards the beautiful and much loved child that slept in Barking burying-ground.

In November 1812, Mrs. Fry and her family left Plashet for St. Mildred's Court, where they were to spend the winter. Four Friends, well known to her, visited Newgate in the month of January. Their representations induced her to visit the female prisoners, for the purpose of giving them some relief during this inclement season. The relief was needed indeed. In two wards and two cells, of which the extent did not exceed one hundred and ninety superficial yards, were confined three hundred women and their children. Some were tried; others still unconvicted; but all lived together, and fared alike: they lived, cooked, and washed in these four rooms. Their clothes were in rags, the floor was their bed, its boards raised for that purpose, served them as a pillow. No employment was assigned to them; they fought, drank, and gambled without restraint. The power of the law literally ceased at the doors of the wards tenanted by this reckless crew. Mr. Newman, the governor, never entered this part of the prison without reluctance. When Mrs. Fry, and Miss Anna Buxton, sister of Sir T. F. Buxton, made their first visit, Mr. Newman, fearing lest their watches should be snatched from them, advised them, though in vain, to leave them behind: Property was not safe in the very dungeons erected by society for the preservation of property. Mrs. Fry was shocked with "the filth, the closeness of the room, the ferocious manners, and the abandoned wickedness which everything bespoke." Her journal, which was more the record of her religious feelings than of her life, is meagre and incomplete on this interesting subject: she knew not to what important results this first step was to lead. Her third visit to Newgate is thus simply mentioned on the 16th of February: "Yesterday we were some hours at Newgate with the poor female felons, attending to their outward necessities; we had been twice previously. Before we went away, dear Anna Buxton uttered a few words

15*

in supplication, and very unexpectedly to myself, I did also. I heard weeping, and I thought they appeared much tendered ; a very solemn quiet was observed : it was a striking scene ; the poor people on their knees around us, in their deplorable condition."

Mrs. Fry did not renew her visits to Newgate until the Christmas of 1816. The physical condition of the prisoners was somewhat improved, but they were still idle, profligate, and fierce. On her second visit, she requested to be left alone with them. She read to them the parable of the lord of the vineyard, and addressed them at some length. They seemed moved ; but some thought themselves beyond redemption : others asked who was Christ. The proposal of establishing a school in the prison, with a schoolmistress of their own appointment for the children, was, however, adopted with tears of joy. An unoccupied cell was granted for the schoolroom ; Mary Connor, a young girl committed for theft, was appointed schoolmistress ; and, on paying her next visit, Mrs. Fry opened the school for children and young persons under twenty-five years of age. Many women asked to be admitted, but could not for want of room. Mrs. Fry was accompanied by her friend, Mary Sanderson, who visited a prison for the first time, and described her feelings in forcible language : " The railing was crowded with half-naked women, struggling together for the front situations with the most boisterous violence, and begging with the utmost vociferation. She felt as if she were going into a den of wild beasts, and she well recollects quite shuddering when the door was closed upon her, and she was locked in with such a herd of novel and desperate companions."

Mrs. Elizabeth Pryor, who long shared the benevolent exertions of Mrs. Fry, beheld one of these desperate women come out and rush round the prison yard with her arm extended, " tearing everything of the nature of a cap from the heads of the other women, and yelling like a wild beast." This same woman left Newgate a reformed character. She married, and often came to see Mrs. Pryor. Her conduct was good, and her appearance most respectable.

In her evidence before the Committee of the House of Commons, Mrs. Fry mentions " the dreadful proceedings that went forward on the female side of the prison ;" the begging, swearing, gaming, fighting, singing, dancing, dressing up in men's clothes," seems too bad to be described, and which prevented the ladies from admitting young persons with them. These fierce and degraded women asked, however, to share in the benefits extended to their children. In opening the school, Mrs. Fry had scarcely hoped for their reformation; the chance was not to be neglected. In April, 1817, she succeeded in forming a ladies' committee, consisting of the wife of a clergyman and eleven members of the Society of Friends. They formed themselves into "An Association for the Improvement of the Female Prisoners in Newgate." The object of this association was, "to provide for the clothing, the instruction, and the employment of the women; to introduce them to a knowledge of the holy Scriptures; and to form in them, as much as possible, those habits of order, sobriety, and industry, which may render them docile and peaceable whilst in prison, and respectable when they leave it."

Even by the friends of the ladies, this scheme was considered visionary and hopeless. The sheriffs, though they had no faith in its success, showed themselves willing to assist, so far as assistance in this case was possible. They met the ladies one Sunday afternoon at Newgate. In their presence and in that of the Ordinary and the Governor, Mrs. Fry asked the assembled women, "whether they were willing to abide by the rules, which it would be indispensable to establish amongst them, for the accomplishment so much desired by them all?" The women fully and unanimously assured her of their determination to obey them strictly. The sheriffs also addressed them, giving the plan the countenance of their approbation; and then turning to Mrs. Fry and her companions, one of them said, "Well, ladies, you see your materials."*

The prospect did not discourage them. They devoted themselves to their task with heroic zeal. They suspended every other labor—they gave themselves no leisure—"they literally *lived* among the prisoners." Mrs. Fry was unremitting in her exertions; but confesses that this multiplicity of cares was like being "in the whirlwind and in the storm." The consciousness of the good effected supported her. She

* Memoir of the Life of Elizabeth Fry.

writes in April : "Already, from being like wild beasts, they appear harmless and kind."

. Religious instruction of the simplest kind, the morals of Christianity, and not the doctrines of sects, was the plan adopted by Mrs. Fry. It proved most successful : the women flocked to hear her read, pray, or exhort. She ruled by the law of kindness ; and yet it was thought "more terrible to be brought up before her than before the judge." The rules were seldom broken—order was preserved ; and of twenty thousand articles of wearing apparel which had been manufactured by them, when Mrs. Fry gave her evidence before the House of Commons, but three were ever missed, and it was doubtful whether the women were guilty. To find them employment had been the first task of the association ; for without work religious instruction was useless. It occurred to one of the ladies that they might supply Botany Bay with stockings and articles of clothing. She called on Messrs. Richard Dixon & Co. of Fenchurch Street, and, informing them that she was desirous of depriving them of this branch of their trade, explained her views, and solicited their advice. So far from opposing this laudable project, they engaged to provide the work. With these two principles—employment and religious instruction—Mrs. Fry and her coadjutors entered on their task.

The improvement which a fortnight effected was wonderful. A gentleman who then visited Newgate gave the following account :—" I went and requested permission to see Mrs. Fry, which was shortly obtained, and I was conducted by a turnkey to the entrance of the women's wards. On my approach, no loud or dissonant sounds or angry voices indicated that I was about to enter a place which, I was credibly assured, had long had for one of its titles that of ' Hell above ground.' The courtyard into which I was admitted, instead of being peopled with beings scarcely human, blaspheming, fighting, tearing each other's hair, or gaming with a filthy pack of cards for the very clothes they wore, which often did not suffice even for decency, presented a scene where stillness and propriety reigned. I was conducted by a decently dressed person, the newly appointed yards-woman, to the door of a ward, where, at the head of a long table, sat a lady, belonging to the Society of Friends. She was reading aloud to about sixteen women, prisoners, who were engaged in needlework around it. Each wore a clean-looking blue apron and bib, with a ticket, having a number on it, suspended from her neck by a red tape. They all rose on my entrance, curtsied respectfully, and then, at a signal given, resumed their seats and employments. Instead of a scowl, leer, or ill-suppressed laugh, I observed upon their countenances an air of self-respect and gravity, a sort of consciousness of their improved character, and the altered position in which they were placed. I afterwards visited the other wards, which were the counterparts of the first."

The ladies continued their exertions, and were rewarded by the gradual improvement of the women. The governor and clergyman at the penitentiary soon noticed the marked difference between those who came from other prisons, and those who had been under their care. Rewards of books and clothing, and good or bad marks, were part of the plan, and succeeded well. The personal influence of Mrs. Fry was great. Learning, on one occasion, that some gaming still went on, she called the women up, and earnestly requested them to give up their cards: she did not expect they would do so; but, to her surprise, five packs were brought to her, with many expressions of penitence. Mrs. Fry stated this interesting fact in the evidence which she gave before the Committee of the House of Commons, "on the prisons of the metropolis," in February, 1818. She dwelt on the necessity of a prison exclusively for women, with none save female officers over them. She also explained the plan on which she had proceeded: it was both simple and judicious; but, to use the language of the committee in its report, "much was to be ascribed to unremitting personal attention and influence." When the experiment had been tried for a month, the city adopted the plan as a part of the system of Newgate; empowered the ladies to punish the refractory by short confinement, and undertook part of the expense of the matron. The cost of the undertaking was still considerable; the ladies quickly exhausted their private resources; a subscription came to their aid; the sheriffs gave £80, and the relatives of Mrs. Fry assisted her liberally. As the means increased, the association extended its labors.

Before the ladies visited Newgate, the female convicts had made it a rule to tear down and burn everything, on the eve of their departure for Botany Bay. They were now, for the first time, induced to leave the prison in peaceable order. Mrs. Fry and her companions accompanied them to Deptford, saw them on board, divided them into classes, made them elect monitors for the voyage, gave them Bibles, established a school for the children, and, finally, provided them with work. This was not the easiest part of the matter; for there were no less than one hundred and twenty-eight convicts. The difficulty was obviated by Admiral Young, who suggested patch-work; it was not only convenient for a long voyage, but it sold well in New South Wales. The Manchester houses in London were applied to; in a few days they had sent a sufficient number of pieces of coloured cotton. Some of the quilts thus manufactured sold for a guinea a-piece at Rio de Janeiro. After five weeks, during which the ship lay in the river, the kind ladies parted from the poor creatures for whom they had done so much. "Mrs. Fry stood at the door of the cabin, attended by her friends and the captain; the women on the quarterdeck, facing them. The sailors, anxious to see what was going on, clambered into the rigging, on to the capstan, or mingled in the outskirts of the group. The silence was profound, when Mrs. Fry opened her Bible, and, in a clear, audible voice, read a portion from it. The crews of the vessels in the tier, attracted by the novelty of the scene, leant over the ships on either side, and listened, apparently with great attention; she closed the Bible, and, after a short pause, knelt down on the deck, and implored a blessing on this work of Christian charity from that God who, though one may sow, and another water, can alone give the increase. Many of the women wept bitterly, all seemed touched; when she left the ship they followed her with their eyes and their blessings, until, her boat having pushed within another tier of vessels, they could see her no more."[*]

From this time it became part of the duties of the ladies of the Association to see to the moral and physical welfare of the female convicts. The convict ship committee, which still exists, was established at a later period. The amount of human misery which these generous women and their successors have contributed to lessen, will never be known until the great judgment-day. They provided the female convicts with food,

* Memoir, &c.

clothing, and employment. Many of these poor creatures came on board chained to each other, and some laden with irons, which they had worn for months. The influence of the ladies caused this evil to cease.

The miseries of the female convicts were frequently increased by a cruel separation from their children. "Often did Mrs. Pryor, and her friend and companion Lydia J——, quit these scenes, in which they had passed nearly the whole day, not to return to their homes, but to go to Whitehall to represent such cases; that the necessary letters should be despatched without the loss of a post, ordering the restoration of these poor nurslings to their mothers, before the ship should sail."

In the convict ship, as well as in the prison, Mrs. Fry was indefatigable. A peculiar blessing attended her labors. Her aspect, her voice, her manner, possessed an indescribable charm. One who had seen her as she returned from a convict ship, still spoke with enthusiasm, twenty-six years after the meeting, of "this beautiful, persuasive, and heavenly-minded woman. To see her," he adds, "was to love her; to hear her, was to feel as if a guardian angel had bid you follow that teaching which could alone subdue the temptations and evils of this life, and secure a Redeemer's love in eternity."

Mrs. Fry was naturally of a timid nature; but now neither fear nor the dearest feelings of her heart could keep her back. On one occasion, she reached Deptford late in the afternoon of a tempestuous day in March; and it was dark when, after being exposed to wind and rain, she returned to shore. But on being pressed to stay for rest and refreshment, by the family of Admiral Young, she refused, and said she was anxious to go home, having left one of her children seriously ill. The answer struck them deeply.

These philanthropic labors occupied some years. The change they wrought in the mode of life of Mrs. Fry—the mistress of a family, the mother of nine children—was great indeed, and felt to be such. Her correspondence alone was a serious matter. She strove to neglect no duty; but the burden was heavy. "Oh! that I could prosper at home in my labors, as I appear to do abroad," she writes, on reaching the close of 1817, that year to her so eventful. "Others," she adds, "appear to fear for me that I am too much divided; but, alas! what can I do but follow the openings." She also dreaded

lest the praise of man; and not the service of God, should
become her aim. Vain fear, with a soul and heart like
hers.

Celebrity found and left her the same humble and devoted
servant of her God. In the presence of a large party assembled at Devonshire House, a noble lord spoke with tears of one
of her Newgate exhortations, and called it "the deepest tragedy he had ever witnessed." Her name was mentioned with
praise and honor in the Address, moved by the Marquis of
Lansdowne, on the State of the Prisons of the United Kingdom. Queen Charlotte spoke to her publicly at the Mansion
House. To know her was held a privilege; to hear her
addressing the women at Newgate was an intellectual treat,
eagerly sought for by the most eminent and fashionable personages. The friendship of the good, the homage of popular
writers, the praise of poets, were and deserved to be her meed.
To her Hannah More very appropriately dedicated her "Practical Piety;" and Crabbe, in his "Tales of the Hall," recorded
her first visit to Newgate.

In time, the fame and moral power of the English Quakeress
spread beyond her own country to foreign lands : in Paris,
Turin, Amsterdam, Berlin, and St. Petersburg, her name was
reverenced, her counsel was asked, and heeded. The Empress Mary Federovna set the greatest value on the suggestions concerning the treatment of the insane, which, through
the medium of Mr. Venning, she received from Mrs. Fry;
whose letters were, immediately on their receipt, translated
and entered in the journals of the Lunatic Asylum. Fourteen rules were thus adopted in one day. In her admiration
and sympathy, the empress could not help once exclaiming :
"How much I should like to see that excellent woman,
Madame Fry, in Russia !" It would indeed have been a
meeting. Ladies' committees were established, with the
happiest results, in St. Petersburg, Turin, Berlin, and Amsterdam. Many interesting communications concerning their
management and success reached Mrs. Fry in England. Her
own exertions, though for some years they remained confined
to Great Britain, were unremitting ; there were few prisons
in England, Scotland, or Ireland, which she did not visit ;
and everywhere she strove to improve the physical and moral
condition of the prisoners, and to establish ladies' committees.

She took a warm interest in every philanthropic cause of the day, and an active share in some.

The abolition of capital punishment and of slavery were always subjects near to her heart. She remonstrated strongly, and for years, on the condition of the female convicts, placed under the care of sailors during the voyage, and unprovided with a home on their arrival. She took an active part in the proceedings of " The British Ladies' Society for Promoting the Reformation of Female Prisoners ;" and, from her own experience, did much to encourage the hopes expressed by " The Society for the Improvement of Prison Discipline, and Reformation of Juvenile Offenders."

She had the happy art of suggesting to others things it was not in her own power to attempt : a conversation with Miss Neave, in which she drew her attention to the great want of an asylum for discharged prisoners, led to the Tothill Fields Asylum. It began with four inmates, and, under the name of " The Royal Manor Hall Asylum," it has contained fifty young women at a time. Another conversation with Mrs. Benjamin Shaw, led to a school of discipline for the vicious and neglected female children of London. Wherever circumstances led her, Mrs. Fry left tokens of her presence. To establish district visiting societies, for the purpose of encouraging industry and frugality amongst the poor, assisting cases of real distress, and preventing imposture, was one of her favorite objects,—if she could indeed be said to show favor when there was good to achieve.

Whilst she was doing these things, the joys and sorrows of domestic life visited Elizabeth Fry as well as any other woman. The birth of children, the death of dear relatives, the marriage of her elder sons and daughters out of the Society to which she was so warmly attached, and which they forsook, one by one ; many cares and anxieties, the censure of some, the exaggerated expectations of others, were obstacles which sometimes retarded the progress of her cherished task, but were never allowed to impede it long. She had repeated attacks of ill-health : but even sickness was made subservient to good. It was at Brighton, where she went in 1824 for the restoration of her health, that the utter seclusion in which the coast-guards spent their days, first suggested to her mind the libraries which were some years afterwards established throughout Great Britain for their use, and chiefly through her means. To the troubles and sorrows from which no human life is exempt, a heavy misfortune was added in 1828: a house of business in which her husband was partner failed. The change thus wrought in her life was much felt by Mrs. Fry, born and bred in a state of affluence which rendered wealth essential to her comfort. Plashet was given up; many dear ties were broken; many tasks of charity were left undone. The visitation, though deeply felt, was borne in a spirit both humble and resigned.

We think that, without seeking for artificial divisions, the life of Mrs. Fry will admit of being considered under two,— distinct and characteristic. Her youth, her first religious feelings, her marriage and its domestic cares, the ministry amongst the Friends, the early visits to Newgate—comprise the first; in the second, we follow a life of settled benevolence in its peaceful flow. The good deeds are there still; but with the novelty, much of the first interest is gone: we admire, but we no longer wonder. All that can be done by one woman in Newgate,—and not in Newgate only, but throughout Great Britain,—has been done by Elizabeth Fry: she has imparted her spirit to sisters in mercy, and to men in authority. She takes her share in the task, but calmly and peacefully,—like one who feels that it might go on without her now. There was a change, too, in public opinion, which she accepted cheerfully. On the first of January, 1831, she writes: " My interest in the cause of prisons remains strong, and my zeal unabated; though it is curious to observe how much less is felt about it by the public generally. How little it would answer, in these important duties, to be too much affected by the good or bad opinion of man !"

Through this comparative repose, there is a spiritual change revealed by the journals. Their tone is more hopeful; there is more real faith ; a spirit more lofty, more enlightened,—more in charity with the opinions and creeds from which it differs. Not in vain has Elizabeth Fry seen fallen beings, moved in the world, and beheld at work the passions of men. The charity so simply expressed, yet so true ; the evident joy with which good is acknowledged and revered in all, is a beautiful feature in her character and religious opinions.

We have dwelt at some length on the early life of Mrs. Fry,—on her first labors and their happy result : we shall be compelled to record more briefly the tasks and events— less important, it is true—which occupied and filled her latter years. In 1827 she went to Ireland, chiefly to exercise the ministry amongst the Friends there, but also visiting the prisons and establishing committees on her way. A second visit, in 1832, showed her that the first had not been unproductive of good. Her third and last visit was paid in 1836. She wished to see the large female prison in Grange-Gorman Lane, Dublin, which was then nearly completed. A prison for women, and as exclusively under the government of women as circumstances would permit, had long been a cherished plan with Mrs. Fry, and she rejoiced in the success of this experiment ; to which her judicious advice much contributed.

In 1833, Mrs. Fry spent some time in the islands of Jersey and Guernsey. She took great pains to establish district societies, and endeavored to improve the prison and hospital, both in a neglected condition. It was not until 1836 that she had the satisfaction of seeing these objects carried out by government. An interesting task in which she was long engaged, which gave her much trouble, which she had to press repeatedly on the attention of persons in office,—libraries for the coast-guard stations throughout Great Britain, was accomplished in the same year. Upwards of fifty-two thousand volumes were thus disseminated amongst the coast-guards and their families.

Although, owing to the great improvement in prison discipline, Mrs. Fry's prison labors were naturally drawing to a close, she took unabated interest in the subject, and exerted in its favor whatever influence she possessed. She visited the prisons of Scotland in 1834 and 1838, and besides suggesting improvements, she examined some of the systems adopted. Mrs. Fry was slow in pronouncing on the silent and solitary systems ; but, after much thought, she concluded against both, as cruel and inefficient : she held, that by treating human beings like machines, the chance of reclaiming them, by an appeal to their sympathies, was wantonly thrown away. The submission arising from sheer terror of a punishment so awful that it drives men mad, was not, indeed, that obedience which she and her coadjutors had found, when they first entered Newgate, and read the Gospel to women fierce, degraded, and amenable to no authority save that of the stone walls, and iron bolts and bars of their prison.

In 1836, Mrs. Fry paid her first brief visit to France. She went as far as Paris in 1838; visited France again in 1839, and extended her journey as far as Switzerland. In the following year, Holland and Northern Germany were visited; Denmark was included in 1841. In 1843, she saw Paris for the third and last time. Wherever she went, Mrs. Fry excited much interest and curiosity, and saw as much as she desired of what is called good society. But her errand was not to them: charitable asylums, and above all, prisons, were the places in which she delighted. Her power to do good was naturally limited by difference of creed, the difficulty of expressing herself in a foreign language, and the shortness of her stay. Much that she saw afforded, however, matter of instruction, interest, and profitable thought. The following just remarks were suggested by a visit to the charitable institutions of St. Omer:—"The sacrifice that must be made to give up the whole life, as the Sisters of Charity do, to teach and bring up the poor children, and attend to the sick in their hospitals, is very exemplary; and the slackness of some Protestants, and coldness of too many, led me to think that whilst, on the one hand, the meritoriousness of good works may be unsoundly upheld by the Roman Catholics, yet, that it stimulates to much that is excellent; and a fear arose in my mind that the true doctrine that teaches that we have no merit in any thing that we do, is either so injudiciously represented, or so misunderstood, that in many cases it leads to laxity as to sin, and a want of diligence in works of righteousness and true holiness."

Some touching incidents marked these foreign travels of Elizabeth Fry. In February, 1838, she visited the great women's prison of St. Lazare, in Paris; it then contained nine hundred and fifty-two inmates. Mrs. Fry asked and obtained permission, that a French lady, who accompanied her, might read to them; and the parable of the prodigal son was chosen. Mrs. Fry commented upon it; the French lady translated every sentence as it was uttered, and the women, and not only the women, but the jailor and the turnkeys, wept as they heard her. The charm of the voice, of the delivery, of the language, always pure and eloquent, were not there: nothing but the earnestness of a rich lady, who had left her home, her country, to address the outcasts of a foreign land. When Mrs. Fry visited St. Lazare again in the following year, she was recognized with delight by many of the women.

In 1843, Mrs. Fry, then on her way to Paris, visited the great central prison at Clermont-en-Oise. Men never enter it; it then held nine hundred women, under the rule of a superior and twenty-two nuns. The superior, evidently a woman of strong intellect, showed the English ladies over the prison. Mrs. Fry greatly desired to see all the nuns assembled; this was at first thought impossible; but as she was going to leave, the superior led her guest into an apartment, around which sat the twenty-two nuns, in their gray robes, and the lay sisters in black. In the centre of the room stood the superior, holding the Quakeress lady by the hand. Mrs. Fry began an address, which was translated by her daughter. She spoke on those subjects to which her best energies had been given, and their whole lives had been devoted. She told them of Newgate, of what the Gospel had done there, and, though daughters of a different creed, the nuns wept to hear her. She concluded, saluting them as "sisters in Christ," with a short blessing and prayer in French. The whole scene was strange, unusual, but solemn and impressive.

It was on her return from this last journey that Mrs. Fry sank into that declining state of health from which she never rallied. She lingered for two years, in much suffering of the body and the spirit. The death of old friends, who had shared her philanthropic labors, or been her companions in the ministry; of grandchildren, dear relatives, and finally of a much-loved son, tried her deeply. It was, as she wrote in her journal, "sorrow upon sorrow."

On the third of June, 1845, Mrs. Fry was, for the last time, present at the yearly meeting of the Ladies' British Society. She was then residing in Upton Lane; and, to accommodate her in her suffering state, the meeting was held at the Friends' meeting-house, at Plaistow, in Essex. The reports on the state of the prisons, and the moral and physical welfare of the prisoners, were deeply gratifying to one who remembered their condition when she visted Newgate, upwards of thirty-three years before. For the last time Elizabeth Fry spoke on "the objects of philanthropy and Christian benevolence, with which her life had been identified." She was not able to stand; but her mind was as strong as ever, her thirst of good unabated.

The progress of her illness during the course of this year showed that her life was drawing to a close. She felt it, and as death approached, the secret fear in which she had always held this solemn change vanished. She expressed to those around her the belief, that whatever human dread remained in her heart would be taken away from her; or that, "in tender mercy to her timid nature," she should be permitted to pass unconsciously through the dark valley. In July she was removed to Ramsgate, for the benefit of the sea air; but her health, and with it the powers of her mind, continued to decline. On the 13th of October she grew much worse. One of her daughters, who sat reading Isaiah to her, heard her saying, in a slow, distinct voice, "Oh! my dear Lord, help and keep thy servant." She never spoke again, but sank into a state of unconsciousness. Her agony was long, but its bitterness was for those who beheld it, not for her. At length, early on the morning of the following day, her bonds were broken: the Master had released his servant.

All that was mortal of Elizabeth Fry now rests by the side of her little child, in the Friends' burying-ground at Barking; but her name, her deeds, her spirit, are with us still. Who shall estimate not only the good which she did, but that to which her example led? How noble, how generous, was the use she made of the personal beauty, exquisite voice, ready eloquence, and many talents with which she was gifted! The extremes which met in her character gave her greater power. Timid, daring, prudent, enthusiastic, practical, equally alive to the beautiful and to the humorous, Elizabeth Fry was eminently fitted for her task. She possessed an insight into character and a power of control which enabled her to influence almost every one who came within her sphere.

This was not simply the result of her earnestness; for others as earnest have failed; but of exquisite tact and judg-

ment. In the year 1835 she chanced to visit the penitentiary at Portsea. The inmates were assembled in the parlor
when Mrs. Fry entered it; two were pointed out to her as
peculiarly refractory and hardened. Of this she took no
notice; she sat down and addressed a general exhortation
to all. When it was concluded she rose to depart, and,
going up to these two, she held out her hand to each of
them, saying, in her simple Quaker speech: ".I trust I shall
hear better things of thee." The manner, the tone, had a
power more deep than admonition or reproach; they both
burst into tears.

This same tact guided her in every thing, and made her
feel at home everywhere. She was as much at her ease in
the palaces of kings, amongst the courtly and the polished of
foreign lands, before committees and public assemblies, as in
the humblest meeting held in a stocking-weaver's room, with
homely " Friends sitting on the stocking-loom for want of
chairs," and the mistress of the place " getting up during the
meeting to attend to dressing the dinner."

But however much Mrs. Fry owed to her natural endowments, to 'penetration, tact, and eloquence, " to the silver
tones of her voice, and the majestic mien with which she
delivered the message of God,"* we do not mean to say
that there lay the secret of her power. We think we can
trace it more surely in the confession which she made to a
friend during her last illness. "Since my heart was touched
at seventeen years old, I believe I never have awakened from
sleep, in sickness or in health, by day or by night, without
my first waking thought being, 'how best I might serve my
Lord.'"

It needs not much faith—not much knowledge of our
nature—to say that she who, for forty-eight years, could
keep one unchanged desire of love in her heart, was indeed
destined to achieve great things, and fit to be a servant of
her God.

* Memoirs of W. Allen, p. 462.

CHAPTER XXVII.

Sarah Martin.

THE labors of Mrs. Fry were limited. She could do much, but not all. Everywhere she left room for individual exertion. It was not always, however, that this indirect appeal was responded to, as in the case, well known, but still interesting, which we will proceed to relate.

In the month of August, of the year 1819, a woman was sent to the jail of Yarmouth, in Norfolk, for having cruelly beaten her own child. The prison of Yarmouth was all that the vices of its inmates and the neglect of its rulers could make it: a den where human beings, covered with vermin, and the prey of skin diseases, spent their days in gambling, blasphemy, and strife; where the purifying influence of labor was unknown, and the voice of God's teachers had never been heard, the very stronghold of moral and physical evil. From this abode the unnatural mother was expected to come forth penitent and amended.

The lamentable state of Yarmouth jail was not unknown in the town and its vicinity. A young woman, who resided with a widowed grandmother at Caistor, had heard of the condition of the prisoners. She was twenty-eight years of age, a dressmaker by trade; Sarah Martin was her name. Devout, sensible, full of tenderness, and yet essentially practical, she was of those whom the high aims of faith early invest with moral dignity. From her nineteenth year she had devoted the Sabbath—her only day of rest after the labors of the week—to the task of teaching in a Sunday-school; she had visited the inmates' of the workhouse, and read the Scriptures to the aged and the sick; but her ambition rose beyond this. "Whilst frequently passing the jail," she wrote in after-life, "I felt a strong desire to obtain admission to the prisoners to read the Scriptures to them, for I thought much of their condition, and of their sin before God; how they were shut out from the society whose rights they had violated, and how destitute they were of that scriptural instruction which alone could meet their unhappy cir-

cumstances. . . . I did not make known my purpose of
seeking admission to the jail, even to my beloved grandmother, until the object was attained, so sensitive was my
fear lest any obstacle should thereby arise in my way, and
the project seem a visionary one. God led me, and I consulted none but Him."

This sensitive fear long influenced Sarah Martin; but
when she heard of the incarceration of the unnatural mother
above alluded to, her heart moved her to go and speak to
her. She asked permission, was refused, and, nothing deterred, asked again; this time the request was granted.
The woman gazed with surprise on her unknown visitor.
Sarah Martin simply told her errand : she was come to speak
to her of her guilt, and of God's infinite mercy. In the simplicity of her pure heart, Sarah does not seem to have
imagined that the criminal whom she addressed might, perchance, not know the feeling of remorse, nor care to be told
that she could yet be pardoned. And indeed it was not so :
she who had violated the dearest laws of nature, burst into
tears on receiving a token of Christian sympathy; and
listened, a subdued penitent, whilst Sarah read the divine
promise of forgiveness recorded in the twenty-third chapter of
St. Luke.

The work thus begun was earnestly continued. For the
first few months Sarah Martin only paid short visits to the
prisoners, for the purpose of reading the Scriptures to them ;
but, desiring to instruct them in reading and writing as well,
she gave up to them one day every week. To this day many
other days were afterwards added ; and though she lived by
her labor, "the loss," she said, "was never felt." Her mode
of teaching was simple : those who knew not how to read she
encouraged to learn, and other prisoners who knew, taught
them in her absence. Thus, also, those who required not her
teaching in writing, were induced to improve themselves by
copying extracts from books lent to them. The prisoners who
could read, daily learned verses from the Scriptures. Sarah
Martin encouraged them by her own example : she learned
her set of verses, and repeated them with the rest. This silenced the pride of many who had at first refused, saying,
"it would be of no use." "It is of use to me," calmly replied
Sarah, "and why should it not be so to you? You have not

16

tried it, but I have." So great was the ascendency which she finally obtained over them, that, during her absence, the prisoners not only learned their appointed lessons, but added to them, in order to please and surprise their kind teacher. Of these labors, and their failure or success, Sarah, at a later period, when she attended the prison daily, kept exact record in an every-day book. The following extract will show her manner of proceeding with her pupils :

May 16.

"Skinner, Psalm cxix., 1 verse.
Beams, John vii., 1 verse.
Whitby, Matt. v., 1 verse.
Doyle, Matt. xx., 2 verses.
Turner, John xv., 14 verses.   Hymn, 3 verses.
Brown, Isaiah li., 4 verses.   Hymn, 3 verses.
Bowlin, Matt. viii., 2 verses.
Howerel, John iv., 4 verses."

" *General Observations.*"

"It astonishes me to observe how strictly and constantly the prisoners labor to learn their verses from the Holy Scriptures every day. Poor old S. takes uncommon pains to remember one every day. T., who, on April 21, could only attempt one, has for some time learned five regularly, and several of Watts' Divine Songs. Since yesterday, he has learned fourteen, from John xv., perfectly. It is no less gratifying and wonderful to observe the success of H., who, with a defective memory, perseveres, by constant study, in furnishing his mind and memory with from two to five verses daily.

"I was particularly pleased with the progress of B.; and the youngest B. had learned perfectly the verse which, as he could not read it alone, I had commenced teaching him yesterday. But when I returned to R. H., a dull person, who has been committed four days, he said he had been so busy mending his clothes, that he had not had time. I entered on the subject, explaining its advantages ; and on his acknowledging that, as an ignorant and guilty creature, he was not happy, that he needed instruction, God's mercy, and to be reclaimed from a bad course, that he had better, knowing the thing to be right, give his mind to what I proposed, and not

consult his inclination, but at once begin to store his mind
with suitable portions from the Testament.

"May 17. This morning R. H. repeated three verses from
Matt. viii."

It was more easy to induce in the prisoners a wish for reading. Sarah Martin procured them tracts, children's books,
and four or five larger volumes; which were great favorites,
and were daily exchanged in every room. For those whom
this supply did not satisfy, she procured more serious works,
chiefly from the Religious Tract Society.

This was not all. No chaplain attended the jail; the Sabbath was broken and desecrated; it was neither the day of
rest nor that of worship. Sarah Martin pressed the prisoners to form Sunday services among themselves. They agreed
to do so; but, to insure the performance of their promise,
she was present. After several trials, they ultimately fixed
upon her as their reader. Laborious as was the task, she accepted and fulfilled it, until the year 1831, when a minister,
who came to reside in her parish, undertook the afternoon
service. Sarah confessed that it was "a timely relief." One
of these Sunday services is thus described by Captain W. J.
Williams in his Parliamentary Reports: "Sunday, November
29, 1835. Attended divine service in the morning at the
prison. The male prisoners only were assembled; a female,
resident in the town, officiated; her voice was exceedingly
melodious, her delivery emphatic, and her enunciation exceedingly distinct. The service was the Liturgy of the Church
of England; two psalms were sung by the whole of the prisoners, and extremely well, much better than I have frequently heard in our best-appointed churches. A written discourse, of her own composition, was read by her; it was of a
purely moral tendency, involving no doctrinal points, and admirably suited to the hearers. During the performance of
the service, the prisoners paid the profoundest attention and
most marked respect, and, as far as it is possible to judge,
appeared to take a devout interest. Evening service was
read by her afterwards, to the female prisoners."

But perhaps it will be asked how this quiet, unpretending
woman had first acquired the power of making herself listened to and obeyed by these lawless beings. She has not told
us how the thing was done. We wonder and admire, and

can find no other explanation than that which lies in the might of faith and charity, even over the most evil and abandoned. Those spiritual labors of Sarah Martin stand the first in order and in honor—but they stand not alone. The charity which teaches degraded creatures that they are beings with immortal souls; which reclaims the vicious from sin to virtue, is by far the noblest charity; and would ever be honored as such, if those who profess it did not so often contradict its teaching by their example, talking of heavenly aspirations while their souls cling to earth. Those whose faith is living are generous in all things, temporal and spiritual: Christ taught sinners and fed the hungry multitude.

Having first made a moral and religious impression on the prisoners, Sarah strengthened it by every means in her power. Idleness was their great bane. She had the art to make them love labor, and was ingenious in finding them work. She first made the attempt with the women. One gentleman had given her ten shillings, and another a pound, for prison charity. It occurred to her to spend the money on material for baby clothes to be made by the prisoners. The experiment succeeded. They soon made shirts, coats, and other articles of clothing; the plan became known under the name of Female Prisoners' Employment. Charitable persons supported it; and the British Ladies' Society made liberal donations. The advantages were twofold: many of the female prisoners learned to sew, and found themselves possessed of a little money by the end of their imprisonment; and the articles thus manufactured were either given to the poor, or sold to them at reduced prices. The original fund of £1 10s. rose to £7 7s., and from the period of its establishment to the time when Sarah Martin wrote her memoirs, £408 worth of various articles had been made by the prisoners and sold for charity.

The men were similarly employed. They made straw hats, bone spoons and seals, men's and boys' caps; the material being old cloth or moreen—whatever, in short, Sarah could obtain from her friends. Some of the younger ones even learned to sew gray cotton shirts, and to make patchwork, sooner than remain idle. Nothing, indeed, was more remarkable than her ingenuity in rendering every thing of use to her great aim: pieces of print for patchwork, scraps of paper or pasteboard, pictures, the leaves of spelling-books, the worn-out Testaments of schools, became in her hands so many instruments of pleasure and good to the prisoners. On one occasion she showed them an etching of the chess-player by Retzch; two of the men, one a shoemaker and the other a bricklayer, desired much to copy it; they were allowed to do so, and supplied with materials. They succeeded so well as to induce a similar wish in others; for a year or two afterwards many prisoners continued to make copies of it.

This is only a meagre outline of the great and heroic labors scarcely dwelt upon in Sarah Martin's brief memoirs, but revealed by her account-books. Strange books these are: besides poems, they contain a considerable number of addresses written for the prisoners, and a large Scripture place-book for daily use. Sarah also wrote down accurate accounts of the funds she received and spent for the prisoners, under the various heads of "The Female Prisoners' Employment;" "Employment for the Destitute, and Donations for General Purposes." The "Every-day Book" records minutely the behavior, good or ill, of the prisoners whom she taught: her patience under disappointment—her constant hope of their reformation; whilst the book entitled "Liberated Prisoners," shows with what earnest and watchful love she followed the steps of those whom she had attempted to reclaim. We have already explained the nature of the accounts kept under the head of Female Prisoners' Employment; the book of Employment for the Destitute, which may be said to continue it, opens with the year 1827. A young girl of loose character had attempted suicide; she was fortunately saved from death; but, on visiting her, Sarah discovered that she needed employment as well as religious instruction. She collected £2 6s., and bought materials for articles of clothing, which the girl made for sale. The same benefit was extended to many female prisoners after their discharge. At a later period, the donations and subscriptions of a few liberal individuals enabled Sarah Martin to adopt a similar plan with those male prisoners who earned nothing in prison, and who on leaving it found themselves destitute. She could thus, while serving them, observe their conduct and strengthen their good resolves.

The time and labor required by each separate charity can

scarcely be estimated. Sarah Martin's account-books are models of accuracy and order. She was never known to have a bill in all her life; she praised and practised the apostolic injunction: "Owe no man any thing, but to love one another." We can see that to keep an exact account of all the money she received and disbursed was no slight task; but the time, thought, and energy which she gave so freely, are things of which she kept no record, and left to conjecture. When she provided labor for the destitute, she had to purchase materials, to cut them out and prepare them. After a day's hard labor, and an evening of writing, she has been known to stand cutting out work until past midnight, or to prepare copy-books for her pupils in the jail,—a constantly recurring task, as she could allow only two sheets of paper at a time, in order to be able to see when part of the quantity was abstracted. This one precaution shows the harassing nature of her self-imposed task. But even this was not all; the liberated prisoners were to be attended to, aided, watched, and strengthened. An honest home and lasting employment were to be found for them, lest they should fall back into evil courses. Dangerous companions had to be removed, friends and masters to be persuaded into forgiveness; and all this was to be effected by a delicate, sensitive woman, who labored for her bread, and who, though she never allowed herself to be dismayed, keenly felt every check.

Her path was beset with irritating obstacles, which chiefly arose from the perverse nature of those whom she endeavored to reform. We have already mentioned that the younger prisoners amused themselves with patchwork. Sarah provided them with pieces to sew together, yet never dared to give them as many as they wished for, lest they should cease to value their occupation. She regretted to leave them often idle; but she knew their wayward temper too well to act differently. Tact and patience were needed to steer her through her difficult course; not less did she require the most ardent faith and charity to endure the things which she braved daily. The prisoners were infested with vermin, and a prey to skin diseases. The horror and disgust of Sarah Martin were the greater that she dared not mention her distress, lest the houses of her customers and friends should be closed upon her. She endured all silently, and commended herself to God. The thought of shrinking from her task does not seem to have occurred to her.

The most serious obstacles with which Sarah Martin had to contend, and the manner in which she overcame them, are frankly set down in her several books. What follows is extracted from the Every-day Book:

"February 2.—I had been accustomed to allow the prisoners, in the middle of every day, to write a copy in my absence, with the view of filling up their time. On Friday, in consequence of a note being sent over to the female prisoners' ward, the governor, to prevent the improper use of pen and ink, took both away, with their books also. Since that day not a single prisoner has learned any lessons. On leaving, after reading with them to-day, I asked why it was that all had done so?—F. J. replied he wished to write, that would do him some good; the other would do none,—so he would learn no more. I reasoned with him; but his reply was, 'I am sure it will do me no good.' I turned to the Bible as a standard to convince him. 'As for that,' said he, 'I won't believe one word of it, it is all nonsense; victuals is what I want.' 'Yes,' replied B., a poor, ignorant creature, 'victuals is what we want, and not to be put in here for nothing; we don't want religion, we want victuals.' I then took pains to show that religion, which enforced justice, industry, &c., brought plenty; and in the absence of its principles, there was want and destitution. I still referred to the Bible; it was my standard, although F. J., in rejecting it, had none. F. J. said, exultingly, 'I have a right to think as I like.' I replied, 'If such be your thoughts, you have no right, viper-like, to cast forth the poison upon other people.' It was remarkable, that when he spoke the most dangerous things, the others seconded him at the beginning of the contest; not so at the end. I requested, as a favor, an answer to one plain question: Did they still wish me to visit them, or was it their wish that I should keep away? If it were the latter, as I would never go where I was unwelcome knowingly, I would never enter the room again until they were gone. All but F. J. eagerly desired that I would still come; that they were quite sure I intended good to them, and hoped I would on no account leave them. I told them it was enough; I would visit them still. J. B. said, 'Al-

though I am bad, and have not followed them up, I am convinced that your views are right:' he acknowledged that
what I taught from the Bible was true, and those who. followed up such views were the best people. All agreed to
this excepting F. J.; and at parting I said, 'If any of you
think proper to learn more from the Scriptures, I shall feel
happy to hear you, except F. J.; with his views, I shall not
hear any from him.'

"February 3.—On entering the middle room to-day, all
received me in the most respectful and grateful manner; all
had learned a lesson from the Scriptures to repeat, except
F. J.; and all except him read a verse in turn in general
reading. As we read, I adverted to what had been said the
day before: J. B., as spokesman, said, 'What you said yesterday, madam, was satisfactory; it removed all doubts;
you are in the right; you can have no motive but our
good.' F. J. did not speak once. One said there must be
a Creator: this opened the way for carrying forward the
subject; the Creator is good; his works are good; man is
not good—hence the need of a Redeemer. W. and all said,
I certainly meant for their good, and thought I was happy
in it: Yes, I said, and if the surface of one's mind be disturbed for a moment, my happiness in the work is not in
human power.; and you can no more touch that, than you
can bring the sun from the firmament."

The offender proved sullen, and several days elapsed before he showed signs of repentance. On February 10, we
find the following entry: "J. B. followed me to the gate to
speak to me in behalf of F. J., who wished I would allow
him to have some conversation with me apart from the rest;
also, that I would receive him again. He wished to retract
all he had said against the Bible and religion. J. B. said:
'F. J. thinks you were wrong in casting him off so hastily,
and,- you will excuse me, madam, I think so too,' J. B.
said, 'F. J. thinks some remarks I made on Sunday were
entirely meant for him, which, however, were unpremedi-
tated.' I asked: 'Do you frequently think me personally
severe, then?' 'We do,' he replied, 'and the prisoners
talk of it.' 'But if they feel offended at the moment, they
feel the justice of it afterwards.' 'That,' said he, 'has
been my own case; but I have done the same thing, and

have been as bad as they.' I went up to the room, and told F. J. I should be happy to receive him again, and he thanked me.

"February 11.—This day I afforded F. J. the opportunity he desired, of some private conversation with me, by asking him to take my Bible up to the gate. He said he should be sorry to bring up his children with such views as he had expressed; that he had reflected, and felt that he had been wrong : he expected to be ridiculed by the other prisoners, but was determined to adopt a new line of conduct altogether. There was deep feeling, thoughtfulness, and strong earnestness of manner : he spoke highly of his wife. Here I asked : 'Do you love your wife ?' 'Oh yes, and my wife loves me.' 'And do you love your children ?' 'Oh yes, I love my children.' 'And were I or any other to say, I hate your wife, I hate your children, would you like it ?' 'No, I should not.' 'And yet you spoke against my God ; and of this lovely book you said, It is all a pack of nonsense, I do not believe one word of it !' F. J. acknowledged the application with much emotion. He said he had been accustomed to sit from Sunday morning till Sunday night in a public house, but would attend a place of worship in future, which his wife had formerly advised in vain. He acknowledged that I was justified in leaving him, after his having spoken of the Bible and of God as he did.'

In the Liberated Prisoners' Book we find F. J. thus mentioned under the date of July 1 : "F. J. has called upon me, and of him I have the highest hope. He was tried and convicted for a felony, and sentenced to six months' imprisonment : his previous character had been bad. At first he was quiet, and for a while I did not discover that he was a scorner of all things sacred. The circumstance which led to this discovery is written in the Every-day Book. After the date of February 11, he seemed a new character, no longer close or shy on the one hand, nor presuming on the other ; but simple, honest, and open. The poor fellow has obtained no work ; his children are ill ; and his excellent wife, whilst rejoicing at the change in her husband, is cast down by extreme poverty. I gave them an order for some flour."

We have extracted somewhat largely, because we think that the preceding passages give a fair insight into the character of Sarah Martin. We see her there in her earnestness; persevering, patient, and forgiving; yet not free from a certain human pride and warmth of temper, which she regretted, but could not always rule. In one of those written prayers and confessions, in which she laid her heart bare before her God, she penitently exclaims: "Oh that I had returned good for evil, and love and gratitude for good! . . . . When I reproved the sinner, I did it not in love, but in the feeling of human vexation, and of human anger: I did not love the sinner, but felt great dislike, yea, aversion to him. Have pity on the lost and guilty one: teach him to pray; and whilst I try thine infinite forbearance as I do, give me the grace of patience and forbearance to others." It was hard, indeed, to see her most earnest efforts often fail: to behold prisoners leave the jail obdurate in evil, and return to it again and again, worse every time they came back. Faith bore her through this trial: that a few should heed her, or rather the truth that spoke through her, seemed ample reward to her humble heart. She tells us herself, in that glowing language which the daily study of the Scriptures had rendered familiar to her, that "the sower is rewarded when, by a power not his own, the grain arises, and is still nourished by the sun and the rain from heaven; what is that to the delight which I have known, when, in my happy course, I could stand still and see the salvation of God!"

This fervent enthusiasm did not unfit Sarah for the more humble duties of charity—attention, prudence, and forethought. A few entries from the Liberated Prisoners' Book will show the minute details into which she daily entered.

"October, 1837:—G. N., a donkey, eighteen shillings.

"October 17.—N. has been in the jail six months for stealing deals out of the sea; he has a wife and four young children, and earned his living by fishing, selling fish, &c. The chief means of their support, in winter, appears to have been that of selling fish in the villages, which was hung in hampers on each side of his donkey. During his imprisonment his wife sold the donkey, as she could not afford to feed it, and wanted the money for her own support. They had a pig also, which she was obliged to sell to procure food for the family. The parish gave them a small allowance part of the time, up to the last fortnight of N.'s imprisonment, which was then withdrawn, as the officers thought his term of imprisonment was six lunar months, and they were calendar. Their distress was relieved by a threepenny loaf each day for that fortnight, at the end of which they must all have gone to the workhouse, except some efficient means of support had been immediately adopted. After considerable attention to the matter, my conclusion was this : I had better set about purchasing a suitable donkey, and let him load it with fish to sell along the villages, by which N. thinks he can honestly keep out of the workhouse.

"October 18.—N. came to speak to me this morning, as I desired ; he was liberated yesterday ; he thought a donkey would save him and his family from the workhouse. I judged the thing worth the trial, and consulted where it would be best to seek one, as I was at liberty, in the hope that he would turn out well, to purchase a donkey at the expense of the magistrates, which, if it answered the purpose, and he used it well, would in the end be his own. His wife's relations, at a village a few miles off, knew of one four years old, which had not been broken down by bad usage, for which the owner asked a pound. He offered to go and fetch the animal for me to look at, which I desired him to do ; and as he had six persons to feed, and was earning nothing, I gave him one hundred herrings to sell on his way. N. came this evening with the donkey and its owner; it seemed a good animal, and I bought it for 18s., the least he would take. He said he would not have sold it in Yarmouth, except where he thought it would be used well. N. sold his hundred herrings on the way, and said he got 1s. 3d. by them. He engages to lead the donkey to my residence frequently for me to see, and inform me of his success."

The little family thus rescued from ruin is again mentioned in the month of March of the following year. We then learn that they still had the donkey, " and valued it greatly." Instances of the kind and grateful feelings often manifested by the liberated prisoners, are faithfully recorded by their friend.

T. E., we are told, came to see her some time after his liberation, "with a new hat on, new blue slop, yellow silk handkerchief, and quite smart. I said: 'You have been to the public-house?' 'Yes,' he replied, 'but not to drink; we have had our making-up dinner; the owners pay for it; I only took a little ale; I was forced to it.' I said: 'Ale is poison with you; I wish you would spare a little money for the savings bank.' He replied: I 'can't, for I bought my mother a gown and a pair of shoes; my sister a new gown and a hat; and my sister's child a new frock, for they are so poor; and I bought myself two such beautiful books; they cost 2s.' 'How foolish! Why not let me buy them for you? What are they about?' 'I don't know; may I bring them and show you? and may I write you some copies on paper, to make you a present of, because you taught me?' I told him to bring the books, as I wished to see him again. His kind feeling towards his mother is right. The public-house was his ruin at first, and, with his want of firmness, much is to be feared."

Another lad, designated as R. H., whose chief fault seems to have been want of steadiness, was practically encouraged to keep his good resolves.

"January 3.—I have provided R. H. with a pair of scales from the liberated prisoners' fund which cost 2s. 6d., also with a pound and a half-pound weight, which cost 10d., and a basket, which cost 1s., to sell sprats. I went also to a fish-merchant's, and paid for a stone of red sprats for him.

"January 5.—R. H. called to inform me of his success: he saved 9d. by the first stone. He then bought a half-stone of sprats, which he sold, and gave his mother the money. I shall see his mother soon, although I believe the boy is going on rightly.

"January 10.—R. H. has obtained work at a twine spinner's, and is to have 2d. a skein the first week, and $2\frac{1}{2}$d. the next. At this season he is to sell sprats, being prevented from working by the weather.

"February 3.—This evening R. H. called to speak to me. He has obtained regular employment in a ropemaker's yard. I allowed him to read a fellow-prisoner's letter I had that day received; having done so, he said, 'It is a nice letter; I wish he could get some work: when people come out of that place it is a hard matter; thank God I have got work. L. and I made vows together that we would never do what was bad after we got out of prison, as we had done before.'

"February 7.—R. H. is conducting himself so much to my satisfaction, that I desired him to bring the duplicate of a jacket and waistcoat which had been pawned, and went myself with him to P.'s, to get them out, for which I paid 2s. 4½d., being aware that he stood in great need of them, without the means of procuring them for himself." .

We cannot help giving one last extract from this interesting book, as it illustrates forcibly not only the hardships of the poor, but the sort of friendship and assistance they require.

"March 22.—W. R. was discharged, after being six months in jail. He called upon me directly, expressed his determination to follow an honest course, and whatever his difficulties might be, not to do wrong with the view of removing them. He has been convicted before, knows no trade, and although he has a home with his father, he is destitute of means of support. His father earned his living by making and selling peppermint-balls. I ordered him a threepenny loaf a day for seven days, whilst seeking work.

"March 26.—W. R. came to inform me that he had entered on board a man-of-war; as there seemed no prospect of his getting work, it appeared the only opening to obtain an honest living. He said he felt more happy in his mind than he had done for years.

"April 12.—W. R., after entering the navy, and leaving Yarmouth, has been returned home, with fourteen others, as more had been received than were wanted, except regular seamen, which is a sad disappointment. I have been to the house: there are three sons without the knowledge of any trade, who have no work. One young man sat with an expression of grief, who was prevented even from going out to seek work, because he was entirely without shoes. I have determined, after much consideration, to venture on the payment of half the price of a half-barrel of herrings, and send W. R. into the country to sell them.

"April 13.—W. R. has made inquiry where he could best get the herrings, and the cheapest likely to answer are 9s. 6d. the half-barrel. I went with him to the fish-office (W. B.'s),

and if his father can either borrow money or get credit for
the other half, he shall start in the morning to sell them in
the villages. The business was managed about the herrings :
I paid Mr. B. 4s. 9d., being my half part. W. R., accompanied by the brother whose shoes were scarcely sufficient,
went out on Thursday morning. They returned to-day, and
he has this moment been to tell me that, after having paid
expenses, they had 3s. to spare."

To another, these duties, which not only required so much
thought and attention, but were also ever recurring, might
have seemed sufficient; yet Sarah Martin found time and
energy to attend a factory girl's evening school, which opened
in 1837. The fatigue, however, proved too much for her,
and at the end of two years she was obliged to relinquish the
school, and devote herself exclusively to the jail. There she
suffered greatly, through the bad character and conduct of
the turnkey.

It was some consolation to her to feel that even he could not
deprive her of the respect of the prisoners; but his power was
great; that power was against her, and as he daily became
worse, anxiety impaired her health. Comfort came to her in a
way which might have dismayed another, but which could only
strengthen the trust of her generous heart : her occupation as
dressmaker daily declined. We have already said how she
devoted one day every week to the prison; a charitable lady
proposed to pay her for another day, to be given to the same
labor; she accepted, and now the four remaining days seemed likely to be left to charity. In December, 1838, Sarah
Martin found herself entirely free : she had literally nothing
to do but to attend the prisoners; she did so daily; and the
introduction of a new and efficient governor tended, as well
as her increased exertions, to produce many happy results.
Her satisfaction was complete.

What, it may be asked, were her means of support ?. The
interest of two or three hundred pounds, inherited from her
grandmother. Prospects so narrow and dismal could not
appal Sarah Martin. In a noble passage of her memoirs we
read the secret of her strength : "My mind, in the contemplation of such trials, seemed exalted by more than human
energy, for I had counted the cost, and my mind was made
up. If, whilst imparting truth to others, I became exposed

to temporal want, the privation, so momentary to an individual, would not admit of comparison with following the Lord, in thus administering to others."

The noble woman's trust was justified. She labored incessantly in that work which was the delight of her heart, of which she fervently declared that "it had afforded her the highest elevation of desire' and satisfaction that she could contemplate on this side of heaven; that it had brought in wealth which the mind of an archangel might fail to estimate;" and the God whom she served did not forsake her. She received presents of clothing and other articles, and so well was she known, that these donations were often accompanied by the express declaration, "that they were not meant for her charities, but for her own exclusive use."

Some years before this, it had been proposed to make a provision for Sarah Martin, from the Borough funds; the design was relinquished, to be resumed in 1841. Sarah opposed it; she wished that the good she did should be freely done. Her objections were overruled; the wife of a magistrate who had brought the subject before the council, wrote to her in somewhat imperious strain: "We consider it impossible, from the manner in which you live, that you can long continue your arduous labors at the jail. Mr. —— and myself will feel angry and hurt if you refuse to accept it."

This threat of anger and wounded feelings, which would be amusing were it not so impertinent, did not affect Sarah Martin; although she declares that the writer was a very dear friend, and one, no doubt, from whom she had derived much valuable aid. She still objected to receive payment for the labor and devotion of a life; and it surely required little tact or delicacy to feel that the refusal was justified. "Such scruples," observes the writer, in the 'Edinburgh Review,' with whom lies the merit of drawing general attention to the history of Sarah Martin, "should have been held sacred. Corporation gratitude should have been exhibited in some way which would not have excited a feeling of self-degradation; but, alas! a jail committee does not enter into questions of feeling. It was coarsely intimated to this high-souled woman,—'If we permit you to visit the prison, you must submit to our terms;' and these worshipful gentlemen, who were then making use of Sarah Martin as a substitute for the schoolmaster and the chaplain, whom it was by law their bounden duty to have appointed, converted her into their salaried servant, by the munificent grant of twelve pounds per annum."

Sarah Martin enjoyed this liberal salary for two years. For the last year of her existence, there was an evident decay of nature's powers, but no diminution of that spiritual strength which had ever sustained her; and which only rose higher at the aspect of death. For this event she had long been prepared, and had herself written her own funeral sermon as early as 1832. A simple inscription, recording her name and age, and recording no more, was likewise prepared by her, and may now be read on a plain stone in the churchyard of Caistor.

She was patient and resigned throughout her whole illness; but the sufferings of her last hours were great: they closed in August, 1843, in the fifty-third year of her age. About twenty minutes before her death she begged for more anodyne to still the pain. The nurse knew with what fearless spirit she had to deal. She told her that the hour was near. "Thank God! Thank God!" exclaimed Sarah; and she clapped her hands in token of victory won—that Christian victory which snatches its triumph from the grave, and says to death: "Where is thy sting?"

CONCLUSION.

With the name of Sarah Martin, an humble working-girl of our own times, we close this series of generous women, who, for eighteen hundred years and more, steadily followed in the path opened by Dorcas, a lowly disciple of the first Christian age.

They were of every land; of every race; of every rank: they differed in aspect; they spoke languages that were to one another as unknown tongues; but they burned with the same spirit, and everywhere they struggled nobly in the same cause. These Daughters of the Cross felt themselves called to a destiny more lofty than a life of pleasure and idleness: they labored from dawn of day, the sun set not on their toil; and behold the things they accomplished! The mansions of their charity outnumber the palaces of kings. The boasted hospitality of Eastern princes and ancient patriarchs sinks into nothing before theirs; for they build dwellings to receive lifelong guests, and glory in the name of servants of the poor.

When men liberate nations and win realms, their names live forever. But who shall count the multitudes these women redeemed from misery? Who shall reckon the souls they conquered to heaven? And yet their memory too often lies buried beneath the dust of past ages, and the worldly indifference of to-day. The ambition, the genius, the very beauty of woman, have had their meed of power or praise; but those do not seem to have been thought of whose glory is, that, like the sisters of Bethany, they received the divine Master beneath their roof: that, like Martha, they labored in his service with zealous love, and yet, forgetting not the better part, humbly sat like Mary at the feet of their God.

Such women dwell amongst us still, as obscure and neglected as their predecessors. Names worthy of record have been omitted with regret; but, besides that I knew how much those who bore them would shrink from observation and praise, I also felt that it was not in their own lifetime they could be judged rightly. When they are fairly in their graves, perhaps their zeal will not be called party spirit, or their charity ostentation : perhaps the good they did may then be confessed ; and what seemed narrow and trifling, indicate a lofty and generous spirit. On this chance let them rest their hope : if, indeed, their hopes are of those that look for the praise and honor of man.

But because such is the case, it does not follow that it need be. Shall spirits so noble, lives so pure, natures so holy and yet so lovely, ever pass away from amongst us, unheeded in life, forgotten in death ? If we but knew it, we could find, even in the imperfect records of the good, the same strange charm which lies in the story of troubled feelings and tragic passions ; for if there we see their triumph, here we behold their subjection. It is not just to them, and it is dangerous to ourselves, to consider them as privileged against either error or temptation. We lose the true lesson of their lives if we look but at the result, howsoever fair and beautiful it may seem ; if, in contemplating the outward victory, we forget the inward cost : the natural longings repressed ; the sinless wishes and pleasures not indulged ; the weariness of spirit and of flesh endured ; the struggles overcome ; the sacrifices daily made, and never repined at : things which, even more than whatever they did, have sanctified the lives of the pure and the good.

INDEX.

Date Due